REGIONAL POLICY AND REGIONAL PLANNING IN GHANA

To my dear mother, Comfort Adwoa Ofori and the fondest, most cherished memory of my late father, Reverend Emmanuel Stephen Ofori

and my dear children:

Kenneth, Andrew, Elsie and Michelle

Regional Policy and Regional Planning in Ghana

Making things happen in the territorial community

SAM C. OFORI
BA (Hons) (Ghana) MSc (UST-Kumasi) PhD MSc (Strathclyde)
CertEd DMS MBA (UCE-Birmingham)
Member; Ghana Institute of Planners (MGIP)

Formerly Lecturer
School of Planning
Faculty of the Built Environment
University of Central England
Birmingham, England, UK

Routledge
Taylor & Francis Group
LONDON AND NEW YORK

First published 2002 by Ashgate Publishing

Reissued 2018 by Routledge
2 Park Square, Milton Park, Abingdon, Oxon OX14 4RN
711 Third Avenue, New York, NY 10017, USA

Routledge is an imprint of the Taylor & Francis Group, an informa business

Publisher's Note
The publisher has gone to great lengths to ensure the quality of this reprint but points out that some imperfections in the original copies may be apparent.

Disclaimer
The publisher has made every effort to trace copyright holders and welcomes correspondence from those they have been unable to contact.

A Library of Congress record exists under LC control number: 2001097976

ISBN 13: 978-1-138-74145-4 (hbk)
ISBN 13: 978-1-138-74144-7 (pbk)
ISBN 13: 978-1-315-18284-1 (ebk)

Contents

Figures and tables

Preface

Formal regional planning has existed in post-colonial Ghana for over three decades. A number of programmes and projects have been implemented in the country in the past and more recent times to improve the well-being of the people in both urban and rural areas. Apart from this, effort has also been made to introduce a planning system and legislative provisions in support of practice and to facilitate the process of socio-economic and physical-environmental development in the localities and regions of the country.

However, a dialectic of these processes is that the perceived levels of disparities and disadvantage within and between communities as well as groups of people in the regions become even more pronounced over time. Indeed, the experiences of socio-economic and spatial development processes in many Third World countries, including Ghana, show that most rounds of investment and initiative hardly achieve the policy and programme objectives. In particular, the socio-economic well-being of the target populations hardly experiences real material change. This trend has been exacerbated in the last fifteen years with the more active pursuance of the structural adjustment policies and economic recovery programmes. The already marginalized, deprived and disadvantaged groups, in particular those in the territorial communities, have suffered greater relative poverty.

A principal aim in this book is to assess the impacts of sector-based and one-off projects on levels and dimensions of socio-economic and spatial disparities between the district localities within the Central Region. A more specific focus related to this is to evaluate the impact of a major and more concrete regional programme on the well-being of communities and groups in a particular sub-region within the Central Region. This whole engagement is set within an assessment of the statutory planning frameworks, contexts and practices. While regional planning is presented as much as possible as a process, it is not set out as being mechanistically unidirectional. The Central Region is used as an exemplar of the region in Ghana.

Methodologically, this scenario poses a greater challenge to the planning process to prove itself dynamic, continuous and legitimate. But reduction or even elimination of the disparities and deprivation depends on the effectiveness and efficiency of the intervention and mediation actions. This, of course, can only be ascertained by a conscious and rational evaluation of the impact of programmes and projects implemented within the statutory regional planning context. It has obvious futuristic benefits for learning from the regional planning actions and processes and enriching policy refinement.

This book is divided into nine chapters. The general introduction to the study and its specific objectives are presented in chapter one. Aspects covered here are the concepts of region, regional planning and the general nature of the 'region' in Ghana. The evolution of the national space-economy is also briefly traced out. The current planning system is presented. Then the backgrounds of the Central Region and more focused sub-region, Lower Denkyira-Twifo-Hemang District, are also set out. The assets and opportunities available to regional development and the challenges facing these in the Region are highlighted.

The methodological and epistemological framework of the book are explained in chapter two. Emphasis is on its particular engagement and distinctive concern. A review of relevant literature contributes to a basis for mapping out these aspects. Chapter three covers the theoretical contexts. The aim is to emphasize the relevance and value of these in guiding policy and strategy in regional planning than being used essentially for explanatory purposes. Thus the important considerations and issues involved in planning the kind of region in context are emphasized. Two underlying hypotheses are also stated.

In chapter four, an attempt is made to explore the administrative, economic and demographic-population contexts of regional planning. Effort is made to identify the occurrence of regional development to the extent that it is reflected in the history of national development planning. The national development policy framework is presented and reviewed. The intent in chapter five is to assess the state and practices of regional planning policy formulation, plan-making and strategies. Another objective is to set out the background to a major development programme implemented in the Central Region. An attempt is made to tease out the possible influences of globalization processes and corporate capital on the regional initiatives.

The first level of regional policy and development assessment is done in chapter six by analysing the disparities between district localities as well as sectors in terms of various data sets. The issues of convergence and divergence, equity and growth are addressed. The impact of the more concrete regional programme is evaluated in chapter seven. The focus is on its various aspects, including the economic, social, spatial, environmental and political.

Chapter eight is centred on an assessment of implementation effectiveness in relation to all the initiatives dealt with in the earlier chapters. An attempt is also made to assess the effectiveness of managing regional change. The main lessons learned in the study are indicated in chapter nine. The assumptions underlying the hypotheses and policy implications of these are pointed out. Finally, a number of policies for future regional planning in Ghana is proposed and a general prognosis made of the strategic implementation of these.

It is emphasized the greater need to ensure that regional planning initiatives are effective and achieve real positive results. A general observation made is that the whole process of regional planning and socio-economic development has been a case of play-it-over-again and *déja-vu*. The development process tends to be made an event of in this situation and poverty suffers greater burdens. Real development hardly takes place, previous initiatives having been non-events. Moreover, policy formulation, practices of implementation, monitoring and programme evaluation have been characterized by ineffectiveness.

This practice and attitude of play-it-over-again, we-have-seen-it-before and the-same-thing-over-again are deterministic, mimetic and stifle creativity as well as limit responsiveness. These attitudes and practices are also obstacles to the effective management of regional change. The territorial communities have held this humdrum recurrence suspect and consider it an orchestration by the public domain and coalitions of elitists. Planning practices and development processes become characterized by slander and tale-telling.

Furthermore, the situation only worsens the polarization in society: between those who have and those who do not; between communities; between the 'powerful' and the 'powerless'. The planning process has a vital role in redressing and restructuring such polarization. Indeed, this history of play-it-over-again is in need of total abolition. Therefore, the tendency or underlying orchestration as well as scenario must be radically abolished in lieu of making things actually happen in the territorial regional communities.

S.C. Ofori
Birmingham, England
November, 2001

Acknowledgements

This work has been accomplished with the help and support of many and I should like to express my sincerest gratitude to them. I am deeply grateful to Professor Ivan Turok who is based at the Department of Urban Studies, University of Glasgow for kindly accepting to review the manuscript version of this book for me and the publishers. Previously, Professor Turok had been my tutor at the University of Strathclyde in Glasgow and did supervise my post-doctoral masters thesis in urban and regional planning at the Department of Environmental Planning, University of Strathclyde from October 1991 till July 1992. We had very useful interactions, heart-warming and trail-lighting discourses relating to planning policy and theory and in particular, research methodology.

In the same manner, I am profoundly grateful to Professor Urlan A. Wannop, OBE, who supervised my doctoral thesis over the period, October 1987 to June 1991. Professor Wannop was the Head of the Department of Environmental Planning (formerly Centre for Planning) which is within the Strathclyde Business School, University of Strathclyde in Glasgow. I have the greatest appreciation for his excellent guidance, distinctive management of my doctoral studies as well as firm support and deeply encouraging supervision of the original thesis from which this book has been created. He also taught me during my post-doctoral and instructional masters course in urban and regional planning which he actively supported me to undertake. These inspiring experiences shall always remain most pleasant, pervasively memorable and usefully shining learning for me.

It will never leave me, gratitude to the Confederation of Scottish Business Schools and in particular, Strathclyde Business School for organising the six-month doctoral programme in research workshops, research design and methodology at the University of Glasgow from October, 1987 to April, 1988. This course, which was an integral part of the PhD programme, included training seminars and hands-on sessions in further descriptive and inferential statistics, applications of the Minitab and SPSS^{X} software systems. I have benefited very much from this rigorous and intensive training, including the Confederation of Scottish Business Schools certification in research and quantitative skills.

I am very appreciative of the kind support given me by Mr. K. Johnfia, Chief Economic Planning Officer, Ministry of Finance and Economic Planning. He had headed the Regional Planning Co-ordinating Unit in the Central Region and was, at the time of my original study, heading the Greater Accra Regional Planning Co-ordinating Unit, where he allowed me a formal interview with him. In the same way, I thank Mr. Osam Duodu who was Principal Economic Planning Officer and Head of the Regional Planning Co-ordinating Unit in the Central Region at the time of the original field work for the relevant discussions he permitted me to hold with him. Similarly, I remain grateful to Mr. G.L. Cann who was Chief Economic Planning Officer and Head of the Regional Resource and Planning Unit at the Ministry of Finance and Economic Planning, Accra at the time of the earlier study for the interview I had with him and the planning and policy documents he made available to me.

I equally acknowledge with abundant thankfulness the support of Professor B.A.W. Trevallion, formerly Head of the Department of Planning at the University of Science and Technology (UST), Kumasi in allowing me beneficial discussions and interview with him. He also provided me with useful documents in relation to national development and planning policy. Professor Trevallion was acting as Planning Consultant to the National Development Planning Commission in Accra at the time of my fieldwork.

In a similar way, I am grateful to Professor Dr. Klaus R. Kunzmann, Director of the Institute of Spatial Planning, the research and service centre of the Department of Spatial Planning within the Fachbereich Raumplanung at the University of Dortmund, Germany for allowing me a personal discussion with him about programme implementation in Third World countries. He was visiting the Department of Environmental Planning at the University of Strathclyde. He shared his personal field experiences and I have found this of valued learning importance.

Gratitude to Professor Clyde Mitchell-Weaver, Director of the Economic and Social Development Programme at the Graduate School of Public and International Affairs, University of Pittsburg, USA for making time to allow me a personal discussion of aspects of my earlier study with him. I am so thankful for his useful instruction on aspects of regional policy evaluation and territorial regional development strategies.

In addition, I am filled with heart-felt gratitude to the memory of the late Professor K.B. Dickson, formerly Vice-Chancellor of the University of Cape Coast for the encouraging discussions, interviews and discourses I held with him on many occasions. These took place in the course of my developing the proposal for my doctoral thesis and, subsequently, during the actual fieldwork. He also shared his direct experience of the Twifo Oil Palm Plantation programme with me.

This acknowledgement would suffer a vacuous omission without my thanking, very much, the entire management of the Twifo Oil Palm Plantation Project (TOPP) company for permitting me to research the programme as a case study. I am very grateful to the Managing Director, the Assistant Personnel Manager, the Commercial and Production Managers as well as the Managers for the Smallholder and Outgrower Units. All of the foregoing are based at the project site at Ntafrewaso in the Central Region. In exactly the same way, I have every thankfulness to the Company Solicitor and Secretary who was based at TOPP's Office in Accra for the useful discussions and interviews he allowed me with him.

I am also very grateful to messieurs Boateng, Otu-Ansah, Ayera-Kwa, Annobil, Kwame Alorvi and the late John Asong who braved the circumstances to act as field assistants for me during the surveys in Cape Coast and, in particular, at the project site, Ntafrewaso. I am, equally, thankful to Hayford Okyere Adomako for collecting further data for me at Ntafrewaso after my original fieldwork in 1989. Subsequently, at the time of writing, Hayford agreed to conduct follow-up interviews at TOPP headquarters, Ntafrewaso, for me. I am also always indebted to George Nyarko and his spouse for providing me with lodging in Cape Coast as well as to Irene Ofori, my sister, with whom I lodged in Accra during the original fieldwork.

I appreciate the assistance of Ann Muir who was based at the Social Statistics Laboratory at the University of Strathclyde for her guidance on the use of the Vax (main frame) computer system. I also thank Don Evans who was based in the central Computer Centre at the University of Strathclyde for his patient guidance and direction on the application of the Plotlib software. In addition, I am thankful to Steve Roddie who is based in the Technical Services Unit within the Faculty of Built Environment at the University of Central England in Birmingham for computer-producing the three maps in the book.

In a similar way, I am grateful to the Business Learning Centre within the University of Central England Business School (UCEBS) in Birmingham for assisting me to scan in most of the figures and all the photographs used in the book. I could not have achieved this without their support.

Further, I remain ever grateful to the Government of Ghana for sponsoring my studies at the University of Strathclyde in Glasgow. This covered the main funding for my original fieldwork in Ghana. I am equally grateful to the University of Strathclyde for supporting me with a travel grant during the fieldwork and, subsequently, granting me a Research Student's Bursary over the 1989-90 calendar year.

Finally, I am sincerely thankful to my publishers, Ashgate Publishing Limited for their encouraging support during the preparation of the book and for publishing it. Any of its limitations remain mine.

1 Introduction: regional planning policy, socio-economic and spatial disparities and statutory planning

This book is about the socio-economic and spatial impacts of regional planning policy on the living standards and well-being of communities within a political-administrative and planning region in Ghana. It is, therefore, centred on the evaluation of regional policy and development programmes as well as assessment of implementation effectiveness. This also addresses the effectiveness of the management of regional change. The whole engagement is set within the framework of statutory planning practice, with an intent to assessing its effectiveness in this regard. Regional planning policy, while addressing the forces that impinge on it, is seen in the context of national development policy. The Central Region is used as a case study of intra-regional change and regional planning effectiveness in a territorial region. Therefore, its external validity for the other regions of Ghana is pointed out as considered appropriate.

The practice of regional planning is assessed in terms of the effectiveness of its legitimacy and the extent to which it results in and promotes the making of policy, design and implementation of development initiatives. The agencies and power relations involved in these processes are as crucial as the quality of the initiatives and the aspects relating to programme financing. Regional planning practice in Ghana has been in much need of assessment, in particular its outputs in terms of refined policies, plans, programmes and projects as well as the socio-economic and spatial changes they are aimed at securing.

The impacts of Ghanaian regional planning on the well-being and standard of living of the regional communities have come into vigorous and valid questioning (Ofori, 1995a; 1991a; Simon, 1990a). This vigour and validity derive strength from the greater concern of the Ghanaian state and external funding agencies for the effectiveness of development policy and the emasculating legislative provisions in support of planning in general and regional planning, in particular. A number of programmes and projects have been implemented in the regions and in the sub-regional zones since the late 1960s. Government has been concerned with knowing what is happening under these programmes and projects. For example, in 1987 a national survey of living standards in Ghana was jointly started by the Ghana Statistical Service and The World Bank (Government of Ghana, 1988a). One of the objectives of the survey was to find out what impact government development policy has had on Ghanaians at the household, community, regional and broad ecological zone levels. It was hoped that the results of the survey would be used in evaluating a national programme which is also aimed at mitigating the social cost of adjustment policies (Government of Ghana, 1987a). Therefore, this book is also intended to be a contribution to the formulation and refinement of more effective regional policy as an output of the planning process. While there may not be any formal and statutory regional development plan, there has been regional implementation of national development programmes.

The regional problem, therefore, is the identification and assessment of the nature and behaviour of disparities in socio-economic well-being and spatial development, over time and under various planning and development policies within the Central Region; also reflective of the situation in other regions of Ghana. This behaviour of intra-regional disparities is tested by the implementation of programmes and projects and evaluation of their impacts, based on identified indicators in the context of national development policy goals and objectives. Provision has been made for some of these functions of regional planning under the newly established planning system in Ghana.

This problem has a number of dimensions. Regional development programmes in Ghana tend to be more regional in scope than area-specific projects. While the former is more infrastructure-oriented and sector-based, the latter is more targeted, affecting identified groups of people and communities. Often regional evaluation research, if any, is seen at the level of the former. For a fuller picture of disparities, evaluation has to be done at the two levels. Second, the problem of socio-economic development is also seen between sectors of the regional space economy. It is therefore important to give consideration to these in an evaluative study of this kind. Third, these evaluations constitute an assessment of regional development and planning effectiveness at a wider level. This is in terms of the effectiveness and efficiency of policies, contexts, frameworks, practices as well as the enabling legislative provisions.

Thus strategic regional change is perceived and assessed in two ways. The first relates to one-off and sector-based disparities in terms of a multiple set of socio-economic and spatial indicators between the districts within the Central Region. The second is at the level of well-being between more specific and local communities in relation to an agro-industrial initiative, the Twifo Oil Palm Plantation (TOPP) project-complex, in the Twifo sub-region in the Region. The first approach is also aimed at emphasizing and justifying the necessity and role of the latter, while demonstrating approaches to assessing planned socio-economic and spatial change within the territorial region in both regards. The latter programme is evaluated in terms of economic, social, physical-spatial, political as well as environmental factors. It must also be emphasized that apart from its value as an instrument of regional planning, the TOPP programme holds critical importance as the Ghanaian state aims at replicating it, upon its success, in other parts of the Region and the country as a whole.

The general approach to the analysis and assessment of regional disparities does not include focus on specific programmes and target populations in many cases. Thus any interpretation of policy functions is not in direct relation to the impacts of substantive and concrete regional programmes (Ofori, 1995a; Simon, 1990b; Rambanapasi, 1989; Slater, 1975). The approach in this book is to relate such studies to real, material initiatives and processes of change. It is in the light of this also that the principal hypotheses tested in this book relate to the two approaches adopted. These are the one-off projects and the more concrete and wider regional programme. These are also aimed at integrating the two forms of inquiry related to the approaches noted.

In explaining the strategic regional changes, use is made of both the more generally established and context-based theories. However, greater emphasis is placed on theory to the extent that it guides and informs planning policy as well as strategy more than a basis for explanation. In assessing the implementation effectiveness of regional programmes, the effort is based on management functions as well as a range of agency roles. These functions and roles are also seen in terms of a matrix of factors. With respect to implementation effectiveness, therefore, the aspects addressed include the nature and quality of planning policy, design of development initiatives and strategies as well as the dialectics and contradictions of the processes of planned change.

On the basis of the various considerations, a set of policies is proposed for a more effective futuristic regional planning. Conclusions are also made in relation to the assumptions and policy implications of the hypotheses tested, the validity of the general themes addressed as well as the theory and methodology of regional planning in its greater emphasis on the procedural aspects. The study is of epistemological value for regional planning in sub-Saharan and other Third World countries. This is because it seeks to contribute to an understanding of the workings of planning policy with consideration for a range of facets at the regional level and in the territorial context. It is also of particular importance in terms of the implementation of regional development programmes and their impacts as well as evaluation methodologies (Simon, 1990b; Folmer, 1986; Slater, 1975; Friedmann, 1973).

'Making things happen' means changing how things are done and achieving the results for which goals and objectives have been formulated. Thus, it imbibes the need for strategic and consistent innovation. Being clear about how things are done, including the strengths and weaknesses relating to these are also essential elements of the effectiveness of planning and its practice. Ensuring that such change takes place, at all, boils down to effective programme implementation and management of change. Therefore, it is fundamental to this process to be aware of the opportunities for strategic as well as tactical interventions. In the same way, it is crucial to achieving the goals to clearly identify the agents and actors who actually make things happen. This must include their roles, relationships and any conflicting interests or value systems. While the nature of change itself may be changing, the objects of change, certainly, change over time. Therefore, it is equally important to change existing knowledge and skills in relation to the tasks and processes involved in making things happen. While making things happen in urban and regional planning is an essence of the proceduralist ethic, the impinging substantive aspects are crucially relevant.

The question of a region

The understanding and clarification of what is a region is fundamental to regional planning. It is ironic that a 'region' tends to have different meanings for various people (Wannop, 1995; Ofori, 1991a; Glasson, 1978). In seeking to clarify this in this book, however, the focus is not on the regional problem, for I see the question of a region as being different from the regional question which has been generally stated already. However, the former contributes to preparing the ground for identifying or shedding light on the latter. There are numerous regional concepts (Teriba and Kayode, 1977; Hilhorst, 1969) and choice is a function of the purpose of study.

The 'region', in general terms, is a relatively large and continuous area delimited under some criterion - criteria - for purposes of sheer description or as a basis for development activity. There is a general agreement on its two main forms: formal or homogeneous; functional, heterogeneous or polarized regions. The former is often based on one or more predominant factors such as population, employment rates and is essentially characterized by homogeneity which is never precise (Hallet, Randall and West, 1973). The latter is based on functionality, usually involving multiple factors constituting an 'interdependent mesh', polarized against the other areas. This type is made up of nodal regions - urban sub-systems - which may be considered a special case of the functional type, but itself can also be considered nodal (Richardson, 1969a). The most typical nodal region is the city-region such as greater Cape Coast or more typically, Accra (Omuta and Onukerhuraye, 1986; Glasson, 1978). In this regard, the metropolitan area which is wider than a single urban centre, yet less so than a political-administrative regional territory, is a typical nodal region.

Hilhorst (1971) has provided a typology of regions in both theoretic or academic and planning terms. The former includes the two main types identified above. For practical purposes, 'programme' and 'planning' are presented as the correlates of the formal and functional types, respectively. The planning region is one that shows coherence of economic decisions, the basis of which may be formal or functional. For example, it may be an area of acute unemployment within industrial and service centres (Richardson, 1969a; Boudeville, 1966). The planning region is often under an executive authority located within the region. On the other hand, the programme region is seen in terms of some central function such as water supply often under a local or central authority. However, it may cover a number of planning regions.

The implementation of regional development policy and initiatives requires the legitimate power to act as this emanates from government and private agencies. Therefore, planning and programming regions must possess administrative status and political jurisdiction of various sizes and scales (Richardson, 1969b). In this sense, the political and administrative region would often coincide more with the planning region than the programming type.

In relation to planning problems, Friedmann (1966) identified a typology of planning regions. One of these is the core region and is an area with high, intensive economic growth with prospects and having the fullest provision of all needed infrastructure. The challenges facing the core region include the absorption of new entrants into the local labour market and environmental problems. The upward-transitional area is presented as one characterized by the possibility of intensive resource use and where there is net in-migration. The development of this type may happen through increasing commercial demand in the core region. The resource frontier region is characterized by the incidence of unsettled areas, the possibility of new settlements needing prime investment in particular activities and in appropriate infrastructure. A further type is the downward-transitional region which is an older, established and settled region with largely rural economies and in stagnation or decline. It may typify problems of both population distribution, settlement, community and rural land-use adjustments. The downward-transitional area could also be a city, metropolitan or territorial area whose economy is in decline. This type of region is actively in need of substantial infrastructure.

All these forms of the planning region can, however, be further categorized, broadly, as core or peripheral regions as the cases may be. While the traditional notion of the periphery is based on distance, it has been seen in socio-economic and endogenous terms. This is in the belief that the periphery is able to improve its status through a self-generating development process by the entrepreneurial and innovative abilities of its residents (Molle and Cappelin, 1988; Wadley, 1986; Teriba and Kayode, 1977).

However, the most effective region, in practical planning terms, is the one that has political power over its jurisdictional area. Since planning problems are not static, it may be necessary to delimit or revise the boundaries of the region, restructure or reorganize it. In this way, it can be seen to respond to dynamic changes, endogenous, exogenous or both (Wannop, 1995; 1988).

The 'region' in Ghana

In the context of Ghana, the 'region' is a sub-national unit which serves both a political-administrative function and sub-national planning purpose. Being dominated by the central state, the Ghanaian region is also weak in political terms. In its dependence mainly on the extraction of resources that provide its exchangeable surplus through export, the prosperity of the region is under the control of international and exogenous forces. Its infrastructure is largely and historically conditioned by this extraction of surplus.

It is also largely unsettled and natural resource-based; those parts that are, in many cases widely spread out. There is thus a dominance of a few towns and cities as well as a host of poorly integrated settlements in spatial-functional terms (Weaver, 1989; Hardoy and Satterthwaite, 1986; El-Shanks and Obudho, 1974). It has a largely rural economy and mostly in a state of decline, having lost a considerable proportion of its resources and possessing little but deteriorated socio-economic infrastructure. The Ghanaian region is also characterized by high rates and levels of unemployment and unexpectedly, low incomes and needing massive investments. Its delimitation has been based on population, cultural and physical factors as well as economic activity. Thus residents of each region generally exhibit some regional consciousness. These attributes make most of the regions in Ghana territorial and the critical forces noted are impinging on its development.

Therefore, the Ghanaian territorial region is also regarded as a resource frontier and downward-transitional area. This also underlies its continued and increasing disadvantage. This has grown worse even under the structural adjustment programmes which are massively funded by international agencies (Gooneratne and Obudho, 1997; Donkor, 1997). Indeed, this landscape of a region is also typical of other parts of Africa (Omuta and Onukerhuraye, 1986; Mabogunje and Faniran, 1977).

In the last ten years, the personality of the Ghanaian region has changed with the creation of new local government areas, District Assemblies. This has meant the emergence of district localities or sub-regions with defined legislative political as well as planning powers (Republic of Ghana; 1994a; Government of Ghana, 1988b; Conyers, 1984). This kind of statutory power is not available to the regional level, yet. However, the emergence of the district, within a programme of decentralization, has strengthened the case for a sharper focus on intra-regional issues as this book purports to do (Rodwin, 1978).

Nevertheless, a critical assessment of the implementation effectiveness of the political and administrative decentralization programmes in Ghana reveals serious constraints and challenges (Ayee, 1994). It has been observed that central government is still involved in controlling local affairs, not yielding power easily and allowing due autonomy required at that level. In fact, the process has been described as one of 'recentralization' rather than decentralization (Ayee, 1994). There has also been competition and conflict between local authority initiatives and those of central government sector departments, especially with the weak control of the former. Ayee (1994) further argues that the decentralization programme is not seen and implemented as a process of evolution and learning which would also permit firm monitoring and effective feedback. This is further used to imply the linear than multidimensional nature of the programme.

Decentralization at the local level has been faced with other technical and political constraints that do not paint a bright future for the districts. This is also because of the lack of monitoring and feedback. Besides, effective public participation in development planning is still constrained. Many of the promises and statements of the District Assemblies remain unfulfilled - the old form of state-level politics resurfaced at the local level. Local government has also been faced with many financial problems which include declining tax receipts and low levels and rates of fund transfer from the state to them. Therefore, their financial position has been seriously weakened. This situation has meant that the District Assemblies have had to exact unfair taxes from the local constituents, a move that has met with vehement local resistance and a further source of conflict. Ayee (1994, p. 203) has also pointed out the fact that local governance has been characterized by high levels of corruption, including embezzlement.

Apart from these, the local government institution has displayed sectionalist and conflicting interests among decision-makers, agencies and the local elite. This also includes a coalition of interests in which the various contenders have been pursuing their own agendas. In this local twirl of affairs, it has been difficult for the local authorities to control the former sector organizations now brought under their control. Meanwhile, the individual 'sector' units are themselves limited in their capabilities. In the same way, the districts are also lacking in well-trained, qualified and skilled personnel. Some of them have been reluctant to be relocated to remote parts of the localities because of the limited nature or non-availability of social and physical infrastructure to make those places attractive enough. Furthermore, resource transfer from the former regional structures to the new local authorities has not been matched by legislation to decentralize political and administrative authority.

The local government system of District Assemblies is a test of any future elected regional government. Indeed, if far-reaching efforts are not made to make them effective and efficient, it is likely that its constraints, as pointed out, would recur. This situation could also be used as a case against elective regional governance. It must be emphasized, however, that this book is neither about decentralization nor regional governance.

New planning legislation also includes provision for other forms of region in Ghana (Republic of Ghana, 1994a; 1994b; Government of Ghana, 1988b). Under the planning system, a Joint Development Planning Area can be created for any area wider than a single district or covering parts of a number of districts within the same or across more than one region. Such an area is based on its contiguity and is defined by physical as well as socio-economic attributes which necessitate its delimitation. The legislation further allows the creation of a Joint Development Planning Board to manage the delimited area.

In the same way, provision is made for the designation of a Special Development Area as may be considered to be in the national interest (Republic of Ghana, 1994a). Under such circumstances, the formal and normal administrative and jurisdictional control of the particular district(s) is suspended in the national interest. Therefore, this implies more of emergency delimitation of a region which may tend to be far more limited in its permanence.

Since the end of the colonialist era, and particularly in the last two decades, the Ghanaian region has been the scene of activities directly driven by external-corporate agencies. This is also part of a global process of restructuring of business organizations as will be further explained in chapter five. These have the potential to determine and control the future development of the Ghanaian region like any other territory, especially in most parts of the world.

There may thus be at any time different regions within or encompassing the politico-administrative one as may occur the problems, including pressures that necessitate their creation. This 'oscillating' or 'osmotic' behaviour of regions also confirms the general ephemeral nature of most regions and regional issues. The observation has been made by Wannop (1995) in a compelling and comprehensive way with respect to the case of Euro-American countries. This characteristic of regions either across or within established regional boundaries also provides a source of dynamism in the process of regional planning. The extent of responsiveness of planners and policy-makers, in this regard, determines the level and rate of strategic effectiveness in the process of development. All theses attributes are critical to determining strategic regional change as well as the effectiveness of its management. This is even more engaging in regions as fragile and fragmented as the Ghanaian types.

Planning in the context of land use and spatial organization

Professional planners often argue and tend to disagree about the meaning of planning. The confusion often caused by the multiplicity of meanings, therefore, requires the clarification of this in context (Conyers and Hill, 1984; Roberts, 1974). In a general sense planning is understood as a deliberate and advance preparation and rehearsal in the mind or mental realm for an action (Rose, 1974). Therefore, it is a process of thinking out prior to the future action (Webber, 1984; Chadwick, 1978; Faludi, 1970).

In relation to land-use planning and spatial organization, this is seen as involving the continuous arranging of spatial patterns, based on the fore-thought. However, the spatial patterns are only the objects of the process based on considered and largely agreed decisions and policies chosen from among a set of alternatives. Indeed, process, in this case, can be seen as independent of objects (Chadwick, 1978, p. 24). Planning is the act, art, science, and process of arranging these spatial patterns.

The making of choices in the face of several options for achieving the objectives of the action thought out is emphasized. This underlies the nature of planning as being a process of decision-making about allocating resources among various contending and conflicting objectives on the basis of which formulated initiatives are implemented. That planning is a 'political-level' activity in this relation also stands out with implications for the equities and equalities needed for the distributive justice normatively required of it. This is also important for the alleviation of poverty, so prevalent in Third World societies and as characterizes the region in Ghana (Todaro, 1989; Balogh, 1978; Ahluwalia, 1976; Roberts, 1974; Baster, 1972).

While the contending and conflicting forces in the process of resource allocation and attainment of such distributive justice indicate the dialectical nature of planning, these also imply the need for effective mediating of the processes. This includes the urgent need for controlling the drifts away from the set goals and objectives. Therefore, the need to intervene in the working of market forces and processes is imperative in planning (Conyers and Hill, 1984; Cooke, 1983). The fact of considering various choices and options about the future implies the need for consistent and continuous policy-making in relation to the situations and trends (Wannop and Smith, 1985; Faludi, 1973a). The tested quality and validity of these policies in responding to the problems at hand are crucial to achieving the set goals and objectives.

These defining characteristics of planning reflect the rational nature of the planning process (Conyers and Hill, 1984; Faludi, 1975; 1973a; 1973b). Rationality, however, is limited by the reality of uncertainties, especially as planning involves making futuristic decisions. In this case, knowledge other than available through rational means, is of vital importance in the planning process. Thus both rational and non-rational means of knowing need be valued in epistemological terms (Ofori, 2000b; Cooke, 1983; Friedmann, 1973). For example, both rationalist and phenomenological epistemologies are relevant in regional planning as in the wider studies and activities. Indeed, rational knowledge and knowing must also be realistic and pragmatic (Ofori, 2000b).

The view of planning in this book is that it is a continuous process of deliberate and sufficiently rational decision-making about the various uses of land and related space, built and non-built. It involves the making of choices from among a set of alternative options about the allocation of resources for the attainment of defined objectives (Gillingwater, 1975; Friedmann, 1973). This process thus denotes the procedural approach to or theory of planning.

Therefore, the initial stage in the procedural planning process is the identification of problems, based on a clear scanning and analysis of the particular and impinging environments. The next stage is the identification and appraisal of various courses of actions that might be taken to achieve solutions to the problems. Third, choosing the preferred course of action from among the multiple set. On this basis, the fourth stage is formulating policies or a policy, including their stated goals and objectives for achieving positive change in the 'problem environment'. Therefore the policy framework provides the basis for the fifth stage: designing plans, including programmes and projects for actually bringing about the preferred change in the 'policy environment'. The sixth stage is the implementation of the chosen plan, programme or project, following which there is need to monitor progress. Subsequently, and in the seventh stage, the planning process, in this way, is tested for overall results through the evaluation function: material changes as well as the reformulation or review of policy and the entire procedural process.

On the other hand, various definitions of planning in particular contexts and in relation to specific strategies provide substantive approaches to or theories in planning. While every form of planning in the context of land use and spatial organization is characterized by the way in which it proceeds - proceduralism - there are as many substantive thoughts as there are persons who make them (Camhis, 1979; Faludi, 1973a; 1973b).

It must to be noted, however, that it is not a unilinear process. While there might be changes between stages, there would be the need for lateral thinking as well as learning. In this way, the planner prepares for uncertainties. This also makes contingency planning a useful approach. Indeed, procedural and substantive planning theories have unity in planning methodology which is also by nature, decision-based (Faludi, 1987; 1986). Nevertheless, this methodology has been criticized for its neglect of important questions of modes of production and distribution. In particular, it has failing in not recognizing power, its relations and distribution in society as well as implementation (Cooke, 1983). Both procedural and substantive planning are relevant in addressing all aspects of the planning process.

All the stages, together, in the procedural planning process have been used to define and characterize the systems approach to planning (McLoughlin, 1969). There is, however, the tendency in this view, for the human factor to be stripped off as it is based on general systems theory which is derived from cybernetics.

It ought to be emphasized that the benefits of the planning process, being both material and intellectual should then provide more evidence for the revision and, if need be, reformulation of the original policies. Therefore, Coleman (1975) has argued that policy is both the input and output of the planning process. Gillingwater (1975) has also argued that policy formulation is the most important component of the planning process, if not its purpose and rationale. He further argues that planning amounts to more than the making of policy and the production of cleverly sparkling plans (Bruton and Nicholson, 1987). While this is a critical component and condition of public policy as well as regional planning, a more important aspect of planning is the impact side of the equation. Gillingwater (1975) points out that this part has been neglected in both theoretical and practical terms. A recognition of this overarching importance also underlines the cardinal relevance of action and implementation. Furthermore, the concrete importance of action, implementation and impacts highlights the critical test through evaluation. Therefore, planning ought to be and is equally concerned with the need to co-ordinate action and intent. It is equally relevant for planning to be concerned with the attempts at understanding the inter-connections between problems, solutions and impacts as between intents and consequences of actions. These further underline the central importance of processes involved in planning.

The rational nature of planning also underlies its normative character in defining how land should be used and space organized than positive in how these actually take place in the real world. The latter is, however, different from the positivist nature of planning in valuing only that which is quantitative. Therefore, the need to appreciate realism and the fact that many issues are socially-constructed contribute to building a fuller view of planning. This provides further emphasis on the value of rational and realist-phenomenological approaches to knowing and learning in planning. These also promote the attainment of integration and co-ordination in the planning process.

Another important part of the meaning and significance of planning is its pervasive importance and instrumental value in creating as well as providing guidance for change. Planning must be capable of achieving this within the structures, processes and systems of which it is constituted and constructed. In this case, it must be responsive to change in the full range of the contextual and impinging circumstances, conditions and political values. In its professional status planning must be capable of continuous and consistent change. This implies that the planning profession must regularly assess the effectiveness of its instruments with respect to the way problems are perceived, and the abilities needed to up-date its state and stock of intellect and knowledge. In this way, planning creates for itself flexibility that promotes the revision both of procedural and substantive theories that bear on valid strategies and legitimate actions. Therefore, planning must be concerned with the changes in the processes of ordering spatial arrangements as it is with the changes in its level of knowledge and intellectual foundations (Ofori, 2000b; Gillingwater, 1975; Webber, 1969).

Understanding regional planning and its nature

In its earliest stage of modern development, regional planning was presented as a process that deals with making of policy and elucidating of objectives for attaining societal well-being within an area larger than a single urban centre (Friedmann, 1975; 1966). This underlines the notion of regional planning as the organization of regional space (Weaver, 1984; 1981; 1978). The important actions to take, in this regard, include identifying the productive and land-use activities to serve as the bases of the organized regional space, how to undertake and manage them. Of all, the location of these activities is critical to determining the development of the supra-urban space (Friedmann, 1966). It is also important to note the functional importance of urban space, within it.

In this relation, regional planning is perceived as a useful and suitable frame of reference for integrating in a balanced way, projects of national scale and local initiatives. That regional planning straddles the two levels is clear. This further gives regional planning both a socio-economic and physical personality, factors which also predominantly mark the ends of the spatial scale (Glasson, 1978).

However, as pointed out in the concept of planning, this view of regional planning tends to ignore real social and political factors, including power-relations especially with respect to growth and development issues (Glasson, 1978; Friedmann, 1974). The need for local or endogenous control of such political power is part of the critical foundation for regional planning (Weaver, 1984). Gillingwater (1975) has argued that regional planning is embedded in politics as well as the political process. This reflects and emphasizes the fact that planning is a political-level professional activity.

Following from the ideas of the 'region' and 'planning', regional planning has been more clearly presented as a process of attaining rationally formulated goals for a region (Rietveld, 1980). A distinctive feature, however, is the nature of the goals being economic, social, physical-spatial and environmental (Ofori-Cudjoe, 1987; Ashcroft, 1983; 1982; 1978). These could also be used to express a political goal. In terms of functional activity, the goals could also be based on production or service functions. These goals may further create various orientations for different regions as well as generate all kinds of conflicts. Thus a vital function of regional planning is resolving these conflicts.

Another essential requirement for planning the supra-urban space is that it should be an area over which effective decisions can be made. In this regard, it has been proposed that regional planning is most effective when a clear spatial basis can be identified at the urban, rural or metropolitan scales of resolution.

The clearer this is the greater the chance of making effective policies and plans for developing the particular region (Tang, 1978; Bunker, 1971). This underscores the fact that while regional planning in developed economies is more urban or metropolitan-based, it is more rural-oriented in most Third World countries (Conyers, 1985). However, like the changing nature of the region this is not a permanent structure. For example, at the time of writing the latest population census since 1984 was undertaken, together with the counting of houses, in Ghana. While sixteen years ago Ghana was only thirty-two per cent urbanized and sixty-eight per cent rural, the population census held in 2000 would show the former to have grown appreciably, an expansion in the urban component of the country.

Another emphasis is made on the role of regional planning in co-ordinating activities and processes in the localities within supra-urban space. This means that there must be administrative structures and procedures for making this co-ordination possible. Indeed, the feasibility of regional planning depends on the existence of these institutional structures (van Stavaren and van Dusseldorp, 1980). These other elements mentioned earlier and the need for political legitimacy define regional planning as a continuous process of policy-making, exercising of control instruments and the creation of systems of effective communication (Gillingwater and Hart, 1978).

In this regard, the policy exists through the initiation of it, articulation and implementation within the supra-urban space, between the administrative and spatial scales both in the present and strategic future. This is a most important driver for directing the energies of the region's administrators and politicians. It further relates to the role of control as expressed in the concrete interventions required to make regional planning happen in material terms. Regional planning could not proceed without the necessary creation and informing communication channels between central and regional-local administrations. While these three processes - policy, control and communication - of regional planning could not be isolated, effective co-ordination must be required to manage the complex relationships between them (Conyers 1986; Hilhorst, 1971).

These views are also reflected in a another important conception of regional planning. According to Dunham (1977), regional planning involves a process of negotiation with many public and private-sector interest groups. Indeed, Wenban-Smith and Beeston (1990) have argued out the importance and processes of negotiation in the planning process in general. Dunham's view relates to the fact that the main aim in regional planning is the production of plans for improving investment decisions, especially in a dependent and underdeveloped regional economy. It is not the view, in this book, that this is the pervasive role of regional planning as noted earlier. However, Dunham (1977) points out that negotiation and management are technical and equally crucial aspects of the regional planning process. He further argues that an objective of regional planning is to influence the decision-making practices and cultures of the elitists and local relations between and within these classes; between all these on one hand and the wider populace on the other. Therefore, Dunham points out that the spatial and economic structure of the region reflects the patterns of decision-making within it. Thus the spatial structure exists in the extent that the various interest groups succeed in configuring it. This process also reflects the bargaining power available to the interest groups. In relation to these considerations, Dunham emphasizes the role of regional planners as managers, negotiators and able technicians. These roles, among others, have also been recognized in planning practice in general (Healey, 1991).

Inter-regional and intra-regional planning One important aspect of regional planning is the distinction between intra-regional and inter-regional planning (Martins, 1986; Conyers, 1985; 1984; Burke, 1980; Glasson, 1978). The latter tends to be homogeneous in scope and has been concerned with the mobility and balancing of national commitment and action between regions. It deals more with distribution and allocation of resources with the primary goal of reducing inequalities in terms of income and other economic factors between regions.

Intra-regional planning is focused on the translation of national policy into regional context with particular emphasis on the implementation aspects of public policy. It is at this level that the need for public participation, co-ordination and management of development initiatives are most present (Conyers, 1985; Gillingwater, 1975). In more material terms, it is at the intra-regional level that physical, environmental as well as socio-economic elements are most clearly expressed. Therefore, the need to be concerned with power and its relations is also more felt at this level. Indeed, Martins (1986, p. 2) has defined regional planning as 'the management of change at the intra-regional level which is achieved by the public sector through the allocation of resources, the shaping of the physical environment and the influencing of economic and social activity'. However, the inter-regional mode emerges now and again and it is important to have it in view. For example, the provision for the creation of Joint Planning Areas and Special Development Areas under current planning laws in Ghana is evidence of this need.

The aim in intra-regional planning, however, is to achieve a beneficial and meaningful relationship between people, jobs, activities and the environment within the region (Glasson, 1978). The specific focus includes allocating resources between various local communities within the region as well as between different policies and sector-based areas. Therefore, the urgent need for generating employment and economic activity in a consistent and sustainable way bears critical implications for the natural and human resources of the region. Thus environmental sustainability could not be ignored. Another important consideration is deciding on the location of new industrial and other economic activity and the settlements in which expansion should take place. Therefore problems and issues such as providing housing, social, cultural and leisure facilities and dealing with diseconomies of congested towns, cities and distribution of investment come into sharper focus at this intra-regional level.

So is the pervasive need to maintain a balanced relationship between all settlements - rural and urban - within the region. An equally sensitive aspect is maintaining the quality of the urban form and being concerned about the environmental impacts of development projects on both the urban and rural centres. The power relations between urban and rural areas has become increasingly important in intra-regional planning because of the greater tendency for the former to consistently siphon out resources and the real benefits of development from the latter. Lipton (1977) has described this behaviour in relation to the former as 'urban bias' and holds it to account for poverty in the latter. However, poverty has far more underlying causes, both endogenous and extraneous (Harris, 1992; 1986; Todaro, 1989; Seitz, 1988; Griffin and Khan, 1978; Balogh, 1978; Ahluwalia, 1976).

The need to integrate and co-ordinate the intra-regional issues and demands through a regional plan is also imperative if there is to be any significant development. This has been pointed out in relation to the meaning of regional planning. Such a plan would have regard, for example, to the allocation of funds for the improvement of the region's transportation networks, water supply and waste management systems as well as other forms of social infrastructure in the rural areas. It would also lead to the generation of employment and income.

As suggested briefly earlier, inter-regional or intra-regional planning may be a matter of emphasis. It appears that there is a historical continuum in the emergence of inter-regional issues initially and the intra-regional later in many Third World countries (Williamson, 1975). The main determining factor, in this regard tends to be political power. The advantages of intra-regional planning, however, include the greater opportunities it offers for the implementation of innovative developments as it involves local initiatives in determining growth and development within the region. Therefore, the institutional frameworks for enabling and promoting this effort are also more crucial in this relation to securing the objectives of regional planning. The multiplicity of issues and the faster rates of processes at the more local and intra-regional level requires constant and consistent monitoring as well as evaluation of developments (Weaver, 1984; 1981; 1978; Mabogunje and Faniran, 1977; Friedmann, 1975).

Regional development and regional planning A further distinction often made is that between regional development and regional planning (Conyers, 1985; Alden and Morgan, 1974). The former deals with the content of plans or programmes and is more concerned with the processes of regional growth and spatial change. Thus regional development denotes the form and level of change or improvement that takes place as the result of planning effort. Regional planning is more concerned with the processes of policy formulation and plan-making. It is equally concerned with the procedures and practices by which the plan, including the programmes and projects it contains, is implemented - and consequently with the total impact it makes on the region. Regional development, in this regard, has been more based on substantive theory and has captured the attention of researchers and planners more than have procedural issues (Conyers, 1985).

There is also the tendency to describe both regional development and regional planning, inidividually, as development planning. In the context of this book as in other planning practices, however, development planning is considered as being about planned regional development that is essentially defined and shaped by a regional plan as the principal instrument of regional change. Indeed, there can be regional development without a regional plan or regional planning. This also emphasizes the statutory planning framework pointed out at the beginning of this chapter for real regional planning. However, as noted already, substantive and procedural approaches are not two necessarily conflicting components. Nevertheless, it is important to underline the fact that procedural planning and plan-based regional change have been largely neglected in many Third World and sub-Saharan African countries, including Ghana. Therefore, this book aims at being much more concerned with this form of planning practice.

Territorial and functional regional planning Two other paradigmatic modes need be clarified based on the terms, 'territory' and 'function'. In their work, *Territory and Function*, Friedmann and Weaver (1979) pointed out the challenge thrown to regional planning by neo-Marxists, who had rejected the 'urban-industrial' focus and approach (p. 175; p. 187). Their criticism was that regional planning was initially characterized by a territorial approach, then was taken over by functional forces with the subsequent re-emerging of territory. It appears, however, the reawakening of territorial thought and practice has come to meet with far stronger functional forces that the two have become locked into a vigorous struggle and conflict. Functional regional planning is based on centrist power, elitist interests, corporate structures and characterized by a high level of self-interest. This is invariably focused on the city or urban base with the concentration of resources, systems and institutional structures (Hebbert, 1982; Hilhorst, 1981; Friedmann and Weaver, 1979; Weaver, 1978). This form of development, of course, does not benefit the majority of the regional community at any time, so the dissatisfaction with it.

Territorial regional planning is based on community involvement in decision-making on the allocation and use of resources, action for improving their own well-being and raising their standards of living. This people-based approach operates largely by selective closure and territorial ownership of productive resources. It is essentially characterized by democratic participation and equal access to socio-political power in sub-metropolitan contexts. Territorial planning is thus based on an ethic of humanism and practice of decentralization, what has been characterized as neo-decentralism (Hebbert, 1982). It addresses itself to basic human needs, local mobilization of resources as well as inward and endogenous development. However, it must be emphasized that the 'territorial' is not another synonym for 'rural' or a homogeneous rural area. It is one that includes many and rapidly growing small and large villages as well as small and medium towns. This will be illustrated in chapter six.

In this regard also, environmental sustainability, appropriateness of technology and innovative development become critical issues as the intra-regional community seek to take control of their regional destiny. Other elements of the territorial mode are bottom-up processes and labour-intensive development. It also has greater concern for personal, group and disaggregated income as for the rural parts. Therefore, it would appear that territorial regional planning has a greater opportunity and promise of reducing poverty (Ofori, 1995a; Hebbert, 1982; Hilhorst, 1981; Stohr and Taylor, 1981; Friedmann and Weaver, 1979; Weaver, 1978).

The territorial mode of regional planning has, however, been criticized on a number of grounds. It appears to be an integration of strands of ideas, in an eclectic fashion, relating to populism and localism. In this regard, it appears that functional regional planning is much less consistent and concrete (Hebbert, 1982). Indeed, Hebbert (1982) has raised doubt about the political and economic realism of such an approach and calls for an incorporation of 'territory' and 'function'. In this way, one can expect realistic and effective regional government and policy. Territorial regional planning has also been dented on the ground that its supposed legitimacy in relation to power is unreal. In the real world, even such territorial power tends to be concentrated in the hands of elitist groups. Hilhorst (1981) argued that the conflict and struggle between functional and territorial powers, in which the latter only tend to relinquish their own, has an opportunity of being resolved in the ratification and clarification of power and power-relations. In this way too, policy-making and reformulation have a greater chance of being enhanced and made effective. Stohr and Todtling (1977) also agree with this approach.

Another critique of territorial thought is in the way it treats external, including international forces. The point here is that the territorial region cannot develop entirely on own resources. In many cases, capital investment must come in from outside. It has even been suggested that the territorial regions must totally cut off relations with international hegemonic centres of economic power: de-linkage. The case of contemporary Ghana, for example, illustrates vividly that this is absolutely unrealistic and not possible. In this relation, 'selective spatial closure' is also not articulated. Indeed, it is doubtful that any territorial region in the Third

World can close itself to and turn its back on external financial resources.

Regional planning is viewed in this book as a continuous process of deliberate, consciously dynamic, sufficiently rational and action-oriented decision-making about improvements in the standards of living and material well-being of the community in a region. The region must have legitimate and sufficient political-administrative jurisdiction as well as a resource base enough to fuel and sustain its growth and development. Decision-making should be operationally based on the formulation of appropriate policies derived from effective, sensitive and sensible identification of social, economić and environmental problems in the region. Therefore, the region must be politically empowered to make decisions about its own development.

The regional policy-making should be guided within the framework of national development policy. The formulated regional policies then provide the foundation and context for designing a regional plan, including specific programmes and projects. These initiatives which are aimed at developing both the rural and urban areas in the region are implemented by suitable planning strategies to achieve the goals and objectives of the plan.

The performance of the regional plan and its implementation must be assessed through effective monitoring and evaluation of the programmes and projects. What is seen as constituting 'improvements in the standards of living and material well-being', in this regard, depends not only on the perceptions and values of the region's endogenous communities, but of the decision-makers and planners who undertake the planning activities with them and on their behalf. The regional planning process may involve conflicts between the various policy areas as well as between sectors and sections of the regional community. Therefore, regional planning should involve effective participatory decision-making and the appropriate resolving of these conflicts.

General underlying and engaging themes in regional planning

A number of themes underlie the analyses and discussions in this book (Table 1.1). These both emphasize and characterize trends as well as perspectives in urban and regional planning in general, Third World regional planning in particular. The engaging motifs are thus used as criteria of further legitimacy and validity in the practice and process of regional planning. In this regard, they are applied in testing out how and the extent to which things are made to happen in the Ghanaian territorial region.

Democratic enterprise in planning This derives from the idealist, normative and prescriptive origins of urban and regional planning (Hyde, 2000; Healey, 1993; Cooke, 1983). The democratic enterprise also stems from the role of the state,

Table 1.1 General engaging themes

Theme	*Characteristic Elements*
Democratic enterprise in planning	Societal participation; territorial empowerment; negotiated and mediated power-relations; shared action, decision-making and experiential learning; team-work among territorial and functional forces; partnership; class struggle and social conflict; dialectical processes
Sustainable development; environmental sustainability	Equities between and within generations; cost-effective and ecologically-wise technologies; conflict in resource use; constraints and hazards; management of carrying capacity; sustainability of built and non-built habitats; economic and environmental sustainability; sustainability of exchangeable surplus
Strategic effectiveness	Appropriateness; implementation; evaluation; legitimacy; capability; competence; quality assurance; monitoring; sustainable material improvement; control; communication; co-ordination; appropriate and valid indicators of policy and programme objectives; long-term and broad-based
Robustness	Comprehensiveness; responsiveness; integration; strategic flexibility; strategic change; variety; coherence; boldness; strategic perspective; validity; feasibility; jurisdictional coverage; non-spatial separatism; effective and functional linkages

Source: Personal creation

that of functional-domination as well as extraneous and social forces in planning (Wannop, 1995; Cooke, 1983). The relationship among the contending forces in the process of planning requires the democratic involvement of all in shared decision-making, action and social learning. While the democratic enterprise includes shared power-relations, it involves a struggle among the engaged forces which also typifies conflict in a socio-political way. There is a dominant focus on the means and benefits of production and utilization of resources. However, there is a tendency for the process to result in a zero-sum game, if not a minimal and marginal benefit for the weakest forces. Thus the democratic enterprise must call for and be aimed at achieving social and distributive justice (Healey, 1993).

The democratic enterprise also implies the recognition of locality and local variation in human and natural resources. Therefore it underlies and denotes the importance of partnerships in regional development (Ofori, 2000a). This brings together the public domain, local community and the private sector. In this way, a real relationship between corporate-functional and territorial forces is forged.

In the same way, the democratic enterprise ethic and practice enshrine the culture of team-working. Hastings (1992, p. 933) has observed that 'This form of collaboration is vital to solving complex problems fast, gaining commitment to change, and tapping the full reservoir of latent energy and ideas possessed' by members of an organization, community or society. A 'team' is larger and meant to be more functional than a 'group'. It may be designated differently, depending on place and context and particular function (Gilgeous, 1987). It is a useful and effective structure for programme implementation and management of regional change. The full range of skills, knowledge and experiences of team members are brought to bear on the problems to be solved . All members of the team must value as well as mutually recognize and respect each other. They must have clarity of intent, effective co-ordination, interdependence, cohesion and purpose as well as commitment to the team's agenda and functions (Gilgeous, 1997; Belbin, 1996). This also underlines the utmost importance of effective inter-personal communication (Gilgeous, 1997; Belbin, 1996). Team-work is essentially participatory and involves shared, respecting and mutual learning.

The democratic enterprise, while recognizing atomism also promotes the recognition and effective inclusion of space in the planning and development process. Regional planning has been heavily criticized for its separation of spatial factors from the wider context, denigration of social, political and overwhelming emphasis on the economic aspect (Simon, 1990b; Gore, 1984; Cooke, 1983; Slater, 1975). This trend and inclination which has been characterized as 'spatial separatism' also underlies the isolation of development theory from spatial planning (Dewar, Todes and Watson, 1986; Cooke, 1983; Massimo, 1982; Mabogunje, 1980). There has, therefore, been the tendency to apply the same policy and strategy to all places without any recognition for their variations and distinctiveness. In fact, this limitation further tends to strengthen sector-based forces at the expense of spatial ones (Simon, 1990a). The democratic enterprise in planning holds a potential for healing the fallacy of spatial separatism.

There is an increasing support for spatial planning in the many new decentralization policies and attempts at empowering local people in territorial communities in Third World countries (Simon, 1990a; Gattoni, 1989). This must also imply the need to introduce structures that promote the democratic enterprise ethic. Therefore, the democratic enterprise provides a useful and appropriate construct for addressing the roles and participation of all the various forces and achievements in the regional planning process. It is thus critical to the understanding in this book to identify and assess the legitimacy and effectiveness of these roles and their consequences on the Ghanaian territorial region.

Sustainable development and environmental sustainability The World Council for Environment and Development (WCED, 1987, p. 43) has stated that 'sustainable development is development that meets the needs of the present without compromising the ability of future generations to meet their own needs'. Therefore, the need to ensure a consistent improvement in the standard and quality of life is underpinned by the effective management of the carrying capacity of the supporting ecosystems. The critical importance of this for regional development and the management of its resources could not be under-emphasized in the territorial context. The territorial region is one that is primarily dependent on the development of its resources. Indeed, it is emphasized that the incorporation of space and spatial relations, in this regard, is as important as the full integration of environmental planning and management in regional development planning (UNEP and UNCHS, 1987). Understanding the use of regional resources accords with the wisest minimizing of the hazards stemming from human action to both natural systems and built habitats. This makes natural resource development and the human effort needed to make things happen of the greatest necessity in this connection.

From the idea of democratic enterprise in planning, it is clear that the value of political power and production relations in the territorial region must also receive due emphasis (Friedmann and Forest, 1988). This aspect also includes an urgency in addressing the conflicts between demanding goals and uses, say socio-economic and environmental objectives; technological practices and quality of the local-regional environment.

The issue of environmental quality relates, in detail, to air, water, land, flora and fauna of the region. Environmental sustainability thus involves the critical need to ensure that the forms, levels and rates of economic activity and the employment so generated are efficiently and consistently maintained. A further reflection of this consideration in the quantitative and qualitative aspects underlies the utilization of regional environmental resources. In the same way, the urgent need to value the equities between individuals and groups of people in the present as well as between such categorizations within the present and future in the territorial region ensures the sustainability of the exchangeable surplus base for the region. A productive and effective relation between functional and territorial forces in the judicious exploitation of regional resources also promotes the attainment of this goal. The management of this relationship, however, has critical implications for the actual value of exchange to the regional populations and in relation to their use of resources.

While the notion and praxis of environmental sustainability provide an effective framework for territorial regional development processes, it is argued in this book that its validity is best borne out through an appropriate regional plan. The importance of this framework is also indicated in the need to integrate all sectors of the region and co-ordinate the various activities within it. More importantly, it creates the foundation for designing programme-based development initiatives from which finer and integrated projects are derived. This approach also provides a realistic basis for the formulation of regional policy goals, programmes and project objectives (UNEP and UNCHS, 1987).

Strategic effectiveness This is used here to mean the fullest and best match between performers of roles and their tasks on one hand, consumers of these activities on the other and over time (Johnson and Scholes, 1999). This is also applicable to the undertaking of any activity against the levels of the requirements, demands and expectations. These mean the ability and capabilities of the planners to take the right decisions and actions in relation to the 'planned for' in the widest range and over the perspective term. A further implication, in this regard, is the essence of ensuring that the right problems in relation to socio-economic, spatial and environmental changes are identified as a basis for formulating the right policies and strategies.

While effectiveness dwells in the actions of individual undertakers and agents, it also characterizes the capabilities and areas of organizational competence and institutional structures in matching the needs of their constituencies. Therefore, strategic effectiveness is the central and pervasive criterion test of regional programme implementation. In relation to this, it is critical to assessing the effectiveness of planning policies and programmes in alleviating the conditions of poverty in the territorial region over time.

In so far as it relates to evaluation, effectiveness is used to mean the ability to achieve the goals and objectives of policies and programmes (e.g. Republic of Ghana, 1970). This implies the ability and capability to reduce, if not eliminate the drift between policy intents and actual attainments (Robson, 1993). The connection between expressed or stated intent and actual achievement as well as the specific indicators of the activities are essential aspects of effectiveness. These elements also measure the appropriateness and validity of the attainment in relation to the defined policy objectives over the short, medium and long terms. A need to clarify the relationship between programme goals and policy objectives also underpins appropriateness (Hogwood and Gunn, 1984). In these regards, strategic effectiveness is enhanced by the appropriate choice of indicators for measuring the attainment of policy goals and objectives in relation to the perspective period. However, it is useful and important to build in evaluation into the design stage of programmes and projects in advance of implementation. This also contributes to ensuring an effective practice of evaluation and strategic effectiveness (Robson, 1993).

Robustness This is widely applied to various situations as for example, in management (Johnson and Scholes, 1999) and urban design (Bentley *et al.*, 1985). In the present book, robustness is used to mean the capability of the regional planning system, practices and processes and the capacity for dealing with a variety of issues and problems that include the linkages among these in the region. The strategic adaptability, flexibility and responsiveness of regional planning practice in addressing the plethora of challenges that face the region are essential elements of robustness (Wannop and Smith, 1985). In this way, regional planning is able to achieve a wider variety, hopefully, of results. These also reflect a wider range of strategic regional trends.

There is a further implication in robustness that the regional plan and other instruments are effective in making the regional planning process plan-led than development-led so that it has consideration for the whole region in material terms. Therefore, the region has the benefit of gaining total coverage under the particular planning instrument and with respect to strategy, even in a targeted form. Robustness thus imbibes a self-critiquing and adjustment mechanism in a learning process than a blue-print. In relation to this, it has the advantage of contributing to the development and review of policy as well as planning methodology (Wannop and Smith, 1985; Skelcher, 1982).

Furthermore, a robust regional planning has regard for all dimensions of the region in terms of its spatial, economic, social, environmental, institutional as well as political factors. Therefore, it has an additional merit of promoting the abolition of spatial separatism. Robustness must also bring regional planning in accord with its constituency and jurisdictional support. In this relation, robust regional planning practice thrives best in the region by sufficiently empowering territory to decide on its own allocation of resources, formulate its own policies, plan and design its programmes and projects.

Evolution of the space economy and development policy in Ghana

The development of the space economy in Ghana, as in many countries of the Third World, is often presented as having colonialist origins in particular. However, it does have pre-colonial as well as post-colonial origins to some extent (Songsore, 1979; Howard, 1978; Hinderink and Sterkenburg, 1975; Kay, 1972; Dickson, 1969). The intention here is to set the background for the focus in this book and to sound out the general influence of the spatial history.

Ghana, before the colonial era was organized into individual kingdoms and nation states which were engaged in a very lucrative trade between the forest and savanna regions, and between these on one hand and the North African coast on the other. This activity was particularly intensive between the eighth and fifteenth century *Anno Domini*. The atavistic rise and fall of these territories coincided with changing levels of prosperity resulting from the regional and international trade. These, however, had the main effect of developing a network of paths and trade routes which connected the earliest ports and other trading posts. Another effect was the emergence of an incipient network of settlements, reflecting the varying levels of territorial power and prosperity (Dickson, 1969). The initial socio-economic and spatial inequalities that developed as a result of these processes were to be pronounced and differently patterned later. The main causal factor, in this regard, was the uninvited European contact with its capitalist forces providing a greater spatial restructuring force (Songsore, 1979).

European contact which appeared in Ghana in 1471, first through Portuguese traders, geared the pre-capitalist and commodity economy to a quasi-capitalistic or capitalistic mode of production. This was done through the introduction of external financial capital, monetized trade and the creation of a labour market (Songsore, 1979; Howard, 1978; Dickson, 1975). Apart from restructuring areas, these processes also created new modes of social class formation (Andrae, 1981; Howard, 1978). Since European penetration came from the coast, the pre-colonial force of gravity shifted from the interior territory to the littorals with the introduction of mercantile capitalism (Songsore, 1979; Howard, 1978; Dickson, 1969). This triggered off both economic and social dominance within and between the inchoate communities (Howard, 1978; Dunham, 1977; Kay, 1972).

The search for the main commodities gold, ivory, and slaves attracted the European traders into the forest belt and Ghana became 'integrated' into the world capitalist system with the extraction of these export commodities (Songsore, 1979; Dunham, 1977). Most of the early societies were not integrated while traditional leaders and earlier elitist classes became part of a wealth accumulation system (Songsore, 1979). This period coincided with the development and consolidation of Western capitalism and capitalist production (Harrison, 1987; Harris, 1986; Songsore, 1979; Dunham, 1977).

Impacts of colonial and post-colonial development on the space economy

The main impacts of these processes on the space economy included the development of a matrix of settlements over the coastal and inland zones which played the role of 'middleman' towns for the channelling of commodities to and from the ports (Songsore, 1979; Santos, 1979; Dickson, 1969). While all these settlements were the beginnings of the present towns and cities, Kumasi particularly acted as the link between the Southern and Northern centres. It has been pointed out, however, the fact that the system of settlements that developed at this time was different in structure and spatial organization from the one that pre-existed (Dickson, 1971; 1969). This underlies the imposition of a new system of settlements on the traditional and indigenous human habitats.

Another impact was the formal political domination with the extension of political jurisdiction and administrative power over the Northern territories (Howard, 1978; Dunham, 1977; Dickson, 1975). There was also a heavy investment in the development of infrastructure, notably transport, in support of the seats of power as well as sources of agricultural commodities and minerals (Howard, 1978; George, 1976; Hilhorst, 1971).

There also emerged an induced social class formation consisting of a petty bourgeoisie of indigenous traders, merchants and scholars and mostly all urban-based. However, these did not succeed in developing into an indigenous capitalist class because they had no share in the monopoly control of the growing international trade. A further phenomenon of this social formation was the stratification of the incipient communities in the peripheral areas into rich farmers, a middle peasantry and an indebted peasantry, apart from a migrant agricultural labour force (Santos, 1979; Howard, 1978). Therefore, there was a corresponding variety of social classes to the scale of settlements that emerged.

In so far as the colonial power came to determine every form of development in the colony, this created a process that has been described as 'combined development' (Santos, 1979; Santos, 1970). The space economy of the latter was geared to that of the former. Indeed, British colonial power that appeared later made it clear that the colony was important to the extent that it served as source of food and raw materials as well as provided market for its own goods. While this was, perhaps, a frank and non-altruistic indication of intent, the attitude and policy were to produce serious consequences for the colony. Thus the extension of the rail from Sekondi in the Western Region to Kumasi in 1903 was also aimed at gaining greater control over gold-mining in the latter. This rail network was further extended from Kumasi to Accra because of cocoa growing in the eastern part of the country. This kind of landscape which characterizes the whole of tropical Africa has not changed, basically, from what it was in the eighteenth century (Dickson, 1969).

The concentration of the export-import activity meant that the colonial state did not allow the mode of production to change by way of diversification in agriculture and industrial production (Howard, 1978). This was also to characterize the creating of a mono-crop economy later. Besides, there was a neat repatriation of huge profits as the people were under-remunerated by unequal exchange (Howard, 1978; Emmanuel, 1972). This is a situation in which goods of equal value, with respect to the labour-power which enters their production in two different countries, are not exchanged for equal prices. In this case, the superior producer or capitalist country repatriates a large amount of surplus value (i.e. profit) from the exploited country. Perhaps, underdevelopment is used to justify unequal exchange. This is not tenable. Indeed, the latter is one of the means by which the former is produced.

Of course, one significant aspect of the process was the siphoning of manpower from the peripheral areas to the core centres (Songsore, 1979). In fact, there was a deliberate as well as autonomous labour migration process from the other parts of the colony to the core centres in the Southern territory. The North and parts of the Volta Region were designed as labour reserves and not, yet, considered ecologically suited to export activity. In this way those territories were neglected, becoming areas of massive out-migration and depression.

The political-administrative regions of Ghana, as they are today, emerged out of these processes and from this territorial organization. Those regions which had the resource potential and were thus favoured by colonial policy have relatively high levels of development (Dickson, 1975; Szezerewski, 1966). However, it must be stressed that these spatial variations in development are only symptomatic of the underlying and characteristic socio-economic conditions.

On the bases of these and functional considerations, Andrae (1981) categorized the Ghanaian regions into various sets. The first one is the Periphery (rural) comprising the Northern, Upper East and Upper West Regions. This set is followed by the Export Periphery (less rural), the Brong Ahafo, northern and north-eastern Volta Region and part of Western Region. The other sector is the Core (far less rural) covering Ashanti, Greater Accra, Central, parts of Eastern and Western Regions. However, Songsore (1979) recognised colonial Ghana in terms of a 'centre' being the forest belt of the South, and a 'periphery' - all other territories, especially northwards. Nevertheless he pointed that, in the neo-colonial or post-colonial state, a different spatial system emerged in which there is a 'new periphery' of cash crop production areas as against the 'old periphery' of non-cash crop producing parts. It must be pointed out, however, that much of the production from the 'old periphery' has the value of cash crop surplus. This is, for example, reflected in current economic diversification efforts in Ghana. Indeed, this categorization also has the potential to obfuscate the reality of the so-called 'non-cash crop' becoming valued and transformed into 'cash crops'.

It is also significant to recognize that the scale of the rural which is also explicit in the former categorization and implied in the latter aspect further reflects a corresponding structure of urban development. The more peripheral the area, the greater the tendency for less urban development to exist. This may well depend on the definition and conception of an urban place. For example, it is somewhat deceptive to consider the Central Region as part of the core, except in consideration of its past glory as the seat of the colonial government between 1850 and 1877 (Dunham, 1977). This picture will be clearer in chapter six. However, the categorizations coincide with the ecological zones which explain their resource potential and their places as objects of colonial development policy. It must be emphasized, the fact that the colonial development process took place in a highly centralized administrative system (Rambanapasi, 1989; Harris, 1986; Songsore, 1979).

In post-independent Ghana, there was a clear investment in and expansion of public infrastructure, especially with respect to some social services and industrial base. The latter was already an area neglected by the colonial state. The taste for imported goods and the existence of a voracious market and negative attitudes towards traditional goods also encouraged this development. Industrial development plans were drawn up in an import-substituted fashion and centred on the already core centres of Sekondi-Takoradi, Accra-Tema and Kumasi. Although not fully implemented, these further exacerbated the inter-regional out-migration process, in which çase the little metropolitan infrastructure was only strengthened by accretions to support the population influxes.

This could be said to have had a double negative effect. There was not the provision of urban infrastructure at the rate of population increase. Second, there has been an overburdening of the existing core, leading to what has been described as the 'ruralization of towns' in Third World countries (Mountjoy, 1976 quoted in Chadwick, 1987). The main strategy was urban-industrial, based on the assumption that 'development' would trickle down to the territorial areas but this has been far less than expected (Rondinelli, 1983a). As would be expected, new business, especially multinational and further petty bourgeoisie activity also continued to be centred on the core areas. Besides, the centralized administrative system was maintained.

What emerged were broad spatial and socio-economic inequalities, not only between Northern and Southern Ghana, and between the regions, but also significantly within the regions - between urban and rural areas (Dickson, 1975). This is seen in terms of, for example, per capita income and social indicators relating to health, education, housing and utility factors (Okonjo, 1986; Kudiabor, 1986; 1977). Indeed, the sentiments of the communities of the regions have been expressed not only in the agitation for the creation of more regions as was the case in Brong-Ahafo and Upper West Regions. There has also been similar clamouring for the creation of more District Assembly areas within the regions (Ayee, 1994). While these social and political pressures may be justified, it is also important to emphasize the point that the structure of the space economy as it emerged in the pre-colonial era did not change much in the colonial and post-colonial eras (Rambanapasi, 1989; Dickson, 1975).

In the post-independence era, therefore, several of the problems of colonial development processes still persist with efficient obduracy. This is shown, for example, in the national core-periphery structure. Many of the settlements in the territorial areas, however, are not integrated into the national and regional space economy. The main reason is that they are engaged mostly in a vertically structured export production activity, especially in the agricultural sector. Otherwise, many of them have no sustainable production and exchangeable surplus. Invariably, this is related to the poorly-developed infrastructure for accessing those areas, while existing spatial linkages are also weak. Their role in the overall social development of the country is still not much appreciated. Therefore the inter-settlement interactions, especially urban-rural in terms of trade, as well as at the inter-sector-based are very low, if not vestigial. Thus trade flows in this connection, if any, are weak.

This further means that the majority of the people who live in the peripheral territories are deprived of basic social and economic infrastructure. Expectedly, therefore, income and employment in such areas are very low and more unsustainable. These are further push factors in the out-migration process. Development has been more sector-based than plan-led. There is little or no economic activity outside agriculture, apart from petty trading and service activities (Ofori, 2000g; Thomi and Yankson, 1985). The migration to the few parasitic towns and cities and consequent burdening of the urban infrastructure and concomitant 'ruralization' of the urban landscape cause further environmental problems (Tang, 1981; Republic of Ghana, 1970). The dismal fact is that the role of Ghana, like other Third World countries, in the international economic system will continue and be more intensified (Gooneratne and Obudho, 1997; Donkor, 1997; Howard, 1978).

These colonial and post-colonial developments are now being complemented by the global and corporate forces through the process of globalization. These business organzations are becoming increasingly powerful through restructuring and greater profitability, therefore able to provide more financial resources. The reality, however, is that they are determining and controlling much of regional development in the Third World. This trend is not likely to diminish and will also be addressed as the analysis in this book progresses.

The Ghanaian state's early perceptions of regional disparities

The earliest reaction of the Ghanaian state to the problem of regional socio-economic disparities in post-colonial times came in the early 1960s. Presenting the seven-year national development plan to Parliament in 1963, the first President of Ghana (Republic of Ghana, 1963, p.15) observed that:

> The development of Ghana has hitherto not been sufficiently balanced between different parts of the country. It is the deliberate policy of this plan to correct this imbalance. Naturally, we must develop in each part the type of economic activity to which it is best suited by reason of natural resources and geographical location.

This statement recognized the unbalanced nature of development and the need for redressing the situation by a consciously and rationally formulated policy for the purpose. It also underlines the need to recognize the distinctiveness of the different parts of the country and in relation to their resource bases as well as spatial location. Importance is attached to the fact that these factors underpin the designing of appropriate production activities.

It was also noted five years later the urgency and importance of reducing income disparities between the regions and persons (Republic of Ghana, 1968, p. 2). The problem was also recognized in the two-year stabilization plan, 1968-70 (Republic of Ghana, 1968, p. 20):

> The geographical aspects of planning have not yet received much attention. The physical planning part of the Ministry of Economic Planning provides a link with the Regional Planning Committees thereby giving a spatial dimension to a development plan. The combination of physical and economic planning on a regional level will help the regions to define the structural problems and to identify their needs. Increasing attention will be given to the geographical aspects of planning but - as experience in other countries has shown - it will take sometime to harmonise economic and physical planning.

The need to recognize the spatial aspects of regional development was again emphasized. This emphasis also applies to harmonizing relationships between economic and physical aspects of regional planning. In the same way, it was also pointed out the greater responsibilities on sector ministries and planning agencies to achieve an integration between sector programmes (vertical planning) and the wider perspective of regional planning (horizontal planning).

The most significant reaction, perhaps, was the one shown by the 1975-80 five-year development plan. This plan had two principal aims. The first of these was strengthening the machinery for regional development planning in Ghana as a tool for plan formulation, and as a frame for plan implementation in each region. The second was progressively reducing the existing disparities in the levels of development and standard of living between regional centres and other urban areas, rural parts as well as gradually between and within the regions of the country. The intention to adopt a regional planning ideology was also declared (Republic of Ghana, 1977a, p.19):

> Ghana's planning experience has shown that regional planning has not received the attention that it deserves in the methodology of national development planning. Sector planning has been emphasised while regional planning has been played down as if they were two opposing approaches ... regional and rural needs do not receive the thorough attention that they deserve through such a planning methodology ... Government is determined during the plan period to employ regional planning to correct it.

It is also important to note the recognition that regional planning was still in denigration in the 'methodology of national development planning'. Methodology in this regard is understood as the nature and practice of the national planning system. This statement also supports the observation made already that one of the legacies of the colonial development process is sector-based planning as pointed out in the 1968-70 plan. Further, it has characterized the non-integrated space economy and has been practised at the expense of regional planning. Indeed, this skewed focus with respect to the former had created the impression that the two modes were antithetical practices. In this confusion, regional as well as rural needs were not receiving due and legitimate attention. The role in rectifying this situation through the instrument of regional planning is then hammered in.

The above statement was re-stated, in part, in the budget statement for 1980-81, under the Government of the Third Republic (Republic of Ghana, 1980, p. 63). The emphasis here was on the decentralization of the institutional framework for regional development. It had been indicated in the constitution of this Republic that regional development was the responsibility of the Regional Councils. Government also declared its intent to implement this general policy through the strategy of integrated rural development as well as rural-regional development.

While the initial concern was with the perceived disparities between the sub-national units of Ghana, the emphasis later included the intra-regional environment, making regional planning even more imperative. The need for the integration of economic and physical planning supports this argument because the former is largely concerned with income distribution, a homogeneous view of the space economy. The latter deals more with infrastructure and spatial issues, focuses on the local situation and essentially maintains heterogeneity. However, as noted already, regional planning in its intra-regional mode is the appropriate strategy to integrate the two (Alden and Morgan, 1974).

The initiation of regional planning practice in Ghana

In response to the problems of disparities in development between and within the regions, the Ghanaian state has taken several strategic steps to make a specific focus on and progressively address these (Table 1.2). Regional planning was introduced in Ghana at the national level in 1965. It was instituted at the regions in 1967 with the creation of Regional Planning Units attached to the Regional Administrative Offices (Bannerman, 1971; Republic of Ghana, 1970; 1968). The Regional Planning Units were placed under the central control of the Regional Resource Planning Unit within the Ministry of Finance and Economic Planning.

The formal introduction of regional planning was to provide impetus and framework for a major resettlement programme which was commissioned in 1966 - impact of flooding caused by the development of the Volta River hydro-electric power project. The planning of this scheme had started in the 1940s, late colonial period. The development affected some 80,000 people from 14,000 households. The resettlement programme involved the creation of over fifty new

Table 1.2 The development of regional planning in Ghana

Year	*Evolution of Regional Planning*	*Policy Focus and Implications for Planning Practice and Strategy*
1965	Introduction of regional planning at national level	Inter-regional development and 'trickle down' approach
1966	Implementation of Volta Basin Resettlement Scheme (planned since 1940s)	Resettlement-based regional planning: resettling some 80,000 people affected by the development of a hydro-power electric system
1967	Establishment of regional planning in the regions	Inter-regional development and 'trickle down' approach; initial concern with intra-regional issues
1968	Inauguration of Regional Planning Committee (RPC) in each region	Earliest post-Independence advisory regional governance: the beginning of substantive concern for intra-regional developments
1972	Declaration to adopt growth and service centre strategy	Policy of integrating national space-economy; urban and rural centres
1973	Creation of Regional Development Corporations (RDCs) in all regions	Expected focus on planned and project-based development and inward investment
1970s to 1980s	Introduction of various other regional-rural development programmes: VORADEP (1970s-80s), URADEP (1970s-80s), NORRIP (1979-80s), CARRIP (1980s; not fully implemented)	Designed in the context of integrated rural-regional initiatives: emphasis on agricultural and small-scale industrial production, services, road and communication infrastructure, agricultural extension
1983	Abolition of RPCs; inauguration of Regional Consultative Council (RCC)[1] in each region	Regional/local issues, programmes and projects; regional security and stability etc; general and wider regional issues
1988	Abolition of RCCs; Introduction of new local government law (PNDC Law 207); creation of Regional Co-ordinating Council (RCC)[2] in each region; creation of District Assemblies and District Planning and Budgeting Units (DPBUs)	1. Decentralized administrative framework; district development planning and popular participation 2. Advisory regional governance and general planning functions 3. Formal and re-organized district planning functions
1989	Proposal for national planning law and the first formal and quasi-legal backing for regional planning	Further emphasis on decentralization; provision for the identification of Special Development Areas (SDAs) and Special State Territories (SSTs); advisory regional governance
1994a	National Development Planning Commission Act: Creation of National Development Planning Commission (NDPC) & National Development Planning Secretariat (NDPS)	Inter-district, intra-regional issues; National and sector-based development plans
1994b	National Planning (Systems) Act: 1. Re-organization of RCC powers; creation of Regional Planning Co-ordinating Units (RPCUs) 2. Re-organization of District Assembly powers (District Planning Authority); creation of District Planning Co-ordinating Units (DPCUs)	1. Re-organized regional planning functions; strengthening of unelected regional governance 2. Legislative provision for creation of Joint Development Planning Areas (JDPA); Joint Development Planning Boards (JDPB); Special Development Areas (SDA) 3. Re-organized local governance and district planning functions

Source: Author's tabulation; (RCC)[1]: Regional Consultative Council; (RCC)[2]: Regional Co-ordinating Council; VORADEP: Volta Regional Agricultural Development Programme; URADEP: Upper Regional Agricultural Development Programme; NORRIP: Northern Regional Rural Integrated Programme; CARRIP: Central and Accra Regions Rural Integrated Programme

towns and villages. Generally, these ranged from main towns with between 8,000 and 10,000 people; service centre villages with 5,000 to 8,000 population; satellite villages less than 5,000 people; farmhouse and housestead at the village level.

Various assessments of this extensive programme indicate that it has been characterized by a number of serious problems. These relate to poor housing structures, inefficient and inadequate supporting infrastructure for economic activities; lack of the resource base to sustain these activities and the settlements are not integrated with existing settlement systems.

Subsequently and on the basis of the comprehensive post-colonial proposals for decentralization and the establishment of a machinery for social and economic development, Regional Planning Committees were established in all the regions in 1968 (Boateng, 1987; Bannerman, 1984; 1971; Republic of Ghana, 1970; 1968). The Committees were composed of the regional administrative officer, regional heads of sector ministries and agencies, private sector representatives, members of regional employers associations and employee unions. Other members were traditional leaders, clerks and chairpersons of principal local authorities, representatives of the banking and financial sector. Further members were leading development-minded or public-opinionated persons and, of course, the head regional planning officer who acted as secretary to the Committee (Bannerman, 1971; Republic of Ghana, 1970).

The functions of the Regional Planning Committees included collecting data on all local resources. These data and the derived information were to serve as basis for identifying potential growth areas and making appropriate development proposals to the respective sector ministries. It was also part of the responsibility in this regard to identify constraints on the expansion of existing agricultural and industrial activities in the region. Another function was the development of human resources of the region, by identifying and solving specific manpower needs of the region in relation to current and strategic economic activities. A further aspect was the co-ordination of regional development programmes and projects of the different government agencies in the region. These initiatives were to be harmonized with those of the private sector. The Committees were also to undertake the implementation of public and private sector projects, including co-operative and self-help ventures. This function also included efficient monitoring of budgetary plans and programmes as well as the preparation of quarterly progress reports. Furthermore, they were to initiate local and regional development by encouraging the growth of new centres of economic activity within the region.

It must be noted that the Regional Planning Committees had not the power to formulate formal and legitimate regional policies or plans. They were thus denied of a vital function of professional and effective regional planning. In relation to this, the opportunity was lost on the Committees to integrate socio-physical and economic aspects of regional development and provide a sustainable basis for regional planning. The Regional Planning Committees also lacked sufficient capitalization. Indeed, the Government recognized this weak financial position in the budget proposals for 1980-81 (Republic of Ghana, 1980). It has also been pointed out that the Committees did not have any statutory responsibility for making formal regional plans. Besides, they did not have executive powers and performed only purely advisory functions. It has been observed that the denial of the former and the mere exercising of the latter also seriously limit implementation effectiveness and success (Armstrong and Taylor, 1985; Friedmann, 1973; McCrone, 1969). In a conversation with the former head of regional planning in the Central Region, the author was informed that the Regional Planning Committees were imposed on a system of government in which they had no legitimacy. The existing institutional structure also did not provide for the co-ordination of ministerial plans. At any rate, these were no more than isolated projects and bearing no evidence of regionalization policy. Bannerman (1971) had, two decades earlier, vividly described the fashion and problem of preparing the budgetary plans which were only collections of isolated and one-off projects.

Apart from the Volta Basin resettlement scheme, a number of other regional development programmes have been implemented over the 1970s-1980s. These are the Volta Regional Agricultural Development Programme (VORADEP), a similar initiative: Upper Regional Agricultural Development Programme (URADEP), the Northern Regional Rural Integrated Programme (NORRIP). Another one is the Central and Accra Regions Rural Integrated Programme (CARRIP) which has not been fully implemented. This author has attempted to make general and individual assessments of these elsewhere (Ofori, 2000a; 1991a); it is not the intent to do this again in this book.

General observations are made in relation to these initiatives which are all of significance in Ghanaian regional planning. First, the programmes were not part of or set within formal and statutory regional planning. Second, these were not designed independently by the respective regional governments; created within the framework of national development programmes implemented at the regional level. Third, all initiatives involve substantial international, bilateral funding, and inward investment. Fourth, the existing structures for regional governance had no control over these programmes - all under specialized executive agencies and not necessarily reporting to the regional administrative and governing bodies. Fifth, the initiatives were all designed and set within the context of government's declared policy and strategy of integrated rural-regional development.

The Regional Planning Committees were abolished in the early 1980s and replaced with the establishment of Regional Consultative Councils. However, like the former, the latter were purely advisory and their functions much more limited in focusing on development aspects. This was because their functions included wider issues beyond planning functions. The Regional Consultative Councils also lacked legal empowerment. Like the Regional Planning Committees, they were severely under-funded. Nevertheless, as the author was informed in an interview with Professor B.A.W. Trevallion in 1989, some of the Regional Consultative Councils played positive advisory roles. These resulted in the initiation of concrete development activities. The Regional Consultative Councils have been replaced by Regional Co-ordinating Councils in the new planning system. This will be presented in a subsequent section of the book.

In 1972, the government had declared its intention to apply the growth centre policy and strategy in the development of Ghana's regions. A system of settlements was proposed. This consisted of a growth pole at the national level, growth centres at the regional level, growth points at district level and service centres at village levels (Kudiabor, 1986; 1977; 1972). The elaborate package has not been implemented as such, although some rural service centres have been established in parts of the country. Since the advent of structural adjustment programmes, substantial investments have been made in social and economic infrastructure in all district and regional centres. The successful impact of any system of growth centres, however, depends on its sustainable generative function (Thomi and Yankson, 1985; Ofori-Cujdoe, 1981; Dickson, 1971).

Further to the regional planning efforts, the Ghanaian state took the strategic action of creating Regional Development Corporations (RDCs) in all the regions of Ghana in 1973 (Republic of Ghana, 1973). These have been given broad and almost vague powers 'to carry on any business of an industrial, commercial and agricultural nature' (Republic of Ghana, 1973, section 2[1]) within the regions. It is also stated that a 'Regional Development Corporation may do all things as are incidental or conducive to the attainment of its objects' (Republic of Ghana, 1973, section 2[2]). The Corporations have the power to undertake property development (section 1[3]) and are expected 'to conduct their affairs on sound commercial lines' (section 3). Provision has also been made for them to enter into various partnerships and joint ventures with other organizations or persons (section 4).

The specific development focus of the Regional Development Corporations has, however, been disputed (Ofori, 2000a; Bannerman, 1984; The Ghanaian Times Corporation, 1982; Republic of Ghana, 1979; Republic of Ghana, 1977b). While it is expected that they focus on the development of the rural areas and inward investment activities, concern has been expressed across the Ghanaian society that they have only engaged in initiatives unrelated to real socio-economic development (Bannerman, 1984; The Ghanaian Times Corporation, 1982). Indeed, calls have been made for a redefinition of the functions of the Regional Development Corporations so they can concentrate specifically on concrete development initiatives (The Ghanaian Times Corporation, 1982). The issues relating to the RDCs will be further pointed out in chapter eight.

Further in support of regional planning in Ghana, the Government has promulgated more significant legislation and introduced innovative reforms in the 1980s and 1990s. In 1988 a new local government law was introduced. While the legislation covered almost entirely the creation and functions of District Assemblies, sections 111 to 116 dealt with the establishment and functions of Regional Co-ordinative Councils (Government of Ghana, 1988a). In 1989, a national development planning law was introduced for the first time. This included provisions for the establishment of a National Development Planning Commission and planning functions of the Regional Co-ordinating Councils which are carried out by the Regional Planning Co-ordinating Units. This legislation included the re-stated functions of the District Assemblies as the District Planning Authorities. The relationship between the local and regional planning authorities and the Commission is distinctively innovative.

Under its Fourth Republic, the Ghanaian state has re-enacted the drafted 1989 planning law into two principal pieces of legislation: the National Development Planning Commission Act and National Development Planning (System) Act (Republic of Ghana, 1994a; 1994a). This variety of legislation indicates a committed and strategic interest of the Ghanaian state in planning, in general, and regional planning, in particular. At least, there is a new attitude on the part of the central state to matters of planning in this regard.

The planning system

The current planning system is now described and the regional planning functions examined more critically (Figure 1.1). As highlighted already, the chief operational centre in the instituted planning system is a National Development Planning Commission which is linked with other statutory and non-governmental organizations. This system is part of the decentralized structure of government institutions. Therefore, the National Development Planning Commission (NDPC) is the co-ordinating fulcrum of the decentralized planning system.

The Commission has an advisory role in informing the Head of State about national development policy and strategy. It also has the function of analysing options for macro-economic and structural reforms in the country in relation to development planning. Thus the Commission's role involves the formulation of national development strategies, programme goals and objectives. The Commission also has the function of making proposals for national rolling plans within a perspective framework. An important function of the Commission, in this regard, is making proposals for attaining the 'even development' of the district localities. This also emphasizes the Ghanaian state's changing view of intra-regional disparities. It is also appropriate that the Commission's functions include the making of proposals for the protection of the natural and built

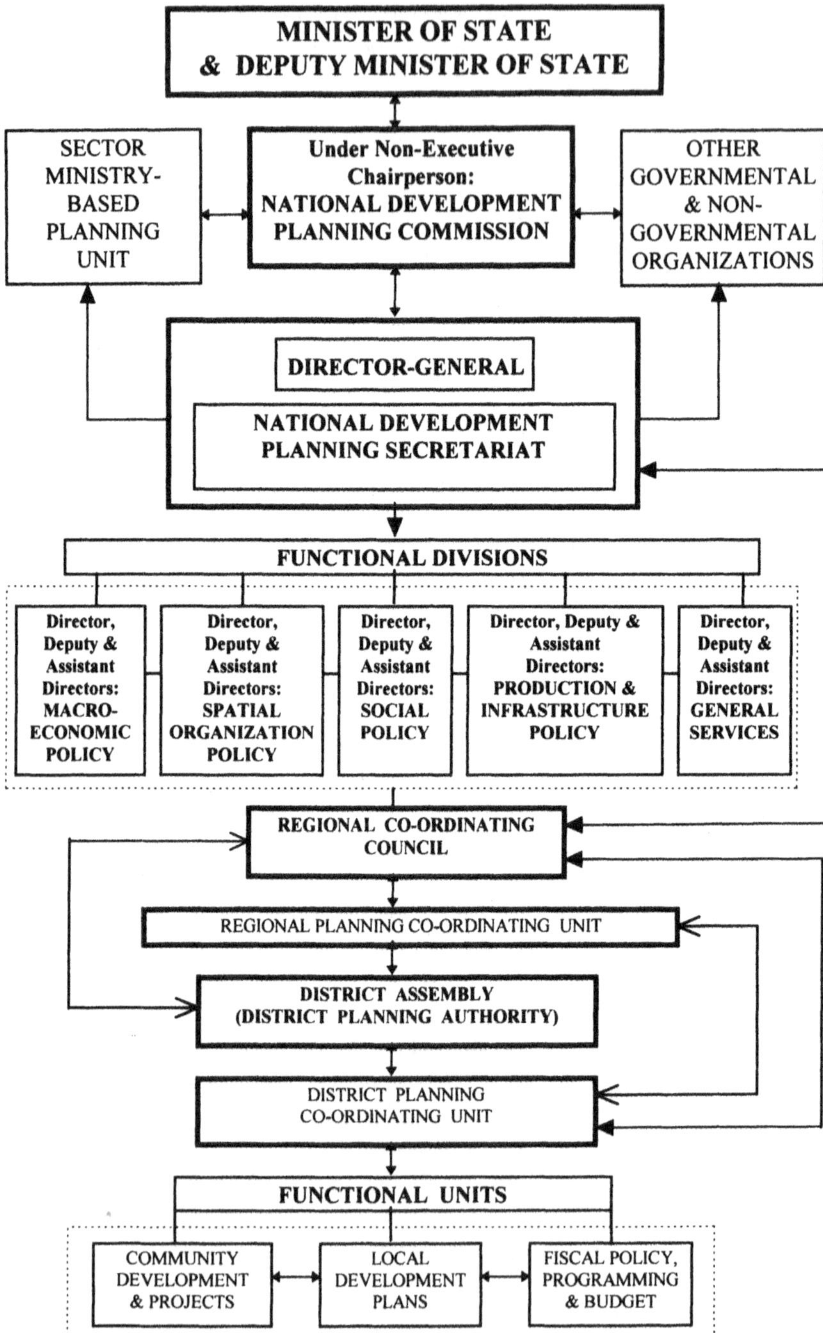

Figure 1.1 The planning system in Ghana
Source: Author's design

environments.

The Commission has a further function in the preparation of national development plans and reviewing them with consideration for all factors that impinge on them. These are the social, domestic, external, economic and political facets as noted already. Furthermore, the National Development Planning Commission has the function of monitoring, evaluating and co-ordinating national development policies, programmes and projects. The operational and management functions here are also related to a further one of making recommendations for socio-economic development. And more, the Commission has call-in powers with respect to the making of local development plans.

Regional planning functions

The regional level of planning is the specific focus in this book. The Regional Co-ordinating Council has the functions of co-ordinating, integrating, and synthesizing planning programmes and implementation processes. Other equally important functions are monitoring and evaluation of development policies, programmes and projects. It is noted here that while the regional-level functions are expected to reflect the guidance and directives of the national level, these do not include strategic regional guidance for the district planning authorities. In the absence of formal policy and plan-making powers, such guidance is essential rather than being steered solely by the national level.

These powers of making policies and regional plans can only be validated and legitimized under a formal system of regional governance that is politically mandated to do so (Wannop, 1995). In this way, the potential effectiveness and robustness of regional planning practice are seriously limited and impoverished. These weaknesses in regional planning further limit the opportunities for practices of effective communication between the regional and local levels. Once again, the non-existence of an elected, more legitimate and directly accountable form of regional government makes only an advisory form of governance and planning administration possible. The lack of executive powers in this regard also undermines and limits the effectiveness of regional planning, in particular programme implementation (Wannop, 1995; Barrett and Fudge, 1981; Lewis and Flynn, 1979; Friedmann, 1973). It will be shown in chapter five that the situation leads to informal and ineffective regional plan-making practices (Bruton and Nicholson, 1987).

However, the current legislative arrangement for regional planning might strengthen aspects of control functions than those relating to policy-making and communication as defined earlier. Perhaps, the current planning structures for managing regional affairs may also be the initial stage of a formal and more legitimate regional governance and with it, an executive form of planning. A greater and distinctive politically-constructed nature of regional planning, unlike other types of planning, holds greater promise of delivering (Wannop, 1995). This is because it offers a wider opportunity for the participation of more localities and various actor-agencies as well as involving a greater range of issues and processes. Indeed, this would also allow flexibility in negotiation and management of strategic change in relation to the participation of all the agencies involved in making things happen. Nevertheless, the sheer existence of more validated and legitimate systems relating to these would not necessarily guarantee the success of regional planning (Wannop, 1995). The powers of the Ghanaian state, through the President, to issue executive instruments and the NDPC to make legislative instruments and guidelines may be considered substitute for the legitimacy being proposed here. Nevertheless, these types of legislation and provision of legal force do not amount to actions of an elected regional government and its planning functions in this context. It has been noted that it is not unusual or impossible for an appointed regional government to make formal policy and produce plans (Wannop, 1995).

The non-elected regional form of governance also has the tendency to limit the democratic enterprise in planning as there is the greater tendency for the interests of minority elitist groups or the powerful to be dominant. This disadvantage also tends to limit the opportunities for bargaining and negotiation in the planning process. Therefore, there is also a greater proclivity for actions to be taken that have no legitimate basis. It is also more likely that the District Planning Authorities would prefer doing business with a wholly or semi-elected regional government which also has policy-making and planning powers. In this case, it would provide a check against possible taking of actions by the regional level not in the interests of the districts. Indeed, as Wannop (1995, p. 193) states, 'The flaws in regional planning have been most frequently failures in governance and in the weak political backing which plans have received'. The consideration being made here would also mean a matching level of legitimacy between the district and regional levels with respect to the making of policies and plans. Besides, these would strengthen the strategic guidance practices of the regional level for the local planning authorities.

The one formidable factor that stands in the way of formally elected regional government and more formal planning powers, in the case of Ghana, is financial independence. Some of the financial problems of the District Assemblies have already been pointed out. Like these, the elected regional governments would have to raise part of their financial resources as the central Ghanaian state might not be able to bear it all alone. In that case, however, the regional community would suffer doubly in fulfilling their tax responsibilities, including district-level taxation.

Furthermore, a more politically accountable form of regional government and planning authority is more likely to promote the attainment of a balanced development of the region, giving equal emphasis to the physical, environmental, economic and social aspects. The opportunities there would be for negotiation, shared agreements and wider representation, in that event, are all favourable factors in making that attainable.

District planning functions

One function of the District Planning Authorities is initiating and preparing district-wide development plans as well as settlement structure plans. In relation to this and wider district planning activities, the local planning authorities are required to undertake research studies including economic, social, spatial, environmental as well as sector-based and settlement policy aspects. These studies must also relate to mobilizing human and physical resources for district development. Provision is also made for the preparation of sub-district or local action plans by local communities. Therefore, the District Planning Authorities have the power of initiating, co-ordinating processes of planning, programming, budgeting and implementing the district plans and development activities.

In addition, they have the function of integrating sector and spatial plans, programmes and projects as well as co-ordinating these with national development planning objectives. A further function is synthesizing all policy proposals into a comprehensive framework for all development initiatives in the district. The Act also requires that these proposals conform to logical and tested criteria of environmental management. In relation to all these, the local planning authorities also have the function of monitoring and evaluating the local development policies and development initiatives.

The District Planning Co-ordinating Unit (DPCU) has the function of advising the District Planning Authority on matters relating to planning, programming, monitoring, evaluation and co-ordination aspects. Therefore, the Unit also has the responsibility of co-ordinating the planning and development activities of all sector-based executive agencies within the district. They also have the responsibility of achieving the synthesis of all the strategies, in this regard, into a full-ranging and cohesive framework. Another function of the DPCU is reviewing and revising aspects of the district plan. Besides, it must maintain an appropriate data base and provide useful information systems.

It is also important to emphasize the fact that meeting budgetary and financial needs is very challenging for the District Assemblies. It has also been observed that their performance in development planning, so far, shows poor internal validity in their design of initiatives and implementation (Ayee, 1994). The continued control of the local by the central state seems ever present. However, a practice of local plan-making is evolving (Mattingly, 1989).

The Central Region

A background context of the case study area, Central Region, is now presented. The emphases here include the assets, opportunities and challenges relating to socio-economic and spatial developments (Ofori, 2000d) as indicated in Figure 1.2. Lying along the central coastline of Ghana, the Region is bounded by the Western and Ashanti Regions to the west and north respectively, the Greater Accra Region and Eastern Region to the east and north-east, respectively (Figure 1.2). The Region extends inland 50-60 km to the east and approximately 90-100 km to the west and 60-80 km north-west in a narrow strip, wedged and jutting out in between the Western and Ashanti Regions. This makes the area of the strip remote from the rest of the Region. Therefore, the general location of the Central Region is relevant to its territoriality. It is particularly crucial to outline its resource base.

The Region has a population of 1,145,520 (1984), 9.30 per cent of Ghana's total. As hinted earlier, the only national population census, since 1984, took place in Ghana in the first half of 2000. The results of this latest census are not available to the present study. Of the 1984 census statistics, however, 28.8 per cent (329,196) of the Region's population was urban and 71.2 per cent (896,041), rural. The Region has an average population density of 65 per km^2. This is generally low to the south and denser northwards. However, when population and its distribution is considered against the natural resource base, then it is generally and sparsely spread out and the Region potentially and richly endowed. It has the second lowest population growth rate (1.8 per cent) after Greater Accra Region (1.7 per cent), based on the 1984 census data. Therefore, the former has been growing relatively less slowly than most other regions.

About 79 per cent of all the settlements in the Region have a population of 2,000 or less. Therefore, based on the statistical definition of 'small village' and 'large village' in Ghana, a predominant number of the settlements in the Central Region fall into these categories, particularly the former. An attempt would be made to shed more light on the urban structure in chapter six. Most of these settlements have only minimal infrastructure, a situation that also typifies the downward transitional nature of the territorial region in Ghana.

Out of the Region's total land area of some 10,000 km^2, over 80 per cent is suitable for farming but just about 40 per cent of this is currently under cultivation. Some 7,510 km^2 constitutes forest zone. There are about 844 km^2 of forest reserves which occur to the central and eastern parts of the Region and are especially concentrated in the Twifo-sub region. A pocket of land, 100 km^2, is also covered by tree crops and planted timber. An area of 2,409 km^2 is coastal savanna. A further area of 198 km^2 is estimated to be non-agricultural land either covered by settlement or unsuited to arable cropping or tree crops.

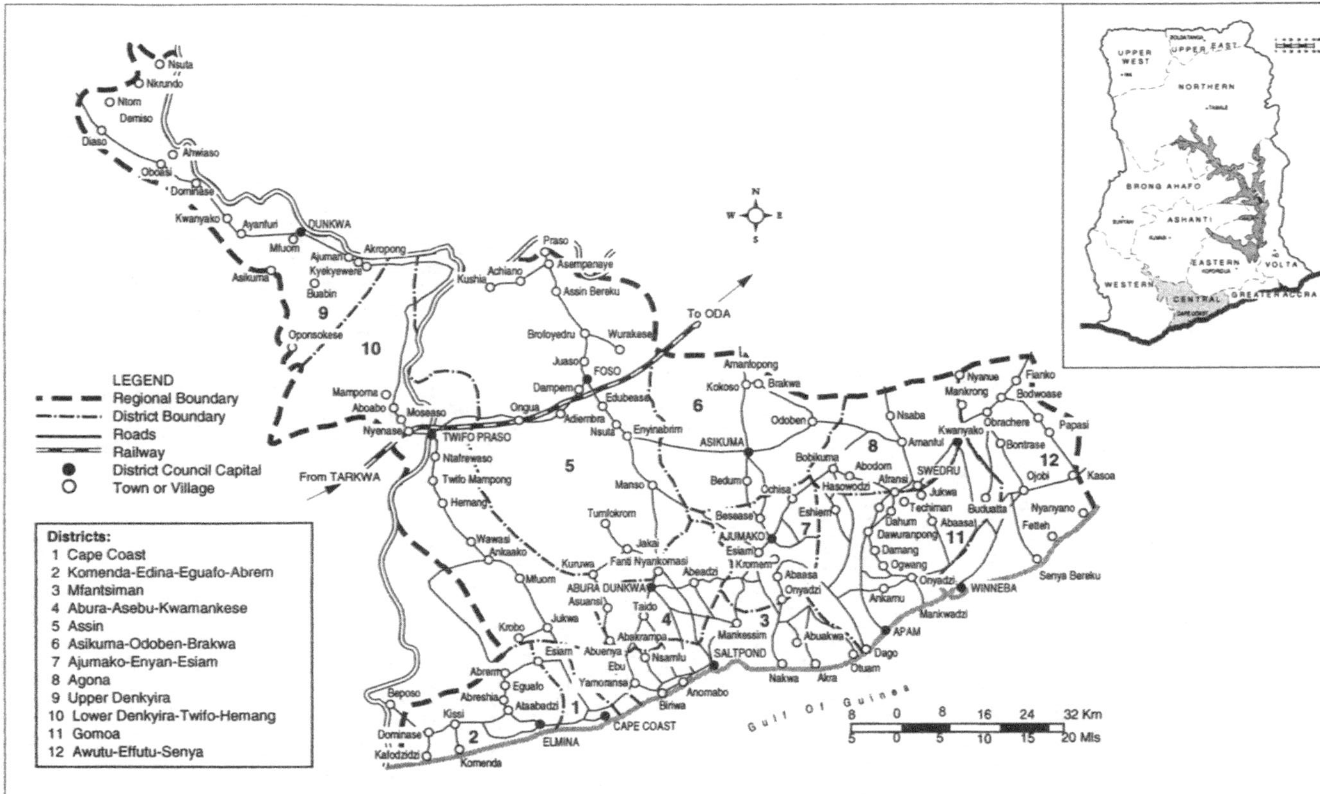

Figure 1.2 Central Region: district assembly areas, main settlements, rail and road network

Agriculture, of course, plays the principal role in the Region's economy, with over 65 per cent of its population engaged in it. The main industrial cash crops are cocoa, oil palm, sugar cane, coconut, pineapple, and çitrus, especially orange. The important foodstuffs include maize, cassava, plantain and vegetables. The main oil palm growing area is centred on the Twifo sub-region as well as along the Foso-Manso axis. Another area of production is centred along the Ochi Nakwa River from Asikuma through Besease, Ajumako, Mando and, south of it. The western part of the Central Region has lost most of its cocoa crop through pest infection and limited farmer investment. Production is now principally focused on the Asikuma-Ajumako areas. Coconut production is prominent along the immediate littoral, especially along the coast of Komenda and Elmina and inland from Dago and Otuam. Marine fishing is also a mainstay of the Region's economy: strewn along its entire coast.

The industrial profile of the Region consists of a few large-scale industries and numerous small-scale undertakings. The former are mostly located within the regional capital and other major urban centres. While the latter are found in these centres as well, they are also predominant in the small and medium towns and particularly, in the rural centres. There has been growth in the pottery and ceramic industries in the relatively more urbanized eastern part of the Region. There are boat-building and repair yards at Elmina, Mumford and Winneba. As indicated, already, the Region is rich in timber, some of which is milled in the Fosu area to the north, the rest serving as log export product for regional and international trade.

The fauna-based and other floral resources also provide a suitable and feasible basis for a tourist industry in the Region. As the initial centre of colonialist settlement and domination, the Region's history has also left it with many forts and castles as landmarks of this heritage. These also provide a viable and sustainable basis for the tourist industry in the Central Region.

Some alluvial gold mining is undertaken in the northern part of the Region (i.e. the Dunkwa Goldfields), where dredging takes place in the Offin River and its basin. Apart from these fields, there are also known gold deposits in the zone centring on Oponsokese, Asikuma and Diaso along the north-western strip of the Region. Limited pockets of gold are also known to occur south of Jukwa and north-west of Mankoadze. In the same way, known diamond deposits occur in a zone to the north-western part of the Region centred on Asaaman and Praso, north of Foso as well as west of Mampong. The salt industry is also important, with the main bases at Elmina, Apam and Mumford (Jumba).

There has also been petroleum-drilling. Production which was started in 1979 stopped in 1986, justified on uneconomic and unprofitable returns to investment (van Buren, 2001; Walden Publishing Limited, 1999). The whole activity did not really appear to have benefited the Region's economy in terms of income and employment or associated services. However, there is continuing to be exploration for natural gas deposits, originally discovered in 1974, around Cape Three Points. In 1997, the Government entered into a formal agreement with two foreign consortia for exploration and production in the off-shore zone. If the exploitation of this resource is linked to the economy of the Central Region, it would create a real and substantial opportunity for its social and economic development.

This brief survey of the Region's real and potential resources show that it has the opportunities and foundations for generating wealth and improving the well-being of all its communities. Environmental sustainability is thus critical in the territorial development processes, in this regard, in the Region. In terms of this potential base, therefore, the Central Region is less disadvantaged than other territorial parts of the country.

However, a number of factors potentially or actually constrain the development of these resources. One of these is the isolation of some zones of surplus agricultural production from consumption areas by insufficient or non-existent transport and communication networks. Another is the high labour:land ratio which has created problems of ecological preservation and maintenance in certain areas as land fallow periods become shorter with increasing population pressures. This also reflects the importance of the issue of environmental sustainability. In link with the regional planning practice, there is also the lack of specific regional planning and development policies which would provide a concrete basis and framework for the integrated planning and design of economic activities and services at the regional level. The continued strengthening of sector-based activities with a number of government institutions reporting individually to central government in the national capital conflicts and competes with regional planning. While this is also an opportunity for central government control of the regional level, it is reflected in the implementation of many strategic programmes.

The lack of specific attention for local level peasants and other smallholders with respect to credit, extension, training, input, supply and marketing advice also constitutes another problem. Further challenges are the competition and conflict between cash-cropping land and food-cropping which also create land shortages with respect to the latter (Ofori, 1991a). This problem has been observed to be characteristic of the Central Region and historically of the entire country (Dickson, 1978; Durham, 1977). The ineffective provision or non-existence of economic and social infrastructure and services is also related to the weak integration of small and medium settlements into the regional space economy. A further implication is that many areas of real and potential local socio-economic development are hardly taken notice of or supported by the public sector (Ofori, 2000c).

It has been observed that the Central Region had inherited a substantially unbalanced social and spatial structure from the colonial period. In relation to this, the concentration and accumulation of wealth in the hands of elitist urban groups is identified as a critical element of this situation. It is relevant to note that Frimpong-Ansah (1991) has pointed out the existence and role of urban-based coalition of elitist forces in a macro-economic context in Ghana (Shillington, 1992; Birmingham, 1990).

Therefore, Dunham has proposed that some of the critical concerns in the development of the Central Region include improving access to markets and urban centres. Another is providing a more efficient and improved distribution of services in the rural areas. A further area of concern is transforming well-selected inward settlements such as Fosu, Asikuma, Bobikuma into functional markets and centres of production, services as well as potential growth. The importance of creating co-operatives and stimulating the production of specific crops is also emphasized. In all these regards, therefore, it is critical to identify and stress on those kinds of activities that link centre and periphery; the impacts of these on all the target population and any positive externalities. On the basis of an earlier argument, these concerns and expectations underline the strategic importance of territorial urbanization with respect to small and medium towns.

Lower Denkyira-Twifo-Hemang District and sub-region This district is located to the central and south-western margins of the Central Region. Part of its northern border is with the Upper Denkyira District and a wedging part with the Central Region's northern border with Ashanti Region. The locality is bounded on its south by the Komenda-Edina-Eguafo-Abrem and the Abura-Asebu-Kwamankese Districts and most of its eastern boundary is with Assin District. The Lower Denkyira-Twifo-Hemang District is the home of a number of sub-ethnic groups including the Twifo, Hemang and Mokwa. While the central mill and immediate estates of the TOPP company are based in the first of the three traditional group areas, the oil palm plantations spread across the whole sub-region.

The case study district and sub-region had a population of 53,066 being 5.9 per cent of the Central Region's total in 1970 and 95,988 - 8.4 per cent of the regional total - in 1984. This shows an increase of 42,922, being 44.7 per cent in only a period of fourteen years. This fast internal rate of population growth is also a challenge for the territorial regional development process. The main settlements in the sub-region are Twifo Praso the district capital, Twifo Hemang, Twifo Mampong, Jukwa, Wawase and Ankaako. Ntafrewaso is one of the smallest rural settlements in the area. The main district is, distinctively, 100 per cent rural as census statistics up to 1984 show (Ofori, 1991a; Dickson, 1978). Therefore, this also marks out its deep territoriality. However a number of these settlements, notably Twifo Praso, Twifo Hemang, Twifo Mampong have the potential to grow into small and medium towns.

The economy of the area is mainly based on primary activities, including lumbering, food- and cash-cropping. The area used to produce between 10-12 per cent of total national cocoa production. As noted earlier, production has now substantially declined. Thus most of the area is now taken up by oil palm and forestry. However, the introduction of oil palm culture also accounts for the reduced interest in cocoa. The district has the highest share of employment in forestry and logging at 16.2 per cent of regional total. It also has 11.6 per cent of regional total employment in agriculture, hunting and forestry, altogether.

Incomes in the district and locality are generally very low, even so by the fact that there is low capital investment in the subsistence economy. The market infrastructure is weak compared with other regions of the country. Roads are mostly rudimentary and accessibility to villages is limited in the more territorial parts. The main Cape Coast-Twifo Praso road has been made appreciably all-weather passable in recent times. As in most rural areas of the country, the local housing is mostly built with bricks made from laterite or to a lesser coverage, cement blocks. Roofing material is in thatching and to a limited extent, iron-sheet roofing.

With respect to utility services, electricity is supplied via the nearest rural feeder line from the national grid. The Twifo Oil Palm Plantation company has a generating and distribution system which provides a limited surplus capacity to a couple of villages. The district capital benefits from a national electrification programme (Government of Ghana, 1984). Several locations were proposed for hydro-power schemes on the Pra River as part of a national water resource study in 1970 (Government of Ghana, 1984). These include one to the west of Twifo Hemang with an installable capacity of 63mw. This project is all part of the long term plans of the Volta River Authority. Under an internationally-funded well-drilling programme, thirty-two bore-holes were drilled along the Cape Coast-Twifo Praso road and hand-pumps installed in 1983. For the majority of the people, it is river and stream water.

There are now a number of junior and senior secondary schools in the area. The adult literacy rate among those aged forty and over is about five per cent. There have been no modern health centres in any of the villages apart from Twifo Hemang and Twifo Praso, where health-posts are established. A medical field unit which is responsible for the control of communicable diseases has also been based at Twifo Hemang. Indeed, the low level of health-care provision is shown in the prevalence of such diseases as diarrhoea, cholera, skin diseases and particularly, malaria as will be further shown in chapter seven.

With respect to industry, trade and commerce, there is no large-scale production, apart from the agro-industrial plant of the TOPP company. As pointed out already, however, there is significant processing of primary agricultural products on cottage industry basis. The TOPP project-complex is also the leading employment generator in the area as will be shown later.

These aspects indicate the general problems facing the Twifo sub-region. One of these is the competition and conflict between cash-cropping and food-cropping as pointed out earlier. This is reflected in terms of land supply and the latter faced with a crisis of shortage. Another difficulty is the limited or non-existence of road infrastructure in most parts of the area.

Besides, economic activity is non-diversified outside agriculture. Therefore, employment is predominantly based in agriculture and limited lumbering activities. This situation also limits the real employment opportunities in the area. The limited employment and income-generation opportunities are low and unsustainable. Besides, part of the available employment is purely seasonal. Furthermore, the need for sustainable development practices and ensuring environmental sustainability are becoming more crucial as agricultural and other resource-based economic activities are intensified.

Summary

The political-administrative and planning region in Ghana is predominantly characterized by territoriality. This has been determined by its history over the colonial and post-colonial eras. While the region displays significant and appreciable resource base, it also depicts a process and state of development constrained by a number of factors. These include an unarticulated and lop-sided structure of spatial organization which also underlies deep social and economic disparities. Another constraint is the ineffectiveness, limited legitimacy and empowerment of regional planning; constraining statutory planning framework. Another element is the limited accountability of regional development institutions. There is also the lack of a more legitimate form of regional governance and political framework, the absence of which the study emphasizes. A further constraint is the state's unnecessary control of regional affairs. Besides, the role of the actual members of the regional community in decision-making is down-graded, while the real benefit they gain from the development process is limited or non-existent. Furthermore, there is a growing re-emergence of external-corporate forces in the national and regional economy. Nevertheless, the vast resource base and deep territoriality indicate the need for committed, sustained, highly substantial funding and inward investment to make things happen. The noted constraints, together, have the potential to limit the opportunities for robustness, democratic enterprise and strategic effectiveness in the process of regional planning. The critical and strategic importance of sustainable development has also been noted.

2 The intra-regional engagement, investigation and inquiry in regional planning

As this book is aimed at presenting an integrated study of socio-economic, spatial disparities and programme effectiveness in the context of statutory regional planning practice and policy evaluation, it is important to provide a conceptual foundation and confirm its distinctive methodology. This is done, initially, by reviewing studies undertaken by other researchers in this regard. These considerations also justify the presentation of an epistemological framework. A clear methodological focus is demarcated on the basis of the epistemology set out.

Reviewing studies on regional disparities, planning and development processes

There has been a growing attention for the intra-regional level of analysis with increasing decentralization programmes and more concern for local-level development in sub-Saharan Africa (Ofori, 2000c; Gooneratne and Obudho, 1997; Gooneratne, 1997; 1991a; Slater, 1975). This trend includes focus on disparities between urban areas, urban and rural areas as well as rural areas and various combinations of these (Gore, 1984; Gilbert and Gugler 1981). However, it is also important to relate, as well, to cases of inter-regional analyses because these may hold useful insights for strategic policy-making and formulation of development programmes. It is crucial in all these regards that the disparity analysis must be related to planning policy impacts, while other effects are isolated (Ofori, 2000c; Cappelin and Molle, 1988).

In his classic work on disparity analysis, Williamson (1975) attempted to identify patterns of income distribution at various inter-regional, national and international levels, using data based on twenty-four countries - both developed and developing economies. Weighted and non-weighted coefficients of variation were computed to measure disparities at the various levels. He argued, in a neo-classical fashion, that the main factors that determine divergence in regional development are labour, capital migration, central government policy and inter-regional linkages. It was also argued that these factors can operate and be controlled to minimize the divergence.

Williamson's arguments are based on the hypotheses derived by historical determinism. Therefore, he concluded that inter-regional income inequalities occur at the initial stages of development, spatial divergence becoming pronounced and being followed by a stage of stability. Then convergence and 'de-polarization' appear towards the latter stages. According to Williamson (1975), the diminution in income inequalities occurs most in mature economies such as those of the developed Western countries. On the other hand, inter-regional inequality is more pronounced in economies with low per capita income as in the Third World countries.

However, Williamson (1975) could not answer the question as to why inter-regional inequality persists nor fully explain the mechanisms behind the evolution of the specific stages. He also stayed away from 'the more difficult task of disaggregation and identification of causation' (p. 159). Besides, income is only a partial measure, even if implicitly associated with other factors. Nevertheless, Williamson (1975) did point out that the larger the geographical size of a country, the larger the inter-regional inequality as well as variations in the natural resource bases. This is because of the longer economic and cultural distances there tends to be between the wider regions. A very important element of this observation is that there is a more powerful tendency for the occurrence of 'localism'.

Similarly, Ahluwalia (1976) studied inequality in relation to poverty and development in sixty countries, including forty in the Third World. He aimed at testing the hypothesis that inequality is pronounced at the initial stages and begins to decline in the latter stages of development (Williamson, 1975). He demonstrated that the process of development may cause not just increasing relative inequality but absolute impoverishment of lower income groups. On the basis of national per capita GNP, Ahluwalia (1976) measured the level of development of each country by multivariate regression analysis. In this way, he estimated cross-country relationships between the income shares of different percentile groups and other variables of the development process likely to influence income inequality. The estimated equations served as a basis for making broad generalizations about relationships between income distribution and level of development.

Ahluwalia made a number of conclusions. Per capita GNP is useful as a summary indicator because of its correlation with most of the processes occurring with development (Thirlwall, 1972). It is noted, however, the fact that this measure is silent about the specific dynamics by which development affects the degree of inequality. Therefore, this justifies the relevance of other socio-economic and demographic variables in providing additional explanation. Aluwahlia confirmed the Kuznets hypothesis tested by Williamson (1975) that the inequality reduction process is prolonged for the poorest groups. Further, he points out that other sector-based shifts are associated with the development process itself and which also affect the state of inequality. These shifts relate to the structure of production, expansion in educational attainment, skill levels of the labour force and decline in population growth rates.

In the same way, Bigstern (1980) in a study of Kenya points out the fact that most of the growth attained by the less developing countries in the 1960s tended to be concentrated in the small modern sector in the most progressive regions. The majority of the people only suffered greater poverty. Bigstern's objective was to analyse the processes determining the development of regional incomes and growth in Kenya's employment. He was particularly interested in analysing the extent of the regional differences and their rates of development as well as isolating the critical dynamics in this regard. The author also meant to establish the extent to which it was possible to influence regional inequality by economic policy. Bigstern observed that regional inequality was particularly severe in Africa and stressed on the fact that a typical feature of growth in the less developing countries is increasing inequality. This is also reflected in the observations made by Williamson (1975).

Bigstern also pointed out the hypothesis that inter-personal inequality as well as regional per capita income first increase and then decrease on reaching a certain level in both cases. He made an important observation that the most crucial determinant of regional inequality in underdeveloped countries lies is in differences in the structure of production. This is consistent with the theoretical and conceptual analyses made by other writers (Sayer, 1988; Massey, 1979).

Further, Bigstern (1980) noted the fact that regional development policy is often associated with infrastructure, apart from elements of fiscal policy. Richardson (1973) believes that investing in the former is the best way for a government to create agglomeration economies, thus leveraging economic activity. Bigstern based his analysis on income, employment, production as well as infrastructure relating to education, health services and self-help projects. He measured inequalities by using the techniques of coefficient of variation, Gini coefficient and Theil indices.

Another major study was presented by Slater (1975) in the context of Third World regional planning. He also pointed out the fact that this kind of study had for long concentrated on inter-regional analysis to the neglect of intra-regional studies. In addition, he observed that the notoriety and persistence of spatial inequality in development constituted constraints on the territorial organization of Third World economies. Thus these attract much attention and interest (Ofori, 2000c). Slater underlined the fact that there is a fundamental difference between spatial inequalities and socio-economic disparities. He realistically emphasized the point that as long as the latter persisted the former would also (Massey, 1979; Coates, Johnson and Knox, 1977).

Slater (1975) based his study on Peru and Tanzania and in relation to such factors as manufacturing establishments, employment, electricity generating capacity, roads and communication, public investment and taxation. Other indicators used are infant mortality rate, number of hospital beds, per capita doctors and schools as well as enrolment ratios and access to public amenities. He applied different methodologies to the two countries: multivariate analysis and coefficients of variation plus z-scores in the case of Peru; historical methodology with Marxist orientation in relation to Tanzania.

Slater failed to answer the question of whether inter-regional inequalities have been decreasing or increasing. It is also not clear whether there was any significant differences among the variables in terms of socio-economic disparity nor to what extent a generalization could be achieved, based on the disparity indicators. However, he clearly identified a hierarchy of regions and discussed the implication of the various categories, especially the lagging ones, for regional planning policy.

Berry and Jackson, (1981) analysed regional inequality between the Provinces of Papua New Guinea. The ‘province’ in that country is a kind of middle level designation between a ‘region’ and a ‘district’. The main aim of the Government is to achieve a progressive equalization of income and decentralization of planning and public expenditure (Conyers, 1981). Berry and Jackson (1981) aimed at establishing the extent of existing inter-provincial inequalities and examining changes in these inequalities, over time under the impact of state expenditure.

The two researchers based their analysis on the following indicators: health status, health services, educational status, road transport infrastructure per capita and per unit area. Others are government staffing per 1,000 population and per capita income, based on export crop. Adopting an interesting methodology, they adjusted these indices and scaled them to a range of 0-100. In relation to this, they calculated various measures for each province, and also produced a composite index. Other measures used are the unweighted mean of values, weighted and unweighted coefficients of variation as well as weighted and unweighted standard mean deviation. The provinces were then plotted on co-ordinates of economic and social sets of composite factor means. However, their method of cluster search is simplistic and naively subjective. The correlation matrix they produced for achieving this shows significantly low correlation, indicating very large residuals. Other indicators used, rather disparately, are per capita development bank lending by province, national public expenditure by province and provincial government revenue per capita. On the bases of these highly quantitative analyses, Berry and Jackson (1981) discussed the implications of their regional inequality studies for achieving an effective decentralization of public expenditure allocations in the country.

In a more comprehensive work, Rao (1984) analysed socio-economic and spatial disparities between districts as well as sub-district units in the Karnataka State of South-West India. Rao examined urban and rural differences along these categories. She developed a wide array of indicators relating to agriculture, education, transport, communication, health, banking, co-operative society services and energy. Coefficients of variation were used to analyse the disparities between the nineteen districts in the State and factor analysis applied to the sub-district units. Rao (1984) then computed a composite index for each sector-based factor by adding up all the standardized factor scores to obtain z-scores. These composite indices were used as a basis for classifying the 175 sub-district units. Each factor is interpreted in terms of its quantitative implication and qualitative relationship with other factors as well as both real and potential impacts.

The classification yielded a hierarchy according to level of development, with emphasis on the identification of 'backward' areas. Apart from offering explanations set in functional and material contexts, Rao (1984) proposed that the sector-based analyses and structure of disadvantage serve as the basis for formulating policies and making regional plans. She made specific recommendations in this regard. However, an integrated study rather than sector-based analysis holds greater advantage for making regional policies and plans. Nevertheless, she makes an important contribution to the intra-regional focus.

In another study, in relation to Algeria, Nacer (1979; Sutton, 1988) based his analysis of inter-regional disparities on the two census periods, 1966 and 1977. The main objective was to evaluate changing regional disparities seen in terms of measures of convergence and divergence. These relate to per capita measures, ratios of social infrastructure and demographic factors. Using standardized z-scores as well as coefficients of variation, Nacer (1979) showed limited decreases in levels of regional disparities over the period. There appeared to be limited convergence in the indicators relating to female access to education, electrification and energy diffusion. Besides, the primacy of Algiers metropolitan area was found to be declining. On the other hand, there was strong divergence with respect to the indicators on industrial employment.

A more critical study was presented by Rambanapasi (1989) in his evaluation of regional development policy impacts on regional planning practice in both colonial and pre-colonial Zimbabwe. His central goal was to 'correctly conceptualize the relationship between the central delivery system and regional development policy and planning practice in Zimbabwe' (Rambanapasi, 1989, p. 1). He considered this realist engagement as a cardinal aspect of regional planning in identifying and specifying the mechanism for making things happen.

Rambanapasi pointed out a number of conflicts and contradictions in the Zimbabwean experiences. One of these is between the politician's view of regional policy and real world practices in regional planning over the two historical eras. Another aspect is between functional regional planning which has created spatial dominance centred on urban areas and the growth sector on one side; territorial regional planning which has been aimed at the distribution-based sector and achievement of horizontal spatial organization, on the other. A further conflict is between material planning processes and the socialist ideologies of national government. Despite the introduction of populist governance in the post-colonialist era, the function-led ethic has dominated planning practices. There has also been conflict in the national-regional economic base between the intensive growth sector and the residentiary (or peasant subsistence) and extensive sector. This also means there has been no mutual benefit between the economies associated with the two structural levels.

The writer identified a number of regional development initiatives that were created both in the colonial and post-colonial eras as the instruments of regional development and pointed out their effectiveness. One of the areas is under the authority of the Sabi-Limpopo Authority focused on the South-Eastern Low veld. The experiences show that despite its defined territorial concerns, the agency only retracted into functional regional roles. Another initiative was the Sanyati Project which was introduced over 1971-74 and based on cotton production in the districts of Kadoma and Gokwe. Again, only functional regional planning emerged under this experiment. The Sebungwe Regional Plan designed for 1979 to 1981 was also focused on four districts, including Kadoma and Gokwe, the others being Kariba and Binga. The strategic and instrumental resource-based activity, in this case, was anthracite coal-mining which supplied the raw material for the production of electricity. Apart from being implemented by a sector-based organization, this regional plan was also weak in its definition and delineation of the 'region' as well as conceptualization of decentralization. These problems also limited the plan's contribution to territorial regional development.

Rambanapasi noted that other provincial-based initiatives displayed similar features of limited effectiveness. Nevertheless, he pointed out that some of the projects had been characterized by robust co-ordination between the various implementing agencies. These have also shown appreciable commitment to both territorial and functional regional planning. This, however, did not remove the dominance of sector-based processes and functional regional development. Moreover, central government planning policies as well as decentralization initiatives remained non-integrated with planning practice. Therefore, these also only bolstered up functional development processes.

Furthermore, the Zimbabwean planning policies and programmes, being sector-based were not effectively co-ordinated and integrated. If these had been done, the effort would have, for example, brought together agricultural development, services as well as urban-industrial developments. Rambanapasi also points out the fact that some of the planning initiatives were not based on a clear and realistic analysis of regional problems and processes. This was reflected in the lack of focus on migratory trends in Masvingo Province, for example.

Another failure of colonial and post-colonial planning in Zimbabwe was the lack of planning systems and structures for development practices. For example, there was no hierarchy of plans at the national, provincial (regional) and local levels. This also meant the unarticulated relationship between socio-economic processes and the spatial factor. All these limitations also typify a state of spatial separatism in Zimbabwean planning. Other difficulties are shown in Zimbabwe's experiences in regional planning during the first years of Independence. These include the emphasis on substantive more than procedural aspects as well as territorial and not functional processes. The pervasive and dominant role of the private sector later meant that planning was only set within it. However, there has also been a more explicit abolition of the dual colonialist practice founded on racial discrimination: trends initiated towards people-based planning and implementation processes.

A review of the trends and situation led central government to emphasize territorial regional planning more strongly in the national development plan for 1986-90. This focus was on raising the living standards of the territorial populations and included the need to redress the social and spatial imbalances. Other aspects of territorial regional planning and autonomous development were included in the plan. In the same way, the issues of environmental sustainability of regional programmes and delineation of clear urban hierarchy were emphasized. The result of these planning efforts, once again, was notoriously characterized by functional processes and sector-centred approaches. Rambanapasi further attributes this to the fact that planning in Zimbabwe has been more articulated at the national and district locality levels than at the regional scale, where it is even less understood. Besides, there 'has been lack of dominant commitment to planning at this level' (Rambanapasi, 1989, p. 291).

The fashion of top-down planning is further reflected in the regional plans for Masvingo and Manicaland Provinces. Furthermore, Rambanapasi points out that the regional plans 'have thus been merely indicative, discretionary or permissive ..., in which implementation is left open to either the private sector or to the provincial development committees' (Rambanapasi, 1989, p. 291). The plan-making processes and activities have also been poorly co-ordinated and inconsistent. This also includes the sheer listing of sector-based projects in the fashion of the 'shopping list' approach that characterized national development plans in Ghana, too (Bannerman, 1971). The first set of regional plans in post-colonial Zimbabwe was also based on the assumption 'that the public sector can plan and the private sector will implement' (Rambanapasi, 1989, p. 282). Development initiative has been in the form of infrastructure provision. There is also a deliberate emphasis on small-scale industrialization in preference to the large-scale one. And this appears to be a reaction to the capitalist undertakings.

Yet, the private sector has maintained a capitalist and dominating ethic and approach to economic and spatial development. Therefore, the apparent contradiction and conflict between policy declarations and real world development processes is more due to the historical strength and unrelenting nature of capitalist forces. The experiences of Zimbabwe clearly hold insightful relevance to the practices of regional planning and evaluation in Ghana.

Szerewszewski (1966) undertook one of the earliest studies on inter-regional distribution of economic activity in Ghana, based on the regional distribution of resources. The analysis was done in terms of gross value added per capita; per capita expenditure and regional labour resources. Szerewszewski (1966) aimed at testing the hypothesis that regional capital intensity determined the level of regional productivity per employed person. He argued that his explanation with respect to capital and labour conformed to economic theory. He also made use of historical explanations. Szerewszewski emphasized the crucial need to lessen the regional as well as per capita differences in welfare and consumption. However, this work was not done within the context of statutory regional planning and policy. Nevertheless, the indicators of disparity are informing.

Ewusi (1976) analysed socio-economic disparities between the regions of Ghana and emphasized the use of social indicators in addition to economic measures. He observed that there had been neglect of the former in this area of research. Ewusi developed a number of indicators to measure levels of socio-economic development. These include average annual earnings per worker, per capita energy consumption, crude employment participation rate, population of employed labour in non-agricultural activity, the rate of urbanization, literacy rate, population density per square mile and the accessibility index of the regions. Others are the number of doctors per 100,000 persons in the regions, and number of hospital beds per 1,000 persons in the regions. He analysed these data by using the technique of simple correlation analysis to show the degree of association between all the various indicators. The Wroclow taxonomic technique was then used to classify the regions into four categories. The study was mainly descriptive and did not identify the dynamics behind the inequalities. Apart from pointing out lagging areas, the wider regional policy implications were not discussed, neither was there any attempt made to evaluate any policy impacts on the regional problem.

Again, Ewusi (1977) analysed inter-regional disparities in terms of manufacturing industries in Ghana. The regions were ranked on the basis of computed location quotients. Apart from being simplistic and partial, this study is equally presumptive because manufacturing activity is obviously minimal as one moves towards the Northern part of the country. Although the study was sector-based, some positive recommendations were made for a better industrial location policy for Ghana.

Furthermore, Ewusi (1986) presented a more comprehensive study on inter-regional disparities in Ghana on the basis of wide-ranging indicators relating to manufacturing activity. These include the distribution of industrial organizations employing not less than thirty persons; value of gross output in constant prices; value added in constant prices; per cent value added; per cent distribution of manufacturing employment. Others are distribution of manufacturing organizations by location quotient; distribution of manufacturing companies employing not less than 100 persons; and not less than 500 persons. He also analysed the forward and backward linkages of manufacturing output.

Ewusi based his explanations for the observed disparities on the volume of production, location of investment, especially private capital; level of industrial concentration, institutional factors, raw materials, markets and agglomeration economies. He also pointed out the historical and deliberate government policy of concentrating manufacturing industrial activity within the urbanized and metropolitan parts of Southern Ghana. It was also emphasized that industrial location must be considered as only a facet within overall regional development and economic planning. Ewusi demonstrated that there was a high correlation between level of industrialization and regional development. However, variation in resource occurrence and distribution must mean that industrial development in some parts of the country must be limited. While this is in support of the ideas of territorial development, it may also be necessary to bring in a significant amount of location inputs from outside a region to some areas. While proposing an 'optimal location policy' for Ghana, Ewusi also pointed out the conflict between the location of private investment decisions and public-sector preferences for community-based local economic initiatives.

Bannerman (1971) pointed out disparities within the regions of Ghana and in relation to regional policy and planning. He pointed out the need for objectivity in these and need to aim at achieving economic growth and development. Bannerman (1971) observed the fact that regional disparities had been a historically notorious problem in Ghana's development. One of the reasons accounting for this is the fact that sector-based planning has been practised more to the neglect of regional planning. He based his analysis on variables relating to land area, population and its density, gross value added, selected skills by sector and capital resources. Although he admitted that the problem could be attributed to differential resource endowment it was also pointed out that the lack of regional policy-making accounts for this situation. Biehl (1980) also made the same observation.

One of the solutions, Bannerman (1971) agreed, is in the devolution of policy and decision-making to district and regional-level authorities. He critically pointed out the fact that the latter had not been allowed to make their own development plans and policy. Bannerman (1971) argued that intra-regional solutions, notably inward investment, were imperative in the regional planning and development processes. He also emphasized the importance of project planning in this context. However, Bannerman (1971) did not assess the impact of any known project or point out the dynamics that induce socio-economic development in relation to any one. He assessed the performance of the regional planning committees and stressed the urgent need to empower them to make regional policies and plans, short of which the effectiveness of regional planning would be seriously limited.

Dugbaza (1978/79) made a sector-based analysis in relation to health facilities in the urban and rural areas of Ghana. He explained the disparities in terms of these and on the basis of differences between the regions of the country. The emphasis was still on the preference of urban locations for the health facilities. While this approach makes an important contribution similar to that of Rao (1984), it remains a sector-based analysis. It is also not set within the context of regional policy and statutory planning.

A spatial analysis of service factors in twenty-four settlements in the Upper West and Upper East Regions of Ghana and centred on the period 1960-80, was made by Adarkwa (1983). The differences between the various settlements were inferred from the context of past rural development policies. He also emphasized the fact that earlier studies of the regional problem had been solely concerned with analysing inter-regional inequalities. Referring to national development plans made from 1920 to 1975, Adarkwa (1983) questioned the effectiveness of these in reducing disparities within and between the regions of Ghana. Like Rao (1984), he focused on the intra-regional level of analysis. Disparity was considered in binary terms, absence or presence of thirty-four socio-economic and unidimensional indicators. Using the Guttman maximal scaling method, Adarkwa (1983) produced isoline maps of synthesized component scores derived from the data. In addition, he produced Gini coefficients to depict wider differences in the distribution of services within the twenty-four settlements.

A number of critically important conclusions were made from the study. While the larger settlements were growing more rapidly and attracting more service activities, the extensive territorial parts of the regions were not experiencing any form of development. The former were the few towns and the latter, rural settlements. Therefore, he identified four levels of settlement development: depressed, transitional, developing and the development stage. Adarkwa's (1983, p. 16) conclusion that rural development policies introduced over the decades studied 'had not been entirely successful in reducing intra-regional disparities', appears rather too optimistic. In view of the fact that the study did not include primary and, in particular, secondary production activities, it was not likely that a faster reduction in such disparities would have occurred. Moreover, some of the settlements lacked even the services analysed. Indeed, the need to integrate service and growth activities in the space-economies of Third World countries has been noted by a number of writers (Dickson, 1984; Rondinelli and Ruddel,

1978; Richardson, 1978a). However, Adarkwa emphasized the critical need for adopting bottom-up development strategies and having consideration for humanistic basic-needs in the two Regions. In this regard, he also pointed out the need for planners and other researchers to collaborate with local communities in the development effort.

An analysis of disparities between the districts in the Central Region was undertaken by Yankson (1986). He emphasized the importance of a multi-dimensional perspective of development and the need to develop the most suitable and effective indicators in this respect. Yankson (1986) based his analysis on ten indicators related mostly to services, apart from non-farm employment and limited manufacturing activities. A factor analysis of these produced three new factors, altogether accounting for 83.73 per cent of total variation. Two of these were named as the 'social services' and 'urbanization' factors. He identified clusters of districts on the basis of the first factor that accounted for most of the variation.

Yankson (1986) explained the observed disparities in terms of a number of factors. One of these is the ineffectiveness of regional planning in inducing distributive justice. It was noted that this was mainly due to the unwillingness of central government to give the necessary power and control over budgetary resources to the regional level. Another factor is the limited level of skilled and trained human resources. An additional one is the failure to adopt an integrated approach to the analysis of and action on the regional problem. This has also meant the popularity of only a project-based approach to regional development, with a concentration of these in the leading urban centres and municipalities. Apart from the problem of insufficient funding, the inefficiency of development companies was also to account for the situation. Other factors relating to this were the interference of central government sector agencies and location considerations based on population size and density. Yankson (1986) pointed out the severely limited database for decision-making in regional planning.

Yankson's choice of indicators is limited in view of the fact that factor analysis requires a more comprehensive data input. He also did not comment on the factors that scored negatively. Some of the results of the analysis were unrealistic: for example, Lower Denkyira-Twifo-Hemang District achieved the highest positive score of 1.24. Yet, it is the least urbanized locality and has the lowest amount of social services on the basis of which it was identified in the analysis. It has already been noted (Adarkwa, 1983) that the dependence on social services for developing a territorial region, like of the Central Region, is limited in its potential and strategic effectiveness. No justification is provided as to why factor analysis is the suitable and preferred technique for analysing the disparities. Besides, Yankson did not undertake a survey of the beneficiaries under the project approach nor of any concrete and wider programme in the Central Region. Nor is there a clear assessment of implementation of the initiatives. He did not also make a clear, concrete and focused assessment of regional policy. Thus there is no clear indication of regional planning as a process, nor is it in terms of the management of socio-economic and spatial change. Indeed, the notion of regional planning is not indicated. The presentation of development as basic needs in terms of theory, policy and strategy is partial.

In a similar study, Dickson (1978) made a strategic and *ante post* assessment of the potential impact of the TOPP programme. He focused on the levels of 'ruralization' among thirteen of the former eighteen local authority areas within the Central Region. This was measured in terms of per cent total population in the locality dependent on direct river water supplies; population density per locality; per cent male working population in three main age categories; per cent population of school pupils. Others were per cent male population of any education and per cent urban population in the locality. The variables were subjected to factor analysis. Perhaps, many more variables could have been used in this socio-economic survey as the successful implementation of an agro-industrial project depends on multiple factors. Besides, the multivariate technique of factor analysis is rather too much an aggregation for a study which involves more qualitative issues. In addition, the *ante post* impact assessed was not done within the context of existing and statutory regional planning and policy. However, potential programme policies and goals were recommended.

Another study of regional disparities in Ghana was undertaken by Aryeetey (1987). He also pointed out the fact that there had been no government evaluation of the regional implications of any of the development plans. It was observed that intra-regional disparities in development were becoming more important than inter-regional ones. Aryeetey (1987) sought to test the hypothesis that the former were growing faster with the latter growing slower than before. Levels of regional disparity were measured on the basis of indicators relating to demographic, socio-technical infrastructure and economic activity.

Aryeetey made three propositions. One was that the peripheral regions of Ghana now have more accessibility to the socio-technical infrastructure and, therefore, depend less on the core regions. Another is that the original core areas, which it is suggested should now be termed 'pseudo-core-regions', are unable to function effectively as a result of declining levels of investment. Third, the centres of the peripheral regions as well as those of the pseudo-core region now all exploit their immediate regions. Would it mean, for example, that there is now a process of 'de-peripheralization'? Would it also mean that there is really a process of inter-regional convergence in Ghana? Would it further mean, in relation to these issues that there is a trend of polarization reversal in the regions? These are pertinent but inconclusive significant propositions which need hard data to be tested.

Aryeetey-Attoh and Chatterjee (1988) analysed socio-economic inequalities between the regions of Ghana and pointed out the policy implications of these. Their objective was to identify trends in the social impacts of spatial inequality with respect to 'wellbeing' and 'deprivation in Ghana' (Aryeetey-Attoh and Chatterjee (1988, p. 31). The two writers emphasize the relevance of alternative planning strategies that depend on the spatial systems as a foundation for achieving social, territorial and distributive justice.

They also point out the notoriety of poverty that poses a severe challenge to planners and policy-makers. It is in this context that they perceive regional development as a process of socio-spatial transformation that includes the reduction of inequalities and the need to raise standards of living as well as welfare across all social groups. The two writers further argue that the variation in resource bases between regions is a dynamic that transforms the issue of 'social justice' into one of 'territorial justice'. However, it should be pointed out that the resource base is only one aspect of territoriality. They perceived 'social justice' in terms of the distribution of benefits as well as allocation of responsibilities or 'burdens'. These also result from the process of production and changes in relation to this as part of the wider process of development.

Aryeetey-Attoh and Chatterjee (1988) argue for an improvement in absolute income levels through the elimination of poverty as well as increase in relative income levels of the poor groups in society through the reduction of inequality. They also argue that while these two goals are related, there is a conflict between them in relation to regional policy.

They also justify the relevance of a number of indicators for measuring regional development, including income, employment, population distribution, gross output per capita and value added by manufacturing activity. Aryeetey-Attoh and Chatterjee (1988) emphasize the use of the Physical Quality of Life Index (PQLI) for the measurement of regional inequalities. Their preference is based on the consideration that it includes such elements as infant mortality, life expectancy and literacy. This index measures output or ends and not input or means. Thus it is also a measure of life changes and economic opportunities.

They identified a pattern of regional inequality at three levels in Ghana: most deprived area; most metropolitan area; capital district-affluent region. They justified these on the bases of the distribution of infrastructure, economically viable urban centres, social services and other facilities relating to 'social justice' and 'economic efficiency'. The noted urban bias stems from the national-level decision-making; the non-adoption of formal regional policy as an instrument of socio-economic change. So they emphasized the ability and capability of the individual Ghanaian region to exploit the political process of decision-making in its interest (Dunham, 1977). The leading role of agriculture in regional development is emphasized as have the Ghana Institute of Planners (1987).

Aryeetey-Attoh and Chatterjee prescribed various regional policy options: redistributing existing assets in favour of the poor social groups for access to socio-economic opportunities; taxing the best-off to improve the socio-economic well-being of the worse-off; making the peripheral parts also benefit directly from the additional income growth in the core regions. Others are the strategic combination of redistributing with basic needs approaches; regional growth with inter-personal income reduction strategies are emphasized. Their work is heavy on substantive theory and lacking in regional planning practice focus. The two writers also did not evaluate any specific regional programme. The emphasis is on regional development and economic policy, not on regional planning policy.

Focus of the present work

Each of the cases attempts to justify the choice of methodology and methods. These have been mostly quantitative-positivistic and based on inferential and multivariate techniques. There is limited emphasis on the qualitative aspects. Again, while all the studies tried to identify, measure, explain the levels and structure of national and regional development, only two of these actually touched on regional policy (Rambanapasi, 1989; Aryeetey-Attoh and Chatterjee, 1988). Yet, still only Rambanapasi (1989) has dealt directly with statutory regional planning policy and plan-making practices. Further, while some of the cases use cross-sectional data, others attempt longitudinal studies with the advantage of showing trends (Adams and Schevaneveldt, 1985). All the noted limitations are part of the strengths of the focus in this book. It is also part of this focus that explanation for the observed changes is embedded in the material context of the programme and planning regions and particular use made of inductive methodology.

The present book is distinctive and explicit in its analysis and treatment of inter-local and intra-regional analysis in its combined use of coefficient of variation and z-score techniques to measure and graphically depict the behaviour of intra-regional disparities in relation to development policy and statutory planning. Other charting techniques are used. This distinctiveness is also reflected in the emphasis on the influences of globalization processes on regional planning and development.

A more distinctive aspect of the book is its specific focus on a target population and community under a clear regional development programme and policy experiment. The objective here is to achieve a full measurement of policy and programme impacts on a sub-regional community. The inclusion of a survey of the target community, in this regard, also marks out the present book from all the other studies reviewed. Indeed, both the special and detailed focus on a regional and sub-regional community based on the use of a direct survey methodology are not covered in any of the studies reviewed. Another equally distinctive emphasis in the book is the approach to assessing the effectiveness of programme implementation and management of regional change.

These various aspects also justify the reference to relevant systems of epistemology. Rambanapasi (1989) based his study on the realist epistemology However, this is emphasized to a greater depth and the importance of other epistemologies pointed out in the present study. Therefore, a context is created for refining, producing as well as testing regional planning knowledge and practices. In clarifying the methodological and epistemological approaches, therefore, this book also contributes to the debate on the management of knowledge in planning practice. In these connections, a firmer case is made for the abolition of the spatial separatist theme.

So another case is made for a realistic, materially-relevant regional planning policy and practice within its statutory context. In this regard, the nature, quality and processes of policy formulation as well as of plan-making are of critical importance. Furthermore, the engagement in this book is more clearly set within the wider framework of national development policy as well as regional planning policy context. Like Rambanapasi (1989), effort is made to assess the effectiveness of regional policy and planning practices. However, the particular difference here lies in providing a foundation for the design of regional planning policies and providing examples of this approach.

In relation to these, therefore, a further distinctive aspect is the comprehensive probing of regional development and planning theory as a guide to policy, strategy and programme design. A particular concern here is to point out the implications of these theoretical constructs for regional policy and planning practice. The specific and distinctive foci and various emphases also contribute to the integration of the spatial, economic, social, political-administrative and environmental dimensions of regional planning policy and regional development in the book (Seitz, 1988; Seers, 1973).

The study is also distinctive in its consideration of a number of themes within the frameworks of the democratic enterprise in planning; robustness; sustainable development; environmental sustainability; and strategic effectiveness in planning and development processes. All these contribute to further embedding the intra-regional focus in its material contexts and engagements.

Epistemological framework

The general themes and facets introduced in chapter one emphasize the multi-dimensional nature and comprehensiveness of regional planning. A reflection of this is also confirmed in the quantitative and qualitative nature of the regional problem and development process. So are the data and information input required for analysing, ratifying and explaining regional change (Ashcroft, 1983; 1982; 1978). Beyond these, however, there is a greater advantage in the opportunity for making more realistic policy proposals for effective practices and material achievements. In this way, regional planning has the merit in gaining from a multiplicity of evidence in support of the research design and methodology used in the book. A pervasive and enriching trend is thus provided in the creation of knowledge about processes, practices and impacts.

The diverse nature of regions and localities and the varying behaviour of development initiatives that might be implemented also invite a focus on the different objects and their specific contexts. A capitalist and homogeneous perspective on phenomena is also abolished in this way (Sayer, 1988). In this relation, causes and effects are context-specific with no intent to provide a grand and umbrella theoretical explanation.

The foregoing elements are appropriately founded in the realist epistemology. Realism aims at grounding theoretical statements and explanation in material processes. It seeks to unearth linkages that connect various successive events. Therefore, it identifies the mechanism which necessitates a cause to precede specific effects. This necessity of occurrence does not reside in logical relations but in real world and material situations (Cooke, 1983). However, this does not necessarily remove the possibility of deriving conceptual relations from real world ones and which could be used as a basis for explanation later. Therefore, the place of regional theory in this book is essentially a guide to policy and strategy and not a determinant of explanation. At best, such conceptual constructs could provide general explanations; what Sayer (1988) has called 'abstract concepts'. These may not coincide with 'concrete concepts' relating to specific situations in the Ghanaian territorial region, for example.

In applying the framework of realist epistemology, effort is made to ensure that the fallacy of reductionism is not committed by not basing explanation on a simplified general mechanism which underpins complex relations. In this regard, every relevant detail is included in the explanation offered for the emerging regional changes. It is also recognized that explanation would not be limited to a dominant and central mechanism. In this sense, other intervening mechanisms, perhaps still influenced by the major one, could offer additional explanation. By so doing, a more realistic foundation is created for policy-making.

Traditional positivist epistemology is not accepted in this book with respect to the view that knowledge is value-free and an objectively given entity. Nor is it appreciated that knowledge is necessarily created solely by empirical verification as the means of validating it and truth through the medium of personal observation. That a systematic build-up of such inferences thus made would necessarily approximate to reality is also not accepted in this book (Cooke, 1983). Indeed, part of the data generated and knowledge derived by researching regional change and programme impacts in the Central Region are provided by alternative sources. However, positivist epistemology is only reflected in the measurement of change, in the testing and part corroboration of truth and knowledge in regional planning.

In this regard, the approach to the creation and validation of knowledge also includes an application of rationalist epistemology without any intent of providing quantitative proofs. It is rationalist, in so far as there is the aim to depicting aspects of the real world in a quantitative way as a means of providing graphic understanding. Thus an attempt is made to show that the graphic display of relationship between district units and certain measurements made on them are borne out in the real world, at least approximations of it. These logical or realistic connections provide important policy and material implications without any strict correspondence meant.

It has already been pointed out, the fact that idealism underpins the origins of urban and regional planning (Hyde, 2000; Greed, 1994; 1993; Healey, 1993; Ravetz, 1986; Cooke, 1983). The idealist epistemology projects a relationship between human consciousness and the external world. In this case, knowledge is not an absolute reality. Such cognitive awareness as represented in the form of ideas, reasoning, constructs and concepts also changes in relation to the external world. There is thus a dialectical relationship between the logical-conceptual and real worlds, with the attendant contradictions. However, it is recognized that logical constructs can hardly exist in a purely deductive way and without material foundations.

Therefore, idealism underlies the hypothetical and theoretical constructs that are reviewed in relation to functional and territorial regional planning. The aim is not to test such theorization but to provide a framework and guide for regional policy and strategy (Friedmann, 1973). As hinted earlier, these may be considered as the 'abstract concepts' suggested by Sayer (1988). While it is not the intent to focus on how concrete situations necessarily fit these abstract concepts, it is also realist to identify linkages between the two. In this sense, regional planning is underlain by normative theory in proposing how the real world should be organized. The elements of 'concrete concepts' suggested and local-regional diversity fully valued also underlie the importance of situation-constructs in this book.

Phenomenology provides a further epistemological framework for this book to the extent that the processes and outputs of regional planning are perceived as being socially-constructed. The phenomenological epistemology allows a more specific focus in a way that can be replicated at other such specific locales. Without bearing any relationship to the positivist epistemology it yields a bigger picture, in this way, from the isolated sites. By the application of this approach, for example, the material processes of change in the Twifo sub-region are brought out. Phenomenology also generates its own 'theory' from initial inquiry, including a general and non-controlled involvement with the objects of study.

Such 'theory' is applied later to the actual and specific case under investigation. The focus is on the perceptions, meanings and understandings that are typified by the objects of study and the way they experience social phenomena. For an outsider to gain an understanding of the situation of the target populations and development processes in the Twifo sub-region, for example, one must 'sink into' the particular contexts. Therefore, this epistemology is suited to small samples, the use of a variety of data-collection methods which also generate multiple sources of evidence. As it involves the recording of the exact statements of respondents, the data tend to be mostly qualitative. Therefore, an attempt must be made to disaggregate and organize them into appropriate categories. In this way, however, phenomenology promotes the use of logical analysis or inference. Further, the phenomenological epistemology promotes the understanding of the attitudes and responses of the target populations to planning policy and development initiatives as well as their feelings about material impacts of these on their socio-economic well-being.

Methodology: programme impacts and strategic regional change

Designing a regional planning investigation This book is primarily designed to be evaluative of the impact of regional policy and programmes. According to Adams and Schevaneveldt (1985), evaluation can be formative and summative. The former involves a continuous feedback for purposes of programme management, in which case, it is more of strategic monitoring. The latter deals more with the 'final' programme outcome. Evaluation is seen as covering the two forms in this book. Indeed, 'effective evaluation is seen by many experts to be a continuous process that includes both forms of evaluation' (Adams and Schevanevelt, 1985, p. 319). It is also important to assess the effectiveness of the various means by which policy objectives are achieved (Ashcroft, 1983; 1982; 1978).

As a case in planning policy research, this book includes other considerations relevant to evaluation practice (Hakim, 1987). It is important to put emphasis on 'actionable variables', which are 'often clearly defined from the ground', rather than down from theory. Equally important is the need to stress on the usefulness of policy research in the generation of knowledge for action because 'it is more important to change the world than to understand it' (Hakim, 1987, p. 4). It is also important, in this regard, to emphasize the point that inductive theory is more useful as it is founded on real world experience. Deductive theory and related research is primarily concerned with explanation and knowledge for understanding. However, established theory may be relevant to embedded and grounded studies.

Design of the present study also includes descriptive and analytical aspects in relation to the regional problem. These set out and strengthen the case for pointing out the dynamics in context and creating a concrete basis for explanation, including the interpretation of the observed patterns. Indeed, the goal of most regional policies is to abolish disparities. Achieving this effectively requires knowledge of the regional system's dynamics.

The study is also designed to be exploratory to the extent that it attempts to cover the evaluation of a major and composite regional development programme in the context of statutory regional planning. As pointed out already, this is a neglected area in regional policy and programme evaluation research in Ghana. This would produce a fuller knowledge and understanding of the regional development processes.

Strategy for undertaking the study Three different research strategies are used in this regional planning investigation: case study, survey and experimental (Robson, 1993; Casley and Kumar, 1988; Casley and Lury, 1982; 1981). The case study is applied to the TOPP programme as an instrument of regional socio-economic development. In this sense, therefore, the programme constitutes a single case study. In terms of its specific projects, it amounts to a multiple case study based on the smallholder, outgrower and main estate components. In both its single and multiple case study aspects, the TOPP initiative provides the opportunity to put regional planning into its real world context and illustrates how the material achievements can be made and enhanced. In this way, it allows the 'development of detailed and intensive knowledge' (Saunders, Lewis and Thornhill, 1997, p. 40). This makes the case study strategy useful for exploratory, explanatory as well as descriptive research designs. The case study also has merit in promoting the application of analytical or logical inference (Sharp and Howard, 1996). In this connection, it is a useful research strategy for realist-based and phenomenological enquiries and in bringing out more the qualitative aspects of the study. In addition, it creates a firmer and concrete basis for generalization (Yin, 1989).

The survey strategy is applied at two levels. The first and general form of this is the set of interviews held with the heads of sector-based government organizations and planners. The main objective in visiting these departments was to collect data on measures of regional disparities and sector-based programme performance as well as relevant practices. The data generated in this way are more quantitative. The other aspect of the interviews with the various officials was aimed at finding out their views, perceptions of planning policies and development processes. This yielded purely qualitative data. A second and more concrete level of survey relates to the three components of the TOPP programme. This generated appreciable amount of quantitative data. Therefore, this combination of survey with case study research strategies contributes to a realistic use of qualitative and quantitative data. This combination of research strategy also allows for the use of both analytical inference and statistical analysis (Sharp and Howard, 1996).

In distinguishing between settled and non-settled smallholder groups and measuring the impact of the TOPP programme on the former, an experimental design strategy is introduced into the study. The two groups thus constitute the 'experimental' and 'comparison' or 'control' groups, respectively (Robson, 1993). In this case, it is important for the 'experimental' and 'control' groups to be equivalent (Rye, 1987). In the same way, the experimental design is generally applied to the estate employees and those who did not get the opportunity to gain such employment. This research strategy is also applied to the outgrowers in active work and those who are not part, yet, of this scheme or are potential entrants into this particular group. In this general case, however, there is no specific identification of the 'comparison' or 'control' groups. The comparison is only inferred (Moser and Kalton, 1996).

In applying this model of experimental evaluation, the focus is also on the conditions 'before' and 'after' the particular project (treatment) (Bowden, 1988; Rye, 1987; Patton and Sawicki, 1986; Casely and Lury, 1981; Freeman, Rossi and Sonia, 1979; Franklin and Thrasher, 1976; Franklin, 1976; Haveman, 1976; Hatry, Winnie and Fish, 1973). In this form as in the experimental and control options, it is important to establish some measurements as in the form of a base-line study prior to treatment being applied to one of the groups.

Robson (1993) and Rye (1987) discuss various approaches to the experimental design strategy of evaluation. However, it must be emphasized that the smallholder and non-smallholder groups are equivalent groups. Therefore the equivalent experimental and control group design is applied to these. The 'before and after' approach is applied in the case of outgrowers and estate employees. The forms of experimental design evaluations indicated here are used for their simplicity, comparability and the particular research context. The chosen techniques are also capable of generalization (Ofori, 1991a).

It is also relevant to point out the notion of 'impact' and 'outcome'. The latter is a discrete occurrence or change as for example, per capita welfare expenditure or per capita health expenditure and so on. Impact is considered as the totality of the changes that occur in the policy environment as associated with implementation of some public intervention. Impact may also be seen in gross terms which includes both direct policy effects - confounding factors - and autonomous elements (Casley and Kumar, 1988; Ashcroft, 1983; 1982; 1978; Casley and Lury, 1982; 1981). Net impact is the direct tangible as well as intangible policy effect on both targeted and non-targeted communities as the intervention may affect the latter in the form of an externality (Freeman, Rossi and Sonia, 1979). Thus the defined impact measure must reflect the policy goal and objective and be sensitive enough for any identifiable and measurable change to be observed in them.

Data and information management The measurements made in terms of regional disparity and programme impact indicators are used to indicate the absence or presence of the particular output or characteristic and dimension or intensity of an output. The term 'disparity' is used to mean difference and includes inequalities, inequities and imbalances (Molle, Holst and Smit, 1980). This also implies its frequency or magnitude. The data generated are more of the ordinal and interval type. The former because they are of ranked nature and the latter because they exist in the form of intervals between two points of a dimension, yet without an absolute zero. While these also provide the basis for making qualitative analyses, however, other aspects of the study also present essentially qualitative data and information. These also imply that various techniques of analyses are required. However, these must be simple and directly relevant to the data systems analysed.

Indicators of intra-regional socio-economic and spatial development The choice of indicators in the kind of analysis in this book is fundamental. This must be done as rationally and carefully as possible because we are abstracting from the real world and may not be able to include all relevant factors in absolute terms. But as much as possible, the residual must be minimised. According to McGranahan (1972, p. 22), the indicator should reflect both the process and dimension of development. It should also express an established or grounded theory as to what constitutes development in all its aspects.

These indicators should also promote the opportunities for policy-making as an output of the regional disparity analyses and programme evaluation. The more effective the choice of the indicators is, the better the opportunities for learning lessons for improving implementation effectiveness. The indicators also measure variously the goals and objectives of planning policy and development initiatives. Therefore, it is crucial for indicators to sensitively relate to policy variables that can serve as performance measures (Rao, 1984; McGranahan, 1972). This is also important in planning if control is to be effectively exercised and impacts successfully measured.

An indicator may be seen as a direct and full measure of a specific aspect of development so that it is useful only to the extent that it is recognized as a goal or element of development. If the real goal or element itself is not fully or partly amenable to measurement, a proxy measure can be used. Further, indicators may relate to inputs or outputs as for example, investments in the case of the former and production or length of roads built in the case of the latter. In addition, Ewusi, (1976) has suggested the use of intermediate indicators. However, Rao, (1984) thinks that there can be duplication if 'input-indicators' and 'output-indicators' are taken together. For example, outputs may not fittingly reflect inputs because of autonomous factor effects.

It has also been argued that indicators for measuring and analysing regional disparities and programme impacts should be chosen from a wide range of socio-economic and production-based sectors with related data (Molle, Holst and Smit, 1980; Holland, 1976b). It also ought to be emphasized that in the kind of focus in this book, the concentration should be on processes of social and economic change rather than the mere spatiality of the processes. In doing this, one is aware of the reality that spatial disparities are only symptoms of deep-seated socio-economic aspects.

In the light of these considerations, the following sets of data and indicators of socio-economic change are used for the various analyses. The focus on national and statutory planning contexts, in chapter four, involves pointing out broad inter-regional disparities in Ghana. These relate to population and demography, regional administration and jurisdiction. Others relate to GDP by sector and regional income. Further variables in this regard relate to poverty as seen in terms of degree of urbanization and ecological zones and determined by income. For all these, the analysis is based mostly on percentages.

In the case of the intra-regional analysis, the indicators of socio-economic development used also relate to population, health, feeder roads and highways, public sector-based projects; employment and unemployment levels. Others are public sector investment; community development projects; urbanization and urban population change.

The techniques of analysis applied here are the coefficient of variation, standardized or z-score, percentages and charting. Coefficients of variation are used to show relative dispersion between one or more dimensions of sets of variables at two-time intervals in each case (Abe and Alden, 1988; Adelman and Morris, 1971). The z-score is more effective than the coefficient of variation in showing disparities. It possesses zero mean and unit variance and presents individual values as standard deviates. Therefore, it is a deviation from the mean stated as a standard unit or score (Spiegel, 1974). A high z-score means that the individual case measured has greater relative standing. It is also useful for showing trends and comparison of distributions. This technique also has greater simplicity in its determination (Baxter, 1976; Yeomans, 1968). Line and bar charts are also used as appropriate.

With respect to the second main focus and special case study in chapter seven, the measures of programme impact used relate to inward investment, employment, income, production and sales of industrial raw material and local food supplies. The other aspects are social infrastructure in terms of health, housing, education, land-use and urbanization effects. In applying the various ways of experimental design, the programme evaluation in chapter seven is based on the techniques of ratios, percentages as well as line and bar charts.

Apart from these main data analyses, two main hypotheses are tested: one relates to the levels of inter-district and inter-sector-based disparities in the Central Region. The Analysis-of-variance (Anova) technique is used to test this with its appropriate F-test of significance. The other hypothesis relates to determining whether the differences among impacts under the TOPP programme are significantly different from zero. Certainly, the Chi-square technique is appropriate for testing this hypothesis.

Sampling of respondents A stratified random sample is used to choose the non-settled smallholders (control group) and the settled smallholders (experimental group). This sampling technique recognizes the heterogeneity involved in the relevant population. As a combination of the stratified and simple random approaches, the sampling technique also has the merit of randomization. The data relating to the two groups are shown in Table 2.1.

Table 2.1 Sample of settled smallholders, non-settled and ejected land-owners and tenants

Settled Smallholders	*Population of Participants**	*Sample out of sub-total*	*% of sub-total of sample*
Twifo Mampong	40	32	74.42
Hemang	3	3	6.98
Sub-total	**43**	**35**	**81.40**
Non-Settled Smallholders			
Ntafrewaso	1	1	0.848
Twifo Mampong	50	17	14.41
Twifo Hemang	60	17	14.41
Eduabeng	7	5	4.24
Sub-total	**118**	**40**	**33.908**

Source: Author's fieldwork; *Only 43 smallholders had been settled in the early half of 1989 when the author undertook the earlier fieldwork; later that year, this shot up to 89 smallholders

There were only 43 settled smallholders, out of the target population of 300 at the time of the earlier fieldwork in 1989. Out of the 43 settled smallholders, 40 were based at Twifo Mampong and 3 at Twifo Hemang. It was only possible to randomly interview 32 or 74.42 per cent of the sample sub-total at Mampong on the basis of respondent availability. However, all the 3 settled smallholders at Hemang, at the time, were interviewed. Similarly, 40 or 33.908 per cent non-settled persons were interviewed out of an 'available' sub-total population of 118 from 4 settlements. Only one person was available at Ntafrewaso, the village where the company headquarters is sited.

The sampled data for the outgrower group are shown in Table 2.2. Altogether, a total of 57 outgrowers were in operation in the 7 settlements, out of which 43 or 75.39 per cent were interviewed. The outgrower project area is, in general, delimited into three zones: the Fosu zone, Jukwa zone and Atieku zone. All the settlements indicated in Table 2.2 are in the first named zone. It was not possible to reach the other two because of accessibility difficulties. Of all the settlements, Hemang has the highest population and largest sample. This is probably because the settlement was not actively involved in the smallholder scheme. Indeed, Hemang showed the highest number of non-settled smallholders at the time of the fieldwork.

Table 2.2 Sample of outgrower producers

Settlement	*Population of Participants*	*Sample*	*% Population Identified*
Twifo Mampong	5	2	3.51
Twifo Hemang	33	32	56.1
Eduabeng	3	2	3.51
Ankaako	3	1	1.75
Watresu	3	1	1.75
Ampenkro	4	3	5.26
Jukwa	6	2	3.51
Total	**57**	**43**	**75.39**

Source: Author's fieldwork

The sample of TOPP estate employees is displayed in Table 2.3. Out of a total estate employee universe of 1,148 at the time, the identified population was 1,102. This was because 46 headmen were away from site on other duties at

Table 2.3 Sample of TOPP estate employees

Category	*Population*	*Sample*	*% Population*
Harvestors; pruners	311	28	2.54
Headmen	23	2	0.18
Loaders	43	12	1.09
Checkers	11	4	0.36
Upkeep Labour	502	24	2.18
Sundry*	79	18	1.63
Mill workers	50	9	0.82
Building	70	8	0.73
Mechanical	13	4	0.36
Total	**1,102**	**109**	**9.89**

Source: Author's fieldwork; *security, health, transport, carpenters, gardeners

the time of the survey. A stratified random sample of 109 or 9.89 per cent of the available population based on the employee categories, was taken and on a *pro rata* basis (Moser and Kalton, 1996). In this case, this is generally used as a sample proportion because much depended on how many of a particular group were available at the time of the fieldwork.

Finally, Table 2.4 shows the number of heads of sector-based departments, administrators, planners and local politicians covered in the survey. The sector-based heads were those of the various ministries and departments from which statistical data on government projects were collected. The sectors covered were determined by data availability. Of the planners chosen, one was an expert-consultant at the national level, two from the Greater Accra Regional Planning Co-ordinating Unit and two others from the Central Regional Planning Co-ordinating Unit. In the case of the two Regions the officials interviewed were the only persons at post. The Greater Accra planning officers included a Chief Planner, who had recently been transferred from the Central Region and was, therefore, very conversant with happenings in that Region. The expert-consultant was an expatriate of long residence in the country and had adequate, competent, reliable knowledge of socio-economic conditions and planning matters in Ghana. The District Assembly Representatives were interviewed about their views on the general and urbanization impacts of the TOPP initiative. Thus out of the population of 40 persons, 33 of them or 82.5 per cent were interviewed, using a structured interview schedule. This type of research instrument allowed in-depth interviews, based mostly on open-ended questions, yielding copious qualitative data. This also made data collection in this way flexible. Altogether, a population of 1,360 potential respondents were identified out of which 260 or 19.12 per cent were interviewed.

Table 2.4 Sample of public sector heads, administrators and planners

Category	*Population*	*Sample*	*% Population*
Sector heads; administrators	7	7	17.5
Planners	8	5	12.5
District Assembly Representatives	25	21	52.5
Total	**40**	**33**	**82.5**

Source: Author's fieldwork

Summary

Various studies of the problem of regional disparities in socio-economic and spatial development have been reviewed with the aim of learning lessons from them and setting out a distinctive context for the focus in this book. While the engagement here relates to some aspects of those studies, the book has its own focus in many respects. This relates to the use of a direct inductive methodology which includes its design, research strategies relating to the survey, case study and experimental approaches as well as wider programme. Another differentiating aspect relates to its epistemological foundations, framework and theory. Others are its application of techniques of analyses; choice of indicators of policy and development impacts as well as emphasis on regional planning policy, related dynamics and statutory planning context. It is also distinctive in emphasizing the procedural planning process and evaluation.

3 Regional development theory and the planning process: informing policy and strategy

Regional development theory is useful in guiding the analyses and explanation of observed socio-economic and spatial changes (Richardson and Townroe, 1986). However, the greatest importance of theory is in guiding policy formulation as well as the designing of strategy and development initiatives. Thus theory is useful in informing planning policy and shaping strategy. In this way, 'theory underpins the criteria by which the goals and objectives of initiatives and social engagements may be assessed' (Ofori, 2000b, p. 19). The intent is neither to explicate nor test theory but to point out and emphasize its implications for regional planning policy and strategy (Hautamaki, 1985; McNeil, 1985). These aspects are also essential for both tactical and strategic planning thought.

Slater (1975, p. 100) has argued that, 'no policy or planning strategy exists in isolation from an underlying and conditioning theoretical base'. Other writers have made the same observation in relation to planning policy in the Third World (Richardson and Townroe, 1986; Gore, 1984, p.81). For example, Cappellin and Molle (1988) find the same observation relevant to regional policy in the European Union. Indeed, it is significant Patton and Sawicki (1986, p. 319) also observe that:

> there must be a theoretical and substantive justification ... Theory is an essential ingredient of the experimental design approach as well as of policy analysis in general. Policies are adopted because we expect them to bring about certain changes. Assumptions and observations led us to develop theories that describe the relationships among variables and specify policies to change or enhance those relationships. After the policy changes are made, we collect data to measure change in the variables and thus confirm or reject our theories.

Thus Friedmann (1973) has argued that while plans could be prepared out of theoretical contexts, it is theory that provides the basis for analysis that can also be justified in the face of any criticism. In this way, theory also creates the framework for defending alternative proposals in technical terms. Within its framework, the planner can reduce the area of choice by indicating and demonstrating the area of feasibility. Another benefit of theory is that it enables the planner to isolate the relevant issues for political decision-making.

Cooke (1983) has also argued the fact that there has been a gap between abstract planning theory and as it relates to material urban and regional development processes (Cooke, 1983). He also argued that there has been an emerging attempt to achieve an integration between the two modes (Cooke, 1983). Therefore, it is necessary to provide integrating solutions to this problem as the implications of the regional theories for policy and connection between the two modes are pointed out. It was indicated in chapter one the need to integrate procedural and substantive planning theories. Cooke further points out the need to integrate procedural and substantive planning theory on one hand and the two with implementation on the other.

He suggests a number of criteria for achieving such integration. One of these is that it must be founded on an embedded and material context. Another is to base it on pervasive as well as interactive and intra-active factors. A further criterion is in actively addressing wider factors such as 'power', 'power relations', 'cultural diversity', 'convergence' and 'divergence'. Therefore, it is logical that a further integrating criterion, in this regard, be one that avoids the strictly deductive and abstractionist constructs which also have the tendency to exclude uniqueness and distinctiveness in processes of explanation.

Ofori (2000b) noted the limitation in Cooke's criteria in the failure to include the processes of policy formation, formulation and development of strategy. It is argued that these two instruments of planning must happen, as much as possible, simultaneously (Ofori 2000b). While helping to explain the processes of regional change and the policy-strategy refinement, theory is useful in accounting for the emergence and evolution of disparities in regional development. It has been argued that the realist and phenomenological epistemologies are also useful in achieving this goal.

Notion of regional policy

While an emphasis in this book is on regional policy, the expression 'policy' has not been explained. A more explicit view of 'policy', in context, is presented at this stage because it is used differently in various contexts. Policy has been defined as 'an implicit or explicit statement or declaration of intent, intended action or commitment on the part of policy-makers to pursue and implement a particular course of action' (Gillingwater, 1975, p. 8). Similarly, Diamond and Spence (1983, p. 8) defined policy as 'an interventionistic statement of intent and act in response to a perceived problem ... it involves the design of programmes to ameliorate or reduce the problems towards the achievement of the desired goal'.

Barrett and Fudge (1981, p. v) observed that 'public policy may be defined as the implicit or explicit intentions of government and the expression of those intentions entailing specific patterns of activity or inaction by governmental agencies'. In a more substantive study, Hogwood and Gunn (1984, p. 22; quoted from Heclo, 1972) state that 'the term "policy" needs to be able to embrace both what is intended and what occurs as a result of the intention; any use which excluded unintended results ... would surely be impoverished'. Thus they point out that '... outcomes of policies require to be studied and where appropriate, compared and contrasted with policy-makers' intentions' (Hogwood and Gunn, 1984, p. 24). However, Scott (1978) has pointed out that policy may be determined solely by politics and not by analysis. These meanings are important in showing that a policy can be an implied or explicit government intervention statement as well as related to intended and unintended actions to solving perceived problems. The unintended effects of policy may also produce externalities or spillover effects (Schofield, 1987, pp. 16-17).

It is important to distinguish between different levels of policy because of the implication for policy-making (Magnifico *et al.*, 1985). Kuklinski (1970) identified two levels as inter-regional policy and intra-regional policy, respectively. In relation to this, the distinction has also been made in terms of what is described as "policy for regional development" at the national level and inter-regional scale; "policy in regional development" at the sub-national or regional-local end. However, in many cases, the latter may derive its strength from the former. Therefore, the two are not mutually exclusive.

Policy must also provide a clear operational basis for strategy. Strategy itself, is 'a set of actions that involve selection and sequencing of instruments and organization to achieve its ends' (Armstrong and Taylor, 1985; Chatterjee and Nijkamp, 1983, p. 4). Therefore, strategy is both an input and a medium for implementing a development initiative.

Theoretical and hypothetical formulations in regional development

Regional development theories exist in more established forms, quasi- or just hypothetical formulations. Thus many of the constructs exist as an eclectic mass and not solidly concrete and consistent corpus of theory. Therefore, there are various ways in which these theoretical and hypothetical formulations may be categorized or organized (Hautamaki, 1986). The classification adopted depends on the objectives of study. The categories used in this book are recognized simply on functional bases as well as from which realm of knowledge they originate. The differences among the various categories examined lie in the varying emphasis with respect to the regional problem for which policy intervention actions are needed. While reviewing these theoretical constructs, it is also borne in mind the basic structural differences between countries of the Third World and the developed ones (Richardson and Townroe, 1986). For example, the goals of spatial equity and efficiency are relatively more reconcilable in developed economies than in Third World countries.

Urban-industrial formulations

These formulations are based on the rationale that an urban basis is a necessary requirement and so is the location within 'urban' of a processing industrial activity. As an urban place is not seen to exist in vacuum but in symbiotic relationship with its surrounding territory, the entire urban-and-region would benefit from the inter-relationships. The urban-industrial formulation provides the foundation for functional regional planning (Friedmann and Weaver, 1979). The fundamental policy implication is that of the need for a 'prime mover' activity in regional development. It must be designed and implemented with the intent to maximize its many-faceted, multiple function and impacts.

Growth pole and centre theory Originally propounded by Perroux, (1955) from his inductive experience of post-war Europe, the approach and strategy originally had nothing to do with Third World countries (Gore, 1984). The basic premise is that economic development does not occur homogeneously and simultaneously. It is essentially heterogeneous and time-scaled, occurring in propulsive or dominant economic units, which as they expand induce growth in other units: firms (Higgins and Savoie, 1988). The propulsive unit is an industrial complex or a set of industries.

Originally conceived in purely economic terms, it was abstract and was later conceptualized into geographic space by Boudeville (1966). So the development pole or *pôle de croissance* located within an urban area and made up of a set of industrial activities is probabilistically viewed to induce growth in its region as it expands through various linkages. In this way, it is expected to attract other firms through the agglomeration economies that may be created. Therefore, the traditional *pôle* is a robust and complex corporate entity. In practice, this complex and growth-inducing economic activity may not be existent nor would a large and developed city-system, especially in the case of many territorial regions of the Third World (Gore, 1984; Friedmann and Weaver, 1979; Richardson, 1978a). Any viable venture, say a sustainable agricultural undertaking could serve as the growth-generating unit. In this case too, any other lower scale of urban centre may serve the functional purpose.

One policy implication of this construct is that it depends on centralizing resources and infrastructure within a few core zones. The infrastructure could be provided by the public agent as leverage to attract sets of economic activities. Another implication is the need to establish a clear scale of urban centres to provide the spatial foundation for the 'mover' and 'generative' activities (Ofori, 2000h).

There have been attempts to fuse the positive aspects of the formulation with the central place theory, a static normative model which seeks to explain the distribution of service activity and settlements (Richardson, 1975; 1973; 1969c; 1969b; Gruchman, 1972). This also has the advantage of fusing growth and service activities. It is the view of the present writer, as held by many, that unless a service activity has the potential to generate growth and development, it could not provide the generative activity basis of the growth pole and centre application. The channels and systems for actually propagating the impulses of development must also be clearly and functionally identified.

A further implication is that the generative activity must be one in which there is consideration for not only the economic but social, environmental or physical and spatial aspects of development. Furthermore, it is important to recognize the possible dilemma or conflict in trying to achieve spatial equity by an 'efficiency approach' (Coffey and Polese, 1985, p. 87). This would have the tendency to induce appreciable divergence and limited in its unity of facets, especially in the initial stages of the development process. In many Third World countries where this theory and policy strategy has been implemented the results have been very minimal or mostly ineffective (Richardson, 1978b).

Circular cumulative causation; polarization and trickling down effects Myrdal, (1957) also accepted the reality that the process of development tends to create spatial inequalities and demonstrated that the process happens by circular cumulative causation. Once certain places have taken the 'lead' by some fortuitous circumstances, any further progression of activity will tend to be focused on and become intensified in such areas. Cumulative causation can be positive in the form of a progressively upward spiral of growth or negative in a downward direction. Myrdal, realistically, pointed out that market forces tend to increase and perpetuate such inequalities between and within regions through the process of circular cumulative causation. He noted that this makes it necessary to introduce a deliberate intervention policy.

As the leading region siphons out resources, in the form of capital, labour and other trade flows from its surrounding region, it creates relative stagnating and regressive 'backwash effects' in those territories. If there is a positive spatial linkage, the regional core can, rather, induce growth and 'spread effects' through demands for its products in its surrounding areas. Thus either way, the effect becomes cumulative, exerting a multiplier effect in that way. Once again, there is the assumption of the existence of an urban-industrial base. But the factors of capital, labour, market forces and trade flows are crucial explanations while the mention of intervention policies is just appropriate. Indeed, Myrdal points out that it is only by such decision-making and related action that Third World countries can rise from their state of less and constrained development.

Hirschman (1958) also accepted the hard reality of economic development and pointed out the polarizing nature of the process. Significantly, however, he admits that the initial 'imbalance' - disparity and divergence - or disequilibrium is an inevitable and necessary condition for growth and its spread. After the leading centre or regional core has grown and become polarized against the remaining territory, growth may 'trickle down' from the former to the latter. If it does not, all the leading node does is to pipe out resources from the surrounding region, leaving it even more seriously regressed than before.

The principal concern here should be with a policy and strategy of controlled investment, with initial selective attention to the 'urban-industrial pockets'. This represents, perhaps, the first spatial exposition of 'unequal' regional development. Again, efficiency considerations are paramount but policy intervention and, in particular, investment are recognized as essential conditions. Since imbalance is a necessary stimulating condition, planners are urged to adopt a policy of 'controlled disequilibrium'. In this way, too, policy should be flexible and particularly responsive to meeting the demands of strategic regional change at all successive stages.

Centre-periphery process The centre-periphery model which was originally proposed by Friedmann (1966) offers more insight into the process of spatial concentration and the phenomenon of socio-economic disparity. His conceptualization includes strands of ideas from other writers (Gore, 1984; Gilbert and Gugler, 1981; Rostow, 1960). According to Friedmann, the leading centre is one of resource concentration and decides on its own development as well as determines the development of its surrounding territory.

This structure evolves in four stages. Stage one postulates a state of primary resource extraction under some exogenous and colonizing power or force within an incipient system of settlements. There is very little industrial activity at this stage. In stage two, there is further concentration of investment in one or two principal centres, marking out a dualistic spatial structure and some intervention in the form of regional policy becomes necessary. Stage three is one of greater regional consciousness of and responsiveness to the problem (Friedmann, 1972). Local initiative and government action may come together to aim at reducing the inequalities through the adoption of regional policy. Friedmann postulated further that in stage four a situation of 'balanced' and integrated space economy would develop, characterized by efficiency in the location of firms and minimal inter-regional disparity. There is also said to be a balanced urban-size distribution in this stage of centre-periphery evolution.

Friedmann's model is inconsistent with historical reality in many Third World countries. It also downplays exogenous forces such as the dynamics of the international economic system. It is not politically realistic in assuming that national governments introduce regional policy because it is in the public interest to do so. Friedmann also perceived poverty in regional rather than in national and social terms. In this way, the wider context of local poverty conditions is not realistically appreciated. This also means any effort to reduce or abolish poverty is primarily constrained and ineffective. Indeed, he assumed that once there is heavy investment in the creation of infrastructure and rise in per capita income and, consequently, a 'spatial integration', poverty would be reduced, if not eliminated. Therefore, personal disparities which are predominant in Third World countries are not dealt with (Bigstern, 1980). Finally, the model, like that of Rostow (1960) assumes a unilinear development process. This is unlikely to be replicated in Third World countries (Gilbert and Gugler, 1981). Nevertheless, Friedmann usefully shows the importance of infrastructure as leverage. The other significant elements are the emergence of a hierarchy of settlements, the regional community as a cultural entity as well as social and political factors.

Regional economic-oriented growth and development

The neo-classical model The neo-classicists explain regional disparities in terms of the availability and inter-regional mobility of production rather than consumption factors (Richardson, 1975; Borts, 1960). Capital and labour would flow where they would earn the highest rate of return. The process is expected to bring about equalization of wages and capital yields and to work towards convergence in regional per capita incomes (Bigstern, 1980). For example, this typifies the behaviour of global corporate organizations. Regional development policy, based on this, is expected to increase returns on investment in the regions to which they move and where capital circulates. The free flow of labour is expected to regulate unemployment in peripheral areas. Regional development policy thus relies on fiscal measures and aims at improving industrial infrastructure.

This model does not answer distribution questions (Holland, 1976a; 1976b; Richardson, 1973). Besides, it ignores the influence of external economies. It does not recognize the other sources of financial resources, including welfare benefit payments, where these are available. It does not also address possible internal community reactions such as employee union pressures for effective regional change (Holland 1976b). In addition, it does not recognize inter-regional innovation diffusion and technological progress, the latter of which may develop locally on its own. Therefore, while emphasizing the importance of providing infrastructure and investing in meaningful production activities, the policy implication also attracts attention to social forces. It is to such limitations as these that the Keynesian model reacts with emphasis on public domain-induced investment and related demand processes.

Export base model The export base concept is premised on the notion that exports of a region are the only and autonomous mover of its growth and development (Cooke, 1983; Glasson, 1978; Richardson, 1973; Lewis, 1966; Friedmann, 1966; North, 1964; Perloff and Wingo, 1964; Borts, 1960). The construct is on the application of the short-run static economic base model to long-run dynamic growth situations. It can be used as the intra-regional multiplier, usually based on employment data. A simpler form of the export base model is applied in the evaluation of the TOPP programme in chapter seven. As the basic and production sector of the total regional economic base responds to external demand by exports, this generates income which as it flows in goes to generate the local and service sector. The process of structural change also induces capital and labour movements. This means the basic sector is the real mover of growth.

The model can also be regarded as the inter-regional or Keynesian multiplier model where the multiplier is equal to regional output divided by total exports. This is more based on income data and explains regional growth by recognizing imports, taxation and savings, all of which affect regional income (Armstrong and Taylor, 1985; 1978; Glasson, 1978). The basic sector tends to have a pervasive effect shaping the scale and location of residential development, as well as influencing urbanization patterns (Cooke, 1983; Richardson, 1973).

However, export base thinking has several weaknesses which also limit its policy applications (Glasson, 1978; Richardson, 1969a; Lewis, 1966; Tiebout, 1964). Some regions may develop primarily on the basis of 'autonomous' service activities. The view in this book is still that if such service activities do not have the potential and reality to actually generate growth and development, they could not provide the foundation for regional socio-economic progress. For example, such service activities should generate local or sub-regional employment rather than, say, public services that bring in employees from outside the region. However, exports may diminish with time as primary activity depreciates in favour of services and other post-industrial processes including tertiary and quaternary activities. Further, the income generated through export activity may not produce any positive effect on inward investment and availability of development funds because of its repatriation as it is earned. As in the neo-classical models, the export base construct disregards the possibility of technical progress including technological innovations being induced within the region. Nevertheless, it is realistic in showing that for most regions their socio-economic progress depends, to a large extent, on external demand via exports of resource-based production. In this way, too, it contradicts the notion of selective spatial closure.

Harrod-Domar model Instead of depending on external demand as the growth mover, the Harrod-Domar approach explains growth in terms of the progressive increase in investments and additions to the capital stock of the region (Todaro, 1989). The investment originates from the performance of gross national product. Therefore, each round of successful performance is supposed to create a fillip for successive stages of investment in the region. Thus the Harrod-Domar model assumes a relationship between the capital stock and Gross National Product (GNP). The relationship is reciprocal with respect to the behaviour of the levels in both the capital stock and GNP.

It is assumed that the rate of GNP growth is determined by a constant propensity to save; equal capital-to-labour ratios. It is also assumed that there is a constant rate of growth in the labour force as a constant proportion of population growth and constant returns to scale. There is also the assumption of homogeneity of labour cost and skill. Therefore, the greater national savings are, the larger the economically-active labour force with uniformity in cost of labour and skill, the greater the GNP growth which is also inversely related to the capital-output ratio.

The net effect is that the higher the rate of national savings, the greater chance of investment as well as level and rate of socio-economic development. In this way, the fast rate of growth would sustain itself. Therefore, where the rate of new capital formation is low, this constrains the development process. Each round of progressive investment and increase in GNP creates the opportunity for factor mobility from the equilibrium, proportional to the capacity created in the region. The demand making this happen would also require necessary levels of technical improvement in the particular centre of production (Cooke, 1983; Richardson, 1969a; 1969b). These ideas underline the importance of national economic context for statutory regional planning.

The effectiveness of investment inducing growth in GNP and consequently, regional development, in this way, has been seriously questioned (Todaro, 1989). It has been argued that other factors and conditions are necessary if there is to be an effective utilization of investment and generation of growth (Todaro, 1989). For example, these include managerial ability, the capability and robustness to plan and manage development projects as well as an efficient public-sector administrative system. Others are appropriate institutional structures and systems, attitudes, competence, skilled labour and efficient transport infrastructure. The one critical challenge to the working of this model is the limited rate of savings and capital formation. This means variations in the propensity to save, consequently levels of investment already imbibe a disparity

(Cooke, 1983). Nevertheless, the role of savings and investment and the various development processes these can generate for regional development are clear.

Radical formulations

In response to the failures and ineffectiveness of the urban-industrial, neo-classical and Keynesian constructs, the radical formulations emphasize neo-populist socio-endogenous factors. Among other elements, these include recognition for more explicit empowerment of the territorial region to manage its own affairs (Seitz, 1988; Gore, 1984; Friedmann and Weaver, 1979).

A political economy model of territorial regional development There has been a burdgeoning emphasis on what is both a dimension and sub-paradigm of territorial regional planning. Friedmann and Forest (1988) have called this the 'political economy model', based on what they describe as 'politics of the region'. The writers see this as one that aims at providing an expanded model of regional planning which had been limited to economic and non-spatial issues.

This perspective is based on the central argument that regional communities have been dissatisfied with and disenfranchized by the failure to deliver for the individual region. The two writers argue that this is supported by the inability of market and political forces to allocate resources effectively and efficiently. The co-operative and collaborative operation of the state with corporate and capitalist forces has only undermined the opportunity for actually improving the well-being of territorial regional communities (Simon, 1990; Friedmann and Forest, 1988). Moreover, neo-classical factor flows only favour inter-regional disparities in an attitude of homogeneity towards the national space-economy.

Friedmann and Forest argue further that many interest groups, classes and parties are challenged in this situation to seek solutions to regional socio-economic disparities. Therefore, in the process of this struggle, the regional problem has become more politicized. The two writers justify this case further on the observation that this political dimension has been ignored in many territorial regions.

The paradigmatic shift represented in the 'political economy model' is centred on achieving regional autonomy as well as asserting a cultural identity. In this context, members of the regional community aim to achieve by engaging in shared debates and deciding together in controlling their resources and process of development. This is also the response of the territorial region to threats and pressures of state and corporate forces in their domination (Ofori, 2000d). Thus the 'politics of place' is also a reaction to the limited effectiveness of functional regional planning and the classical urban-industrial doctrine in making things happen. It also seeks to promote the democratic enterprise in the region. Thus it contains a focus on wider issues of power, including contention with various interests as well as values and class struggle.

For example, Gooneratne (1997) has pointed out the failure of central and national governments to bring about effective regional planning in sub-Saharan Africa. Under the structural adjustment programmes, it has been observed that the disparities between urban and rural areas has been widening (Gooneratne, 1997; Harris, 1992). It is also noted that regional communities are increasingly and rapidly being faced with the impoverishing and dominating influences of globalism and eco-capitalism (Ofori 2000d; Gooneratne, 1997; Gooneratne and Obudho, 1997).

The focus of the political economy model is also on proactive and not reactive planning. Therefore, the emphasis is also maintained on a shift from purely economic issues to the more complex and wider factors that denote the priorities of the particular territorial region. There is a shift from supply factors to demand-side regional economics. And the region controls its own resources and trade as well as determines the power relations involved in improving the material conditions of the regional populace equitably.

The state still has a role, for example, in the form of initial investment as shown in the case of the Harrod-Domar model. But this role is subordinated to the politicization of the region. Indeed, a distinctive emphasis in this model is on the factor of politicization by which the region is organized and contained within the structure of wider or global economic relations.

Another emphasis is on creating employment for people where they are located instead of moving them to where jobs may be sited. The latter option thrives on the circulatory and restructuring behaviour of capitalist forces. Therefore, a labour-intensive form of work is preferred to a capital-intensive one. This provides a further support for the rapidly growing practice of local economic development and planning (Gooneratne, 1997). The model also puts much emphasis on regional resource development, including landscape and environment and the relationship between these and production as well as socio-cultural initiatives. This underlines the significance of environmental sustainability in it.

Indeed, Friedmann and Forest (1988) point out that the political economy model also generates a new form of planning and role for planners. This requires an engaging dialogue between planners and clients. The former must also be more creative and gain mastery of effective bargaining and negotiation (Ofori, 2000b). The political economy model, however, does not provide a clear process by which this kind of regional development takes place. It consists of strands of ideas. Nevertheless it is applicable to regions in the Third World.

Marxist perspective on regional disparities and development The most radical alternative view of regional development and socio-economic disparities comes from the Marxists. They hypothesize that regional inequalities are the result of class inequalities, resulting from the capitalist mode of production. The poorer regions suffer because part of the value of what they produce is appropriated by the capitalist class of regions at the national and international scales. This consistent and progressive trend of exploitation leaves the peripheral country in a state of regression and so its regions do not benefit from it.

This structural development of the dominant and subordinate modes of production also determines social formation in the peripheral, Third World territories. The extent of social class conflict and the needs of the dominant mode of production only contribute to this process of social formation (Poutlantzas, 1973). Further, the extent of social class conflict and the needs of the dominant mode of production determine the relationships between the main actors: multi-national corporations, the state and the poor as well as all these with elitist classes within the peripheral territory. In each situation and round in the process, the most powerful are the dominant forces: all the dominant centre does, in this state of exploitation, is to siphon out surplus from the peripheral country. As the former accumulates surplus and aims at managing this process, it looks for further external expansion of its investment activities and intensification of exploitation.

Neo-Marxists point out that this process also thrives on unequal exchange in which labour in the exploited region is substantially under-remunerated (Todaro, 1989; Emmanuel, 1972). Meanwhile, the export commodities of the periphery are under-priced by the capitalist exploiters. The process of exploitation and domination is also sustained by the operations of elitist groups which represent the interests of the capitalists in the peripheral territory.

The capitalist mode of production concentrates the means of production within sectors and sorts out society into various classes. As the dominant mode of production changes through time, the method of surplus extraction and the social formation also change (Castells, 1977). The sector-based concentration of the means of production is made possible by the mass-scale adoption of mechanization and other capital intensive activities, apart from the capitalist system of global trade. Consequently, surplus agricultural labour is recruited, as much as possible, into a swelling manufacturing proletariat. Apart from the resulting spatial division of labour, this generates formidable urbanization processes (Massey, 1979). It also stifles cottage and small-scale industrial development as well as increasing regional disparities, impoverishing the poorer regions by a very high rate of surplus extraction.

In this scenario of underdevelopment, neo-Marxists believe that the solution lies in a restructuring of the global capitalist system. Only this, they argue, would liberate the dependent territories from the direct and indirect capitalist domination and the activities of their domestic representatives. In this state of affairs, development in the dominated periphery is 'impossible' except such restructuring takes place. Although the national government or state is expected to act in favour of the poor, it may tend to work in collusion with the dominant and capitalist classes (Miliband, 1977; 1969; Poulantzas, 1973; 1969).

Neo-Marxists further point out that this notion of 'impossible development' is flawed. Rather, it is the operation of certain other factors that created the situation of 'inappropriate development' in the peripheral country and territorial regions. These include the low wages, the lack of entrepreneurial skills and limited administrative talent plus other aspects of managerial competence. Therefore, the dominated region is not able to break out of its vicious circle of poverty. Of course, there is also the question of the ownership of the means of production.

The considerations, so far, are also reasons why Marxists accuse regional theorists of being preoccupied with spatial issues. In this way, the latter ignore the underlying dynamics of the real world structure (Gore, 1984; Cooke, 1983; Massimo, 1982; Massey, 1979; Coates *et al.*, 1977). For example, it has even been pointed out that the terms 'urban' and 'regional' 'point to a spatial mode of thought about processes that are social rather than spatial' (Cooke, 1983 p.132; Massey, 1978). It has been argued that the spatial element in such thinking is only strong at the international and national scales, not at the regional and local levels (Massimo, 1982; Holland, 1976b).

Marxist thinking, of course, further justifies the need for active and policy intervention in the process of territorial regional development. It is also severely critical of self-adjustment. For example, the internal spatial configuration of Third World countries is part of the world system of production and consumption. It is by this configuration that the surplus generated through the establishment of business ventures is transferred abroad through all kinds of networks (Cardoso, 1972; Santos, 1970). The surplus is also appropriated by the local elite groups mainly concentrated in the major cities, rarely benefiting the periphery (Gilbert and Gugler, 1981).

Therefore, the sheer reduction of per capita or inter-group as well as inter-personal income is not the way towards greater equity. The critical determinant of the problem may be some structurally dominant class, controlling power and wealth. Thus to regard the reduction of inequalities as a minimization of spatial inequalities is to commit an ecological fallacy. What should be of concern in the process of regional development and poverty alleviation are the 'processes of social and economic change, questions about the spatiality of the processes' (Gore, 1984, p. 75).

However, modern Marxist analysis is based on social classes and groups rather than individuals (Joseph and Sumption, 1979). In fact, this represents a contradiction in relation to the Marxist view. Planning is interested in groups and classes as well as individuals in all their association with areas. Therefore, class or group alone cannot be a unit of analysis in this context. The historical methodology of the Marxists also does not always apply since different sets of dynamics may operate on various time patterns: there may be significant breaks and intervals in a critical path. In addition, the picture created by the Marxists that there would be no regional disparities under a non-capitalist system is more of theory than practice (Giese and Hecht, 1983; Hilhorst, 1969). Nevertheless, the Marxist perspectives more critically address many of the issues noted in the 'political economy model'.

Endogenous and sub-regional development processes Endogenous regional growth and development theorization is more recent (Cappelin and Molle, 1988). The sets of theoretical constructs described as such strongly focus on the local economic development end of the intra-regional engagement. For example, Wannop (1995) has emphasized the occurrence of this stage in the process of regional planning policy and development. These also reflect many of the aspects of the political economy model and Marxist perspectives.

Endogenous development is based on the assumption of a stable regional environment characterized by such factors as skilled labour force, technical and organizational know-how, social and institutional factors. Emphasis is on the productivity of local physical resources, settlement system, economic structure, public infrastructure and fixed private capital stock (Biehl, 1980). The difference between the 'exogenous' models and the 'endogenous' ones is illustrated by what has been termed 'competitive' and 'generative' regional development, respectively (Richardson, 1978b, pp. 145-146; 1973, p. 86).

Indeed, recent regional development emphasis has shifted to innovation-oriented approaches. This includes the importance of new technology, investment in human capital, venture capital and entrepreneurial factors. These introduce a very important dimension being organizational and enterprise management. Therefore, this relates to the effectiveness of regional development agencies, for example. The endogenous approach is also focused on the critical importance of inward investment and the development of the local economy as either an absolute reality or as an incubator-oriented step from 'maturity' of activity at one plant or activity and diffusion to another or others (Cappellin and Molle, 1988; Thwaites, 1982; Ewers and Wettmann, 1980; Leone and Struyk, 1976).

The relatively older endogenous formulations are the sector and stages theories. The former associates a rise in per capita income with fall in primary activities, a rise in manufacturing and consequent regional growth. The latter sees the growth process in five stages from a subsistence economy; through those of local trade and specialization; inter-regional trade; declining agricultural activity and intensive industrialization; to growth in services (Glasson, 1978). In the stages view, industrialization is considered a necessary requirement at some stage as a result of population growth, failing which population pressure results. The two views are unilinear and appear untenable in the real world. The stages model cannot stand in the face of the Boserup (1965) thesis. This suggests that development of technological capability and capacity in the use of land to meet food needs can occur without industrialization, except where necessary investment is available. However, I will not go any further with this argument.

A more specific endogenous development model proposed by Coffey and Polese (1985; 1984) is based primarily on economic considerations and associated socio-cultural characteristics. They focus on locality economic development in an individual territory or 'micro-region' (Coffey and Polese, 1984, p. 2). The two writers define the local activity as 'an event or action which is initiated and/or sustained by the population of a sub-regional unit' (Coffey and Polese, 1985, p. 86). The goal is to achieve 'self-development of small regions - the development of localities' based on a free market system (Coffey and Polese, 1984, p. 2). However, they are flexible in recognizing the importance of external factors. The two researchers also describe 'local factors' in terms of the socio-cultural and behavioural attributes of the local population and not the geographic and physical characteristics (Coffey and Polese, 1984).

The conceptualization of Coffey and Polese (1985; 1984) is a contribution to the explanation of the 'residual factor' in the territorial development process (Denison, 1974). Development often amounts to investment in the provision of physical infrastructure which may not be really relevant to people or their human capital (Weaver, 1984). It has been pointed out that any regional development policy should not only address the physical infrastructure aspects; it must also include actions aimed at improving the productive and entrepreneurial capacity of members of the local community (Martinson and Schulman, 1977). These other factors which affect the per capita income, yet often left in the background, constitute the residual factor (OECD, 1988).

In relation to these considerations, Coffey and Polese emphasize three foundations in their model. The first one is the fundamental need to increase entrepreneurial ability and know-how. Another is to promote the expansion of local enterprise under migration which, it is held, results in distribution and re-distribution of static production factors. The other aspect is the spatial expansion and development of spatial linkages. This includes a distance-deterring factor resulting in inward investment.

According to Coffey and Polese, the locality would grow and develop in four stages. These include the emergence of local entrepreneurial ability; rippling out of enterprise beyond the locality; and effective local control of the emergent enterprises. Fourth, a regional economic structure 'composed in large part of local firms, together with a labour force and a local entrepreneurial class capable of adapting and modifying the output and the structure of the region's economy' would emerge (Coffey and Polese, 1984, p. 8).

The policy implication of the formulation is that localities or sub-regions can develop comparative advantages, based on endogenous enterprise. The policy focus is on human resource and institutional development rather than on capital subsidies and physical infrastructure. However, Coffey and Polese (1984) suggest that the problem of measuring levels of 'entrepreneurship', innovation, and other factors could create difficulties for the implementation and evaluation of such policies. I think this problem could be solved by the use of surrogate measures. Cooke and Hulme (1988, p. 228) have observed that the model may provide the basis for 'regional policy that complements a market-oriented macro-economic philosophy'. On other hand, Cooke and Kirkpatrick (1988) warn against both extreme intervention and a pure market-oriented approach.

Another focus of the endogenous development formulation is on the urbanization of the periphery of the territorial region. Johnson (1970) argued for the need to stem urban primacy, check rural-metropolis migration and bridge the gap between centre and periphery. In this case, the latter consists of villages and small towns. He advocates a development policy which is aimed at creating a matrix of small market towns and integrating them into larger units which have promising potential to deliver.

The construct and strategy are essentially infrastructure-based. The critical resources, in this regard, include the availability of financial institutions and social services; electricity, roads and industrial estates for small-scale factories. These are to be co-ordinated with capital investment in large-scale projects such as oil mills, the kind of TOPP. It is proposed that this strategy must be founded on market centres and agrarian commercialization. It is also proposed that peripheral space should be delimited into 'functional economic areas', i.e. small towns with their complementary zones. The construct also represents an application of the central place and growth centre theories.

It is noted that the implementation of this strategy requires co-operation between local and regional planning authorities. The reality is also accepted that the strategy can breed its own disparities. It is the view in this book, however, that such divergence would be more pronounced in the initial stages, depending on the level of success.

The wider application of this strategy in the territorial region has been described as 'integrated regional development'. In proposing this strategy, Rondinelli and Ruddel (1978) also emphasized focused development of urban places in the rural parts of the territorial region. They stressed on the critical importance of a number of factors, including the need to build on local cultural resources and specialized production aimed at achieving comparative advantage. Others are the cardinal roles of innovation and transformation with consideration for technical, political, economic, administrative and spatial aspects. These writers also put emphasis on the need for flexibility, adaptive and responsive processes. The model also includes particular emphasis on the provision of various linkages relating to physical, economic, population movements, technological, social interaction, and service delivery. Others are those that promote political administration, spatial and institutional organization, as well as social equity and accessibility to productive activity.

All the theoretical and hypothetical formulations considered have certain general characteristics. These include the critical role of 'town' at various scales; infrastructure as leverage and substantive resource; production-based activities; and inward investment strategies. Others are the development of human capital, entrepreneurial ability, skills, consistent training and development, enterprise, and managerial capabilities. The regional development process is effective if it addresses power and power relations, cultural diversity, autonomous initiative, democratic enterprise in planning and environmental sustainability. It takes robustness to put all these together and manage them effectively in a process of strategic regional change.

Hypotheses: material socio-economic context of the Central Region

This book is aimed at investigating the impact of regional development and statutory planning policy on inter-local and inter-group disparities with respect to selected socio-economic and spatial indicators. The following underlying hypotheses are meant to guide the inquiry and interpretation of the observed changes and provide a further framework for the choice of analytical tools.

First hypothesis The intent, here, is to show whether there has been positive regional change in terms of the levels and dimensions of socio-economic as well as spatial development. The discussions and reviews show the increased recognition and policy support for addressing intra-regional disparities in Ghana. This, in particular, relates to the more downward-transitional areas. These reactions on the part of the public domain give an impression and view that inter-local socio-economic disparities have been and continue to be minimized.

Therefore, it is hypothesized that intra-regional disparities in socio-economic and spatial development within the Central Region have decreased in favour of the less urbanized and more deeply territorial areas as well as sectors of their space-economy; in this case, a further aspect of this hypothesis is that there is a reduction in divergence and increase in convergence with respect to socio-economic and spatial development in the Region.

This hypothesis is based on the following assumptions. The first one is that the 'favoured' localities are not the urbanized areas and which have not continued to receive more investment and development projects. Another one is that the levels and rates of socio-economic and spatial disparity have not increased rapidly in favour of the core areas. The third one is that the availability of central government funding has become greater in the amelioration of socio-economic disparities with respect to the non-core urban places. Fourth, that the extent of intra-regional socio-economic and spatial disparities reflect the level of the effectiveness of project and programme implementation. A fifth one is that local community-induced initiative constitutes an equally differentiating factor which also favours the less urban localities.

The policy implications of the hypothesis include the need to significantly increase investment levels in the peripheral regions and to phase sustained commitment to a number of sectors by keeping to a structure of priority areas; it is by sustained and heavy investment in social and productive infrastructure in the disadvantaged areas that real regional development in the more territorial areas will occur. Another policy implication is the need to achieve an effective horizontal development of the sector-based functions through a formal regional development plan. A further implication, here, is the need to design and implement functional-urban development initiatives and strategies, particularly in the disadvantaged areas with emphasis on the small and medium settlements. Furthermore, it is crucial to encourage the participation of the local communities and the private sector in the processes of regional development.

Second hypothesis It was pointed out, in chapter one, that the evolution of the space-economy from colonial times to the present has structurally integrated Ghana's economy into the international economic system, in a way that even periphery-based production goes to satisfy that system. This is also consistent with aspects of the theoretical and hypothetical formulations particularly in relation to territorial regional development. Apart from the spatial impact, it also has serious effects on personal income and welfare. One way in which this may be solved is to implement regional development programmes and projects which would not isolate the 'region' from the international system but redefine the productive roles of the people in the regional community in a more direct and beneficial way to them. All the cases and theoretical constructs reviewed indicate the dialectics in relation to regional initiatives, the kind of TOPP.

Therefore, it is hypothesized that socio-economic development and well-being at the community, group and personal levels in the Central Region are being maximized most rapidly and effectively by implementing local resource-utilizing programmes and projects such as TOPP. Conversely, it is further hypothesized that the project-complex is not making significant impact on the specifically targeted populations, including the smallholders, outgrowers, main estate employees and the Twifo territorial sub-region.

The following assumptions underlie the hypothesis. One is that such projects and programmes as TOPP are formulated without adequate regard to the socio-economic development of the people and the area so as to achieve regional planning policy and development goals. Another one is that the projects under the TOPP programme are not effectively set within the statutory regional planning practice and policy in the Central Region, under the guidance provided by national development policy. In addition, all project participants have not experienced a real positive change in their well-being since the initiatives started. Furthermore, there is no effective monitoring of the well-being of the target groups and communities under the programme as a basis for feedback into the socio-economic development and implementation processes.

The hypothesis has a number of policy implications. Large and more concrete regional development projects should be seen as integrated within the region's planning policy. These should also be formulated with regard to productive activity in the local-regional economy and overall regional strategy. Another implication is that such investment activities should not be just economic but include articulated social as well as environmental aspects, beyond profits and value added. Further, the investing agencies, public and private, should be obligated to make additional mandatory contributions at a certain proportion of their profits and/or investments to the development of the programme area - as a social responsibility. This also supports the implication that these initiatives should be firmly set within statutory regional planning. Besides, the policy implication of the urgent need to include the local communities formally and actively in the planning and implementation processes is critical to making things happen.

Summary

The relevance of both established and grounded theory in the context of regional planning is to guide policy and shape strategy. Such strategic regional planning guidance should be comprehensive, co-ordinated and robust. It should address both substantive and materially-based goals and objectives, including inward investment and socio-economic well-being. It should also address wider factors of power, cultural diversity and the democratic enterprise in planning. It is also emphasized, the importance of ensuring environmental sustainability in all regional development plans and programmes. The constructs also underlie the need to ensure that development initiatives are appreciably production-based. Therefore, the need for providing relevant infrastructure both in substantive and leverage terms is also emphasized. These aspects also link up with the urgent need to promote urbanization processes in the peripheral parts of the regional territories. More radical regional theory emphasizes the need for regional communities to have control over their resources and be responsible for their development processes. More recent theorization has also put greater emphasis on 'human' and 'soft' factors, such as managerial abilities including effective administrative, project management and organizational abilities. Other elements emphasized are attitudes, enterprise, training, human resources, including skills and entrepreneurial abilities. The hypotheses formulated will be tested later.

4 National development planning, policy framework and contexts

The contexts of 'policy for regional development' and statutory planning are now set out. This includes outlining the national development plans in Ghana from the earliest to the present. The objective is to identify the rates of implementation success in the regions and validity of the plans to the material conditions in intra-regional planning. Therefore, the objective includes a consideration for the effectiveness of the plans in reducing socio-economic and spatial disparities.

The more specific contexts of socio-economic and spatial development are also presented in relation to the demographic, administrative and economic aspects. With respect to the economic part, there is general focus on the notion of poverty and its variation between and within the regions. The intent is to emphasize the general conditions in the regions and to highlight the place of the Central Region and general welfare levels between its urban and rural areas. These considerations set out the background for presenting the national development policies. Further, a comment is made on the extent to which the contexts and the Ghanaian state enable effective regional planning.

National development plans: focus on socio-economic and spatial change in the regions

Ghana is reputed as being the first country under British colonial rule and one of the first in the modern world to make a national development plan (Waterston, 1966; Birmingham *et al.*, 1966; Niculescu, 1957 quoted in Ewusi, 1973). It is shown in Table 4.1 that Ghana has had some eleven development plans since 1919. Since the early to mid-1980s, however, the practice of real national plan-making has been overtaken by the overwhelming emphasis on macro-economic aspects under the pressures of international financial

Table 4.1 Ghana: national development plans, 1919-89

Title of Plan	*Scheduled Implementation Period*	*Actual Implementation Period*
Guggisberg ten-year development plan	1920-1930	1920-1927
Ten-year development plan of welfare for the Gold Coast	1946-1956	1946
Ten-year development plan for the economic and social development of the Gold Coast	1951-1961	1951
First five-year development plan [for economic and social development of the Gold Coast]	1951-1956	1951-1957
The consolidation plan	1958-1959	1958-1959
The second five-year development plan	1959-1964	1959-1961
National physical development plan	1962	Not implemented
The seven-year development plan	1964-1970	1962-1966
The two-year development plan	1968-1970	1968
One-year development plan (stabilization)	1970-1971	1970
Five-year development plan	1975-1980	1975
Five-year development plan (proposed)	1981-1986	Not implemented
Special Economic Development Programmes:		
Economic Recovery Programme (ERP 1): Stabilization phase	1983-1986	1983-1986
Economic Recovery Programme (ERP II): Structural Adjustment Programme (SAP) phase	1987-1989	1987-1989

Sources: Author's tabulation from Ewusi, K. (1973); Adarkwa, K. (1983); Government of Ghana (1983a; 1983b); Republic of Ghana (1977a; 1977b; 1970; 1968; 1963)

arrangements. Nevertheless the economic recovery programmes constitute a form of national 'development plan', heavier emphasis on the economic facet.

Gordon Guggisberg's development plan of 1920-30 for the Gold Coast (Ghana) created and provided the foundation-stone for the initial infrastructure of Ghana's space-economy. The forms include harbour facility, railways, roads, water supply and sewage systems, public buildings, communication systems mainly in the urban areas (Ewusi, 1973).

The policy goal under this plan was not only to develop trade between the coastal and hinterland areas but also to improve the standard of living of the people of the colony. However, the plan favoured only core areas and resource zones of interest to colonial policy. This reflects the observations made in chapters one and three in relation to the material and theoretical contexts, respectively, of regional planning and development in Ghana. Even this plan was implemented for only 75 per cent of the scheduled period. Although this was an appreciably high rate for its time, it also indicates that the objectives of the plan were not fully met. Moreover, it had spelt out a core-periphery structure of the country's space-economy.

The next 10-year plan, 1946-1956, had similar objectives but was more of a listing of sector-based projects. The practice of listing schemes to be undertaken actually began with the first ten-year development plan (Ewusi, 1973, p. 4). This plan had to be terminated after 1946 for the 1951-56 plan to be introduced in place of the 1951-61 plan which had been previously proposed (Ewusi, 1973; The Gold Coast, 1951a). This was probably due to the fact that the first African (Gold Coast) government took up initial power in 1951. In effect, however, the various colonial government departments continued to undertake their listed initiatives as if a plan actually existed. Therefore, progress reports were maintained on the 'plan's implementation' from 1947 to 1950 (Ewusi, 1973). The 1951-61 itself, was implemented for only one year and the first five-year plan was introduced in its place (The Gold Coast, 1951).

The 1951-56 plan, in practice, ran into 1957, year of Ghana's Independence (The Gold Coast, 1951). Even so, this plan is described as having been 'substantially completed' (Ewusi, 1973). This first five-year development plan was the one to be fully implemented over the scheduled period. Apart from continuing to lay the physical foundations of Ghana's space-economy, this plan was also to fossilize the practice of plan-making by mere listing of initiatives. Following the fashion of the first ten-year plan, this plan was to further emphasize the core-periphery structure of the socio-economic and physical development landscapes.

The 1958-59 consolidation plan was actually designated to cover the period 1957-59 (Ewusi, 1973; Government of Ghana, 1959). It was meant to be a transitional planning instrument to allow the new government to prepare a more elaborate plan. The plan's stated policy goal was that (Government of Ghana, 1959, p. iii):

> it should show what we have to do ... to give us a standard of living which will abolish disease, poverty and illiteracy, give our people ample food and

housing ... we want to develop strong basic services - communication, power and water - so that we can provide a real and effective foundation for the industrialisation of our country.

In this regard, the plan was aimed at addressing the material well-being of the newly-independent country. It was also characterized by comprehensiveness with significant validity. Nevertheless, apart from being transitory, its making did not depart from the fashion of mere listing of one-off projects.

The second five-year plan for the 1959-64 period also did not see much light of day. The making of a new plan was proposed in the third quarter of 1961 (Ewusi, 1973; Government of Ghana, 1959). This was part of the attempt to reorganize and rationalize the plan-making process and practices.

The 1962 national physical plan was aimed at settlement development, based solely on central place considerations but was not implemented. It was aimed at providing the basis for the implementation of the growth centre policy and strategy. As noted in chapter one, this was only to be formally declared in 1972. Grove and Huszar (1964) had proposed an analytical basis and framework for implementing a form of this strategy with emphasis on the provision of services. They had identified two types of centres: an intra-regional settlement that serves a town and its immediate vicinity; an inter-regional centre that engages predominantly in basic more than non-basic activities. These two writers, however, argued that both basic and non-basic settlement functions could be combined in particular centres. They proposed this as a third option within the growth centre strategy in which both service-based and production activities become fused together. Basing their analysis on service centre theories, Grove and Huszar (1964) argued for the location of these activities in various grades of settlements (Ofori, 2000g). The 1962 physical development plan was not implemented as a whole.

Perhaps the most professionally formulated post-colonial development plan was the seven-year, 1964-70 plan (Republic of Ghana, 1963). It was the only one that had some clearly articulated objectives. These were the achievement of full employment; structural change in the economy from the rigid primary commodity export. Another objective was distributive justice with respect to income, essentially through a socialist ideology. The highest priority was given to promoting the establishment of as many as 600 factories to be within the Accra-Tema, Kumasi and Sekondi-Takoradi incipient metropolitan zones. The predominant emphasis was on industrial development, an area of the economy which was ignored by deliberate colonial policy as pointed out in chapter one. However, the plan did not run its full course due to the 1966 *coup d'état*.

The two-year stabilization plan, 1968-70, took a different ideological stance in primarily aiming at the expansion of investment in the private sector (Republic of Ghana, 1968). The policy aim here was to stimulate economic, social and cultural progress which would provide higher standards of living for Ghanaians in a way compatible with human dignity, still based on equity and full employment. Direct policy intervention was not discounted by the government. The specific objectives were to check migration to the urban areas; to reduce income inequalities between regions and persons; and to stimulate small, medium industries with the objective of generating employment in this sector.

Further, it is significant to note that the long term objectives of this plan were the development of rural areas and the diversification of the export base of the economy. Significantly, it was at this time that Regional Planning Committees were inaugurated. The Committees were given the responsibility of making advisory and informal regional plans. Therefore, this short-term plan was to break away from the earlier tradition of putting emphasis on the development of the urban and metropolitan areas as the leading centres of the national space economy. On this basis, therefore, it was an indication of the trend towards territorial planning.

The 1970-71 development plan was to pick up the tone of the 1968-70 one and did not differ markedly from it (Republic of Ghana, 1970). The emphasis was, again, on efficiency and private sector-led production. Improving the living standards and the quality of life of Ghanaians, especially those in the rural areas, was the main policy goal for this plan. Somehow, the period coincided with a time when development focus at the international level was shifting to rural development (Brown, 1986). Again, the role and responsibility of the Regional Planning Committees was emphasized.

The 1975-80 plan was the most comprehensively formulated, respecting the science and art of plan-making, since the 1960s (Republic of Ghana, 1977a; 1977b). The guideline for the plan was published in 1975 but the real plan came out in 1977 when its implementation was supposed to have started two years previously. The investment policy under the plan, *inter alia*, aimed at the satisfaction of the basic needs of the mass of the population and re-investment of significant proportions of the profits generated. Other objectives were the spreading out of income, consumption and the creation of employment. It has already been pointed out in chapter one that the most articulate official reaction to the problem of disparities in intra-regional development was made at this time. However, it is doubtful whether this plan was implemented at all since large wage and salary increases plus some sector-based projects were outside the plan (Huq, 1989).

The new government which came into power in 1979 prepared a plan for the period 1981-86 but it did not really see the light of day. This was because that government had barely settled when it fell with the coming in of a new military government. Although the 1981-86 proposed plan was not implemented, an examination of it shows that it was another departmental listing of projects, especially as there was the tendency to rush its preparation. Nevertheless, it had a local-level development focus. At least, the government declared its 'regional development policy' focus as being on 'integrated rural development' (Republic of Ghana, 1979). Thus the government of the day was declaring its intent to adopt a rural-regional development policy (Conyers, 1985). Therefore, emphasis was put on a switch from 'top-down' to 'bottom-up' development policy and strategy. These declarations and intents expressed the deep-seated need to actively pursue territorial regional planning and development practices.

Economic recovery and public investment programmes

It is the view in this book that these instruments of socio-economic development introduced by the Provisional National Defence Council (PNDC) military government and subsequently pursued by the government of the Fourth Republic can be considered forms of national development plans (Government of Ghana, 1987a; 1987b); at least, quasi-development plans. The public investment programmes have been used to make annual presentations of the projects under the Economic Recovery Programmes (ERPs) with all detailed indications of costing and funding.

ERP I, the stabilization phase of the whole programme, was introduced in 1982-83 to cover the period 1983-1986 (Government of Ghana, 1983a; Government of Ghana, 1983b). ERP II, the strategic growth and development phase covered the period 1987-1989 (Government of Ghana, 1987c; Ewusi, 1987). It is thus the Structural Adjustment Programme (SAP) stage of the ERP. Actually, they are Ghanaian versions of the African priority programme for economic recovery. Briefly, ERP I was aimed at stopping the unparalleled decline in the economy, especially in the industrial and export commodity sector. ERP II put special emphasis on the development of social services including education, health, housing and utilities such as water supply. Other aspects of ERP II covered developments related to cultural facilities, sports and the mass media. Further aspects of this programme relate to decentralization, district level and rural focus with consideration for the economic, social and political aspects of these initiatives. A specific and target population under these programmes were the underprivileged, deprived, vulnerable and poorer sections of the rural populations as well as urban informal sectors. At least, this was the government's declared intent.

There is no direct evaluation of the impacts of the ERPs and SAP available to this book. However, it is worth learning from studies undertaken by other researchers (Donkor, 1997). The objective in this regard, is to note the general impacts and point out the implication for territorial regional planning. Initially, the general positive impacts of the economic plans and programmes must be noted. A certain level of stabilization has been achieved. But for drastic changes in the international commodity market, the Ghanaian economy has enjoyed some growth again. Much of general infrastructure has been renewed or newly provided.

The productive capacity of the country, productivity and production levels have also shown appreciable increases as there have been in domestic commodity pricing for producers to achieve significant benefit of their output. A trend of diversification is also beginning to show in the production of what are described as non-traditional commodities such as semi-processed cocoa, dried spices and the like. For selected sections of the populace, there has been some improvement in incomes and welfare. Of course, there has been the greatest infusion of investments from the international sources, especially the World Bank and International Monetary Fund (IMF) (World Bank, 1989a; 1989b). Literally, Ghana has been the doyen of these institutions, under the economic and adjustment programmes. Considering the sordid state of the Ghanaian economy before the ERPs and SAP were introduced, one is left in no doubt that there has been some improvement than total decline and retrogression (Ofori, 1991a; Government of Ghana, 1987c).

These instruments have generated volumes of statistics in terms of programming and initial assessments. However, as far as territorial regional planning and socio-economic development are concerned, 'the more complex questions of how to achieve balanced development where progress is measured less by economic statistics than by the level of social well-being' (Harsch, 1989, p. 22) is the critical issue.

The other side of the economic changes, however, show the urgent need to be concerned about the strategic future in this relation. The observations made here relate to various aspects of the programmes. The unfettered liberalization of the economy has almost eliminated any direct state intervention and form of control. While this has been seen as absolute solution to the plethora of problems, it has created its own effects. In this particular consideration and in relation to the theoretical and practical considerations in the earlier and this chapter, it means the opportunity for intervening in the territorial regional planning process has drastically been vitiated. Indeed, this prospect has receded further as the market is much depended on for the allocation of resources. Thus the economic recovery and adjustment programmes have introduced a serious conflict between planning and state intervention on one side, between the former and market forces on the other.

The case of Western countries shows that the privatization ethic and related practices of the 1980s bred such unpalatable consequences and near outrage as to bring down conservative governments. Indeed, the numerous negative impacts of the privatization agenda and programme of the last Conservative Government in the United Kingdom have been critically pointed out (Thornley, 1991; Barnekov, Boyle and Rich, 1989). These two cited works have, in particular, assessed the influences of the market-oriented ideologies and rolling back of state involvement on planning policies, systems and practice.

It has been emphasized already, the fact that a limitation of Third World and Ghanaian regional development is the lack of attention for the 'human capital' aspect. The recovery and adjustment programmes have also dampened the chances of addressing this limitation. Indeed, relatively less and marginalized investment has been made in this. As Donkor (1997, p. 192) notes, the programme is more 'geared to growth rather than development'. This situation also implies a further innate conflict between the quantitative and qualitative dimensions of national well-being and welfare. There has been overwhelming concentration on growth and intensified extraction of export commodities. On the other hand, there has been rather minimal or a tendril linkage between this production and the rest of the space economy, especially in the most territorial regions (Donkor, 1997). In fact, the limited attention given to the 'human capital' is reflected particularly in the adjustment state of the economic programme in relation to health, education and training. Nor has this been more so with respect to research in support of social capital developments.

Ghana's economy has become vulnerable to the international commodity market in producing, increasingly, more of the same primary and export-based products. Therefore, the benefits of any increased production is determined by the behaviour of the global market for the primary products in which case projections of earnings can be most unreliable. The export-based and Keynesian theories are reflected in this situation. When there is a fall in prices, especially in times of glut, there is a direct reduction or drying up of revenues. The cycle continues into far limited or no investments and consequently, the diminished chances of the socio-economic and spatial development taking place in the territorial regions.

Apart from the limited revenues and investment funds derivable from this kind of economy, the structure of export trade also remains not significantly changed. The three commodities - gold, cocoa and timbre - have commanded eighty per cent of export earnings achieved under the recovery and adjustment programmes. Meanwhile, the dependence on this export base is justified in terms of the country having a comparative advantage. This is one perception and construct by which the international market and dominant economies perpetuate the dependence of a Third World economy such as Ghana's. While this limits the chances of diversifying the sectors of comparative advantage, it further limits the chances of developing industrial linkages in the domestic economy, emphasis on the manufacturing sector. The colonial and structural domination remains persistently more pervasive (Singer and Ansari, 1977).

An essential aspect of the recovery and adjustment programmes is external finance with overwhelmingly predominant reliance on this source of financial resources. Indeed, these sources have as a condition, pressurized government to intensify the privatization initiatives and trends. Non-conformance would not only mean limited or no availability of the funds but diminished and much more weakened capacity of the state for domestic capital formation. Of course, this would also further limit investments, in which case the condition for development as specified in the Harrod-Domar model would not be provided. Indeed, Donkor (1997) has pointed out that private sector savings have been no more than the level of these in the era before adjustment. Therefore, this has also limited the potential and real contributions of the manufacturing sector. Once again, this shows conflicts between the public and private realms as well as between the state and global capitalism. In this situation, the opportunities for planning success are also diminished. This conflict enshrines a dilemma. The case of unequal exchange explained earlier and the reality of lost commodity price and earnings mean that Ghana's economy would have to perform at a fantastic rate to pay off its external debts. Yet, the financial resources and related facilities tie up Ghana's economy to Western and European economies, a further deepening of the dependency situation.

A further adverse impact of the adjustment and recovery relates to the area of taxation. Donkor (1997) has pointed out the terms of the new taxation Act meant to support the programmes for Ghana's economy. This has meant the further loss of revenue. There is a generally low tax rate, in particular in relation to duty on commodity exports. Indeed, the rates are, perhaps, among the lowest anywhere in the world. The Act has reduced the cost of production drastically as a way of encouraging greater participation rates and higher volumes. If these taxation rates are to be progressively reviewed, there might be a chance of revising them in a more realistic way to the greater benefit of the nation's economy. Furthermore, the extension of the privatization of some social services and to the poorest sections and rural communities has burdened the territorial populations more.

The production of foodstuff, livestock and fish-products has not improved under the recovery and adjustment programmes, especially considered in per capita terms (Donkor, 1997). This situation is explained in terms of a weak internal trade system and limited availability of farmer credit. Meanwhile, there has been a substantial importation of food as a proportion of export earnings. The position that Ghanaian regional planning should be based on agriculture and related activities has already been pointed out. As many projects have an agricultural basis, therefore, this situation vitiates the foundation of effective territorial regional planning.

The adverse impacts of the economic plans and programmes is also shown in wider industrialization and the process of change from primary agricultural production. In fact, the rate of industrial growth has slackened in relation to population growth. Besides, the government has deployed a corporate-level retrenchment strategy of divestment under which there has been mass disposal of state-owned businesses. This is also a dimension of the liberalization and privatization agenda coupled with the rather low taxation rates. Much more so, many of these companies are going into external ownership. Donkor (1997) cites the example of the sale of cocoa factories at Tema to German interests. This is only an infinitesimal fragment of the whole thing and further promotes the opportunities for transferring profits abroad. While promoting efficient production and ensuring profitability, it might be better for Ghana to have any genuine indigenous ownership acquire the poorly-performing companies and turn business round instead of divesting them. This is also a challenge to Ghanaian managers and entrepreneurs to prove and maintain competence in managing business profitably. Obviously, the current situation, in this regard, does not favour indigenous industrial development.

Nor has the employment scene fared well in both the formal and informal sectors. The public sector has suffered more job loss as a result of reorganization strategies aimed at instilling efficiency in the various organizations affected. The losses have not been matched with significant creation of alternative employment. Across both fronts, employment is also growing below the rate of population growth. In fact, the recovery and adjustment programmes have had a weak and severely limited employment creation aspect.

Ghana's experience shows the lack of attention for environmental sustainability under the recovery and adjustment programmes. The concentration on growth and quantitative aspects of development mainly account for this trend. For example, the intensified surface mining has caused appreciable air, soil pollution and degradation; there has also been water pollution from heavy metals and cyanide. Such mining as took place could have been undertaken as deep or shaft mining. In the same way, intensified timber production has induced a wider-scale deforestation as well as reduction in woodland stock (Donkor, 1997).

The foregoing general survey of development and focused economic plans illustrate some pervasive characteristics and trends. One of these is the limited or non-implementation of development plans. Another is the drastic change to whole plans being replaced or superseded by new and supposedly more robust ones. There is also the gradual and increasing concern rising from inter-regional and intensely towards intra-regional contexts. This also emphasizes the increasing need for effective intra-regional planning policy. Another element is the constraining nature of the external economic systems as well as the influences of domestic economic management. These two aspects create further constraining impacts on the possibility, practicability and success of planning programmes, especially in terms of inward investment and development financing. I think that all these trends and characteristics further emphasize and support the case for formal regional plan-making. After all, this is in accord with the increasing and logical need for real regional policy formulation and effectiveness of its practice.

Administrative and socio-economic contexts of planning

Development planning does occur within specific contexts. These include the economic, demographic-population, political-administrative and geographical components (OECD, 1988). Therefore, it is relevant to explain these contexts as further background to the case of territorial regional planning in Ghana. However, only the demographic, administrative and economic contexts are dealt with here because these have a more direct and relevant bearing on the focus in this book.

Demographic and population context

The data considered in this section relate to the period, 1960 to 1984. The latest national population and housing census since 1984 was completed in mid-2000 in Ghana. At the time of writing, details of the latest statistics are not available to this book. Table 4.2 shows absolute populations and regional proportions of the national total, regional densities, rate of increase, as well as the regional growth rates over the 1970-84 period.

Table 4.2 Ghana: population by region, density, rates of increase and growth, 1970-84

Region	*1970*				*1984*				
	Area	Population	% total	Den-sity	Population	% total	Den-sity	Inc. %	*Growth Rate*
Western	23,921	770,087	8.9	32	1,157,807	9.42	47	33.0	2.7
Central	9,826	890,135	10.4	88	1,142,335	9.29	117	22.1	1.8
G. Accra	3,245	903,442	10.6	278	1,431,099	11.64	438	37.3	3.3
Volta	20,570	947,268	11.1	46	1,211,907	9.86	86	21.8	1.7
Eastern	19,323	1,209,828	14.1	63	1,680,890	13.67	87	24.8	2.4
Ashanti	24,570	1,481,696	17.3	61	2,090,100	16.99	86	29.1	2.5
B-Ahafo	39,557	766,509	8.9	19	1,206,608	9.81	50	36.5	3.1
Northern	70,381	727,618	8.5	10	1,165,183	9.48	17	37.6	3.4
U. West	18,476	319,865	3.7	17	438,008	3.56	24	27.0	2.3
U. East	8,842	542,858	6.3	61	772,744	6.28	87	29.8	2.5
Country	**238,533**	**8,559,331**	**100**	**36**	**12,296,681**	**100**	**51**	**30.4**	**2.6**

Source: Absolute statistics from Population Census Reports, 1970 (Vol. II); 1984, Ghana Statistical Service, Accra; proportions, author's calculation

Ashanti Region is the most populous in the country, with more than 16 per cent of national total in both the 1970s and 1980s. The Eastern Region held

14.1 per cent of national total in 1960 and fell to 13.67 per cent in the 1980s. The Central, Greater Accra and Volta Regions contained between 10 and 11.2 per cent each of national total population in the 1970s. While Greater Accra maintained an increasing hold to 11.4 per cent in the 1980s, the Central and Volta Regions fell below 10 per cent in the same period.

All the other Regions had less then 10 per cent of national total population in both census periods, with minimal significant increases in the 1980s. The considerable increase in population density in the regions over the 1970-84 period shows the growing pressure on land and space resources. This is further reflected in the per cent increases in the 1984 figures over those of 1970. Furthermore, the rates of growth range from the least, 1.8 per cent, to the highest, 3.4 per cent in the Northern Region. The national growth rate of 2.6 per cent is also appreciably high by standards in the Third World and typically, sub-Saharan Africa. This is another challenging hurdle to the regional development process in Ghana, especially with respect to demographic and urbanization trends.

Table 4.3 shows the various levels of urban and rural populations over the 1960-84 period. Apart from the Greater Accra and Western Regions, there is a consistent trend of urban population growth in all the other regions. Even so, these two indicate the same trend over 1960-70. The decline in this case is due more to out-migration, with other regions as destination. Certainly, the massive rural population presence of the country is confirmed by the data in the table. The overall picture shows that the national urban population increased from

Table 4.3 Ghana: population by region, urban and rural areas (%), 1960-84

Region	*1960 (%)*		*1970 (%)*		*1984 (%)*	
	Urban	Rural	Urban	Rural	Urban	Rural
Western	24.7	75.3	27.6	72.4	22.6	77.4
Central	28.0	72.0	28.5	71.5	28.8	71.2
Greater Accra	78.8	21.2	85.3	14.7	83.0	17.0
Eastern	20.2	79.8	24.6	75.4	27.7	72.3
Volta	13.2	86.8	16.0	84.0	20.5	79.5
Ashanti	25.0	75.0	29.7	70.3	32.5	67.5
Brong-Ahafo	15.6	84.4	22.1	77.9	26.6	73.4
Northern	13.0	87.0	21.2	78.8	25.2	74.8
Upper West	5.0	95.0	6.7	93.3	10.9	89.1
Upper East	3.9	96.1	5.8	94.2	12.9	87.1
Country	**23.0**	**77.0**	**28.9**	**71.1**	**31.9**	**68.1**

Source: Proportions, author's calculation, based on population census statistics; Ghana Statistical Service (1984) Population Census, Preliminary Report

23.0 per cent in 1960 to 31.9 per cent in 1984. Therefore, the national rural population also decreased from 77.0 per cent to 68.1 per cent over the same period. This situation is consistently reflected in the case of the Central Region, even with the least rate of population growth. It will be further noted in chapter six that this increasing urban population is confirmed in the growth of medium and small towns. This also adds greater weight to the debate and case for territorial regional planning.

Administrative context

The sub-objective in this section is to present a snapshot of the sub-regional jurisdictional and administrative basis for planning (Figure 4.1). As indicated already, Ghana is delimited into ten political-administrative and planning regions. These sub-national units are, in turn, divided into 110 District Assembly Areas (DAAs), the level at which effective sub-national statutory planning now operates (Table 4.4). Furthermore, there are 1,106 sub-district units - Town and Area Councils: TCAs and ACAs - within the framework of a national decentralization policy. The TCA is based on the general and

Table 4.4 Ghana: political-administrative units, planning regions and sub-regional structures

Political-Admin. Unit: Planning Region	*District*		*Town or Area Councils*		*Zones*		*Units*	
	no.	%	no.	%	no.	%	no.	%
Upper East	6	5.5	69	6.2	323	6.5	951	6.0
Upper West	5	4.5	49	4.4	176	3.5	660	4.1
Northern	13	11.8	124	11.2	134	2.7	1,012	6.4
Brong-Ahafo	13	11.8	143	12.9	759	15.2	1,962	12.4
Ashanti	18	16.4	196	17.7	899	17.9	2,724	17.2
Western	11	10.0	118	10.7	493	9.8	1,829	11.5
Central	12	10.9	110	9.9	489	9.8	1,463	9.26
Eastern	15	13.6	142	12.8	868	17.3	2,206	13.9
Greater Accra	5	4.6	46	4.2	237	4.7	1,238	7.8
Volta	12	10.9	109	9.9	630	12.6	1,879	11.8
Total	**110**	**100**	**1,106**	**100**	**5,008**	**100**	**15,798**	**100**

Source: Absolute figures provided by Ministry of Local Government, Accra (1989)

statistical definition for townships: 5,000 population. The ACA covers a set of villages or households of between 1,500 and 3,000 population. The TCAs and ACAs are further delimited into 'zones'. In all, 5,008 zones have been identified and these are further broken into 'units'. Each unit is supposed to

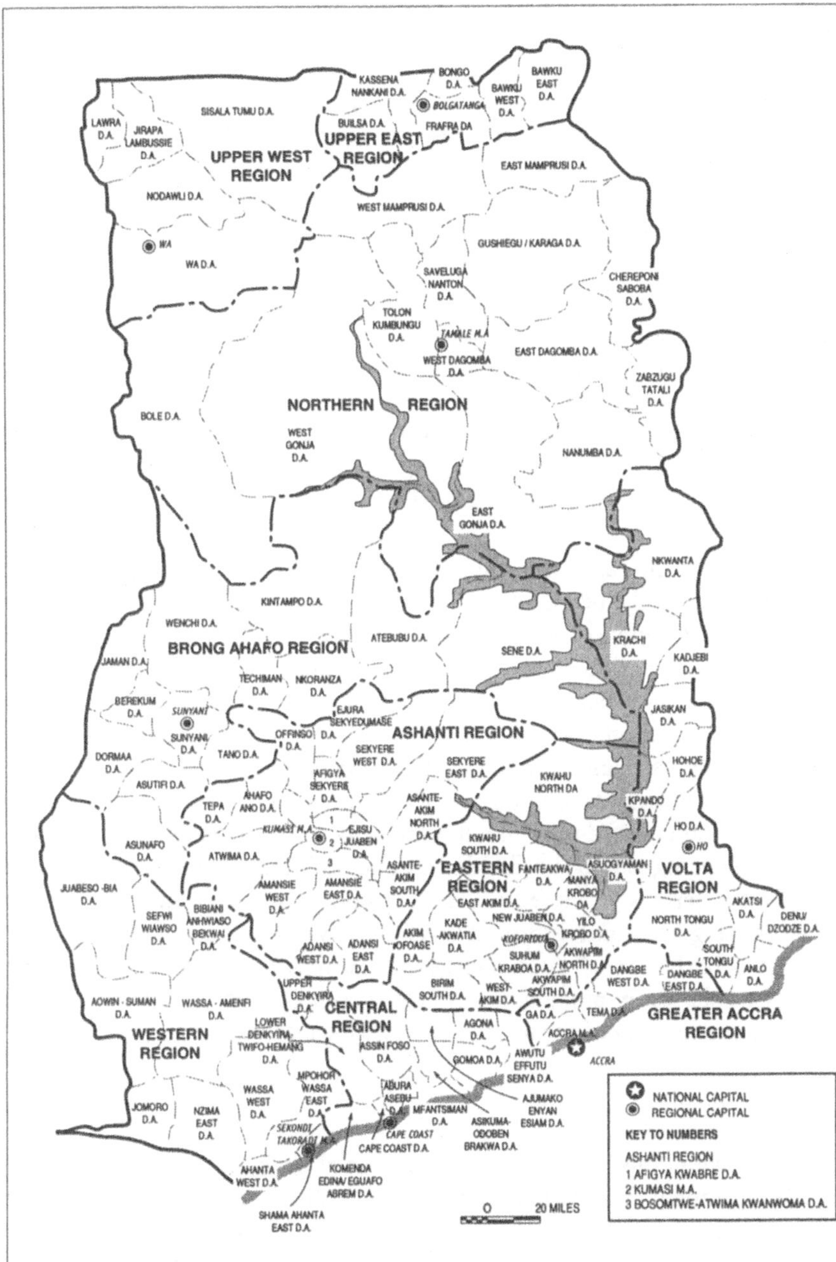

Figure 4.1 Ghana: political-administrative and planning regions and district assembly areas

consist of between 500 and 1,000 persons. The statistics referred to in this relation may have been revised by the time this book is published.

Thus there is appearing a multi-level regional and local delimitation, which it is hoped would facilitate regional planning and policy determination based on participatory development. Indeed, this is reflected in the criteria underlying the present decentralization in response to the centralization of decision-making and planning in Accra; the stifling of local-level initiative. However, regional decentralization, so far, has been purely administrative and advisory:

> It is the devolution of the central administrative (Not Political) authority to the local level (Regional, District/Local) in order to ensure popular grass-root participation in the administration of the various areas concerned from the standpoints of planning, implementation, monitoring and achievement of those services which go to improve the living conditions of the people and the orderly, fair and balanced development of the whole country concerned (Government of Ghana, 1982, p. 3).

In the light of the case for territorial regional planning, so far, if this practice is to be effective, the denial of significant and legitimate political power to the regions would seriously hamper the achievement of planning objectives. In fact, it has been pointed out how this has limited effective regional planning over the years in Ghana. In an observation on the wider explosion of the decentralization trend over the Third World, sub-Saharan Africa in particular, Gattoni (1989) has pointed out that this form of devolution alone does not go far enough. Political devolution has also been thought essential, especially in the case of sub-national planning. It is the view in this book that if a multi-level regional planning is to be useful, this question of political power to the regions has to be seriously addressed. This would also promote the effort at decentralizing economic and productive activity (Thomi and Yankson, 1985). The net contribution of these changes in the institutional and administrative aspects would surely promote the effectiveness of territorial regional planning and make things happen, better, for the more local areas.

Economic context

The objective in this part of the study is to emphasize the economic context of regional planning. The basic premise is that if the economy is not performing well enough, planning initiatives are not likely to be made or implemented. It has already been noted how social programmes tend to be given less importance than economic aspects (Ofori, 2000a).

Tables 4.5 and 4.6 show the structure of the Gross Domestic Product (GDP) over parts of 1975 to 1997. Table 4.5 confirms the agriculture-dependent nature of the economy which proportion increased from 47.7 per cent to 50.7 per cent over 1975 to 1986. Over the same period, there was a decline in manufacturing from 13.9 per cent to 8.9 per cent. There was also a trend of increase in wholesale and retail trade, hotel and restaurants. These fall more within the informal and private sector and may typify the increasing trend in self-employment. And so there was an increasing trend in government services which may be a reflection of the volume of work associated with the various economic recovery programmes and adjustment processes. Obviously, there was a relative growth in services and a decline in primary and secondary production.

Table 4.5 Ghana: contribution to GDP by sector (%), 1975-86

Sector	*1975*	*1980*	*1984*	*1985*	*1986*
Agriculture, forestry, fishing	47.7	53.4	53.4	51.6	50.7
Mining, quarrying	2.0	1.3	1.1	1.1	1.1
Manufacturing	13.9	10.4	6.9	8.5	8.9
Electricity, gas and water	0.6	0.8	0.9	0.9	1.0
Construction	4.4	3.7	2.7	2.5	2.3
Wholesale, retail trade and hotels, restaurants	12.2	10.0	9.8	10.7	11.1
Transport, storage and communication	3.9	3.0	4.0	4.3	4.3
Finance, insurance, real estate and business services	5.2	6.7	8.7	8.6	8.8
Government services	8.2	11.0	13.9	12.8	12.5
Other services	1.5	1.1	1.4	1.6	1.8
Imported bank services charges	-1.4	-2.9	-3.7	-3.8	-3.8
Import duties	1.8	1.5	0.9	1.3	1.3

Source: Ghana Statistical Service (1987), *Ghana in Figures*, Ghana Publishing Corporation, Accra, p. 17

Table 4.6 shows the situation in the 1990s in absolute statistics. There was a steady increase in the contribution of the agricultural sector to GDP as indicated by the first component of the table. This pattern is repeated for the industrial and service sector. Although there are no comparable data from 1997 to date, it is likely that this pattern has continued. In either case, it also means the further intensified extraction and production of export commodities. This also confirms the fact of the economy's return-to-growth since 1983, up to which period it had fallen in the worst doldrums (Ofori, 1991a; Government of Ghana, 1987c).

A more varied set of statistics is shown in Table 4.7, in part, for the period 1980 to 1998 and other, 1993 to 1997. GDP by share of sector indicates that there has been a relatively slight and steady decline in the proportion held by agriculture and services while industry shows mostly stable and minimal

Table 4.6 Ghana: contribution to GDP by sector, ¢billion current market prices, 1993-97

Sector	*1993*	*1994*	*1995*	*1996*	*1997*
Agriculture	1,430.0	1,971.2	3,006.0	4,470.0	5,050.1
Agriculture and livestock	1,994.0	1,307.0	1,827.0	2,750.0	3,192.6
Cocoa	108.1	235.2	524.0	690.0	656.1
Forestry and logging	107.7	139.0	211.0	297.0	477.2
Fishing	220.2	290.0	444.0	680.0	724.2
Industrial	961.1	1,294.0	1,882.0	2,673.0	3,622.6
Mining and quarrying	211.4	293.0	371.0	536.0	719.8
Manufacturing	363.3	472.0	723.0	979.0	1,277.5
Electric, water and gas	99.6	139.0	206.0	302.0	427.7
Construction	286.8	390.0	582.0	856.0	1,199.6
Services	1,065.8	1,420.8	2,152.6	2,977.0	3,935.8
Transport, storage, communitn.	166.0	224.0	303.0	423.0	580.4
Wholesale, retail trade	224.7	297.8	465.0	654.0	917.0
Financial, property, bus services	158.8	209.0	302.6	430.0	586.6
Public admin., defence; other	409.5	540.0	825.0	1,124.0	1,377.0
Community, social, personal	70.8	103.0	185.0	249.0	341.6
Private non-profit services	36.0	47.0	72.0	97.0	133.2

Source: International Monetary Fund Staff Country Report No. 99/3, p. 97

increase. Real GDP by sector for the 1990s indicates a slight increase in agriculture's share from 1994 to 1996 and a decrease in 1997. If this has continued in the rest of 1990s and 2000, it would confirm a gradual and slight decline in the share of agriculture. Again, in terms of real GDP, industry shows a stable and relative increase as do services. Therefore, a trend of relative increase in the two sectors and decline in agriculture may be beginning to emerge in the Ghanaian economy. If this really happens, it would reflect the theoretical formulations in development economics that aims at analysing and depicting the process of economic growth and related structural change (Todaro, 1989; Harris, 1986). These might be indications that planning programmes may become less based on agriculture. The data so far, however, are anecdotal. Perhaps, this is also confirmed by the substantial increase in self-employment and small-medium businesses noted earlier.

The data relating to domestic savings reflect the return-to-growth status of the economy, a steady performance between 5.0 per cent and 7.0 per cent over the 1980-1998 period. Similarly, domestic investment shows a steady increase from 6.0 per cent to 17.0 per cent. If this trend has also continued, it is further confirmation of the trend of growth comparable to the performance of even the newly industrializing economies of East Asia (Wonnacott and Wonnacott,

Table 4.7 Ghana: principal economic indicators, 1980-98

Item[1]	*1980*	*1985*	*1990*	*1998*	-
GDP by sector: % share					
Agriculture	58	45	46	44	n.a.
Industry	12	17	16	17	n.a.
Services	30	38	38	29	n.a.
Domestic savings: % GDP	5.0	7.0	6.0	7.0	n.a.
Domestic investment: % GDP	6.0	10.0	15.0	17.0	n.a.
Item[2]	*1993*	*1994*	*1995*	*1996*	*1997*
Per cent of real GDP					
Agriculture	36.9	37.8	38.8	39.0	35.8
Industry	24.8	24.9	24.3	23.6	25.7
Services	27.5	27.3	27.8	26.3	27.9
Annual per cent change					
Nominal GDP	31.1	41.6	48.9	46.3	24.7
Real GDP	5.0	3.3	4.0	4.6	4.2
Exports (volume)	21.7	2.6	0.3	12.5	-0.6
Imports (volume)	17.1	-12.4	-0.5	13.8	13.7
Prices (billions of Cedis)					
Central govt finance					
Revenue and grants	1,743	1,160	1,865	2,289	2,709
Expenditure, net lending -	1,124	1,622	2,359	3,370	4,002
of which: current expendt.	694	930	1,271	1,861	2,364
Surplus of deficit	-382	-462	-495	-1,082	-1,293
In % of GDP	-10.4	-9.3	-6.7	-9.5	-9.2
Foreign financing (net)	241	236	336	418	509
Domestic financing (net) -	45	-39	-28	531	762
of which: banking system	-22	-44	-67	226	528
Further indicators[3]	*1981-90*	*1992*	*1993*	*1994*	*1995*
Regional growth: % change	2.5	0.8	0.7	2.7	3.7

Source: (1) Barclays Bank Plc, 1999, p.3; (2) International Monetary Fund Staff Country Report, 1999, No. 99/3, p.5; (3) Barclays Bank, 1998

1990; Harris, 1986). However, there is a deficit between savings and investment.

The annual per cent change in nominal GDP indicated more explosive change in the mid-1990s and a decline in the latter part of the decade. In a similar way, real GDP decreased from 5.0 per cent in 1993 to between 3.0 and 4.0 in the mid-1990s. It shows a slight increase in 1996 and a further decline to 4.2 per cent in 1997. In effect, there has been a decrease in the rate of GDP growth. Over the same period, there is appreciable decrease in the rate of growth in exports, but for 1996. On the other side of this equation, there has been a greater increase in imports. This also confirms the generally declining performance in the economy.

All the other parameters relating to prices in billions of *Cedis* show increases over the period 1993 to 1997, particularly in its latter part. There is greater public expenditure than revenue and grants which also accounts for the increasing deficit and its share of GDP. It might be an indication of spending money that is not available to the economy. The general trend here is that planning and social programmes tend to suffer in relation to funding.

A further interesting aspect of the data in Table 4.7 relates to the per cent change in regional growth. The rates show that this remained at 2.3 per cent over the 1981-90 period and decreased to 0.8 per cent and 0.7 per cent in 1992 and 1993, respectively. These also coincide with the period during which the economy performed relatively better, apart from the domestic financing and surplus of deficit. Therefore, this may be an indication that lesser emphasis tends to be given to the disaggregated regional economy. This also tends to obfuscate the need for targeted funding for regional programmes and projects. Again, more comprehensive and time series-based data are needed to test and confirm this observation.

More recent trends At the time of writing, the Ghanaian economy, like that of any other Third World country's, is going through its typical changes. These include a fall in export commodity prices, a loss of some fifty per cent value of the *Cedi* as well as the world-wide price increases in petroleum products and of course, hiking inflation (Moyo, 2000). Thus the foreign exchange rate, particularly in relation to the dollar and sterling is currently explosive (Moyo, 2000). Therefore, the government has increased the newly introduced value-added tax from 10.0 per cent to 12.5 per cent. There has also been an increase in the reserve ratio of commercial banks and interest rates and special taxation on imports due to the increase in this regard, which also confirmed the data analysed earlier. Furthermore, there is a general increase in unemployment, with a significant proportion of the redundant entering the informal economic activity sector. Meanwhile, there has been a reduced inflow of external funds. This situation has really weakened the economy in recent times (Kafe and Nuer, 2000). While some of these trends may be 'cyclical' in Third World as well as global economic terms, others are more structural features such as dependence, over-dependence on raw material and primary commodity exports. Therefore, the current and perhaps medium to long-term emphasis would be on economic growth and the relatively less concern for social development programmes.

A general profile of poverty The arguments, reviews and analyses so far, emphasize the particular situation of poverty in the Third World (Todaro, 1989; Harris, 1986, Lipton, 1977). Indeed, the studies reviewed in chapter two emphasize the need to critically address the problem of reducing poverty under all planning programmes and projects. This should remain an absolute and pervasive dimension of these initiatives.

Without entering into the theories and concepts of poverty, however, it is relevant to observe that it can be understood in a number of ways. One of these is the traditional notion of subsistence. This presents poverty in terms of the minimum nutritional needs of any person per day: quantity and quality of food. This can also be represented in terms of the amount of money needed to satisfy this standard of living. In fact, international organizations, including the World Bank and IMF, view this approach in terms of income needed to provide adequate and nutritious food as other needs such as shelter and clothing. The subsistence view has the demerit of ignoring the economic roles and civic responsibilities of the individual.

Another view of poverty is that of basic needs. Apparently, this is reflected in part of the subsistence approach. In this case, poverty is typified in terms of a list of items. These include adequate food, shelter, clothing and necessary household furniture. Others are safe drinking water, sanitation, public transport, health, education, leisure, recreation and such factors. However, the basic needs approach includes the factors of political and social freedom for individuals and nations to be independent. In particular, for the former to be able to determine and manage their own welfare and well-being. Promoting the availability and variety of choice in relation to all the needs is also a fundamental aspect of this view. Under the approach, then, the individual should have the economic opportunities to be able to contribute to the improvement of welfare in their own communities in a responsible way. Thus a limitation of this approach lies in the inadequacy or non-availability of economic opportunity and income for individuals and groups of persons to make meaningful contributions in this regard. For example, it has been shown in previous studies how small firm owners contribute to the funding of self-community-initiated development projects in their localities in the Eastern Region of Ghana (Ofori, 1994; Ofori-Cudjoe, 1981).

Poverty has also been presented in terms of relative deprivation and as founded in particular socio-cultural contexts. In this case, the welfare and well-being of the individual is based on specific conditions of living. These include diet, amenity, standards as well as services which support and promote their responsible membership and participation in social and cultural life. This also implies that people are expected as well as supported to behave in the way the particular society expects them to do. This idea of relative deprivation lends itself to the convenience of measurement and monitoring as to how the welfare of individuals performs. On the other hand, therefore, there is the situation of absolute deprivation when the poverty-stricken persons have no access, at all, to any of the conditions and standards of life.

I also think that poverty can be studied in terms of personal as well as group income in relation to their needs and wants. In the case of Ghana as in other Third World countries, this must depend on the economic opportunity available to people for them to be in sustainable and gainful employment in both formal and informal activities. The other aspect of this notion is to what extent the public realm provides for its citizens in terms of basic needs. Another relates to the encouragement it gives to the private sector to create competitive businesses and related employment. The studies on the Eastern Region cited already showed typical forms of such informal activity and employment.

Aspects of poverty studies The Ghana Living Standards Survey (GLSS), originally undertaken in the late 1980s, for example, provided some statistics relating to the subsistence indicators of basic needs and poverty (Ofori, 1991a; World Bank and International Finance Corporation (IFC), 1988; Government of Ghana, 1988b). This was aimed at providing a data base for assessing the social effects of adjustment. For example, part of this data show distribution of households by locality and by source of drinking water. This is based on 'inside plumbing', 'water vendor/truck', 'natural sources' and 'other sources' (Ofori, 1991a). While Accra city has 47 per cent of inside plumbing, other urban with 21 per cent of it, the rural areas have only 1 per cent and the country as a whole, 10 per cent (Ofori, 1991a; Ofori, 1991b; World Bank and International Finance Corporation, 1988). If there has been no improvement since the time of the survey, this level of poverty has grown worse. There are no recent data on this to indicate the current situation based on this view.

Another aspect of poverty presented by the GLSS is the distribution of households by locality and by the most frequently used type of fuel. This is based on a variety of fuel sources: wood, charcoal, gas, electricity, kerosene. While 93.1 of wood-fuel users were based in the rural areas, 1.4 per cent were in Accra city and 74 per cent for the whole country. For charcoal-fuel, 81.3 per cent were in the capital city, and 4.5 per cent in the rural areas. There were 2.8 per cent consumers of electricity in Accra, 1.2 per cent in other urban areas and 0.1 per cent in the rural communities; only 0.6 per cent of all households used electricity (Ofori, 1991a; World Bank and IFC, 1988). This also gives a snapshot of poverty in relation to the basic needs approach.

The data on housing further emphasizes the pattern and prevalence of poverty. The GLSS survey also indicated that 85.4 per cent of Accra's population lived in non-self contained quarters (rooms), 9 per cent in flats, 2.1 per cent in single family lodging and others in huts and buildings within the same or different compounds (Government of Ghana, 1988b). For the rest of the country at the 'other urban' and 'rural' levels, the proportion for people who live in rooms and flats decreases as those in single family accommodation increases, from the base statistics indicated for Accra city. This underlines the relatively poor quality of housing further, out of Accra. This is not to say that it is an easy experience finding accommodation in the capital city. For the whole country, 55.4 per cent live in non-self contained type of accommodation, 'room'; 24.8 per cent in huts/buildings that are not within the same compound as do 14.2 per cent in single family lodging; the remaining 2.5 per cent in other huts/buildings. Therefore, the majority of people live in 'rooms' which do not typify the basic standards of housing such as water supply, sewerage systems and toilet facilities, both urban and rural areas.

The issue of standard in material terms and as an instrument of development and planning control, particularly in relation to housing is a very crucial one. This also underlines the notions of poverty, especially under the relative deprivation approach. The case further emphasizes the fact that standards for welfare, well-being and responsible citizenship are critical to the process of socio-economic development. This remains a challenge to national planning and, in particular, the District and Metropolitan Assemblies as the local planning authorities.

Furthermore, the GLSS survey provided important data in relation to the distribution of poverty by urbanization and ecological zone as indicated in Table 4.8. In terms of the former, 50.2 per cent of the poorest Ghanaians live in the rural areas, 30.2 per cent in urban areas and 19.6 per cent semi-urban settlements. Again, the poorest 30 per cent as well as the poorest 10 per cent live in the rural areas. The data for the semi-urban areas are 15 per cent and 17.2 per cent respectively. This means that while the poorest live in the rural areas, the semi-urban dwellers are relatively well-off than the urban populations. By ecological zone, the majority of 60.3 per cent of the poorest 10 per cent are in the savanna zone areas. This is also true of the majority of 42.0 per cent for the poorest 30 per cent, with 26.6 per cent of the poorest in the country living in this zone.

However, in relation to this poorest 10 per cent group, there is greater poverty in the savanna areas and relatively more so in the coastal part than the forest belt. As 43.1 per cent of the poorest, overall, are in the forest areas and 30.3 per cent in the coastal areas, this means the former ecological zone has a higher concentration of poverty. Indeed, this pattern is reflected across the poorest 30 per cent for the whole country. This distribution has a link with land-population relationships: it is not the intent to enter into this analysis. There is a trend of increasing poverty in the forest zones. This may further relate to the depleting resources, especially of timber and limited land supply as a result of increasing pressures and changing farming cultures in those parts. The stress is

Table 4.8 Ghana: poverty by degree of urbanization and by ecological zones

By urbanization:	*Poorest 10 %*	*Poorest 30 %*	*All Ghana %*
Urban	19.2	19.8	30.2
Semi-urban	15.0	17.2	19.6
Rural	65.8	63.0	50.2
By ecological zone:			
Coast	20.2	17.2	30.3
Forest	19.5	40.9	43.1
Savannah	60.3	42.0	26.6

Source: World Bank/IFC (1988), *Ghana*: *Preliminary Results of Living Standards Survey*, Washington, p. 23

on the point that the Central Region has all three ecological zones, especially forest and coastal. Therefore, it typifies all classes of the poor with the potential of an increasing trend over the strategic future.

In completing this section, further information on the poverty profile of the country is derived from rather limited and cross-sectional data based on inter-regional and mean regional per capita expenditure. Of course, the statistics referred to here would have changed astronomically, by now, since the time of the original GLSS in 1987-88. Indeed, the dismal situation relating to inflation and exchange rate have already been pointed out. The available data show that Greater Accra had the highest mean per capita expenditure of ¢92,828 with Accra city, itself, standing at ¢106,273. Tema city plus other parts of the capital city region ranged between ¢70,000 and ¢81,000. Only the Western Region, of the remaining sub-national areas, came close to this high level of mean per capita expenditure of ¢81,940. The Eastern Region had ¢63,364. The Brong-Ahafo, Volta and Upper West Regions showed mean per capita expenditures between ¢50,000 and ¢55,000. The Ashanti, Northern, and Central Regions were between ¢40,000 and ¢50,000. However, Kumasi city indicated a figure of ¢60,325 and other parts of its metropolitan area, ¢44,105. Upper East Region had the least mean per capita expenditure of ¢37,594 (World Bank-IFC, 1988).

This also confirms the observation made in relation to the data in Table 4.8 that there is relatively greater poverty away from the forest zones; also a trend of increase in poverty within the forest area. However, while the higher mean per capita expenditure may be considered as a measure of relatively more income, it is also the indication of greater cost of living in the forest ecological zones. It has already been suggested that poverty, after all, may be on the increase in these zones. In fact, the mean per capita expenditures show a trend of decrease towards the Northern parts. This picture further indicates the scenario that may face the Central Region over the perspective term. The analyses and observations made, so far, in relation to the various contexts of regional planning in Ghana confirm and consolidate the background for the formulation of national development policy.

National development policy

The analyses and reviews, so far, indicate the general behaviour of the national development process from the colonial times to the present. Initially, the focus and ethic were on top-down trends. Subsequently, there has been increasing consideration for bottom-up and territorial approaches to development (Rondinelli, 1983a). These strategic changes also add to the emphasis in this book on the pervasive importance of the territorial ethic and focus. These current emphases are indicated in the national development policy framework which is set out in Figure 4.2. I will address its wider context before attempting a specific analysis of it.

The various policy documents from the 1980s to date indicate various contexts that provide the rationale for the national development policies. One of these is creating a basis for social justice and equality of opportunity for all members of the national society. As indicated earlier, the special focus is on the most deprived groups in the national community. Another rationale is instituting a planned and co-ordinated programme of economic and social development. A further one is managing the national economy efficiently to achieve the greatest welfare, freedom and happiness for the national populace.

It is also a fundamental rationale for national development policy in aiming to provide adequate means of sustenance and suitable employment for the largest numbers of the economically active as well as giving necessary assistance to the needy. In this connection, it is also essential to recognize the need to provide educational and supporting facilities for all. The aim of achieving full employment and encouraging the development of individual as well as group creative potential is part of this rationale. The element of 'full employment' is, at best, a driving ideal. In fact, this is rarely achieved even in the economies of the most developed countries. Nevertheless, the state recognizes its cardinal responsibility in this regard. Furthermore, it underlies the national development policy matrix that the government aims to ensure health and safety for all, especially in the workplace (Government of Ghana, 1994a; 1994b; 1989; 1987a; 1987b).

Based on these contexts, the main current public sector policies are aimed at improving the allocation of capital and recurrent expenditures, particularly to agriculture, health, and education. With respect to the first, the policy aim

NATIONAL DEVELOPMENT POLICY GOALS	NATIONAL DEVELOPMENT POLICY OBJECTIVES		
	ECONOMIC	**SOCIAL & POLITICAL**	**SPATIAL & ENVIRONMENTAL**
RATIONALIZING AND HARMONIZING SMALL, MEDIUM, LARGE-SCALE PRODUCTION	-Promote a dynamic, mixed economy for self-sustained growth and development; -Introduce innovative, financial, fiscal and monetary policies for development and growth; -Promote labour-intensive methods of production and employment	-Improve public sector institutional structures and practices to ensure enhanced support for and faster responsiveness to private sector needs	-Provide the climate for facilitating higher levels of private sector involvement in land-use based developments; -Integrate rural and urban economies; -Strengthen the role of human settlements as integral parts of the national space economy
TRANSFORMING THE NATIONAL ECONOMY BY PLANNED, SUSTAINABLE, STRUCTURAL CHANGE	-Promote diversification of production; -Enhance the harnessing of more human resources for development; -Promote achievement of greater cost effectiveness of investments in human settlements; -Promote labour-intensive production and improved productivity	-Intensify efforts at progressively reducing levels of dependency; -Promote effectiveness of mass literacy campaigns; -Provide better balance of resource investments for development by greater emphasis on social sectors	-Promote the integration of urban and rural areas; -Promote an efficient spatial distribution of human population; -Promote equitable distribution of investments for greater growth and employment; -Restructure and strengthen rural economies
TRANSFORMING THE STRUCTURE OF SOCIETY FOR PROMOTING SOCIAL HARMONY, EQUITY & DEVELOPMENT	-Increase investment in economic welfare for all sections of society; -Transfer about 2.0 per cent of wealth from the well-off to the poorer section of society (e.g. by taxation)	-Encourage value systems which facilitate change, growth and development; -Emphasize support for more able, capable and poorer sections of society; -Strengthen devolution of decision-making & democratization of society & increase levels of people participation in planning processes	-Promote more equitable distribution of opportunities for all in society
PROMOTING ECOLOGICAL BALANCE BETWEEN SOCIETY AND NATURE	-Promote cost-effectiveness and ecologically-wise technologies for the exploitation of the natural resource base and for ensuring environmental sustainability	-Improve and strengthen the institutional machinery from national to community levels for effective resource conservation, protection and eco-management, including monitoring	-Promote research into forest land in various eco-zones for sustainable environmental development; -Promote ecologically-wise, sustainable farming practices and technologies; -Improve technologies at enhancing carrying capacity of land and effective resource use
RADICALIZING IMPROVEMENT OF THE BUILT ENVIRONMENT	-Consistently investing in sustainable development practices, including appropriate public education	-Provide the institutional machinery at the district level for the involvement of local communities in sustainable development practices in human settlements	-Promoting action at improving the quality of the built environment in rural and urban settlements, emphasis on health and amenity; -Promote and disseminate research into sustainable levels and uses of open forests in settlements

Figure 4.2 Ghana: matrix of national development policies

Source: Author's creation

includes ensuring the effective contribution of agriculture to the country's balance of payments. Another aim is establishing an effective linkage between agriculture and industry for the former to provide raw materials efficiently for the latter. A further aim is generating a multiplier effect from the growth of agriculture on the demand for industrial goods and improving real income levels, especially of the producers. A policy aim relating to all three named sectors is improving the planning and implementation of public investment in order to maximize returns (Government of Ghana, 1987a; 1987b).

Thus the government has stated that (Republic of Ghana, 1994a; 1994b; Government of Ghana, 1982) national development policy is underlain by the following goals (stated by national planning consultant on interview):

> to reduce poverty, improve living standards and the quality of life by a substantial and sustained increase in GDP and the more equitable distribution of the benefits therefrom ... to redress extreme disparities in standards of living and socio-economic well-being between and within regions (i.e. urban and rural areas) and between groups of people.

These reflect the objectives in the various national development plans and programmes reviewed, so far, as they do the elements of the other studies reviewed in chapter two. These goals are, therefore, legitimate and valid in the context of national development and the territorial ethic emphasized. In this regard, the goals of national development policy have essential strategic importance in the country.

Another goal of the national development policy is radically improving the performance of the general national economy with focus on social and spatial equity. This dimension and context has also been emphasized in this book as an enabling force in planned development. One of the objectives under this goal is to strengthen public sector and statutory planning. A second objective is to promote locality-based and popular participation in rural development. Third, to strengthen state institutions that provide training and consultant-based services in relation to national development, including spatial planning. While commercial and public agencies are important, in this connection, urban and regional planning education should also receive paramount attention.

Matrix of national development policies The details of Figure 4.2 are now more directly addressed. The policy matrix is structured into five main horizontal goals and three main facets of objectives. The latter are the economic, social-political and spatial-environmental aspects. The first principal policy goal puts emphasis on streamlining and co-ordinating industrial production at the small, medium and large scales. This accords with the argument made in this book about basing the development process on production activities across all three scales of industry.

The second goal aims at transforming the national economy by planning and sustained change through all its components. This relates to a process of transmission and generative change. In this way, a view of strategic change and long-term development is maintained. The thrust of the third policy goal is on equities, equal opportunities in society and transformation of social structure.

Sustainable development, in particular, its environmental sustainability mode is emphasized as the fourth principal goal in the matrix: 'ecological balance between society and nature'. The need to radically improve the built environment is aimed at under the fifth policy goal. This also relates to the spatial elements as well as the needed details of local planning instruments.

The specific objectives under the three main columns in the matrix are now addressed in terms of their general flavour. The economic objectives include achieving mixed developments and economy, labour-intensive development initiatives and diversified production. Others relate to employment-generation and improvement in productivity; promoting and supporting welfare as well as poverty reduction. And other objectives are to achieve cost and investment effectiveness in town and rural development. However, this could conflict with areas of the more traditionally subsistence economy and where market pricing mechanisms are only new, thus creating greater burdens for the local residents. While introducing these communities to new marketing systems and practices, there should also be stronger public and development policy support for their needs. This is particularly relevant to the basic needs approach to poverty reduction. For example, this has been reflected in some of the effects of the structural adjustment programmes and policies indicated earlier in this chapter. A further objective is to consistently invest in all activities aimed at improving sustainable development practices. Another objective here is to achieve environmental sustainability, including effective land utilization and technologies that are sensitive to the integrity and quality of ecological systems.

The socio-political parts emphasize improvements in public institutional structures for addressing private sector needs. An objective relating to this is to promote emphasis on social as well as environmental aspects of development in balance with the hitherto pervasive concern for economic outcomes. An additional objective here is to promote greater support for the poorest and most disadvantaged sections and areas in society. A further objective is to improve the devolution of administrative power and democratization of social and decision-making processes.

One of the objectives, under the spatial-environmental component of the matrix is to promote the integration of urban and rural economies and localities with greater focus on restructuring the latter. Another objective is to intensify and bolster up the role of human settlements and achieve an efficient distribution of population. A further objective is to promote the participation of the private sector in land-based development. A fourth objective is to promote the most equitable distribution and optimal location of investment activities. Others are to support and promote forest-land management studies and sustainable farming practices as well as promote all effort at improving best use and carrying capacities. A further objective is to support and promote all comparable practices relating to the improvement of environmental quality in all rural and urban settlements.

These policy goals and objectives indicate substantial potential for meeting the material needs of the Ghanaian economy and society. In this connection, they show appreciable validity and concretion. On the other hand, the lack of political devolution, especially at the regional level of governance is more likely to hamper the achievement of the various policy aims. This is because the situation limits the legitimacy of the political decision-making and governance. Indeed, the quality and essence of the policy goals and objectives in Figure 4.2 strongly suggest the need for more valid political practices. In particular, there is need for political devolution. This would provide a more responsive and sufficiently legitimate body for regional decision-making, including policy-formulation and plan-making (Ofori, 2000b).

All the noted policy goals and objectives aim at reducing, if not eliminating the various disparities in society as pointed out in chapter one. Indeed, the national-level planning consultant interviewed stated that the overall goal of national development policy is to 'to progressively redress extreme socio-economic disparities within and between regions, between groups of people and between communities - urban and rural'.

Principles and concepts underlying the policy matrix The various points made in relation to the national development policy goals reflect the importance of the relevant underlying principles. These have also been explicitly indicated in government policy documents (Republic of Ghana, 1994a; 1994b; Trevallion, 1989). They have also been pointed out elsewhere (Ofori, 1995a; 1995b).

The first of these principles is 'decentralization' as indicated already (Government of Ghana, 1982). It also involves the devolution of decision-making to local levels and is intended to work in both a vertical and horizontal way. However, with respect to the horizontal part of reaching a wide array of sectors, many government departments have been reluctant in allowing their organizations to be decentralized in all the localities. This tends to affect data and information collection and availability. Therefore, this principle shows that its style and form imbibe the potential to limit the achievement of policy goals and objectives in the inter-locality levels.

The second principle is that of 'comprehensiveness' which is used to indicate the continuous planning process and its consideration for all levels as well as totality of economic, political, social and spatial aspects of development. As indicated in chapter one, this is not exactly the same as robustness. The usually greater concern for the economic aspects of programme output in Ghana has already been pointed out (Ofori, 2000a). This, in itself, constitutes a matrix of intents and purposes. Therefore, unless the principle of comprehensiveness is effectively applied, the potential for delivering the greatest beneficial impact of development would be hampered.

The principle of 'integration' is used to mean that all planning processes and procedures provide, together, the framework for both analysis and synthesis of all facets of the development process into a singly unified activity. Indeed, an additional aspect of integration is the heuristic nature of the interaction of its composing processes. These work to facilitate the rationalization and harmonization of development strategies and learning in the planning process.

In the principle of the 'balanced' development process, the aim is to eliminate conflicts, as much as possible between various policy objectives and strategies. These relate to the social, economic, environmental and political aspects. Others are production, services aspects and achieving appropriate relative output levels. It also relates to achieving a meaningful trade-off, for example, between agricultural production and environmental sustainability; as between, say, the education sector and employment opportunities and so on.

The principle of 'problem-solving' is aimed at setting the whole development process within a material context of people and which accords with their priorities. This culture of engagement should, as much as possible, exclude abstract conceptualization in the purely deductive sense. It should not be and as a matter of sheer idealism as is often imposed on the 'planned for' in the sole perspective of planners. In this way, a context-contingent and responsive planning practice is maintained (Ofori, 2000b).

The Ghanaian state and enabling of regional planning in the contexts

A significant question to ask is the extent to which the various contexts and statutory framework considered in this chapter promise to promote and deliver effective practice and achievement of the goals and objectives of regional planning. The inconsistent making of national development plans has removed the opportunity of co-ordinating all development polices and activities within a single statutory instrument. Nor does the attempt to substitute macro-economic programmes for national plan-making achieve the aim.

The overwhelming reliance on macro-economic policies and strategies sponsored by international financial institutions obviously ties the Ghanaian state to these organizations and seriously reduces its economic independence. Still in relation to national development plans, the inconsistent and in some cases, appreciably limited rates of plan implementation also limits the effectiveness of the national and statutory spatial planning. Moreover, the non-existence of established methodology for evaluating development plans over the decades further contributes to this ineffectiveness of the statutory planning practice. The focus on national-level planning also indicates the vacuous absence of formal plan-making at the regional level.

The drastic reduction in the national resource base, especially under the macro-economic programme sponsored by the international financial organizations also limits current real and future potential opportunity for resource development and a basis for planning initiatives. Unless the effort at providing a consistent flow of inward investment funds is sustained, the achievement of national as well as regional development goals and objectives would be severely limited. The structural adjustment and recovery programmes have been characterized by insufficient as well as inconsistent funding.

Macro-economic policies, unfettered liberalization and privatization and the strategy of divestment have been used to dispose of many state-owned businesses into substantially foreign ownership. These do not promise to prove beneficial to national, regional, and local development in Ghana. Indeed, the strategy and practice re-introduce a trend of capitalist ownership that further promote the massive transfer of profits abroad. Some of the new owners of the divested companies are part of global corporate organizations which only seek to extend their exploitative tentacles into every corner of the world. These aspects will be further highlighted in chapter five.

Furthermore, the vulnerable nature of the Ghanaian economy to the dictates and behaviour of the international market-place makes the dependence on one or a couple of export commodities dangerous. It has been emphasized that Ghana, like many other Third World economies, has greater potential for success in a diversified economic and production base. The manufacturing sector has appreciable promise in contributing to achieving the goal of diversification. Yet, the various macro-economic policies are in conflict with those that relate to this sector. Fully-empowered regional planning does hold greater potential to contribute to the effective diversification of the national economic base through creating a more varied and wider foundation for development programmes and projects (Ofori, 2000b; 1991a).

Summary

The practice of national development plan-making has not been consistent nor encouraged formal plan formulation at the regional level. The implementation performance of the plans has been limited in effectiveness and in reducing appreciably the disparities, especially between urban and rural areas and the various groups of people. While suitable demographic and administrative contexts appear to have been provided for planning, the rate and level of population growth are still constraints on the process. The economic contexts show minimal achievements and fairly bleak scenarios for the strategic future. The national development matrix, its rationale and underlying principles reflect appreciable validity and concretion. However, these are undermined by the limited legitimacy they provide for regional planning, especially in relation to political decision-making as well as the formulation of policies and plans. Therefore, the conflicts introduced by national statutory planning practices, including economic management approaches on one hand and the lack of effective regional governance and plan-based development processes on the other are constraints on effective regional planning practice.

5 Regional planning policy, regional plans and development programmes

From the considerations at the national level in the previous chapter, I now begin to sink into the central core of this book: intra-regional planning and development processes. The engagement in chapter five is with regional planning policy and plan-making practices, problems of regional development, types and nature of regional development programmes and projects. In relation to this, an introduction to the major case study is presented. The involvement of global corporate organizations in regional development is also highlighted. The strategic implications of this emasculating and dominating role are pointed out. All the analyses and observations provide useful lessons.

Regional planning and development policy

The emphasis in this section is on policy relating to both regional planning and regional development. An attempt was made to clarify the distinction between these in chapter one. The relevant observations are made with reference to Figure 5.1 which indicates the regional planning and development policy framework for the Central Region. The details, here, also reflect the kinds of policies formulated in the other regions of Ghana.

Based on the overall national policy framework indicated in chapter four, the regional planners in the Central Region also stated the development policy for the Region as (Central Regional Administration, 1987, p. 15):

> increasing the capacity of the region to be self-sufficient in food production and meeting the basic needs of specific target groups of rural people for them to experience real improvement in their quality of life measured in terms of more and better food, better shelter, better public health and

	REGIONAL POLICY OBJECTIVES	EXPECTED OUTCOMES
REGIONAL DEVELOPMENT AND PLANNING POLICY GOALS: REDUCTION IN EXTREME DISPARITIES IN SOCIO-ECONOMIC WELL-BEING BETWEEN SOCIAL GROUPS AND BETWEEN URBAN AND RURAL AREAS; SUSTAINABLE AND MASSIVE FLOW OF CAPITAL AND INWARD INVESTMENT	• To improve agricultural production • To provide social infrastructure: e.g. housing, health, education • To provide economic infrastructure, including industry and roads • To promote the development of small, medium, and large-scale enterprises • To develop tourism and tourist-based resources • To monitor, co-ordinate and evaluate the implementation of district plans and projects	• Development of growth-and-service centres; urban renewal • Employment generation • Personal and regional income generation • Agricultural raw materials for domestic industrial use and export • Increased food supplies for domestic consumption and export • Small and medium enterprise production • Boost in tourism • Increase in levels of social and economic infrastructure • Improved implementation performance

Figure 5.1 Central Region: framework of regional planning and development policies

Source: Author's creation

> appropriate education ... as well as sustained generation and increase in levels of employment and income.

This regional development policy is more focused and territorial as it cascades down from the national through the regional levels, at least in theory. So one sees, for example, that the policy statement as presented by the actual regional planners is more specific than the inter-regional policy indicated by the national planning consultant.

This means that the emphasis of the regional planners in the Central Region is clearly on three main aspects. These are food production, poverty reduction in terms of meeting basic needs and improving the quality of life in the specific terms stated (Johnfia, 1983). The first component of the regional policy goal is a challenge to the Region's development with respect to production and distribution of food (Ofori, 1991a; Dunham, 1977). While a significant proportion of the economically active are in marine-based activities, part of the Region's land is under a number of cash crops and include cocoa, coconut and the fastest growing oil palm. It will be demonstrated in chapter seven how the competition among some of these land-uses is affecting the supply and availability of food-stuff. Therefore, the regional policy goal stated by the regional planners reflects the criteria of appropriateness, validity, relevance and concretion as it directly addresses the material conditions of the regional community (Ofori, 2000g; 2000b; 2000c). Indeed, the focus is also more directly on rural development in a Region where the urban population was between 28 per cent and 29 per cent and the rural population between 71 per cent and 72 per cent over the 1960-84 period. The 2000 population census may produce a similar pattern of urban-rural population distribution (Ofori, 1991a). The planners are in touch with the realities of the Region's situation.

Therefore, the policy objectives as presented in Figure 5.1 match the details of the policy goal. While the first five objectives would be typical of the other regions in the country, the one relating to tourism is more special to the Central Region as will be shown later in this chapter. Thus these objectives also appreciably stand the test of validity and appropriateness. Besides, the objectives address the production basis of regional policy and relate to the elements of basic needs and poverty reduction measures.

The urban renewal outcome includes a programme of site-and-services improvement and slum-upgrading in the urban areas. It would be interesting to evaluate this kind of initiative and to transfer the experience and learning in relation to other towns. The objective relating to the planning function and policy is an equally critical and built-in aspect as a self-assessment and learning mechanism. Thus the expected policy outcomes also serve as measures of implementation and project performance in fair balance with the indicated objectives. In a way, these outcome measures also give some glimpses of targets and prepare the background for setting these.

The main strategy for implementing all these regional policies is by integrated rural development with agricultural development as its focus. This is linked with the development of the necessary infrastructure as well as settlements (Central Regional Administration, 1989; 1987). One aspect of this integrated approach is decentralization in economic and administrative terms as a basis for reducing intra-regional disparities and for the effective planning and implementation of rural development programmes. Another part is the co-ordination of sector-based investments. A further aspect of the strategy is the integration of all initiatives of non-governmental organizations (NGOs) with the other planned programmes.

At the time of proposing and formulating these policies and strategies, the Central Regional Administration thought that the Central Regional Development Corporation and the Rural Banks could be used to generate investment funds for implementing some of the projects. How this was to be done was not clarified, e.g. whether through loans to individuals or groups of undertakers. However, at the time of the original fieldwork undertaken by the author, the Central Regional Administration was initiating a regional raffle competition as a way of raising funds for regional development. It was assumed that this would produce a viable source of regional development funding. Again, there is no information available to the present study about extent to which this was patronized by the regional community and how effective it has been. If this source did not yield the expected income, the effectiveness of regional programme implementation and adaptability would be limited or hampered.

These constraints would, in the same way, limit the achievement of the policy outcomes as indicated in Figure 5.1. The effort at generating funds in this way highlights the formidable problem of funding regional and local development programmes in Ghana as in other Third World countries. It also shows the fact that the budgetary resources provided by central government have been woefully inadequate in meeting the cost of the regional development programmes. Securing appropriate funding is as challenging as managing its efficient and effective utilization. The situation relating to development financing, indeed, introduces a lot of uncertainty in the regional planning process (Lichfield, Kettle and Whitbread, 1975).

The formulation of the policies considered, so far, was based on general guidelines provided by central government. The Central Regional Co-ordinating Council (RCC) based its decisions on these as well as those made by the Central Regional planners. In this case, the agenda was set by the Regional Planning Co-ordinating Unit (RPCU) in consultation with the Regional Administrative Officer, for the consideration of the RCC. The practice shows significant input into and managing of a situation that is only statutorily advisory and informal. It is the view in this book that this is a case that requires a closer and more responsive negotiation. The importance of negotiation in the planning process was explained in chapter one. The role of the regional planner in this situation is far more than agenda-setting as part of issue search in the policy analysis process (Hogwood and Gunn, 1984). Nevertheless, it is also a form of policy-tuning. This also indicates the informal nature of policy formulation in the regional planning process.

Statutory regional planning and plan-making practices

The observations and arguments, so far, in relation to the science, art and practice of plan-making at the regional level have all emphasized the point that the statutory provisions have not yet allowed it to happen. It has been pointed out how this applies to the formulation of formal regional policy. The case relating to the making of regional plans is addressed with reference to the data indicated in Table 5.1. Three types of planning devices are shown in the table: an informal short-medium term plan, an informal strategic guidance, and self-initiated regional development programme. The main critical parameters are indicated in the left column.

Table 5.1 Central Region: informal regional planning instruments

Parameter	*Type of Planning Instrument*		
	Short to medium term regional plan	Strategic planning guidance	Development programme; project
Date of approval	February, 1981	February, 1987	May, 1989
Time scale	1981-1986	1987-1989	Open but phased
Initiators	Regional Planning Committee	Regional Consultative Council	Central Regional Administration; Regional Development Commission
Legitimacy	Informal	Informal	Informal
Funding	Central government; Regional Administration	Central government; Regional Administration	UNDP; Central government

Source: Tabulated and created from policy and programme documents

By the time of the original field-work for this study, the Central Regional Administration and advisory regional bodies had produced one informal regional plan and a strategic regional guidance, both in the 1980s. The first one was a medium-term plan for 1981-86. As stated by the Central Regional Administration (1987, p. 14), this plan was intended 'for incorporation into a national 5-Year Development Plan. This is the closest the Region has ever come to preparing a comprehensive Regional Development Plan'. In fact, this regional instrument was actually a set of 'proposals for a Five-Year Development Plan 1981-86' (Central Regional Administration, 1987, *Addendum*). The second instrument in the table was a short-term plan for the period 1987-89. This was considered as serving the purpose of a development plan for the time that the actual plan, the preparation of which it was intended to guide, was being formulated or not made.

The latter was actually a strategic regional planning guidance for the preparation of another short to medium-term plan for the first half of the 1990s. Such guidance may now be provided by the National Development Planning Commission (NDPC). However, the RCC at the time did not have any higher level context for such guidance. Therefore, they had to create their own guidance system, based on general government policies. There is no more information about the fuller regional plan made by the Central Regional authorities for 1981-86 than is reported in Table 5.1. There is much more information in relation to the strategic guidance instrument. Therefore, much of the lesson to be learnt here is based on this foundation.

Basically, the strategic guidance which was a separate document was aimed at empowering the Regional Planning Co-ordinating Unit to initiate the process of preparing the draft of an actual regional development plan. It was also intended to legitimize the informal process as for example, providing a backing for any attempt to collect data from the local authorities and relevant sector organizations. This is an indication that the regional advisory body would, by its own discretion, initiate such actions as it considers legitimate in the preparation of informal plans. Even this minimal effort is innovative by Ghanaian regional planning standards and experience. Although this aspect is not based on a general survey of regional plan-making, casual observation shows that the preparation of informal plans is not a common practice.

In fact, the function of the strategic guidance is confirmed in the following statements made by the Regional Economic Planning Officer at the time in the Central Region. These are contained in the *Addendum* to the 1987-89 strategic regional guidelines (Central Regional Administration, 1987, *Addendum*, items 2 and 3):

2. However unlike the 1981 work the present work does not propose actual projects but rather provides guidelines for possible sectoral and zonal programmes of integrated nature.

3. It is expected that from this work a few programmes could be identified for more serious study with a view to further identifying individual projects for implementation in line with the general principles.

The regional plan and strategic guidance instruments shown in Table 5.1 were initiated by the erstwhile Regional Planning Committee (RPC) and Regional Consultative Council (RCC), respectively. The regional development programmes to be discussed later in this chapter were proposed directly by the Central Regional Administration. The important point in relation to these facts is that the RPC and RCC were all advisory and non-elected. Each time they tried to create a planning and development instrument, they required some form of legitimacy. Therefore, such legitimizing which is substantially, if not wholly lacking in informal planning approaches, far more weakens the outputs of this kind of process (Ofori, 2000d).

The funding for the proposals and programmes indicated in the first two planning instruments were to be provided by the same initiators and aided by central government in the form of annual budgetary financial resources. The special development programme designed in 1989 was to be funded mainly by the United Nations Development Programme (UNDP) as a result of the initiative, drive and negotiation ability of the then Regional Secretary. The lesson to be learnt from this is that formal and statutory planning systems would require a specific budget for funding development initiatives from whichever sources. Indeed, the spending arrangement and channel would provide a reliable instrument for co-ordinating all the public investment activities.

Apart from the non-statutory plan-making, strategic guidance and development programming, other informal instruments could take the form of regional reporting on topical issues such as specific land-use problems. Other forms could be development briefs and urban or regional design guides. All these forms apply in the case of regional planning practice in Ghana. A general observation need be made on some of the merits and demerits of informal planning practices, including the instruments indicated.

In this connection, it is relevant to refer to important studies relating to informal planning and instruments in comparison with statutory ones undertaken by other researchers and writers (Wannop, 1995; Bruton and Nicholson, 1987). The informal plan-making could be an earlier phase of the statutory planning system and practice in absence of the latter or where one is, yet, to be legislated. Where the regional planning authority has direct development control functions, the plan provides the clearest opportunity for ensuring legal enforcement. Indeed, the statutory system provides a more legitimate and incontrovertible basis of investment activities for all development agencies. Thus this gives the regional planning authority the legal power to respond effectively to any challenges to its planning functions.

The informal plan-making systems could also exist alongside a formal and statutory one. This is practised by a number of local authorities in the United Kingdom, especially at earlier stages of the local planning process when many localities were not yet covered by development plans. This also builds greater flexibility into the planning process (Bruton and Nicholson, 1987). This further allows more contingency-based actions in the local planning process, especially under high levels of uncertainty (Christiansen, 1985). For example, while it is easier to revise an informal planning instrument, it is more difficult revisiting all the processes and procedures for making a formal one in a shorter period. The informal system may also be used to undertake specific and localized studies. Nevertheless, the informal practices, in this case, work better when a clear and firm formal plan-making system has been established.

Currently planning law in Ghana only allows the regional planning authorities the functions of co-ordinating, monitoring and evaluation (Republic of Ghana, 1994b). There is no indication, yet, about the future of formal plan-making as well as policy-formulation functions. Therefore, in the Ghanaian case, it is not a question of two systems of planning co-existing. Simply, the informal plan-making practice is substituted for a statutory and formal one. However, the review shows that a statutory planning system is comparatively more efficient and better than the informal practice. Nevertheless, the value of the latter is evident. This alternative practice is also related to the form of regional planning governance. Without appropriate reforms and corresponding change in this regard, it may be impossible to institute a formal and statutory plan-making system at the regional level (Wannop, 1995).

A more specific focus is now made on the strategic planning guidelines for 1987-89. This is the best example of a regional planning instrument available to the present study as indicated in Table 5.2. The main emphasis of regional policy goal is still on the rural communities which have constituted over 70 per cent of the Region's population. The strategic intent is to make them experience development in its totality and in the face of all strategic change. Thus stated, the aim is to propose and create those programmes and projects that contribute to achieving this goal. The specific objectives of the strategic guidelines reflect both material and non-material elements. The former includes those aspects mentioned, so far.

Other aspects in this connection, are the development of efficient regional transportation systems and sustainable management of the Region's fuel-wood stock. The latter includes the encouragement for and sustaining of a 'spirit of

Table 5.2 Central Region: strategic regional planning guidance, 1987-89

Item	*Details*
Planning instrument	Guidelines for three-year regional development plan
Goal	'the main thrust of the Development policy for the Region is the improvement of the quality of life of the rural dweller which would greatly assist in the overall development of Central Region' (p. 16)
Objectives	• to meet the basic needs of the rural people; • to improve the quality of life in terms of better food, better shelter, better public health and more relevant and appropriate education; • to support and strengthen rural service centres, small and medium enterprises; • to create sufficient and industrial raw material surpluses for export; • to raise relative income levels of farmers; • to support and promote education in general and vocational training, especially of children and the youth, in particular; • to generate and sustain a spirit and practice of self-help development initiatives and leadership in the local communities; • to continue creating better and efficient transportation systems within and outside the Region; • to consistently renew the stock of fuel-woods so as to maintain the ecological balance of the Region's forest ecosystems; • to provide more appropriate facilities in support of tourist development, including renovation of castles, forts and catering houses.
Strategies	• Integrated rural development and planning, main focus on agricultural and infrastructure-based development; also seen as essential leverage for and part of regional industrial development; using 'agricultural development as a lever for industrialization and development of social services' (p. 18); • Realistic identification and designation of development centres: creating growth for infrastructure-targeted investment, including 'site and services' improvement initiatives in the towns; • Extensive and focused development of tourist bases within the Region; • Institutionalization of appropriate agencies for the arts, museums and monuments.
Implementation	• Co-ordination of all sector-based district locality programmes within composite budget (e.g. single regional generation budget); • Integrating all NGO programmes in relation to objectives of regional plan; • Management for co-ordination of farmer support centres; • Multidisciplinary technical team: development committee of Regional Consultative Council.

Source: Tabulated and created from Central Regional Administration (1987)

self-help' and leadership in the development of the more deeply territorial communities in the Region. This also illustrates the importance of this non-material aspects which, after all, underlie and support the material aspects. These two aspects are also further illustrations of the qualitative and quantitative aspects of regional planning and development processes. The intended strategy of integrated rural development does involve a targeted focus. This also supports the objective of strengthening rural towns and service centres as much as specific activity localities.

Therefore, there is need for strong co-ordination function in the implementation of the programme and project proposals, based on the strategic guidelines. Indeed, the formulators of this planning instrument did propose the creation of a multidisciplinary technical team and management body. This consisted of the regional administrative officer, regional planning officer, regional director of agriculture, managing director of the Central Regional Development Corporation. Other members of the plan implementation and management team were a representative of the private business sector, the director of the Centre for Development Studies at the University of Cape Coast plus a representative of the District Secretaries within the Region. Despite the attempt to make this body representative, it did not go far enough to include many other sections of the regional community. The team's legitimacy was limited because it was not part of a formal and legally empowered regional government.

Their principal function was to co-ordinate the activities of all the organizations involved in the implementation of the proposed programmes and projects. This kind of body could be likened to an economic and social development committee within a properly elected or more legitimate regional governing body. Otherwise, any specific programme would need its own implementation co-ordinating body. The lack of more legitimate governance as well as formal policy formulation and plan-making by the existing regional body further contribute to the level of uncertainty, in this regard, in Ghanaian regional planning. It also makes the process less flexible. As Lichfield, Kettle and Whitbread (1975, p. 208) observe, flexibility is 'the capacity of a plan to cope efficiently with uncertainty about the future'.

A number of principal projects were proposed under the strategic guidance and regional plan framework. These include the Ghana Seed Company at Winneba, Twifo Oil Palm Plantation (TOPP), Ghana Sugar Estates Limited (GHASEL) at Komenda, Okyereko irrigation project, Mankessim irrigation project and Elmina fishing harbour. Others were Yamoransa-Foso road, Cape Coast-Twifo Praso road, Twifo Praso-Dunkwa road, Cape Coast District water project, Foso District water project, Ankaful brick and tile project as well as the development of Cape Coast Polytechnic.

An earlier survey undertaken by the author prior to the principal field-work showed some of the projects which had been successfully implemented under the 1981-86 regional plan framework in the Central Region (Ofori, 2000c). These are listed in Table 5.3. The projects were all funded by central government. While some of these were new projects, others were continuing initiatives that did not need prime-funding. These characteristics are clear from an examination of the programmes and projects proposed under the 1987-89 regional plan framework. The projects cover production, irrigation, coastal protection works, health delivery and water supply services as well as construction of feeder roads. These show a fair spread in distribution. Nevertheless, they are more single-faceted and one-off type of projects.

Table 5.3 Central Regional Administration: projects implemented, 1981-87

Project	*Implementation period*	*Location*
Vegetable development project	1981-87	Gomoa Nsuaem
Mankessim irrigation project	1980-84	Mankessim
Coastal protection project	1985-86	Elmina
Primary health care project	1978-87	Nyakrom, Abrem Agona, Enyan Abaasa, Moree, Kyekyewere, Anomabo
Water supplies	1980-87	Brimsu (Cape Coast), Fosu, Senya Bereku
Feeder roads	1980-87	Ankaako-Atobiase-Dumama; Winneba-Ojobi complex; Enyeme-Hasowodze-Mampong

Source: Regional Economic Planning Office, Ministry of Finance and Economic Planning, Cape Coast

Again, these are more of initiatives included in the yearly government budget than concrete projects specifically formulated for parts of or the whole region. Therefore, the lesson here is that the regional plan framework only served to create a context for identifying and co-ordinating these kinds of public-funded projects. It is clear that the private sector was not involved in these initiatives. It may have been to correct this that a member of the regional private sector was included in the implementation and management team of the 1987-89 regional plan framework. It has been shown elsewhere that there is a concentration of small and medium-scale industrial undertakings in the Region (Ofori, 2000c). In fact, these small-medium undertakers are driving the economy and environmental developments in many of the localities within the Region. The presence of the private sector in the regional-scale development programmes, in the context of the data and information available to this study, is also an attempt to widen the democratic enterprise in regional planning. A lot more is needed to effectively involve the private sector than this kind of gesture. The programme implementation and management team is also not a substitute for the economic development committee within a formal regional governance system which would have the power to formulate policy and make development plans. This is reflected in the introduction made to the role of team-based management of programme implementation in chapter one.

It must be emphasized further that the lack of formal policy formulation and statutory plan-making at the regional level will hamper the function of co-ordination. It was pointed out in chapter one that the District Assemblies are having a challenging time in coping with the task of managing the development processes in their localities. Indeed, local development planning is almost facing a crisis with many localities lacking the professional planners to inform and guide the process. The situation has bred its own problems. Therefore, this requires a strong and statutory strategic guidance; at best a regional plan prepared and issued by the Regional Planning Co-ordinating Unit.

In fact, without the statutory and formal powers, the districts would not find it committing to comply with the informal instruments. There is the tendency for them to argue that the sole role of the regional level is that of co-ordinating, monitoring and evaluation which are more passive than active with respect to policy-formulation and plan-making. On the other hand, this situation also creates much more room for negotiation between the regional and district levels. This would be more burdening on the regional level. As this is the increasingly emerging situation, the mechanism of negotiation is becoming an important aspect of the regional and local planning processes in Ghana. Indeed, its place, in this regard, was pointed out in chapter one. Wenban-Smith and Beeston (1990) have pointed out this tendency, among others, in relation to the role of negotiation in the planning and development processes. However, there is also the tendency for this to generate its own politics that may weigh down on and constrain the processes.

Regional planning policy and the development of 'depressed' areas

It has been pointed out that one aspect of national development policy is a specific attention for the areas described as 'depressed' (Republic of Ghana, 1994b). The nature of the 'region' in Ghana as outlined in chapter one highlights the fact of the existence of localities and territories in greater decline, deprivation and poverty. Regional planning policy in Ghana, in general, and the Central Region, in particular, is partly based on this kind of problem. It is noted in the strategic regional guidance for the Central Region, 1987-89, that the defunct Regional Planning Committee and the Regional Development Corporation aimed at developing 'socio-economically depressed areas in the Region' (Central Regional Administration, 1987, p. 13).

The depressed areas in the Central Region, as in other regions in Ghana, are seen in terms of poor social infrastructure, employment structure, low income levels and standard of living. Other attributes are the weak local economic structure, minimal or no functional urbanization and low level of utilization of available resources. In a term, these areas are in a state of structural downward-transitional decline. For example, the Twifo locality was identified as the most depressed area in the Central Region before the introduction of the TOPP development instrument which is a principal case study in this book (Ofori, 2000h). Glimpses were given into the sub-region's socio-economic and environmental problems in chapter one. Apart from the basic needs of the area, the sub-region has one of the lowest income levels, per capita and group-based, despite its rich natural resource base (Ofori, 2000h; Government of Ghana, 1984). With respect to the latter, however, it is also largely a frontier region.

The population census statistics up to 1984 showed that the Lower Denkyira-Twifo-Hemang District had an absolute zero with respect to urbanization. By the time of the earlier field-work for this study, however, there were beginning to be signs of urban emergence. Moreover, the area faces one of the major constraints of development in all regions of Ghana, as in other Third World countries - rapid population growth as pointed out in chapter four. This may be partly accounted for by the magnetic pull of the TOPP agro-industrial activity (Government of Ghana, 1984). It does not appear that this explosive growth of the locality's population could have occurred through natural increase alone. The significant point here is that the high and rapid rate of population increase compounds the problem of socio-economic development. The district locality was the most disadvantaged in terms of almost all the relevant variables mentioned, so far, before the TOPP initiative was launched. Therefore, there is greater need for sustained inflow of investment funds in the development of the sub-region as in other such areas in the country.

Growth and service centres: policy and strategy A specific aspect of regional policy and strategy for generating growth in the 'depressed' areas of the Region is the growth centre and service approach (Linn, 1979). The system of centres in use in the Central Region is shown in Table 5.4. Apart from Cape Coast, the regional capital, there are three other levels of centres: district, zonal and large community. The district centre has population of 5,000 and is the capital town of

Table 5.4 Central Region: proposed hierarchy of growth and service centres

Hierarchy	*Functional criteria*	*Settlements*
Regional capital	All regional agencies; co-ordination of policies and programmes	Cape Coast
District centre	Multi-purpose agricultural co-operatives; district agricultural office; senior secondary school; technical institutes; level 'C' hospital; district water supply systems; continuous electricity supply; commercial and development banks; daily markets	All district capitals: Cape Coast, Elmina, Saltpond, Abura Dunkwa, Foso, Asikuma, Ajumako, Swedru, Dunkwa, Twifo Praso, Apam, Winneba
Zonal centres	Multi-purpose agricultural co-operatives; farmers, farmers/fishermen input depots; junior secondary school; senior secondary school; level 'B' health centres and posts; treated water supplies; rural electrification; commercial banks; rural banks; twice-weekly markets	Diaso, Ayanfuri, Awisam; Assin Bereku, Assin Manso, Fanti Nyankumasi; Twifo Hemang, Jukwa; Elmina; Moree, Abakrampa, Mankessim, Enyan Abaasa, Bisease; Asikuma Brakwa; Nyakrom; Senya Bereku, Bodwease, Kasoa; Apam
Large community centre	Farmers and fishermen services centres; rural extension service; junior secondary school; level 'A' health delivery system; shallow wells and bore-holes; rural electrification; rural banks; weekly markets	Opponsokese, Asikuma, Kyekyewere, Moseaso; Kushea; Anyinabrim; Twifo Mampong; Jukwa; Mfuom; Komenda, Abrem Agona; Asebu, Abura Dunkwa; Essuehyia, Otuam; Enyan Denkyira, Anyinasu, Ochiso; Abodom, Nsaba, Kwanyako, Mankrong Nkwanta; Dawurampong, Potsin; Ojobi, Awutu, Nyanyano; Bedum, Odoben

Source: Created and tabulated from Central Regional Administration (1987)

a District Assembly area. The zonal centre has a population of between 2,000 and 4,999 and the large community centre below 2,000. The various selected settlements at each level of growth-service centre are also indicated in the table.

The strategic guideline for the 1987-89 regional plan did not clearly distinguish between growth and service centre (Central Regional Administration, 1987). It appeared to mean the latter but the strategy is actually discussed under the section on 'growth centres'. The objective was to create 'a four-tier service hierarchy throughout the Region' (Central Regional Administration, 1987, p. 26). The criteria for identifying the centres are mostly service-based. Besides, the only criteria relating to production are agriculture-oriented. The argument is emphasized, here, that the most rewarding approach to regional development is the one that is based on real production activities, whether industrial or agricultural. This has also been underlined in the earlier chapters of this book and elsewhere (Ofori, 2000c; 2000a). This does not underplay the need to create relevant infrastructure and leverage, including basic services. In fact, this may be an initial step in the process of poverty reduction. Many of the distinguishing variables are characteristic of the theoretical constructs reviewed in chapter three, especially relating to the endogenous development models. This aspect on locality development and socio-economic generation processes has come under greater focus in other studies (Ofori, 2000h; Coffey and Polese, 1985; 1984).

Two of the criteria are more vivid and effective in showing the scale of the centres. These are health services and markets. The former ranges from level 'A' service at the large community centre through level 'B' type at the zonal centre to level 'C' hospital at the district centre level. In a similar way, the large community level has a weekly market, the zonal centre a twice-weekly market and the district centre, a daily market. The paramount importance of these markets in the functioning of intermediate settlements, as seedbeds of territorial socio-economic development, has been emphasized by a number of writers (Weaver, 1989; Hardoy and Satterthwaite, 1986; Rondinelli and Ruddel, 1978; Johnson, 1970). Therefore, it should be part of the regional policy objective aimed at developing such areas to bring about an improvement in these characteristic factors and to create more production-based and mover activities.

Principal regional programmes and projects

Various cases have been made for the efficient and effective design of regional development programmes and projects. Those considered, so far, in this chapter are more one-off and single-function based. The emphasis on integrated development as well as the brief review of the Central Region's growth-and-service centre strategy emphasize the need for multi-purpose development initiatives. Two examples of this type of instrument are now reviewed for the purpose of learning further lessons in practical regional planning and development (Rondinelli, 1983a).

Central Regional integrated development scheme

This programme was first proposed in 1989 by the then Regional Secretary (now Regional Minister) for the Central Region (Table 5.5). At the time of the original fieldwork for this study, the Secretary was in the process of setting up the institutional and organizational structures as well as seeking funding from the United Nations Development Programme (UNDP) and Non-Governmental Organizations (NGOs). Despite the attempt to integrate as many projects as possible, it appears that the principal concern was with developing the tourism sector of the Region. This is the most consistently and concisely listed out in the original programme document (Central Regional Administration, 1989). The information used in this book does not include any on the actual implementation and developments that have taken place since the programme was launched. The information is only analysed to demonstrate some of the limitations and merits of formulating regional development initiatives.

Table 5.5 Central Regional Integrated Development Scheme components

Major project component	*Specific initiatives and focus*	*Implementing agencies*
Tourist development scheme	Renovation of museums, monuments and other heritage sites; development of wildlife and ecological parks; urban renewal sites and services; development of arts and crafts, local and regional culture; development of other recreational and leisure centres: beaches, resorts, hotels and catering houses; relevant employment training; tourism marketing	Tourism development scheme for the Central Region; (subsidiary company within the scheme) (TODSCER)
NGO-sponsored and funded projects	Small-scale kaolin production; fish curing and processing; production of tree crops and fruits on outgrower basis; production of cassava-based products; production on smallholder basis; small-scale gold and diamond mining; construction of children playgrounds	NGOs
Linkage projects: Central Regional Development Corporation initiatives	Cold stores and ice-making plants; farmer-support services; livestock breeding and production; plant pool services; palm kernel processing and refinery; allied salt and chemical industries; small-scale mining and quarrying	Central Regional Development Corporation (CEREDEC)
Other linkage projects	Twifo oil palm plantation and mills; Elmina lagoon fishing port; production of salt and allied chemicals; fruit juice processing companies; marine stock exploitation research based at the University of Cape Coast	Various public and private sector companies

Source: Author's creation from programme document

The Central Regional Integrated Development Scheme does include a distinctive project unit for tourist development as well as a collection of various small-scale undertakings and two 'linkage' project components as shown in Table 5.5. The small-scale initiatives were to be funded by NGOs. One of the linkage projects was the entire portfolio of the TOPP project-complex which is, generally, under CEREDEC on behalf of central government. The other was a set of existing public and private-sector projects and companies. These two linkage projects were meant to provide appropriate and robust support for the first two parts of the whole Scheme. Its other parts were to be funded by the UNDP and the Government of Ghana. The executive and principal spending agencies are the Linkage Project Authorities, CEREDEC and TODSCER. It was intended that these three organizations would be funded by the Government of Ghana and initially, by the UNDP.

The Scheme was meant to be under the direct control of the Central Regional Administration which was also expected to provide political guidance, general policy formulation and monitoring of progress. However, it is under the executive management of an advisory organization, the Central Regional Development Commission (CEDECOM). This is composed of a representative of the University of Cape Coast; a representative of the Regional Co-ordinative Council, managing director of CEREDEC and the Regional Economic Planning Officer. Others are the regional director of the National Council for Women and Development (NCWD), two representatives of NGOs, a representative of the business sector in the region, a representative of the Regional Administrative Officer as well as a separate representation appointed by the Regional Secretary (Regional Minister). The Commission was also given the mandate to co-opt the head of any sector department as it deemed appropriate. CEDECOM is meant to be an independent organization with its own headquarters and secretariat.

The functions of CEDECOM are supposed to include policy and programme formulation, in this regard, for the 'total economic development of the Central Region and as such ... directly responsible for the development and implementation of the UNDP-sponsored Integrated Development Programme for the Central Region' (Central Regional Development Commission, 1989, pp. 3-4). Other functions of the Commission are maintaining a link with agencies and ministries of central government. In the same way, it is to keep a link with the UNDP as well as other multilateral and bilateral development agencies, thus giving it an international dimension and flare. Further functions of CEDECOM are the designing, co-ordinating, managing and monitoring of projects in the Central Region. Apart from its own projects, the Commission is also expected to implement national strategic development initiatives in the Region. In this case also, it would need to maintain a link with the National Development Planning Commission. Besides, the CEDECOM is to supervise directly the set of projects funded by NGOs and scattered all over the Region.

The initial activities of the Commission were phased out as indicated in Table 5.6. The details in the table confirm the more legitimate and independent functions of CEDECOM. Unlike the programme implementation and management team of the Regional Co-ordinating Council, CEDECOM is able to initiate its own process of development ranging from the production of policy and programme documents to implementation. It also has independence with respect to its resources. For example, one of the problems of regional planning and development facing the Regional Planning Co-ordinating Units as well as the Regional Development Corporations is the lacking of transport facilities for their officials and project managers. Therefore, they are not able to undertake effective site visits and project monitoring (Ofori, 2000a).

Thus CEDECOM is meant to fill in a gap created, by default, in the non-existence of a legitimate and formal regional government. While the existing Regional Co-ordinating Council (RCC) has no strong political or economic powers, CEDECOM has both enshrined in its independence. The Commission and its outfit represent a well-thought out, strategic and yet 'subverted' effort at providing substantive and sufficient legitimacy for the regional development process in the Central Region. The creation of CEDECOM also introduces a

Table 5.6 Planned phases of Central Regional Integrated Development Scheme

Phases	*Details*
One	Consolidation of co-ordinating and implementation agencies, following project identification and baseline work; these included staffing and setting up of office facilities, relevant employment training, acquisition of vehicles for transportation
Two	Sponsorship for preparation of final project documents and funding of final feasibility studies
Three	Initial implementation of approved projects

Source: Tabulated from programme document

clearly founded robustness into the regional planning and development of the Central Region. However, in its design, it appears over-ambitious as it brings numerous organizations, including private and public ones as well as NGOs together and under one umbrella structure.

There are likely to be conflicts between these individual companies, especially the public and private sectors. There is also likely to be a conflict between the NGOs and CEDECOM because the former are usually more in touch with the local realities and conditions. The NGOs relate to and work more closely with the local residents. They also tend to operate in more realist-phenomenological ways and situations. This has been shown in other African countries and not unusual in Ghana (Ofori, 2000h; Ng'ethe, Mitullah, and Ngunyi, 1990). The success of this kind of CEDECOM would depend on the extent to which it is able to withstand the tests of management, planning and the development function. Anyhow, it needs responsive co-ordination and flexibility to deliver.

Special focus of CEDECOM: trends in national-level development of tourism It has been indicated that a special and principal focus of the Scheme is tourism for which the Central Region has an appreciably viable resource base. The trends in the development of tourism as a basis for regional development is a reflection of the increasing attention for the growth of the sector at the national level. Indeed, tourism in Ghana is now growing at the rate of eight per cent per year. In 1993, there were 80,000 visitors which increased to 372,000 in 1999. The tourist sector is now the third biggest earner of foreign currency, after cocoa and gold, for the country (Moyo, 2000). The Central Regional Administration (1987, p. 11) has stated that:

> The Region receives over 40% of the tourist arrivals in the country due to the special attraction of historic castles like the Elmina Castle, Cape Coast Castle and the Forts at Anomabo, Kromantse, Apam etc. which are all relics of the Slave Trade. The Region also boasts of pleasant and scenic landscapes as well as beautiful safe sandy beaches but nevertheless its tourist infrastructure is still poorly developed. There are only a few excellent Hotels and Restaurants in the Region.

Central government has taken a number of significant steps to promote the development of the sector. One of these was the introduction of the 15-year national tourism development plan in 1996. This is focused on the various market segments in the sector and general strategies for achieving targeted growth up to 2010. Another relates to the undertaking of various projects, based on the national plan. An aspect is the restoration of thirty castles and forts dotted along the coast of Ghana. Over 160 kilometres of Ghana's coastline is covered by the Central Region (Central Regional Administration, 1987). The heritage sites are particularly of value and importance to the history of the slave trade and colonial domination. While some of these are being fitted with new facilities, other catering and rest houses are also being renovated. There is also a training programme for tourist guides and assistants. Emphasis is also being put on the development of eco-tourism particularly in terms of wildlife, including plant protection and the management of national resource and forest reserves.

Tourism studies and hospitality management studies would be viable areas of academic study and training in relation to these developments in the Central

Region. This scenario could be further promoted through the TODSCER arm of CEDECOM.

The Twifo Oil Palm Plantation and development programme

The Twifo Oil Palm Plantation programme (TOPP) was started in the late 1970s. It was one of four such initiatives set up, on a pilot basis, in various locations in the country. The others are the Benso Oil Palm Plantation (BOPP) Limited and the National Oil Palm Plantation (NOPP) Limited, both in the Western Region. The other one is the Ghana Oil Palm Development Company (GOPDC) at Kade in the Eastern Region. Like TOPP, the other programmes were also aimed at developing depressed areas and producing much needed raw material for domestic industries and international export.

TOPP is the largest agro-industrial complex in the Central Region. The programme was born out of the entrepreneurial spirit and professional planning drive of a former managing director of CEREDEC (Bannermann, 1984). The Government of Ghana, Commonwealth Development Corporation (CDC) and the European Union entered into an agreement on the understanding that the lands in the area which had been acquired by the Government of Ghana in 1975 would be leased or sub-leased to TOPP. The TOPP company was established in February, 1987 and the first CDC management personnel started work in August, 1978 (Harrisons Fleming Advisory Services, 1985). The Government acquired the lands partly because of the local conflicts among the Twifo sub-groups and partly owing to the fact that the area had been identified as being suitable for oil palm cultivation. The earlier dominant cash crop of cocoa had also been hit by a pest epidemic.

The programme is funded, under a broad ‘partnership’, involving the Government of Ghana, two private Dutch organizations, the Commonwealth Development Corporation and the European Union (EU). Under a Ghana Government Special Agricultural Scheme, foreign parents of locally established companies were encouraged to take up shares in TOPP. The main investors and shareholders in the programme are Mobil Holding UK which is part of the global Mobil Corporation; Paterson Zochonis Plc (UK) and Pasico Elders International. UniLever (Ghana Limited) recently acquired 50 per cent out of the 80 per cent shares controlled by CEREDEC for central government (Table 5.7). Figure 5.2 shows a pie charting of the equity investors and shareholders. The data in Table 5.7 are now more vividly illustrated: UniLever (Ghana) now having a lion’s share, followed by CEREDEC - for the Government of Ghana - the rest fall in.

Before its acquisition of the shares, UniLever was only a regular and leading customer of the TOPP company as will be further shown in chapter seven. It would appear that UniLever had always been eagle-eyed on the goings-on in the TOPP company. It seemed to have considered it opportune to have leapt rightly when 'it was learnt that the Company was listed for divestiture' in 1993 (interview with managers at TOPP Headquarters, Ntafrewaso, 1998). No more information has been forthcoming from TOPP about the possibility of its full divestment. It may be the Government's intent to divest all the palm oil production companies in the public sector.

Table 5.7 TOPP development programme: equity investors (%)

Investors		*% shareholding*
Foreign:		
	Mobil Holding (UK) Limited*	15.0
	Paterson Zochonis Plc, UK	1.0
	Pasico Elders International (Australian)	1.0
	UniLever (Ghana Limited)	50.0
Local:		
	State Insurance Corporation (SIC) and National Investment Bank (NIB)	3.0
	Central Regional Development Corporation	30.0
Total		**100.0**

Source: Author's fieldwork; *Equity share could not be confirmed at time of the follow-up fieldwork in September, 1998

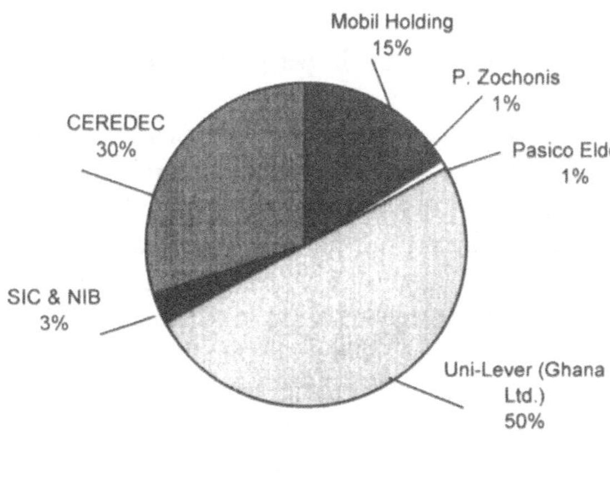

Figure 5.2 TOPP: pie chart of equity investors and shareholders

However, at this rate and level of share, UniLever (Ghana Limited) may be on the way to acquiring more or the full share in the TOPP company. If this happened, it would shift decision-making and control dramatically and overwhelmingly in favour of UniLever. Depending on the behaviour of UniLever in this regard, this trend might not be in the interest of the socio-economic development of the area. For example, an attempt has been made to demonstrate the partnership orientation of the TOPP programme complex elsewhere (Ofori, 2000a). If UniLever did take over all the shares in the TOPP company, that would limit partner participation. With the possible withdrawal of the Government of Ghana, the bargaining position of the local community is likely to be much more weakened. Indeed, the Government's withdrawal is also likely to undermine the active participation of the Lower Denkyira-Twifo-Hemang District Assembly and the Central Regional Co-ordinating Council. Already their roles have been more passive than otherwise.

The TOPP company could not confirm the continued participation of Mobil Holding (UK) during the last follow-up field interviews in the latter part of 1998. If this loan investor had decided to withdraw from the programme, it would appear to stem from a reorganization of its own parent company, Exxon-Mobil Corporation. It could also stem from disagreement over the entry of UniLever and its acquisition of the greater part of the shares in the TOPP company. Of the two Dutch organizations involved in the TOPP programme, NIO is still a loan investor and FMO which originally funded the purchase of the palm oil mill has had its loan fully paid off by TOPP. The CDC and EU are still loan investors. The other loan investors and shareholders in TOPP are locally-based and public organizations, the State Insurance Corporation (SIC) and National Investment Bank (NIB). CEREDEC only holds 30 per cent of the shares on behalf of the Government of Ghana.

TOPP is managed by an eleven-member Board of Directors, on which Ghana Government is represented by the Ministry of Economic Planning and Finance, through the Regional Co-ordinating Council (RCC). Other members on the Board are the Lower Denkyira-Twifo-Hemang community, the District Assembly, CEREDEC and Central Regional Administration. The technical consultants to the TOPP company are based in Malaysia, a country that has an international reputation in the palm oil production business. Expatriate employment recruitment and international consultant service to the TOPP company is provided by Harrisons Fleming Advisory Services Limited, based in London, England. The TOPP company, has been headed by a British manager, with other expatriates involved in aspects of its operations and are all resident at the project site. Thus the total work-force of the TOPP company also has an international mix and provides an opportunity for learning for all managers as well as employees.

The foregoing facts and characteristics of the TOPP programme indicate its strategic proportions and international dimensions. These include a fairly wide variety of stakeholders at the international, national, regional and local levels. These also indicate various levels of power, authority and roles which further reflect the real intentions of the various partners (Ofori, 2000a). Thus it is important to clarify and rationalize the roles of all the stakeholders as much as the objectives of the whole TOPP programme (Ofori, 2000a; 1991a).

The entire TOPP programme comprises three project components: the core and main TOPP estate, the smallholder and outgrower units. Figure 5.3 shows the locations of the main estate and palm oil processing site, with other plantations developed in the 1980s as well as the smallholder project and the main Cape Coast to Twifo Praso Road. The Assin Attandansso and Kakum forest reserves are to the west of the sub-region and oil palm zones. The principal project consists of the main plantation, nursery fields and a large oil mill with capacity for processing 20 fresh fruit bunches per hour. Apart from producing over 1,000 tonnes of palm oil per year, it also has an output of more than 300 tonnes of palm kernels annually. The acquisition, by compulsory purchase, of the Twifo lands for the purpose of establishing TOPP, involved ejecting some 300 landowners and tenants from their lands.

The smallholder project is meant to cater for the ejected farmers. The unit started in 1982 and involves the allocation of 4 hectares of land for selected farmers for the purpose of cultivating oil palm which is pre-planted for them. Each farmer was supposed to be given an additional hectare of land solely for food-cropping. It must be noted that the process of selecting the programme participants unfairly left out some of the ejected people.

Outgrowers are regarded as independent oil palm cultivators who may decide to sell their produce to the central mill, or dispose of them elsewhere. This project was initiated because the estate and smallholder parts could not meet the input requirements of the palm oil mill. Outgrowers are distributed mainly on either side of the road link between Twifo Praso and Cape Coast, from Twifo Praso to Jukwa in the south. Jukwa is to the south-south-east of Mfuom, itself further south-east of Ankaako (Figures 5.3 and 1.2).

There are three groups of outgrowers. The first group are the co-operative outgrowers, located outside the 50 kilometre range of the central mill. These are given technical aid and extension services, marketing facilities as well as occasional sales and supplies of inputs such as fertilizers and other chemicals. Second, the rehabilitee outgrowers who are given what is called 'supervised credit'. That is, they personally invest in their farms under supervision and are later re-imbursed. The reimbursements averaged ¢18,732 per hectare per year, each participant taking about ¢66,228 annually. The third group consists of 'new planter' outgrowers: those who take up 'supervised credit' of ¢100,000 per hectare per farmer, yearly, to develop entirely new farms.

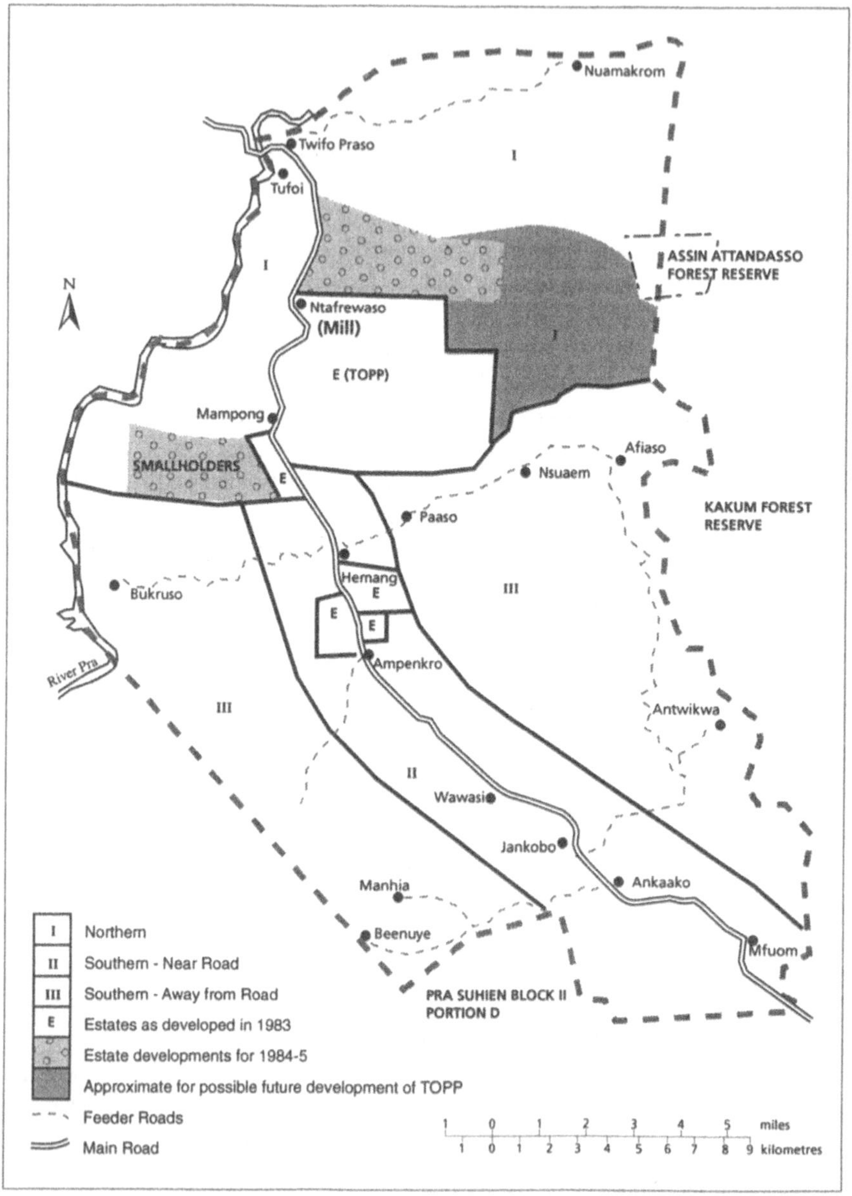

Figure 5.3 **Lower Denkyira-Twifo-Hemang District: location of oil-palm plantations and mill**

Hemang oil palm estate Apart from the three components, CEREDEC has its own and separate oil palm project, east of the settlement of Hemang. The Regional Development Corporation has a total concession of 220 hectares but had developed 162 hectares of it. However, this estate is poorly developed in comparison with the TOPP project-complex. The difficulties with the Hemang estate include relatively poor soil quality, limited oil palm plant growth and development. Others are poor road network and accessibility as well as low oil palm production per hectare annually. However, the Hemang estate has created some 90 jobs. This includes managers, administrative staff and plantation employees. This separate project is not included in the evaluation done in chapter seven of this book.

Programme goals and objectives The specific objectives of the TOPP programme are now examined. This is done within the framework of regional planning and general development policy as well as on the merit of the stated programme goals and objectives.

The role of TOPP as an engine of socio-economic development has not been well-articulated at any particular time. Rather, bits and pieces of statements have come from various sources. For example, according to Dickson (1978), in an *ante post* socio-economic assessment of the project-complex, the principal goal is to strengthen the rural economy and by that raise rural living standards, especially in the programme region. The specific objectives include raising family net incomes in the rural locality, establishing a firm basis for an agro-commercial economy in the perspective term and intensifying food-cropping as well as raising productivity per hectare of land. Other objectives, according to Dickson (1978) are facilitating the development of agro-technical activities, improving road net-work connectivity and thereby, the accessibility of the major agricultural areas. The other aspect of this objective is developing an efficient marketing system to support the farming and agro-technical activities. Furthermore, strengthening the regional role of Cape Coast, particularly by the location of higher level manufacturing activities and which depends on agro-technical activities within the capital town.

While these objectives relate to the material context of territorial development problems in the light of the considerations in chapter three and the present one, some of these amount to an overloading of the expectation from the programme. TOPP was seen as the engine for generating rather too many benefits. For example, the trends in national economic performance and in the expansion of global corporate operations limit the achievement of all the objectives. The particular aspect has been highlighted earlier in this chapter and will be further elucidated in the following section. The creation of agro-technical activities and the consequent generation of growth in the urban economy of Cape Coast have been limited in both substance and potential.

Similarly, Bannermann (1984b) discusses the policy strategic nature of TOPP as a tool for the development of peripheral areas with emphasis on income and employment generation. Indeed, this has been the focus of the growth centre-service strategy and the regional programmes reviewed in this chapter. The more critical importance of these types of regional initiatives in developing and generating growth in the deprived, declined, and downward-transitional territorial areas is much emphasized in this book.

The TOPP company, itself, accepts the pervasive need to raise the rural producer's income level as the dominant objective for setting up agro-based industries (TOPP, 1989a). Therefore, the low income levels are perceived as the source of the structural and continuous poverty of the rural producer. The absence or low level of income is also seen as the main push factor in the rural-urban migration process. The company also considers the project as a producer of industrial raw materials as part of government policy in this regard (TOPP, 1989b). The public investment programme (Republic of Ghana, 1987) clearly states that the project is commercial and part of a major oil palm expansion programme in the country and emphasizes the position of TOPP as a key element in the macro-programme.

Further, in a personal interview with the managing director of the TOPP company, he stated the following as the programme's objectives: (a) 'to produce palm oil for consumption in Ghana'; (b) 'to produce raw materials for industries'; (c) 'to develop the oil palm industry, extending help to smallholders and outgrowers and to encourage them to go into oil palm cultivation'. The managing director added that 'our main purpose is to look after the interest of shareholders'. However, he indicated that the programme had 'an adjunctive objective' of improving the living standards of the local communities. This is seen in terms of employment, income, social and economic infrastructure (TOPP, 1988a). The management consultants also recognize these objectives (Harrisons Fleming Advisory Services, 1985).

The managing director, is of course, right in putting emphasis on the company's responsibility towards its shareholders and the commercial function of TOPP as a business entity. However, as the socio-economic aspects of the locality's development are perceived as only 'adjunctive', this means that these have been grafted on the original purposes and functions. It is realistic to accept that the TOPP company can only be a useful generator of regional development if it is managed efficiently and successfully. The latter is the *sine qua non* of the former. However, the analyses, reviews and discussions in this book, so far, show that without specifying the socio-economic aspects and being given the same status like the more valued and purely commercial consideration, the former are only given a secondary and down-graded place. Thus the TOPP company and all its components are not committed to actually making things happen in relation to the social aspects of territorial development. There is also no legitimate foundation to really hold them responsible for not doing so. In the same way that it is essential to clearly specify the roles of executive development agencies, so it is critical to stating the exact function and responsibility of the TOPP company in the development of the Twifo area and wider Central Region.

The TOPP Board Chairman, who is a professional accountant as well as a local chief, articulated the socio-economic objectives of the programme. These are more of his own views. In an interview with the Chairman, he stated that (quote):

> First of all, it will provide employment for thousands of workers and thereby reduce urban drift. Secondly, it will provide multidisciplinary training for engineers, accountants, mechanics, agronomists and agricultural managers. Thirdly, it will provide medical facilities in the form of a hospital. Fourthly, we are providing decent housing for our workers. Fifthly, we are involved in education by establishment of primary and junior secondary schools.

The principal aspects of the programme are indicated in the above statement: employment, multidisciplinary training for various professions, hospital, as well as housing and educational facilities for the TOPP and Twifo communities. While this emphasis on employment generation is a pervasive aspect, the Board's chairman was distinctive in pointing out the benefit of the programme as a breeding and training ground for the various professional groups. The income variable is implied in employment, in this case. The Chairman's statement is the most appropriate and comprehensive in relation to the socio-economic and territorial aspects, so far. Nevertheless, it has already been pointed out that it is these aspects that have been given a secondary, adjunctive or background status in the scheme of making things happen in the territorial sub-regional community. In so far as these aspects are not given the same status as the economic and commercial components, the former lack legitimacy that is enshrined in the latter.

Another significant statement of the project's objective was stated by the head of state of Ghana at the commissioning of the TOPP mill. He put emphasis on the development or opening up of 'depressed areas' through the establishment of various companies (TOPP 1988b). In this case, the idea of developing depressed areas by this approach is not only an objective but also a policy (Hogwood and Gunn, 1984; Bannermann, 1984). The institutional role of CEREDEC in this regard was firmly acknowledged. This also means that the development of these depressed and such other territorial areas is tied up with or depends on the creation of special development organizations or companies. If this is the case, it implies that the territorial and land-based development functions of these organizations have to be explicitly and formally spelt out.

Furthermore, the possible impacts of the TOPP programme are recognized in the framework of the Central and Accra Regions Integrated Programme (CARRIP) (Ofori, 2000a; Government of Ghana, 1984; 1983c). CARRIP was formulated in the 1980s for parts of the Central Region and Greater Accra Region. It was primarily aimed at the socio-economic development of a wide territory considered to be mostly depressed (Ofori 2000a; 1991a). The main elements of that inter-regional programme were focused on socio-demographic changes, economic structural changes and employment. The other factors are growth of commerce, trade and urbanization, general government and financial services, as well as pressure on land availability and supply. Some of these aspects are recognized as the areas of impact under the TOPP programme as will be shown in chapter seven. As part of the CARRIP framework however, the Central Regional Development Corporation expected the central government to provide leverage in terms of social infrastructure in the Twifo area.

The strategic importance of the TOPP programme and its value as a pilot undertaking, however, has been stated as part of the wider CARRIP initiative that (Government of Ghana, 1984, p. 2):

> It must be stated ... that the scheme *[TOPP]* is of special significance to CEREDEC. CEREDEC is committed to the development of the region. Its function in this effort is to act as a catalyst to improve the living standards of the people of the area ... should this project succeed ..., it will be replicated in other parts of the region.

It ought to be noted that CEREDEC has no total control of the TOPP programme. Besides, there are indications that the Government of Ghana might pull out as an equity investor. It is important to note that the TOPP initiative is seen as a "policy experiment" (Rondinelli, 1983b).

This review of the TOPP programme goals and objectives clearly shows variations and conflicts between and within them. There is a disagreement between the social and economic aspects; between the social and business aspects; between the economic-industrial and the social-territorial. Indeed, there is a conflict between the corporate and the territorial aspects (Ofori, 2000d; 2000a). There is further conflict between the corporate-industrial values and those of territorial governance (Ofori, 2000d; 2000a). The consultants and project management see it basically in commercial terms, based on the notion of efficiency. The general public, including the local community, put greater emphasis on socio-economic developments. Although the project managers do recognize the social aspects, those are not clearly part of the terms of reference, but rather, grafted or added on.

The socio-economic aspects are also part of the expectations of regional and central governments. But the project, as originally formulated did not include these conflicting aspects in a more balanced way (Bannermann, 1984). The lack of this balance also limits the comprehensiveness, robustness and strategic effectiveness of the TOPP programme as an instrument of regional development.

This scenario looks even more bleak with the change in the structure of shareholders and possible withdrawal of some stakeholders, including the Government of the people. The corporate forces and corporate-industrial values are gradually becoming more dominant and supplanting the social-territorial ones in either consideration.

The interest in this book in evaluating the impact of the TOPP programme is not based on its agrarian aspects, but on its socio-economic and environmental outcomes (Helmsing, 1986). Nijkamp and Pelt (1983) have made a case for urban and regional policy impact studies in the Third World countries in terms of changes in indicators of socio-economic development. Conyers and Hill, (1984) emphasized these aspects as including income levels and distributive effects, increase in employment, rural accessibility and road infrastructure. Factors such as these will be emphasized in chapter seven.

Involvement of global corporate organizations in the TOPP programme: globalization and territorial regional planning

The involvement of global-level corporate organizations in the TOPP programme is also of critical importance to territorial regional planning (Friedmann and Weaver, 1979). An attempt is now made to outline the stature and underline the global-strategic nature of the principal equity investors in the TOPP programme in the context and processes of globalization (Ofori, 2000e; 2000f; Hampden-Turner and Trompenaars, 1998; Hill and Jones, 1995; Bartlett and Ghoshal, 1989). These are Mobil Holding (UK Limited), part of Exxon-Mobil Corporation; Paterson Zochonis Plc (UK); Pasico Elders International (Australian) and UniLever (Ghana Limited).

Business organizations, especially in Western capitalist countries are re-defining their market boundaries and product markets in response to the forces of competition and strategic change. Nationally-based market boundaries are increasingly being replaced by global ones. The formerly country-based and nationally 'bordered' product-markets are becoming 'borderless' (Ohmae, 1990). In other parts of the world, governments and nations are being compelled to open up their protected and controlled borders to the operation of market forces and enterprise. Corporate organizations are now having to identify and concentrate on their core competence and strengths, including product and process technologies as well as marketing strategies. These pressures of strategic change have created powerful forces of competition. A principal feature of this process is the taking over of weaker companies by the more powerful and competitive ones. Other structural changes include mergers, joint ventures, and partnerships. In expanding their product markets, these large corporate enterprises are also entering and competing in wider cultural environments.

The 'bordered' world had been dominated by multinational monopolies. There were only fewer dominant products. Buyers had limited choice, including limited information and knowledge about products and markets. The customer was rather 'peripheral' to the real interests of the organizations. National markets were particularly isolated from each other while many national governments protected their economies by erecting stiff and high tariff barriers (Hill and Jones, 1995; Ohmae, 1990). Therefore, the current process of globalization is a change from multinational monopoly and oligopoly to global competition.

The process of globalization has two main aspects relating to production and markets. The globalization of production involves the relocation of divisions or branches of businesses by the corporate organizations to various places on the globe. The strategic aim is to operate at less cost, meet the specific needs of segments and earn greater profits. Indeed, as the global markets become increasingly fragmented, many organizations are aiming at achieving total globalization of their activities (Jeannet and Hennessey, 1994). The globalization of markets means that the barriers of trade, distance, time and culture are no longer impenetrable boundaries. National markets are coalescing into one massive global marketplace. Another implication of this strategic trend is the fact that consumer tastes and preferences are converging on a global scale (Hill and Jones, 1995; Ohmae, 1990). These changes also mark out the fact that in contemporary capitalism, wealth is no longer necessarily created in individual organizations, rather among networks and coalitions or clusters of companies.

For example, Mobil UK is part of Mobil Corporation and the whole organization started in 1866 (Mobil Corporation, 1998). The parent company operates in 140 countries spread across Europe, Asia-Pacific, United States and other parts of the world, including Nigeria, Venezuela, Canada. Others are Sao Tome and Principe, Kazakhstan, Abu Dhabi, Equatorial Guinea and Angola. The Corporation's businesses are in energy and petrochemicals with focus on petroleum exploration and production, marketing and refining as well as chemical manufactures. Mobil Corporation had a network of 23 refineries dotted round the globe which process crude oil into fuels, lubricants and petrochemical feed-stocks. The organization has a total annual revenue of 53 billion dollars. The group merged with Exxon Corporation, in 1999, to create Exxon-Mobil. Thus the parent company's growth reflects the trends in globalization outlined.

It is this stature of a global organization that has had 15 per cent share of equity investment in the TOPP company. This has been the third largest share in TOPP's equity investment after UniLever and CEREDEC (for central government) (Table 5.7 and Figure 5.2). In late 1998, TOPP could not confirm Mobil's continued investment. Mobil Holding's participation is minimal compared to its interests in other businesses across the globe. Nevertheless, its participation at 15 per cent is significant in context. However, Mobil's interest in TOPP is more in making profits. Therefore, its current uncertain presence in

TOPP may be due to the fact that a glut of palm oil on the national and domestic markets has affected this company's performance and profits in recent times. In fact, it will be shown that this trend has caused TOPP's suspension or termination of its 'social' projects. It could also be due to the reorganization of Mobil Corporation. The point is that this type of corporate organization has not the intent of really being involved in the socio-economic and territorial development in the Twifo sub-region.

Paterson Zochonis Plc (UK) is part of the parent company that operates in countries across Europe, Australasia and the Pacific as well as Africa (Paterson Zochonis Plc, 2000). The parent organization groups many companies, including Cussons, Roberts Pharmaceuticals, Fragrance Chemicals, Sipca S.A. in Cameroun, Thermocool Engineering in Nigeria and many others (Paterson Zochonis, 1998). There are two main branches of Paterson Zochonis Plc in Ghana: Paterson Zochonis Ghana Limited in imports-exports merchant business and Paterson Zochonis Industries (Ghana) Limited which manufactures proprietary medicines and toiletries. The principal activities of Paterson Zochonis Plc (UK), like many other branches of the parent Plc, feed on substantial input of palm oil. The company's one per cent share is rather token, considering its global stature. The point here is that this low level of equity investment must mean that TOPP is still a significant source of profit. Yet, TOPP is rather insignificant compared to many other ventures undertaken by Paterson Zochonis Plc. This further plays down any real interests in direct socio-economic development of the Twifo area.

Pasico Elders International operates mainly in Europe, South-East Asia, Australia, Greece, Poland, Indonesia and Thailand as well as other countries in Africa. Like Paterson Zochonis, Pasico's main products are soaps, toiletries, edible oil, detergents, cosmetics, pharmaceuticals and confectionery. Others are packaging material, refrigerators and air conditioners, general merchandise and household goods. This organization also demands appreciable quantities of palm oil. Again, like Paterson Zochonis, its share of one per cent is still less than one would expect. The level of its investment is also a measure of the premium it puts on TOPP and further indication of the nature of this interest.

UniLever (Ghana) Limited is part of the global organization (UniLever, 1994). The parent company operates in countries across Western Europe, Central and Eastern Europe and North America. It also operates in other markets across Africa and the Middle East, Latin America, Central Asia as well as in East Asia and the Pacific. The group's principal activities are in a wide variety of food preparations, detergents, soaps and toiletries, specializing in chemicals and personal products. Like any company of global size, UniLever has been going through structural and strategic changes including mergers, acquisitions, joint ventures and terminations. It now consumes a more substantial share of TOPP's palm oil output. Before it directly acquired a share of equity investment, it used to be the major customer of TOPP's. Its further interest is also related to the lower prices of palm oil it enjoys. Indeed, the company stated in 1997 that: 'We acquired a substantial interest in oil palm plantations to safeguard raw material supplies and disposed of brewery and textile interests' (UniLever, 1997, p. 16). Indeed, by acquiring 50 per cent share in TOPP, UniLever (Ghana) may be on the way to taking over the company and adopting the corporate-level strategy of backward integration (Porter, 1998; Hill and Jones, 1995; Doyle, 1994). It has already taken control of Benso Oil Palm Plantation Limited in the Western Region. By this, UniLever would be able to control its source of supply as well as have much more stake in decision-making and management of TOPP. Its increased power in TOPP would also influence the price of palm oil in its favour (Porter, 1998; Doyle, 1994).

These trends are real in practice as they are in related regional theory. For example, Holland (1976a) has argued that classical economic theory is limited in including the influence of institutional factors, especially capital markets, on the spatial orientation of capital flows. Such theorization thus excludes social, cultural, political factors as well as elements, for example, relating to public taxation. In doing so, government tends to be a weak provider of leverage for development activities (Allen, Bachtler and Yuill, 1988; Holland, 1976a). Therefore, all other theories that have consideration for intervention contribute to providing a basis for the making of regional policy. Holland (1976b) further pointed out and emphasized a fundamental assumption in classical regional theory that regional inequality is self-correcting. In this perception, therefore, the focus is on the economic aspect of regional investment to the neglect of such elements as he pointed out in his other work (Holland, 1976a).

This argument faces a dilemma and irony of regional investment in capitalist economies. On one hand, the classical theory assumes that a certain amount of inequality acts as a 'dynamic' for self-adjustment. Therefore, unequal regional development is a necessary and contributing factor to the dynamic of growth. In relation to this, therefore, a greater and direct capitalist involvement in the regional development and investment activities in a Third World territorial region has to be managed with strategic caution.

On the other hand, the involvement of central government is essential in leveraging and supporting such developments in order to achieve a real amount of balanced development benefit for the target population. This also contributes to promoting the co-ordination between regional policy and regional planning, while providing more significant support for leveraging (Allen, Bachtler and Yuill, 1988). This kind of government attention too has the greater potential and reality to promote the achievement of environmental sustainability in having regard to both socio-political and environmental aspects of regional investment activities. While there may not be a direct causal relationship, leveraging through infrastructure creates an important condition for regional investment activities

(Allen, Bachtler and Yuill, 1988).

International capital tends to have an efficiency and commercial enterprise motive more than equity issues. It is the only way that hard results are attainable and returns on investment and recovery made. This is the reason why the investment activities should be more production-based and productive. These should also be robust and comprehensive enough to meet the multiple and widest range of regional planning and development objectives.

Summary

Effort has been made by the regional planners and advisory regional administrative structures in the Central Region to design various instruments for initiating the development process. These include an informal regional plan, strategic regional guidance for preparing the plans as well as one-off projects and multiple objective-based programmes. However, in absence of formal regional governance, including powers for policy formulation and formal statutory plan-making, all the available instruments remain informal and have not the same legal value and force as formal versions. The situation also has constraining effects on funding systems as the advisory administrative structures have not the financial resources to implement their programme and project proposals effectively. It also affects aspects of development strategy in implementing initiatives with multiple objectives for, say, depressed areas.

The introduction of rather wider regional programmes such as CEDECOM and TOPP are different in attracting external funding and investment. These have greater potential for inward investment. However CEDECOM kind of initiative is more ambitious in seeking to bring many organizations under its umbrella. Nevertheless, it illustrates the effort in trying to overcome the political difficulties involved in working with a rather advisory informal system of regional governance. TOPP illustrates one of the most practical instruments in developing a downward and transitional area such as the Twifo sub-region. The conflicts involved in defining the programme's range of objectives have been pointed out. There are various conflicts between the social and economic as between corporate and territorial-political forces. These also weaken the potential benefits to the target communities as well as their socio-political standing in the structure of the power relations.

6 Impacts of regional development policy on inter-local spatial-socio-economic disparities: trends in convergence and divergence

The aim in this chapter is to make an assessment of the impacts of regional planning and development policy on socio-economic and spatial disparities between the district localities in the Central Region. It must be emphasized that the analysis in this chapter, as in most parts of this book, is aimed at learning lessons from past trends and practices in regional planning in the Central Region. It is also partly intended to demonstrate various approaches to data analysis as part of policy assessment and project evaluation in regional planning.

Depending on the available data, the units of observation used are based on programme area districts of sector organizations, semi-decentralized or fully-decentralized jurisdictional districts. Full decentralization, in this context, means that the particular data set relates to the existing 12 District Assembly areas. The sector-based and inter-district changes, under the development policy impacts, are analysed in terms of disparities between various data sets and indicators. These relate to health facilities, road infrastructure, employment and unemployment, public capital expenditure and investment, public sector-initiated projects, community-initiated projects as well as urbanization (e.g. Allen, 1979).

An attempt is made to assess the trends in socio-economic and spatial convergence or divergence, as may be the case. This includes attempts at explaining the disparities in terms of the stated regional development policies as well as relevant constructs and historical contexts. In this relation, the issues of equity and regional growth are also addressed. Furthermore, the first of the two hypotheses stated in chapter three is tested.

The various ordinal, nominal and categorical forms of data are analysed as in chapter two. The principal objective is to do a comparison of the situation before (time T_1) and after (time T_2) the policy treatment for almost all the sets of data and selected indicators. The absolute values are transformed into z-scores which are then plotted in the form of various charts. The plotted z-scores are then interpreted in terms of change in categories of districts. Changes in the indicators or elements of the composite sectors are shown by the coefficients of variation and between localities with respect to the z-scores which are obtained from a 'transformation' of the original data. It must be stated that the z-score levels are arbitrarily set by the researcher. Despite the subjectivity there may be in this, an objective basis exists. The combination of techniques of standardization and measure of dispersion as well as percentages with categorical data is intended to provide greater objectivity and check. Further objectivity is achieved by the comparison between the results achieved in using the various techniques. Generally, the analyses cover the period 1960-1984, in particular 1970-84.

General urban-rural population structure and inter-local disparity

The inter-district population distribution is now analysed to identify the urban and rural orientation of the localities and to set a background to the rest of this study (Table 6.1). Therefore, only percentages are used (Ofori, 2000c). Data for 1960 are not included because these are not available. The available data show that the most urban districts in the Central Region in 1970 were Cape Coast, Awutu-Effutu-Senya and Agona with between 53 per cent and 73 per cent urban population. These three districts remained the leading urban localities in 1984 with between 53 per cent to 67 per cent urban population. By the 1980s, Cape Coast District had lost 6.2 per cent of its 1970 population and Awutu-Effutu-Senya District, 11.8 per cent of its 1970 level. The urban lead of these districts is due to historical factors by which they had 'luck' in taking off ahead of the rest of the region. This 'inertia of luck', generally, persists.

This loss of population in these two districts is more due to their having become more downward transitional and the lack of appreciable manufacturing activity. Another factor is the decline in the old cocoa trade (Dunham, 1977; Hinderink and Sterkenburg, 1975). A further factor is more likely due to out-migration. However, Mfantsiman and Ajumako-Enyan-Esiam Districts showed appreciable growth in population in 1984, both localities ranging between 35 per cent and 38 per cent. In-migration is most likely a factor behind these trends. This appears more valid, especially with the general growth in small-medium undertakings, distribution services, other commercial activities, administrative functions as well as other services in more recent times.

The expanding regional educational industry has also been partly centred particularly on Cape Coast and Awutu-Effutu-Senya Districts (Ofori, 1991a). Apart from a high concentration of local educational institutions, the localities also contain educational institutions of strategic national importance.

All the remaining districts were much more rural and had between 71 per cent and 91 per cent population in this regard. This pattern was maintained in 1984

Table 6.1 Central Region: urban-rural population structure by district, 1970-84

District	*1970*		*1984*	
	% Urban	% Rural	% Urban	% Rural
Cape Coast	73.1	26.9	66.9	33.1
Komenda-Edina-Eguafo-Abrem	26.1	73.9	29.1	70.9
Mfantsiman	28.6	71.4	35.7	64.3
Abura-Asebu-Kwamankese	11.4	88.6	22.2	77.8
Gomoa	13.5	86.5	16.9	83.1
Awutu-Effutu-Senya	65.1	34.9	53.3	46.7
Upper Denkyira	27.5	72.5	24.7	75.3
Lower Denkyira-Twifo-Hemang	0	100	0	100
Assin	9.2	90.8	8.4	91.6
Asikuma-Odoben-Brakwa	10.2	89.8	9.4	90.6
Ajumako-Enyan-Esiam	25.3	74.7	35.4	64.6
Agona	53.2	46.8	53.9	46.1
Whole Region	**28.5**	**71.5**	**28.8**	**71.2**

Source: Absolute data from 1984 Population Census data, Ghana Statistical Service, Accra

with minimal decreases in Ajumako-Enyan-Esiam, Gomoa, Abura-Asebu-Kwamankese and Komenda-Edina-Eguafo-Abrem Districts. Since 1984, all these other rural districts have ranged between 64 per cent and 92 per cent in population. It is clear that Lower Denkyira-Twifo-Hemang District has registered 100 per cent rural population in 1960 and 1984.

The data show that the Central Region has not fallen below 28 per cent nor been above 28.8 per cent urban population since 1970. In a similar situation, the rural population of the Region has not been less than 71 per cent nor been more than 71.5 per cent. This shows a trend of general 'stability' in the region's urban-rural population structure. Indeed, the Central Region, like many others in the country, is more rural-based as the population data show.

Disparities in health facilities

The data shown in Table 6.2 cover the early half of the 1980s when the public health sector was based on only four programme districts. The general quality of data indicated for 1980 and 1984 show the trend in the development of health facilities. There were higher values for doctor population, total nurse population and total hospital-bed population for both 1980 and 1984, with varying differences between the two time-points in relation to the indicators. It is more obvious that these were fewer facilities with respect to total number of hospitals,

Table 6.2 Central Region: health indicators by programme district, 1980-84

Programme district: 1980	*Total doctor pop.*	*Total nurse pop.*	*Total hospital-bed pop.*	*Total no. of hospitals*	*No. of health centres*	*No. of health posts*
Cape Coast	28	294	600	2	n.a.	n.a.
Winneba	5	217	145	1	1	6
Saltpond	3	67	90	1	n.a.	n.a.
Dunkwa-on-Offin	3	64	125	2	1	n.a.
CoV (%)	**125.2**	**71.1**	**100.5**	**38.5**	**0**	**0**
Programme district: 1984	*Total doctor pop.*	*Total nurse pop.*	*Total hospital-bed pop.*	*Total no. of hospitals*	*No. of health centres*	*No. of health posts*
Cape Coast	28	215	236	4	1	11
Winneba	5	170	149	1	1	8
Saltpond	3	64	91	1	n.a.	6
Dunkwa-on-Offin	4	49	125	2	1	2
CoV (%)	**120.3**	**64.9**	**41.2**	**70.7**	**0**	**5.9**

Source: Absolute figures from Ministry of Health, Cape Coast; Coefficient of Variation (CoV), author's calculation

number of health centres and health posts, with only minimal increases by 1984. These six variables indicate that the few public health providing centres were rather crowded with health workers and beds during the period. The absolute statistics show that Cape Coast and Winneba programme districts were in the lead, with Saltpond and Dunkwa-on-Offin vying for third position between 1980 and 1984. This limited pattern of socio-economic disparity is only characterized by a wide divergence.

The main dynamic, in this case, is historical and the case that subsequent administrative services in these main urban centres continued to function under the inertia created in colonial times. This situation also meant the continued concentration of resources within the centres of historical inertia in the post-colonial era (Kiamba *et al.*, 1990).

The coefficients of variation for 1984 indicate, generally, lesser dispersion than those for 1980. This confirms the observation made that the regional development policy objective of providing adequate health facilities showed, at least, an accretion of improvement over the situation in 1980. The multiple line charting of the z-scores of the data is presented in Figures 6.1 and 6.2. Two critical bi-polar levels are set for the scores: 0.0 to 1.5 and 0.0 to -1.5 being the limits of the plots. The lines are differentiated in terms of texture and annotated naming. In this way, the z-scores are used to identify categories of districts.

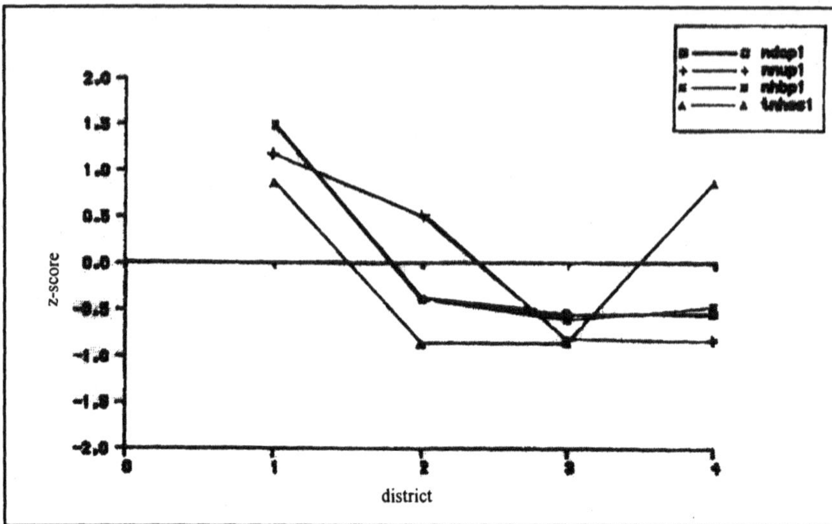

Figure 6.1 Divergent line chart of z-scores on health indicators, 1980

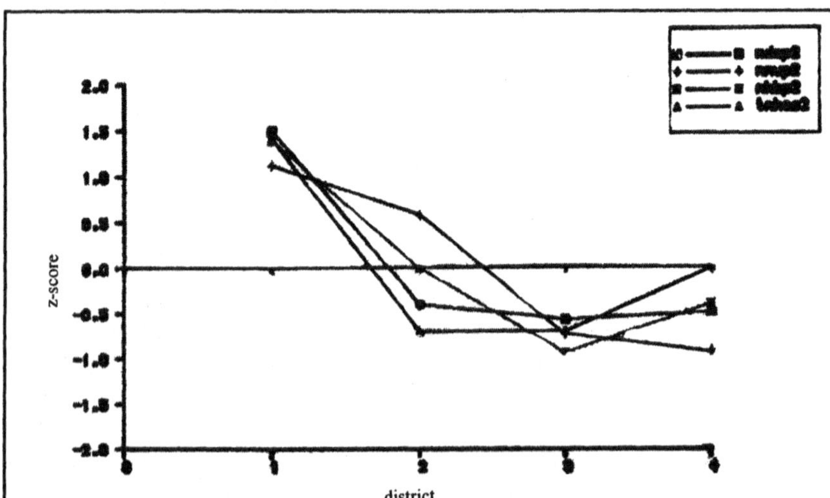

Figure 6.2 Divergent line chart of z-scores on health indicators, 1984

The chart shows the dominance of Cape Coast and Winneba programme districts, with Saltpond and Dunkwa-on-Offin in the second. The same pattern is maintained by the areas over the period. However, Winneba programme district placed higher in relation to the number of hospitals and number of hospital beds; Dunkwa-on-Offin declined on all indicators. Therefore, the line chart shows that there were no significant changes in 1980-84, apart from the minimal shifts between isolated indicators. In this sense, the pattern of divergence was maintained. Therefore, there was no significant attainment in terms of the regional development policy objectives. This is also an indication that the z-scores provide a more rigorous check on the sheer absolute figures.

By the middle to latter part of the 1980s, the four health programme districts had been loosened up into 9 jurisdictional district localities as shown in Table 6.3. The health indicators for the period 1985-88 show far greater dispersions. In 1985, there was much more variation with respect to total doctor population and hospital bed population in 1988. However, only indicators for the number of hospitals and number of health centres actually showed less variation. In this case, there was no aggregate regional change except with respect to these two indicators. Thus it is concluded, again, that the objectives of development policy were achieved only to a very limited extent. Nevertheless, the paucity of data also affects the results.

The interpretation of line charts for 1985-1988, as shown in Figures 6.3 and 6.4 is based on chosen z-score levels of 1.1 to 2.7, 0 to 1.0 and 0 to -1.0. In 1985, Cape Coast, Awutu-Effutu-Senya-Gomoa and Upper Denkyira Districts appeared in the top category. However, Cape Coast easily dominated in the group. Mfantsiman and Assin Districts were in category two. The remaining localities fell in the third category: Agona, Ajumako-Enyan-Esiam, Asikuma-Odoben-Brakwa, Lower Denkyira-Twifo-Hemang Districts.

A similar pattern was displayed in 1988. Cape Coast appears in the first category; the second category contains Awutu-Effutu-Senya-Gomoa, Mfantsiman, Assin and Upper Denkyira Districts. Category three includes Agona, Ajumako-Enyan-Esiam, Asikuma-Odoben-Brakwa and Lower Denkyira-Twifo-Hemang Districts. This pattern reflects the fact that the coefficients of variation for 1988 show wider dispersions for most of the indicators used. This indicates that there were greater inter-local disparities in the latter part of the 1980s. Therefore, there was no significant aggregate or inter-local change over the period and at the level. Once again, the main factors that explain this concentration are those of historical inertia and urbanization.

The analysis is supplemented with an earlier observation made on the morbidity situation of the Region (Ofori, 2000h; 1991a). This was based on variations in whooping cough, infectious hepatitis, malnutrition, anaemia, hypertension, respiratory infection, pregnancy disorders and skin diseases. The variations are very high at the aggregate regional level, reflecting the higher degree of

Table 6.3 Central Region: health indicators by district, 1985-88

Programme Area: 1985	*Total Doctor pop.*	*Total nurse pop.*	*Total hospital -bed pop.*	*Total no. of hospitals*	*No. of health centres*	*No. of health posts*
Cape Coast	28	n.a.	992	2	3	2
Mfantsiman	1	64	97	1	n.a.	7
Awutu-Effutu-Senya-Gomoa	3	160	119	2	n.a.	4
Agona	1	n.a.	n.a.	1	1	3
Assin	n.a.	n.a.	n.a.	1	n.a.	3
Ajumako-Enyan-Esiam	n.a.	n.a.	n.a.	n.a.	n.a.	3
Asikuma-Odoben-Brakwa	n.a.	n.a.	n.a.	1	n.a.	2
Lower Denkyira-Twifo-Hemang	n.a.	n.a.	0	0	1	2
Upper Denkyira	n.a.	n.a.	n.a.	2	2	5
CoV (%)	**168.1**	**60.6**	**153.3**	**56.6**	**54.7**	**46.9**

Programme Area: 1988	*Total Doctor Pop.*	*Total nurse pop.*	*Total hospital/ bed pop.*	*Total no. of hospitals*	*No. of health centres*	*No. of health posts*
Cape Coast	20	311	939	3	3	2
Mfantsiman	1	85	116	1	n.a.	5
Awutu-Effutu-Senya-Gomoa	3	132	182	1	n.a.	4
Agona	1	59	64	2	1	3
Assin	1	63	88	1	n.a.	4
Ajumako-Enyan-Esiam	0	37	17	n.a.	n.a.	3
Asikuma-Odoben-Brakwa	1	19	101	1	n.a.	2
Lower Denkyira-Twifo-Hemang	0	23	23	1	1	3
Upper Denkyira	2	97	142	2	1	2
CoV (%)	**197.4**	**98.5**	**154.7**	**50.4**	**66.7**	**33.9**

Source: Absolute Figures from Ministry of Health, Central Region, Cape Coast; CoV: coefficient of variation, author's calculation.

divergence and the poor provision of the health facilities (Ofori, 2000h; 1991a). In this aspect of the study, Cape Coast District dominated in terms of having the lowest rates of morbidity; Mfantsiman, Awutu-Effutu-Senya-Gomoa Districts appeared in the second group. The worst-off group included Assin, Ajumako-Enyan-Esiam, Asikuma-Odoben-Brakwa and Lower Denkyira-Twifo-Hemang Districts. However, Agona and Upper Denkyira Districts displayed a split standing in both the second and third categories. This categorization and ranking of districts is appreciable, similar to those produced in relation to Table 6.3. It still confirms the more urban districts are the favoured and still leading localities in this regard.

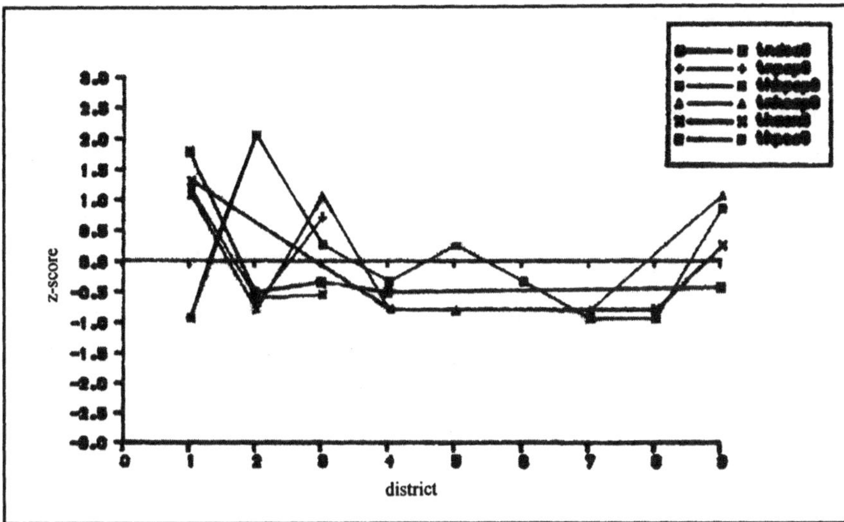

Figure 6.3 Divergent line chart of z-scores on health indicators, 1981

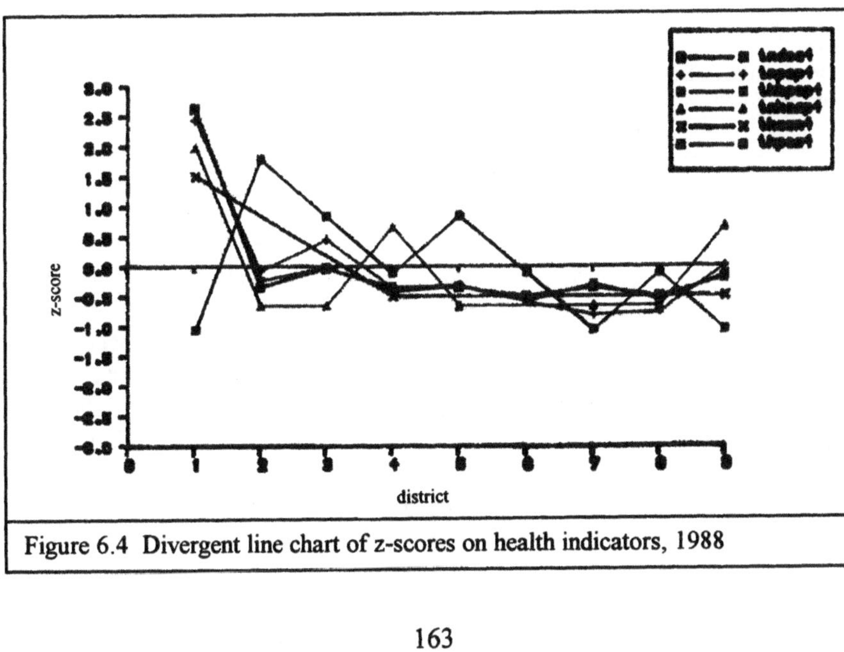

Figure 6.4 Divergent line chart of z-scores on health indicators, 1988

Disparities in road infrastructure

Feeder roads The available data on feeder roads cover the 1980s as indicated in Table 6.4. The absolute statistics show only relatively minimal provision in 1981 than in 1988. This is confirmed by the coefficient of variation which shows greater dispersion in 1981 for all the three variables than for 1988. It is a further demonstration of, yet, another regional aggregate change in terms of feeder road length, percentage district stock and feeder road length per 1,000 population.

Table 6.4 Central Region: feeder roads by absolute length, % total length, length per 1,000 population and by district, 1981-88

District	*1981*			*1988*		
	Road length (km)	*District % of total regional road*	*Feeder road per 1,000 pop.*	*Road length (km)*	*District % of total regional road*	*Feeder road per 1,000 pop.*
Mfantsiman	66.29	12.5	0.940	233.4	12.6	2.810
Cape Coast	15.0	2.8	0.186	39.0	2.1	0.426
Komenda-Edina-Eguafo-Abrem	32.0	6.0	0.445	124.0	6.7	1.510
Awutu-Effutu-Senya	133.96	25.2	1.580	187.6	10.1	1.960
Gomoa	20.60	3.9	0.167	299.7	16.0	2.080
Upper Denkyira	73.60	13.8	0.214	155.1	8.3	2.210
Lower Denkyira-Twifo-Hemang	29.85	5.6	0.329	214.8	11.6	2.090
Assin	74.80	14.0	0.640	385.7	20.8	2.910
Abura-Asebu-Kwamankese	9.0	1.7	0.080	22.9	1.2	0.179
Agona	12.80	2.4	0.110	41.5	2.2	0.310
Asikuma-Odoben-Brakwa	29.60	5.6	0.356	81.6	4.4	0.865
Ajumako-Enyan-Esiam	34.64	6.5	0.601	73.0	3.9	1.120
CoV (%)	**82.2**	**82.3**	**91.6**	**73.3**	**73.5**	**61.7**

Source: Department of Feeder Roads, Cape Coast; percentages and (CoV) coefficient of variation, author's calculation

The conclusion is that there is a generally positive development in relation to feeder roads in the Central Region. The trend of increase here illustrates the national and regional development policy aim of increasing rural accessibility, improving urban-rural linkages and facilitating the transport of regional products from producing to consuming areas. The coefficients of variation for 1981 range between 82.0 and 92.0 per cent. These show far less dispersion in 1988 for which year coefficients of variation range between 62.0 and 74.0 per cent and confirm the accretion of movement in the provision of feeder roads within the Region.

The identified z-score levels are 1.1 to 2.7, 0 to 1.0 and 0 to -1.5 as the fourth unit of observation is much higher above the others in the positive field of the chart (Figure 6.5 and Figure 6.6). It must be pointed out that the line graphs for district share of regional stock and feeder road length per 1,000 population closely coincide on the charts for both 1981 and 1988. Therefore, for the first z-score level in 1981, Awutu-Effutu-Senya was the leading District. The second category is taken up by Upper Denkyira, Assin and Mfantsiman Districts. Category three includes Cape Coast, Komenda-Edina-Eguafo-Abrem, Gomoa, Lower Denkyira-Twifo-Hemang, Abura-Asebu-Kwamankese, Agona, Asikuma-Odoben-Brakwa and Ajumako-Enyan-Esiam Districts. It is a bit unusual to find Cape Coast District, being the most urbanized locality, fall in the third category. This may be explained by the fact that this District depends relatively less on feeder roads.

Nevertheless, this analysis shows that the dominance-divergence structure still persists: only a few districts could be said to be well off, with the majority lagging behind in terms of the provision of feeder roads. The leading districts are those that are less urbanized than Cape Coast District. Indeed, the more rural localities tend to have more feeder roads. However, the relatively more urban areas still harbour significant rural parts that should be in greater need of feeder road infrastructure. In terms of the relevant regional development policy objective, therefore, it is concluded that there was a slim reduction in the disparity.

Highways The data on highways cover the same period, 1981-88, for almost all the localities, except two districts in 1981 (Table 6.5). In terms of the sole factor, road length, all absolute figures for 1988 show increases over those of 1981. This is reflected in the coefficient of variation which shows greater dispersion for 1981, 103.9 per cent, and lesser dispersion, 67.3 per cent in relation to 1988. Thus at the aggregate regional level there was a positive change during the period. In this case, the related objective of the regional development policy was achieved in a minimal measure as reflected in the increase in regional stock of highways.

The critical levels of z-scores chosen are 1.0 to 2.5, 0 to 0.5 and 0 to -1.0 as indicated by the behaviour of the districts in Figure 6.7. Data were not available for two of the district localities in 1981. Cape Coast as well as Mfantsiman Districts appeared in category one for 1981. The second category includes Asikuma-Odoben-Brakwa, Assin and Ajumako-Enyan-Esiam. The remaining districts are diverged in the third category. These are Komenda-Edina-Eguafo-Abrem, Awutu-Effutu-Senya, Gomoa, Upper Denkyira, Lower Denkyira-Twifo-Hemang, Abura-Asebu-Kwamankese and Agona. By 1988, this structure of districts had changed by an accretion. Category one, apart from Cape Coast and Mfantsiman, includes Awutu-Effutu-Senya. Category two contains Assin and Asikuma-Odoben-Brakwa Districts. Ajumako-Enyan-Esiam had dropped into the third category. The remaining ones in this group are Komenda-Edina-Eguafo-

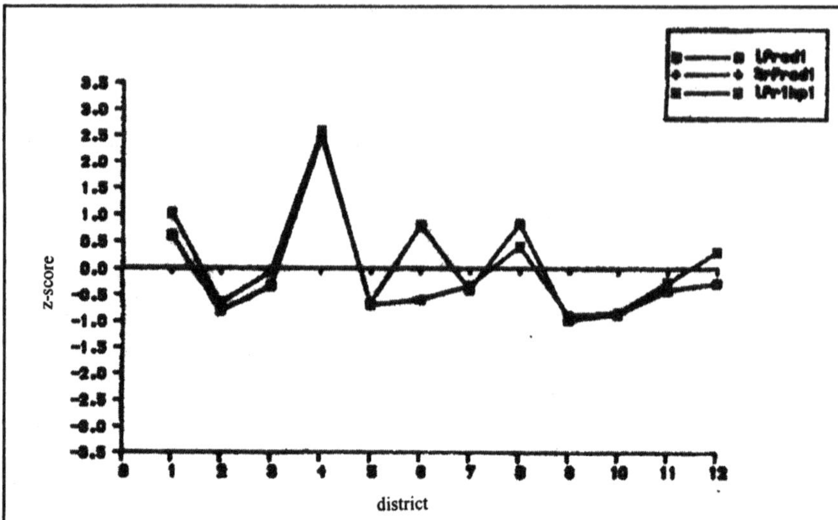

Figure 6.5 Divergent line chart of z-scores on feeder road indicators, 1981

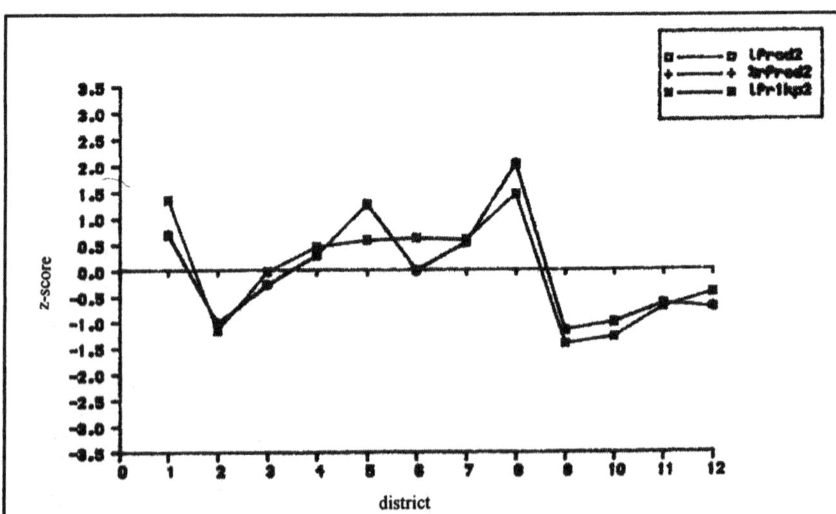

Figure 6.6 Divergent line chart of z-scores on feeder road indicators, 1988

Table 6.5 Central Region: highways by absolute length and by district, 1981-88

District	*1981*	*1988*
	Length of Highway	*Length of Highway*
Mfantsiman	86.6	155.6
Cape Coast	134.0	214.0
Komenda-Edina-Eguafo-Abrem	11.0	58.0
Awutu-Effutu-Senya	10.0	147.5
Gomoa	19.2	32.43
Upper Denkyira	33.6	54.8
Lower Denkyira-Twifo-Hemang	10.0	58.0
Assin	49.0	93.0
Abura-Asebu-Kwamankese	30.0	33.0
Agona	11.0	43.0
Asikuma-Odoben-Brakwa	n.a.	80.0
Ajumako-Enyan-Esiam	n.a.	60.0
CoV (%)	**103.9**	**67.3**

Source: Ministry of Roads and Highways, Cape Coast; Regional Economic Planning Office, Cape Coast; CoV: coefficient of variation, author's calculation

Abrem, Gomoa, Upper Denkyira, Lower Denkyira-Twifo-Hemang, Abura-Asebu-Kwamankese and Agona. This group of districts includes many of the more rural districts. However, the appearance of Awutu-Effutu-Senya in category one shows its better performance in 1988 than in 1981, in this regard. Nevertheless, the dominance-divergence structure is displayed, again, with the most urban districts maintaining the lead in this structure of disparity.

Although there was a regional aggregate change, this does not seem to have affected the relative position of the districts as at 1981, when 75 per cent of them were worse off. By the latter 1980s, 58.3 per cent of the districts were now worse off in relation to the provision of highways. This confirms a relatively minimal improvement in relation to this infrastructure. There is still dominance with the more urban districts in the lead. As in the case of feeder roads, however, it is argued that the highways are more typical of urban areas. Therefore, apart from the usual concentration of divergence in relation to the rural localities, the analysis of disparities in highways would still, without any bias, be against the position of the rural localities. Therefore, it is concluded that there was relatively less divergence and a minor fractional indication of a trend towards convergence. In this way, the indicated regional development policy objective was achieved to a slim-minimal extent. Such level of attainment, minimal yet, is still better than no achievement at all.

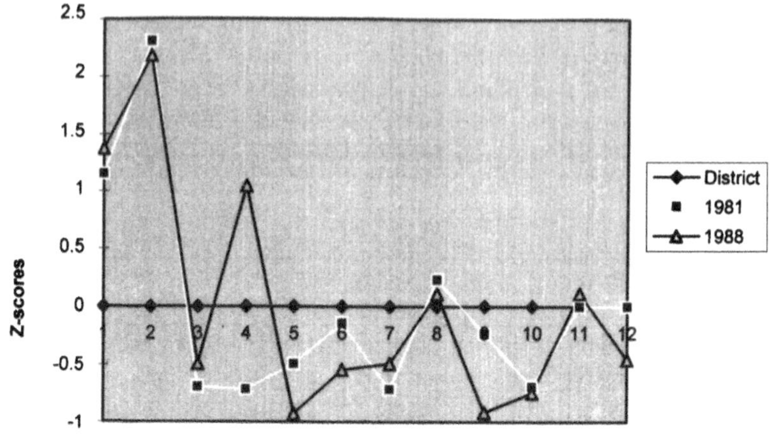

Figure 6.7 **Divergent line chart of z-scores on length of highways (kilometres), 1981 and 1988**

Disparities in employment

Employment by industry group Employment is one of the principal traditional indicators of regional economic growth as well as socio-economic development (Higgins and Savoie, 1988, p. 5; Armstrong and Taylor, 1985). The available data relating to employment by industry group are extracted from the 1984 population census and assembled in Table 6.6. As these are only cross-sectional, they only show structure instead of changes on a longitudinal basis. The coefficients of variation show very high dispersion for all categories of employment, in particular for agriculture-forestry-fishing; mining-quarrying; water works and supply. Others are paper products, recreation and cultural services. This means greater disparities between the district localities in relation to these sectors.

The structure of the inter-local disparity is shown in Figure 6.8. Only divergent bars, based on z-scores, are used in this case. Four critical z-score levels are chosen: 11.0 to 20.0, 0 to 10.0, 0 to -10.0 and -11.0 to -20.0. These relate to the behaviour of the bars in each part of the graph-field and create four categories of districts, altogether. The localities of Cape Coast, Agona and Abura-Asebu-Kwamankese fall into category one, in terms of the level of employment by industry. Category two contains Gomoa, Awutu-Effutu-Senya and Mfantsiman. The third category includes Komenda-Edina-Eguafo-Abrem, Assin, Upper Denkyira and Breman-Odoben-Brakwa. Category four contains Lower Denkyira-Twifo-Hemang and Ajumako-Enyan-Esiam.

Table 6.6 Central Region: employed persons aged 15 years plus, by industry and by district (%), 1984

Sector	*Cape Coast*	*K-E-E-A.*	*Gomoa*	*Awutu-Effutu-Senya*	*Mfant-siman*	*Abura-Asebu-K*	*Assin*	*Upper Denky-ira*	*Lower D-T-H.*	*Breman -O-B.*	*Ajuma-ko-E-E.*	*Agona*	*CoV (%)*
Agric., hunting, forestry, and fishing	5,901	19,232	42,348	22,344	15,490	33,338	44,056	19,962	37,764	30,615	19,841	34,205	131.7
Fishing	2,353	2,994	4,165	4,568	2,714	3,114	12	18	11	18	11	45	108.9
Forestry, logging	39	34	38	38	22	42	197	94	116	35	32	67	80.7
Mining, quarrying	66	212	185	14	46	45	22	1,111	9	8	2	5	217.5
Food Manufacture	2,283	2,043	1,826	1,952	2,056	4,315	932	914	503	1,098	911	2,471	57.9
Beverage, tobacco	135	96	127	57	340	218	247	145	142	151	94	198	47.7
Textile, weaving, leather	953	600	127	901	774	1,251	952	530	612	693	585	1,427	43.9
Wood products manufacturing	375	374	576	506	452	790	352	209	290	330	233	554	39.4
Basic metal industry	80	176	221	182	124	373	79	60	95	183	73	205	57.9
Electric, gas, steam	136	22	30	39	40	34	18	44	5	22	7	65	90.7
Water works, supply	317	26	17	45	59	47	9	98	10	24	14	88	144.3
Construction	1,403	623	533	615	571	658	311	270	204	232	183	458	66.1
Wholesale, retail, restaurant and hotel	9,362	7,139	10,342	9,788	9,780	11,234	2,995	2,927	1,971	3,039	2,114	8,675	55.6
Transport, storage and communication	1,097	477	1,166	719	795	1,059	586	716	330	596	417	1,287	40.8
Recreation, cultural services	243	76	45	64	30	66	22	39	5	47	17	128	99.4
Personal, household services	1,313	421	684	593	631	1,096	462	390	222	437	326	3,197	58.9
Manufacturing: paper and paper products	128	5	21	9	9	20	12	15	7	11	15	31	142.7

Source: Proportions based on absolute figure extracted from Ghana Statistical Services (1984), *Population Census Report*, Accra; CoV: coefficient of variation

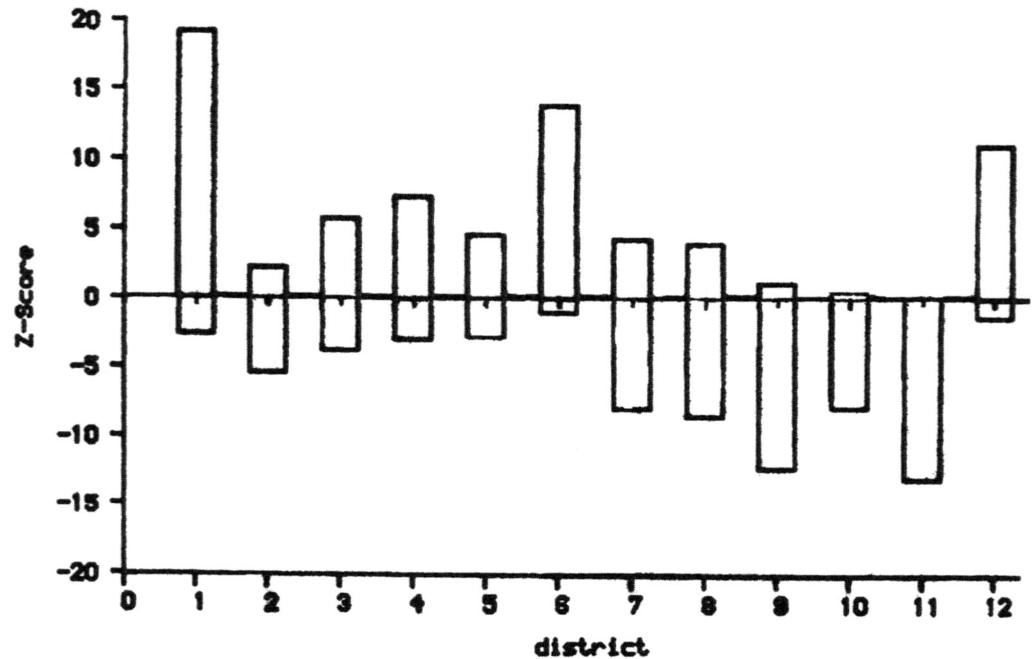

Figure 6.8 Divergent bar chart of z-scores on employment by industry, 1984

While two localities of the three in the first category are among the most urban-based in the Region, all four categories show a general mixture of both the urban and rural localities. This structure is not surprising since the top districts are more urban and have greater magnetic influence on employment. Gomoa and Awutu-Effutu-Senya localities which used to constitute one District, together, still appear in the same category. Once again, the position of Lower Denkyira-Twifo-Hemang reflects most of the observations made, so far, with respect to other aspects of intra-regional socio-economic development. Thus it has the least concentration of overall employment on the basis of industry group.

Employment by sector and programme district For the period, 1978-88, the available data are only based on programme districts of the Department of Employment as shown in Table 6.7. It must be stated that the data represent only persons reporting unemployed to the Department and gained employment through the same government organization. The Department was not decentralized at the time of the survey to allow the collection of data on the basis of political and administrative districts. The data covered five public sectors as well as the private sector of the regional economy.

The coefficients of variation relating to the 1978 data are fairly high, mostly in relation to industrial manufacturing and the private sector. In terms of both public and private sectors, the former is a far less developed component of the regional economy and show less employment in comparison with the primary sectors. However, there was lesser dispersion in the first four sectors for 1988, with greater dispersion for the construction and service industries. This is also reflected in the absolute statistics. Both levels of analysis show that there was greater disparity in relation to these two sectors in the late 1980s. Indeed, there was relatively more growth in service-based employment. This appears to continue to be the case as observed elsewhere (Ofori, 2000c). On the basis of all the data for 1978 and 1988, however, there was relatively more employment in the latter year than the former. This followed the introduction of the economic recovery and structural adjustment programmes which most likely accounted for the slight increase in employment.

Nevertheless, the general national trend in relation to industrial manufacturing sector is also reflected in the 1988 data when there was a decline in the sector, especially in relation to Saltpond and Komenda as well as Dunkwa-on-Offin programme districts. These rates of decrease have to do with the general cycles of retardation and decline. Nevertheless, these also typify and underlie the general lack of industrial manufacturing in the Central Region.

The charted z-scores are shown in Figures 6.9 and 6.10; the chosen levels are: 2.0 to 5.0, 0.0 to 2.0 and 0.0 to -2.0. For 1978, only Saltpond scored in the first category and with respect to industrial manufacturing. Effectively, however, it falls into category two with Assin and Dunkwa-on-Offin. Category three consists

Table 6.7 Central Region: employment by sector and by programme district, 1978-88

Programme district: 1978	*Public sector*	*Agric. sector*	*Industl. Manuftg.*	*Private sector*	*Con-struction*	*Services*
Agona Swedru	53	60	28	2	30	46
Assin Foso	14	35	11	7	32	129
Saltpond and Komenda	54	18	130	4	50	99
Dunkwa-on-Offin	94	59	25	14	21	102
Cape Coast	29	45	30	4	25	120
CoV (%)	**62.3**	**40.5**	**107.6**	**75.9**	**35.3**	**32.5**
Programme district: 1988	*Public sector*	*Agric. sector*	*Industl. Manuftg.*	*Private sector*	*Con-struction*	*Services*
Agona Swedru	60	38	28	3	63	112
Assin Foso	30	19	33	19	11	70
Saltpond and Komenda	58	44	71	10	91	121
Dunkwa-on-Offin	56	31	17	11	74	112
Cape Coast	30	24	56	6	60	253
CoV (%)	**32.9**	**32.5**	**58.6**	**61.8**	**49.9**	**52.1**

Source: Absolute figures from Department of Employment, Cape Coast; CoV: coefficient of variation, author's calculation

of Agona Swedru and Cape Coast programme districts. By 1988, none of the programme districts 'qualified' to enter the first category on the basis of the chosen z-score levels. The localities of Agona Swedru, Saltpond, Dunkwa-on Offin and Cape Coast fell in category two. However, Cape Coast and Agona Swedru Districts took on a split standing as they appeared in category three, together with Assin District. Therefore, there was no significant change in the categorization of districts with respect to the inter-local employment situation, but for two of the programme areas which show a slight relative movement. This analysis further demonstrates the structural-divergence nature of the intra-regional disparity.

Unemployment The data here are also discriminating with respect to the localities and useful in further showing the nature of the intra-regional disparity. By a 'converse approach', this relates to the role of general regional development policy in ameliorating the unemployment situation (Armstrong and Taylor, 1985; 1978). The data used for this purpose cover the period 1978-88 as indicated in Table 6.8 and Figure 6.11. The coefficients of variation shows higher dispersion for 1988 (31.5 per cent) than in 1978 (25.1 per cent). Therefore, the unemployment situation grew relatively worse in 1988 as reflected in the absolute figures for the two points in time. Apart from 1979 all the other years registered

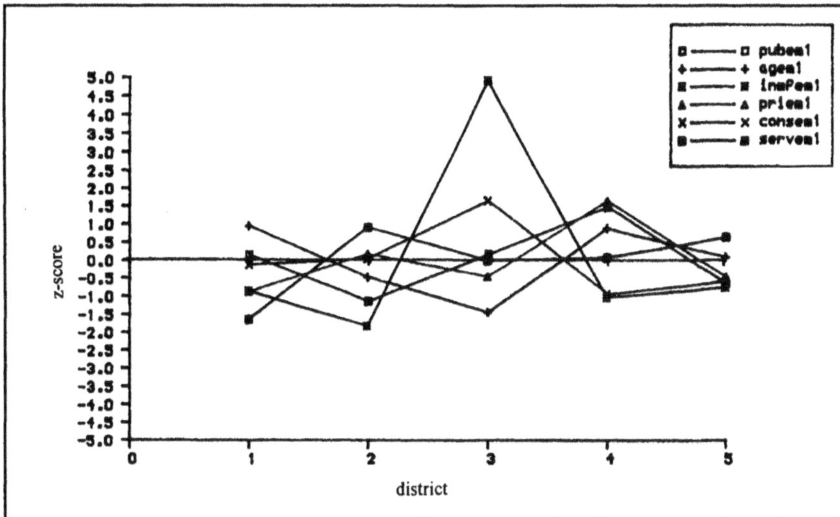

Figure 6.9 Divergent line chart of z-scores on employment by sector, 1981

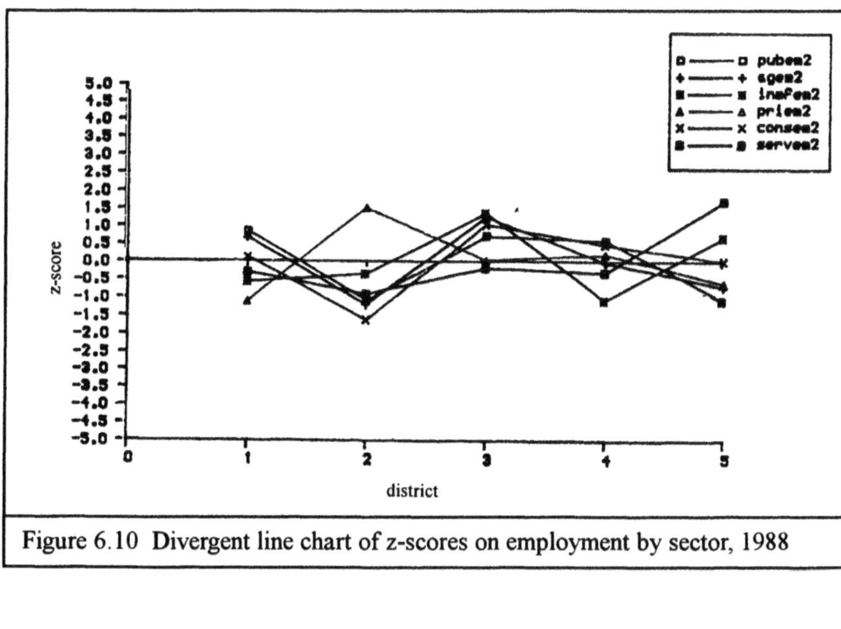

Figure 6.10 Divergent line chart of z-scores on employment by sector, 1988

values between 19.0 to 35.0 per cent with an oscillation in between.

Table 6.8 Central Region: registered unemployed by programme district, 1978-88

Year	*Districts*					
	Agona Swedru	Assin	Saltpond	Dunkwa	Cape Coast	**CoV (%)**
1978	3,329	2,014	2,804	3,786	4,000	25.1
1979	4,328	2,280	3,367	4,020	4,500	52.7
1980	3,907	2,369	3,401	2.987	3,800	24.4
1981	4,129	2,016	3,677	2,388	3,000	19.2
1982	3,820	2,088	3,676	3,708	2,900	29.8
1983	4,056	1,713	3,893	3,708	5,270	22.8
1984	4,156	2,254	3,893	3,303	3,269	34.4
1985	4,538	2,334	3,517	4,293	4,569	21.7
1986	3,258	3,707	3,715	5,131	5,330	24.6
1987	2,460	2,370	4,350	4,857	7,258	22.2
1988	3,624	2,467	4,145	4,840	6,020	31.5

Source: Absolute figures from Department of Labour, Cape Coast; CoV: coefficient of variation, author's calculation

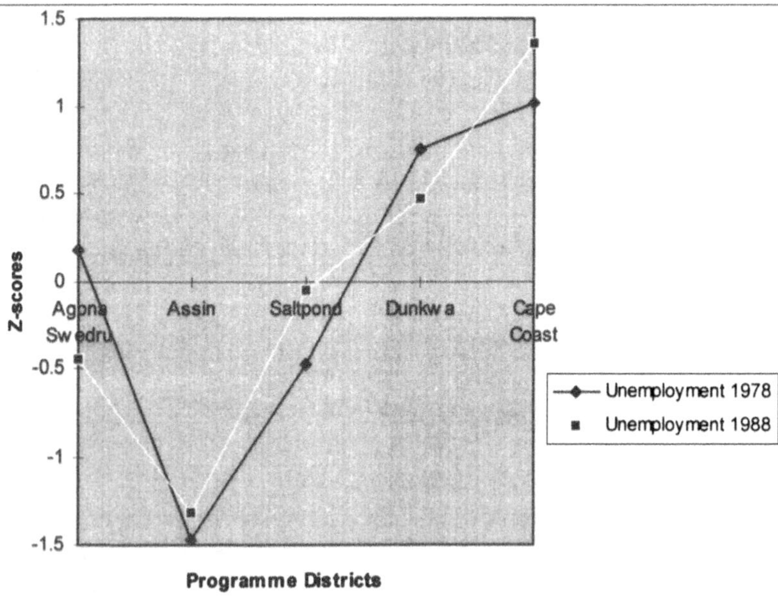

Figure 6.11 Divergent line chart of z-scores on unemployment, 1978 and 1988

The z-score levels chosen are: 1.0 to 1.5, 0 to 0.8, 0 to -0.6 and -1.0 to -1.5 as charted in Figure 6.11. An analysis of the chart shows that in 1978, Cape Coast and Dunkwa-on-Offin District fell in category one in this consideration. Agona Swedru District appeared in category two; Saltpond District in category three and Assin in category four. In 1988, Cape Coast District remained the leading locality in terms of unemployment, Dunkwa-on-Offin District had slipped into the second category; Agona Swedru District also fell into category three with Saltpond District. Assin District still remained in category four. The leading position of Cape Coast District is due to the fact that it has a relatively limited primary sector. It contains greater employment in non-primary activity, which when it declines indicates more unemployment. This also explains why Assin District, the most rural locality, remained in category four over the period.

Disparities in public expenditure and investment

Whilst serving as a substantive form of regional and local investment, public capital expenditure is also seen as surrogate regional income. Data on central government's capital expenditure relating to six sectors in the Central Region are shown in Table 6.9. The disparate nature of the coefficients of variation reflects the incomplete assembly of the original data. However, on the basis of the measure of variation, there was less dispersion in 1988 than in 1981 with respect to highways, health and to a slim-tendril extent, agricultural sectors. The other sectors of feeder roads, water supply and education show greater dispersion.

Nevertheless, on the basis of the coefficients of variation, the overall structure of inter-sector disparity still reflected the characteristic divergence by the latter part of the 1980s. This is also related to the nature of the data which is to a large extent incomplete. It took considerable effort to extract these from equally incomplete records of the Regional Planning Co-ordinating Unit (RPCU). The tables reveal the fact that a number of districts did not receive any capital expenditure and such investment at all. There was no data for other localities, despite whatever funds they had received from central government.

The z-score charting of the sector-based expenditure and investment are shown in Figures 6.12 and 6.13; the chosen critical levels are 1.5 to 3.25, 0 to 1.49 and 0 to -1.0. Cape Coast District is in the first category in terms of its 1981 data and scores on fifty per cent of all the indicators. Category two includes Mfantsiman, Komenda-Edina-Eguafo-Abrem and Awutu-Effutu-Senya Districts and scored on some 33.7 per cent of the indicators. Category three comprises the district units of Assin, Ajumako-Enyan-Esiam and Agona. The others are Lower Denkyira-Twifo-Hemang and Gomoa. These show a mixture of leading urban as well as largely rural districts. The structure of disparity did not change significantly in 1988, apart from minimal inter-category shifts. Cape Coast,

Table 6.9 Central Region: public expenditure and investment by sector and by district, ¢mill, 1981-88

District: 1981	*High-ways*	*Feeder roads*	*Health*	*Water supply*	*Agri-culture*	*Educa-tion*
Mfantsiman	29.9	2.4245	0	1.7663	2.544	0
Cape Coast	9.2	2.587	4.1714	8.6008	3.1305	39.9074
Komenda-Edina-Eguafo-Abrem	0.3338	4.0869	0.18	2.9811	1.6772	1.4199
Awutu-Effutu-Senya	0.213	8.3031	0.2698	1.8133	1.5537	5.3876
Gomoa	0.238	3.4096	0	1.0593	0.0222	0
Upper Denkyira	0	2.9171	0	0.036	0	0.7209
Assin	0	7.5703	0	1.2881	0	0.4798
Ajumako-Enyan-Esiam	2.8765	2.8765	0	0.38898	0	0
Abura-Asebu Kwamankese	0	2.1427	0	2.2018	0.095	0.9575
Agona	0	2.2814	0	4.2206	0.114	4.1414
Lower Denkyira-Twifo-Hemang	0	0	0	0.2239	0	0
Asikuma-Odoben-Brakwa	0	0	0	0.3948	0	0.9599
CoV (%)	**245.9**	**78.2**	**310.5**	**115.1**	**151.2**	**250.9**

District: 1988	*High-ways*	*Feeder roads*	*Health*	*Water supply*	*Agri-culture*	*Educa-tion*
Mfantsiman	225.94	216.14	31.618	195	37.738	18.2
Cape Coast	73.506	9.535	233.218	705	43.518	13694.9
Komenda-Edina-Eguafo-Abrem	0.709	44.188	0.360	184	366.85	139.7
Awutu-Effutu-Senya	4.775	55.028	64.687	92	161.69	1.4
Gomoa	178.965	214.55	2.413	43	161.69	1.4
Upper Denkyira	120.315	61.263	3.713	65	3.064	136.0
Assin	999.424	643.281	14.958	41	n.a.	1.3
Ajumako-Enyan-Esiam	4.924	20.176	12.4	44	n.a.	0.2
Abura-Asebu-Kwamankese	8.383	10.241	98.472	251	0.240	39.0
Agona	149.88	73.38	33.016	352	13.494	160.6
Lower Denkyira-Twifo-Hemang	70.84	306.439	n.a.	25	0.300	68.9
Asikuma-Odoben-Brakwa	42.208	41.789	n.a.	814.554	1.977	106.3
CoV (%)	**176.1**	**130.9**	**144.9**	**346.4**	**150.97**	**326.39**

Source: Regional Economic Planning Office, Cape Coast; CoV: author's calculation

Mfantsiman and Assin Districts now appeared in category one and scored on some 33 per cent of the indicators. Awutu-Effutu-Senya and Gomoa Districts are placed in the second and the other localities in category three. These are Abura-Asebu-Kwamankese, Lower Denkyira-Twifo-Hemang, Upper Denkyira,

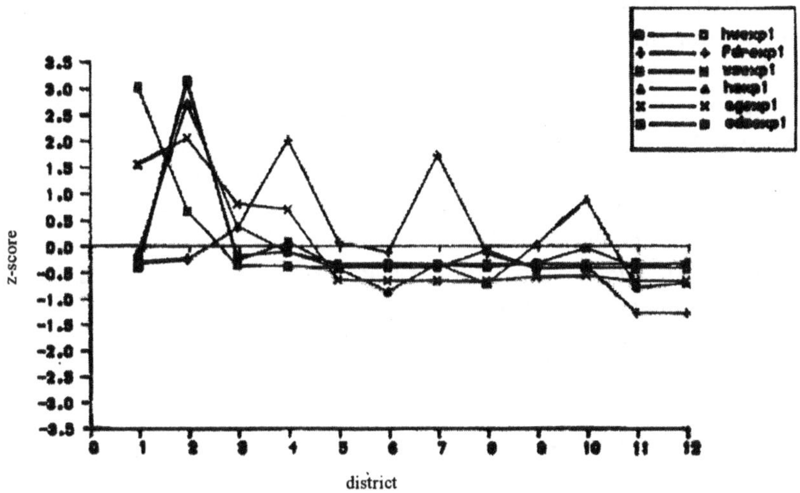

Figure 6.12 Divergent line chart of z-scores on public expenditure by sector, 1981

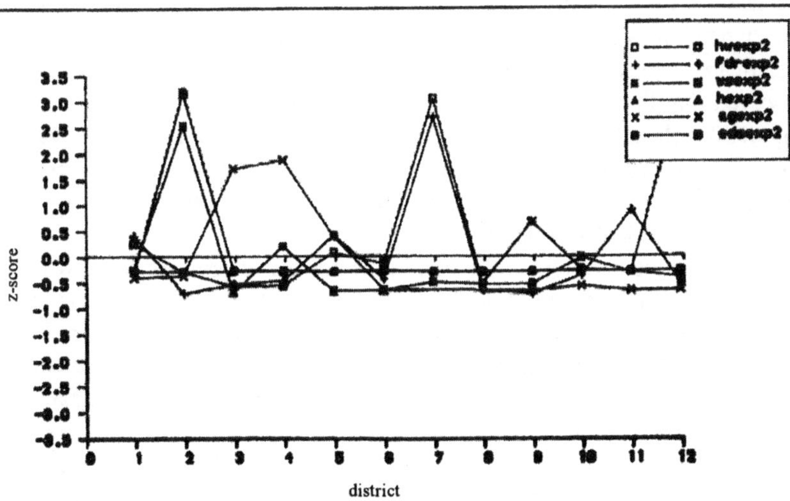

Figure 6.13 Divergent line chart of z-scores on public expenditure by sector, 1988

Agona, Ajumako-Enyan-Esiam, Abura-Asebu-Kwamankese, Komenda-Edina-Eguafo-Abrem, Asikuma-Odoben-Brakwa Districts. Once again, there is a mix of both urban-oriented and rural district localities in the category.

Therefore, it is concluded that there is a general dominance-divergence pattern depicted over 1980s with respect to the levels of public capital expenditure and investment. In this case, there was no major change over the period with respect to the public sector investment aimed at injecting social and productive infrastructure into the Central Region. Therefore, the achievement of the regional development policy objective, in this regard, was also much limited. Indeed, this issue of funding remains a challenging one in the territorial regional development process in Ghana as in many other Third World countries.

Disparities in public sector-funded projects

The number of projects per district over time is directly related to the level of public expenditure and investment dealt with already. Quite apart from indicating the number of sector-based projects, the data assembled in Table 6.10 also show the rate at which government has provided the necessary infrastructure and other facilities. The data relate to highways, feeder roads, water supply, health, agriculture and education.

The coefficients of variation show wide dispersion for both 1981 and 1988, in particular, relating to the agriculture and education sectors. These two areas show greater dispersion for 1988 than 1981, despite the appreciable and general increases in the number of projects in the latter part of that decade. Nevertheless, the dispersion is relatively less in relation to most of the six areas, indicating significant change in 66.7 per cent of the indicators used in Table 6.10. Thus it is observed that the trend shows that there was a minimal aggregate change at the regional level. In this regard, there was significant improvement in the number of public sector projects and an incremental achievement of regional development policy objectives. The quality and specific types of projects have not been indicated due to lack of relevant data.

The plotting of z-scores on the various sector-based projects are now presented in Figures 6.14 and 6.15. For the purpose of interpreting the line charts, three z-score levels have been chosen: 1.5 to 3.0; 0 to 1.49 and 0 to -1.5. For 1981, Cape Coast District appeared in category one with respect to 33 per cent of the indicators; category two consists of Mfantsiman, Komenda-Edina-Eguafo-Abrem and Awutu-Effutu-Senya. The third category is taken up by the other localities of Gomoa, Upper Denkyira, Assin, Ajumako-Enyan-Esiam, Abura-Asebu-Kwamankese, Agona, Lower Denkyira-Twifo-Hemang and Asikuma-Odoben-Brakwa. The same structural dominance in favour of the more urban localities, in particular Cape Coast District, is typified by the charts relating to 1981.

Table 6.10 Central Region: public sector projects by district, 1981 and 1988

District	*1981*						*1988*					
	High-way	Feeder roads	Water Supply	Health	Agriculture	Education	High-way	Feeder roads	Water Supply	Health	Agriculture	Education
Mfantsiman	2	3	0	6	1	0	15	32	16	99	16	8
Cape Coast	1	1	4	9	3	6	23	18	52	161	17	168
Komenda-Edina-Eguafo-Abrem	1	1	1	4	4	2	2	19	7	48	42	25
Awutu-Effutu-Senya	1	2	1	2	2	7	16	11	19	48	33	43
Gomoa	1	2	0	2	1	0	18	41	3	37	53	0
Upper Denkyira	0	3	0	0	0	1	33	23	3	16	8	32
Assin	0	8	0	0	0	2	37	74	20	48	7	10
Ajumako-Enyan-Esiam	0	1	0	0	0	0	1	13	17	16	1	0
Abura-Asebu-Kwamankese	0	1	0	3	3	1	7	5	22	60	9	16
Agona	0	0	1	1	1	4	51	14	22	64	9	25
Lower Denkyira-Twifo-Hemang	0	0	0	0	0	0	17	20	0	12	1	5
Asikuma-Odoben-Brakwa	0	0	0	1	1	0	5	26	0	27	4	12
Total	**6**	**22**	**7**	**28**	**23**	**23**	**225**	**296**	**181**	**636**	**200**	**344**
CoV (%)	**134.8**	**124.5**	**199.6**	**108.5**	**92.6**	**133.7**	**81.1**	**74.2**	**96.2**	**79.2**	**101.8**	**159.8**

Source: Regional Planning Co-ordinating Unit, Cape Coast; CoV: coefficient of variation, author's calculation

The data for 1988 also show the dominance of Cape Coast District as it scored on 50 per cent of the indicators for the first category. Category two, for the latter part of the 1980s, includes Mfantsiman, Awutu-Effutu-Senya, Assin and Agona Districts. All other districts fall in category three. These are the mostly rural localities of Komenda-Edina-Eguafo-Abrem, Gomoa, Upper Denkyira, Ajumako-Enyan-Esiam, Abura-Asebu-Kwamankese, Lower Denkyira-Twifo-Hemang and Asikuma-Odobeng-Brakwa. However, Mfantsiman also appears, for the other 50 per cent of the indicators in this category. Therefore, it also has a split standing but it is left in category two because it has greater presence in the positive component of the graph-field. Overall, 33.3 per cent of the districts appeared in category 2 as against 25 per cent for 1981 and 58.3 per cent of the districts for category three as against 66.7 per cent for 1988. The minimal inter-category shifts imply that the affected localities have either become better or worse-off as the particular case may be.

Therefore, it is concluded that that the dominance-divergence structure is still typified. The minimal shifts in the categories of localities do show relatively better performance of the individual districts affected by these. However, with respect to the achievement of the general objectives of regional development policy, there is no significant change. The results achieved in these analyses also have their limitations originating from the imperfection of the data used. Again,

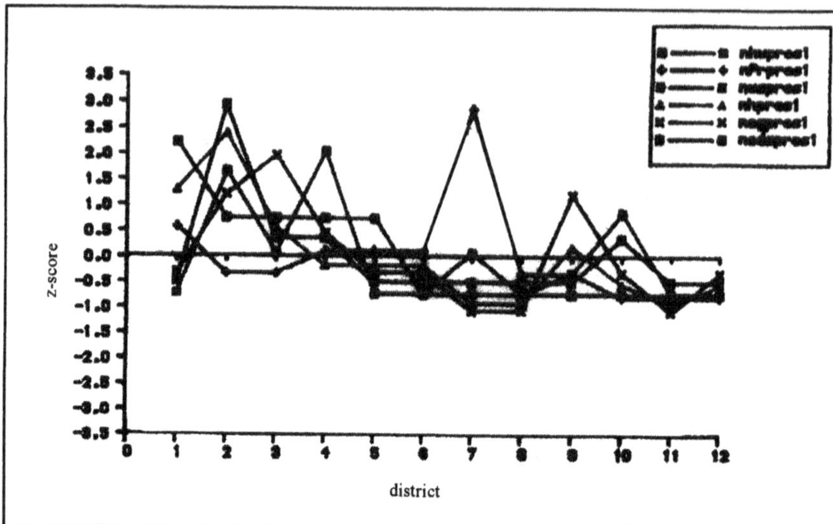

Figure 6.14 Divergent line chart of z-scores on number of public sector-based projects, 1981

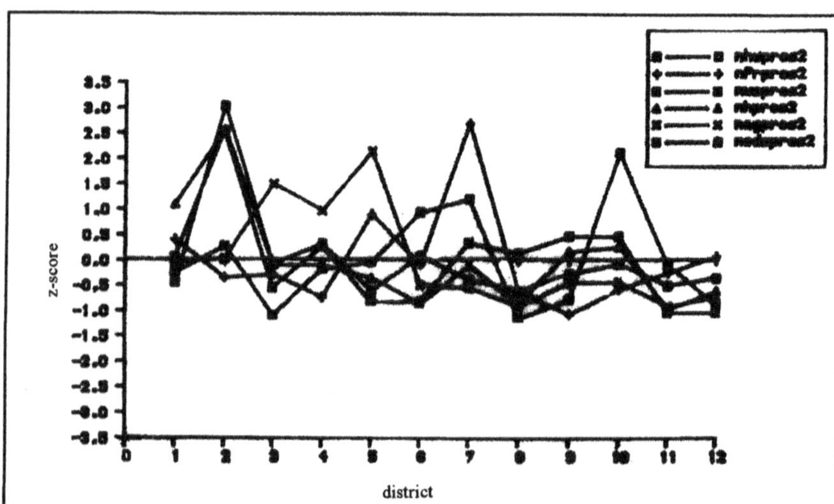

Figure 6.15 Divergent line chart of z-scores on number of public sector-based projects, 1988

it took much effort and arduous search to collect data from the records of the Regional Planning Co-ordinating Unit.

Despite the slim and minimal improvement in central government's project funding, the financial input is still limited in bringing about a real reduction in the inter-sector disparity. There is a close relationship between the categories of districts achieved in the analyses relating to public capital expenditure and the numerical standing in public-sector projects. The only minor difference is between the first and second categories in both cases. In either case, Cape Coast District and the leading urban districts are in the top categories, with the generally more rural localities in the third groups. This is reflected in part of the assumption underlying one of the hypotheses stated in chapter three.

Disparities in local community-initiated projects

Regional development initiative in the Central Region, as in other regions of Ghana, has been led and driven by the public realm. Indeed, private sector and local community initiative have not been accorded the same recognition. This has meant that the analyses of regional development policy impacts on socio-economic well-being in the past have been based solely on the public sector activities. This attitude has also meant a weak, if not lacking public support for the private sector and for the local communities to emerge as real forces in the process of regional planning and development.

For example, studies of small-scale industrial activity undertaken by the present author indicate that this vigorously growing and local economic force barely receives any recognition from local, regional and central government (Ofori, 1994; 1981). If the public effort is itself insufficient as sounded through the analyses and arguments, so far, this gaping absence of private sector and local community efforts further limit the development effort and effective achievements of the regional planning policy goals (Ofori, 2000c).

However, Table 6.11 provides some fragmentary information on what territorial communities can achieve on their own initiative. Figure 6.16 shows a charting of the absolute distribution as well as percentage of total cost and investment, consolidated for the 1981-88 period, based on only nine district localities. Data were not available for the other three districts in the Region. For the purpose of analysis, three categories of total investment levels are chosen in lieu of z-scores. Category one is over ¢15 million; category two, between ¢4 million to ¢7 million and category three less than ¢4 million. On this basis, Mfantsiman District made the highest investment in community development initiatives; Cape Coast District was second in this regard. The third category includes Upper Denkyira, Assin, Komenda-Edina-Eguafo-Abrem, Asikuma-Odoben-Brakwa, Ajumako-Enyan-Esiam and Lower Denkyira-Twifo-Hemang Districts.

Table 6.11 Central Region: community development projects, 1981-88

Item	*Cost of Projects:* ¢*million*	%	*Project and Operation*	*Site and Settlements*	*Initiators*
Mfantsiman	15.865	38.1	School buildings culverts, community centre, hand-dug wells, KVIPs*; Improved school facility; improved public sanitation	Egya and Ekurabadze, Anomabo, Mpeduase, Ekumfi, Abor,	Local community;
Cape Coast	4.995	12.1	School blocks, hand-dug wells, KVIPs:	Enyinasin, Apewosika, Ewim, Akotokyere	Local community; health post; local school
Komenda-Edina-Eguafo-Abrem	2.585	6.3	Nursery centres; KVIPs	Elmina, Brenu, Akyinu	Church; local school
Upper Denkyira	3.500	8.5	School blocks	'Agona Port'	Improved education facility
Lower Denkyira-Twifo-Hemang	7.000	17.0	Health Post	Frami	Local community
Assin	3.500	8.5	School block	Basofi, Ningo	Local community
Breman-Asikuma-Odoben-Brakwa	1.945	4.7	Hand-dug wells	Amoanda, Supunso, Sowutuam, Asabiam, Wansa-biampa, Enyinahu, Etuaduadu, Asikuma	Local community
Ajumako-Enyan-Esiam	1.770	4.3	KVIPs	Enyan Obonster	Roman Catholic Church
Awutu-Effutu-Senya	0.025	0.06	Hand-dug wells	Department of Animal Husbandary	Department of Animal Husbandary

Source: Author's tabulation from various records of the Department of Community Development, Cape Coast; *Kumasi-Ventilated-Inverted-Pit system of human waste disposal

While it is seen as part of category three, Awutu-Effutu-Senya made the least investment of 0.6 per cent of the total investment made by all the nine districts. Apart from Ajumako-Enyan-Esiam which is 35.4 per cent urbanized, on the basis of the 1984 census data, all the other districts in category three are the more rural localities. The case of Cape Coast trailing behind Mfantsiman may be an indication that the most urban centres are not necessarily those of the highest rate and level of community-initiated developments.

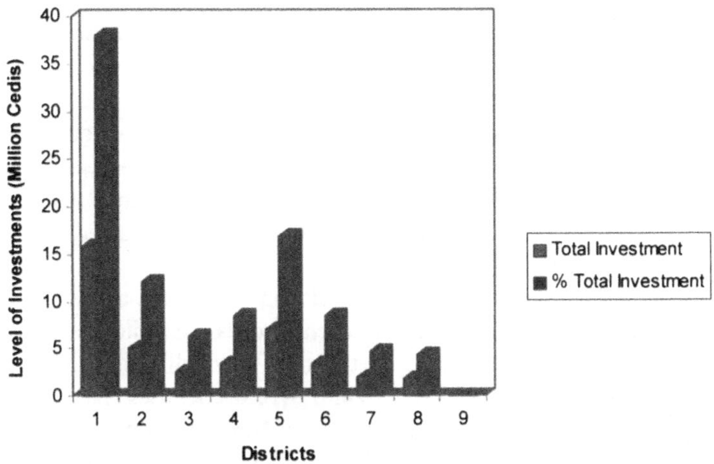

Figure 6.16 **Bar chart of number and percentage of community-initiated development projects, 1981-88**

Nevertheless, the aggregated data for the period 1981-88 do indicate that the local communities, on their own initiative, do constitute a significant source of development initiative which makes a real and differentiating contribution to the public sector efforts within the localities. Indeed, the community-induced initiatives in Table 6.11 include improved school and day-care facilities; improved facilities for human waste disposal; improved water supply and quality; improved health facilities; improved street drains and provision of a community centre. These are reflected in the regional planning policy and development objectives as stated and analysed in chapter five. Interviews held with community development officers in the Central Region indicate that all the projects had been completed and were in operation. Therefore, these local communities have the potential to contribute effectively and immensely to the overall regional planning effort in the Central Region as in the other regions.

Disparities in intra-regional urbanization

The evolution of the regional space economy in the regions of Ghana, as in many Third World countries, has been characterized by the persistent existence of a multitude of small and medium settlements (Ofori, 2000g; Ofori, 1991; Ofori-Cudjoe, 1990). The structure of settlements also includes a host of small and large rural villages. These systems of human habitats create a non-articulated and inefficient spatial system. Thus there is need to recognize and focus on the development of both urban and rural settlements within the national development policy framework. It is also part of the policy goal to integrate urban-rural economies and improve the linkages therefrom. The relevance of these has also been pointed out in relation to the theoretical constructs reviewed in chapter three and noted elsewhere (Ofori, 2000h).

The theoretical views underline the consideration that the urban settlement is a critical factor in the regional development process, despite the defects in the 'urban-industrial' approach. In fact, the role of small and medium towns in regional development, especially in Third World countries, has been receiving increasing attention in planning policy and urban development research (Ofori, 2000h; Weaver, 1989; Hansen, 1988; Rondinelli, 1987; 1983b; Hardoy and Satterthwaite, 1986; Linn, 1979). Therefore, the number of recognised towns and the level of urban population is closely related to intra-regional socio-economic change, due to the impact of general public policy thereon as well as private sector initiatives (Harris, 1992; 1990). Another point is the fact the dominance of the more urban districts has been demonstrated throughout the inter-district disparity and between-sector analyses.

National development policy is aimed at strengthening the role of human settlements by the promotion of action to improve on the quality of the rural-and-urban built environment. Within this framework, regional development policy in the Central Region is aimed at generating growth and service centre functions of the urban centres as well as renewal of these settlements (Ofori, 2000h). These policy considerations make the urban centres more attractive, congenial as well as functional for the population both within it and in its surrounding territory (Ofori, 2000g). Most public policy has been focused on services and productive activities and bound up with the development of urban centres (Harris, 1992; 1990; Hardoy and Satterthwaite, 1986).

Further, the case can be supported by the argument that regional development is often seen in 'peripheral terms' because the urban sector is blamed for the disparities between regions. But a case has been made for the effective role of urban centres as they always lead in productive and socio-economic life (Harris, 1989). At any rate, the level of urban development and population growth reflect the general level of socio-economic development and the growth or decline of the national-regional space economy (Hardoy and Satterthwaite, 1986). These discussions and cases underpin the relevance of analysing the disparities in regional urbanization in terms of changes in population growth.

For this aspect of the analysis, total district urban population for 1960 to 1984 as well as the number of towns and their populations within the districts are used. The coefficients of variation in Table 6.12 show that there is less dispersion in relation to 1960 with respect to inter-district urban population growth. The values dropped from 83.5 per cent in 1960, 80.9 per cent in 1970, to 76.1 per cent in 1984. This implies a relatively slim decrease in the inter-local disparity in urban population within the Central Region.

Table 6.12 Central Region: urban population change, 1960-84

District	*1960*	*1970*	*1984*
Cape Coast	41,200	51,700	57,224
Komenda-Edina-Eguafo-Abrem	12,800	17,400	22,257
Mfantsiman	15,300	17,700	27,670
Abura-Asebu-Kwamankese	14,500	10,100	26,542
Gomoa	17,400	17,500	22,700
Awutu-Effutu-Senya	39,100	46,900	47,700
Upper Denkyira	12,700	15,400	16,905
Lower Denkyira-Twifo-Hemang	0	0	0
Assin	5,300	7,200	10,425
Asikuma-Odobeng-Brakwa	5,400	6,900	8,270
Ajumako-Enyan-Esiam	7,500	13,000	21,553
Agona	43,600	49,200	66,120
CoV (%)	**83.5**	**80.9**	**76.1**

Source: Absolute statistics from 1984 Population Census Preliminary Report, Central Bureau of Statistics, Accra; CoV : coefficient of variation

Actual trends in the urban population growth are now shown in Figure 6.17. The line chart shows the structure of four sets of districts. The leading localities in urban population growth are Cape Coast, Awutu-Effutu-Senya and Agona Districts over the three census periods, 1960-84. The next set includes Komenda-Edina-Eguafo-Abrem, Mfantsiman, Gomoa, Abura-Asebu-Kwamankese and Upper Denkyira. The third category consists mainly of Assin and Asikuma-Odoben-Brakwa Districts; Ajumako-Enyan-Esiam straddles between the second and third categories of districts as its 1984 population increased significantly from 15.3 per cent in 1960 to 35.4 per cent in 1984. However, in terms of its 1960 and 1970 growth, it remains largely within the second category of districts. The fourth category is easily taken up by Lower Denkyira-Twifo-Hemang District. The absence of urbanization, in terms of the population data from 1960 to 1984 in this district has been firmly established in the discussions and analyses, so far.

Therefore, the line chart in Figure 6.17 sorts out the range of districts within the Central Region from the most rural to the most urban on the basis of population over the three census periods. This trend may well be reflected in the recent population census which took place in the first half of this year in Ghana. It is most likely that Lower Denkyira-Twifo-Hemang District has, since 1984, shown real evidence of urbanization. Processes related to and underlying this observation will be pointed out in chapter seven.

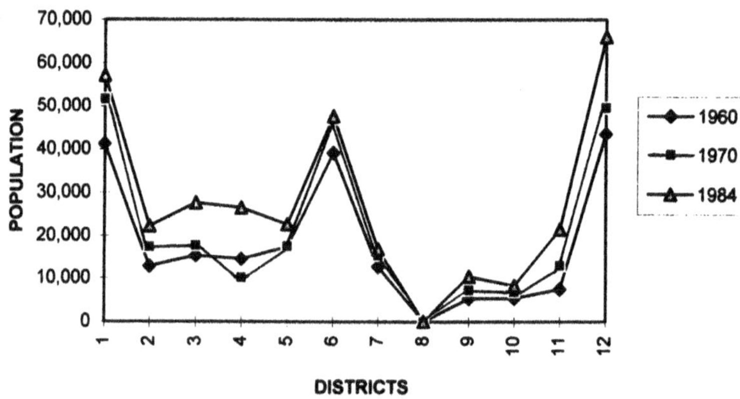

Figure 6.17 **Line chart of regional urban population, 1960-84**

A more critical issue is the change in the number of settlements, in particular towns. Table 6.13 shows the number of small, medium and large towns on district basis. For general statistical purposes, the small town has a population between 5,000 and 9,999; medium-sized town between 10,000 to 19,999; large town between 20,000 to 49,999. In a similar way, a large-sized village is defined as one with population between 2,000 and 4,999 and small rural villages with population below 2,000. The data in Table 6.13 show that the number of small towns remained the same in 1960, 1970 and 1984, that of medium towns grew from 5 to 11 over the same period. As for the large-sized town, only the regional capital qualified to be and remained the sole one over the period.

As demonstrated elsewhere, this shows that medium-sized towns have been growing faster than the small-sized ones in the Central Region (Ofori, 2000g; Ofori-Cudjoe, 1990). The highest concentration of all towns was in the Mfantsiman, Abura-Asebu-Kwamankese and Awutu-Effutu-Senya Districts with three towns each by 1984. However, between these three districts, there were five small-sized towns and four medium-sized ones.

Table 6.13 Central Region: level of urbanization by district, 1960-84

District	*Level of urbanization*									
	1960			*1970*			*1984*			
	ST	*MT*	*LT*	*ST*	*MT*	*LT*	*ST*	*MT*	*LT*	*Total*
Cape Coast	-	-	1	-	-	1	-	-		1
Komenda-Edina-Eguafo-Abrem	1	-	-	1	1	-	1	1	-	2
Mfantsiman	1	1	-	1	1	-	2	1	-	3
Abura-Asebu-Kwamankese	2	-	-	-	1	-	2	1	-	3
Gomoa	2	-	-	2	-	-	-	2	-	2
Awutu-Effutu-Senya	2	1	-	2	1	-	1	2	-	3
Upper Denkyira	-	1	-	-	1	-	-	1	-	1
Lower Denkyira-Twifo-Hemang	0	0	0	0	0	0	0	0	0	0
Assin	1	-	-	1	-	-	-	1	-	1
Asikuma-Odoben-Brakwa	1	-	-	1	-	1	-	-	1	1
Ajumako-Enyan-Esiam	1	-	-	2	-	-	2	-	-	2
Agona	1	-	-	2	-	-	2	-	-	2
Total	**13**	**5**	**1**	**13**	**7**	**1**	**13**	**11**	**1**	**25**

Source: Count made from 1984 Population Census statistics, Preliminary Report

This trend is now applied to all settlements as indicated in Table 6.14. On the basis of this consideration, there were six large villages in 1960, three in 1970 and none in 1984. It is suggested that all the large villages grew into small towns or decayed. In fact, a number of large villages in 1960 grew into small towns by1984. These include Komenda, Mankessim, Abura Dunkwa, Brakwa, Bobikuma, and Agona Nsaba (Ofori, 1991a). There were 13 towns in 1960, increasing to 14 by 1970 and then decreased, again, to 13 in 1984. As pointed out already, the medium town is the fastest growing type of settlement as shown in Table 6.14. There were five of these in 1960, seven in 1970 and eleven in 1984. For example, the following small towns grew into medium ones between 1960 to 1984: Elmina, Moree, Mumford, Apam, Senya Bereku, and Assin Foso. However, one settlement, Tantum, changed from a small town in 1960 to a large village in 1970 and then regressed into a small town by 1984, on the basis of its population changes. However, small villages - with population below 2,000 - are still preponderant. Table 6.14 shows that there has been only one large town, Cape Coast, since 1960. As the regional capital town, it is the only town-size of its type. The small and medium towns together grew from 72 per cent of the total number of towns in the Central Region in 1960 to 84 per cent in 1970, and to 96

Table 6.14 Central Region: structure of settlement change, 1960-84

Level of urbanization	*1960*		*1970*		*1984*	
	No.	*%*	*No.*	*%*	*No.*	*%*
Large town	1	4	1	4	1	4
Medium town	5	20	7	28	11	44
Small town	13	52	14	56	13	52
Large village	6	24	3	12	nil	0
Total	**25**	**100**	**25**	**100**	**25**	**100**

Source: Personal tabulation

per cent in 1984. This confirms the observation made with respect to the rapid growth in number of small and medium-sized towns in the Region.

It has also been demonstrated elsewhere that there has been a greater rapid growth in the number of medium-sized towns in the Eastern Region as for the Central Region (Ofori, 2000g). It is also generally typical of the trend in the other regions of Ghana. On the basis of this general trend in the evolution of towns in the Eastern Region and particularly in the Central Region, it is hypothesized that small villages tend to grow into large ones which in turn grow into small-sized towns, then into medium-sized ones; the process may not always be a unilinear one. This would require a separate and specific study to confirm.

The main dynamic driving this trend of rapid growth apart from the basis of population, is the general increase in small-scale undertakings. In view of the fact that the period 1970 to 1980s coincided with the worst times in the national economic decline, it is suggested that these local individual and community-driven undertakings have managed to stay the times.

Aryeetey (1989) has pointed out the deterioration in general infrastructure in the fabric of small and medium-sized towns, particularly over the period of national economic decline. While he also pointed out the fact that medium-sized towns are driving the territorial urbanization process, he argued that the decrease in the growth of these settlements is due to the lack of government support in terms of continued investment. Aryeetey (1989) puts overwhelming emphasis on the limited or lack of support from central and local government, especially in terms of social, economic and technical infrastructure. In fact, he emphasized the point that whenever government failed to create the necessary services and activities, these small and medium towns declined in growth and development. This is seen, in particular, in terms of what Aryeetey (1989) describes as 'modern government activity', say in the introduction of forms of local governance and decentralized political administration. He also argued that the activity or inactivity of government has actively encouraged and, on occasions, induced social as well as economic relations in the towns. Therefore, any change in the level and rate as well as effectiveness of the government activities have a reciprocal effect on the functions and structures of the towns.

While the public sector provision of the necessary infrastructure is crucial leverage for local settlement development, it is not that pervasively sufficient dynamic for positive change in these towns. In fact, it has been pointed out that many of these local human habitats manage to stay the more difficult times of economic decline and that local private effort largely accounts for the success of the towns in doing so (Ofori, 2000g; 1994). The public sector-provided infrastructure is, certainly, critical to leverage and local economic take-off. While this does not usually come through private sector initiatives, however, local urban growth processes do not necessarily and largely depend on the availability of the various forms of infrastructure.

Aryeetey (1989) also emphasizes the fact that there is greater rate of growth in non-basic or residential activities in the small and medium towns. Simultaneously, it is noted that there has been a failure to develop the basic sector (Aryeetey, 1989). The growth in services tends to be more associated and correlated with the initial provision of basic infrastructure and the creation of administrative functions. Therefore, the initial government support does create a critical level of leverage for development processes. However, as emphasized elsewhere by the present author, the real impulses and processes of growth have promise in production-based than service-oriented activities (Ofori, 2000g; 2000c; Ofori-Cudjoe, 1981). It is also in relation to these that the role of the private sector, especially the small-scale industrial undertakings, is critical. In this connection, therefore, whatever public leveraging or other support would better promote the private sector-based undertakings (Ofori, 2000g; 2000h).

Aryeetey gives rather less emphasis to the role of the local private sector and individual as well as community-based efforts in the process of small-and-medium town development and growth. Contrary to the views he presents, the small firm in the intermediate towns managed to stay the times. This is an indication of their capability to cope and ability to provide significant sources of local urban development and growth (Ofori, 2000g; 1994; Thomi and Yankson, 1985). There is need to study the start-up and failure rates of these small enterprises (Ofori, 1998). This also promotes the awareness of the need to diversify the economic base of the small and medium towns (Ofori-Cudjoe, 1990). In this connection, the crucial importance of the agro-industrial basis for driving the production-based activities is also emphasized (Ofori, 2000g; Thomi and Yankson, 1985). A further benefit in this lies in the creation of effective inter-activity linkages within the small and medium towns (Ofori 2000g; 1994; Thomi and Yankson, 1985; Ofori-Cudjoe, 1981).

Indeed, the failure of capitalist development in colonial Ghana, notably the neglect of industrial development contributed to the lack of consideration for the small and medium towns, especially in the territorial regions. As pointed out in chapter one, these aspects continued to characterize national development policy in the early post-colonial times. This residual problem has persisted and becomes particularly apparent when government support systems, if any, fail to deliver leverage and other services in these towns. It is also due to the fact that the private and local community sectors have not been actively encouraged to make an effective contribution to the development of small and medium towns. These also emphasize the fact that the contribution of the private sector has not been given due recognition in the territorial urban development process.

The intra-regional analyses have also shown that the urban districts continued to head the dominance-divergence structure in relation to almost all the sets of data throughout the periods under consideration. In the case of aspects such as feeder roads, the fact that the infrastructure is much more provided in the rural localities limits the 'urban lead' in a minimal way. Therefore, there is need for an active policy of urbanizing the periphery. Nevertheless, there tends to be only minimal shifts between sets of districts, especially between the third and second categories, in relation to many of the data sets analyzed. Moreover, there is a consistent concentration of the more rural localities in the third category in almost all the cases. Nevertheless, the minimal inter-category shift does indicate the possibility that with consistent and continued investment and management of inter-local change, this socio-economic and spatial shift between the districts would be enhanced and promoted.

For example, in terms of the total number of rankings achieved per locality, the leading ones are, dominantly, the three most urbanized areas of Cape Coast, Mfantsiman, and Awutu-Effutu-Senya Districts. The second set of districts, on the basis, includes Assin, Agona and Abura-Asebu-Kwamankese. The third category of districts, with respect to the total number of rankings based on the data sets consists of Upper Denkyira, Lower Denkyira-Twifo-Hemang, Asikuma-Odoben-Brakwa, Ajumako-Enyan-Esiam, Komenda-Edina-Eguafo-Abrem and Gomoa Districts. The second and third categories of districts contain both urban and rural districts. This structure confirms the observations made already.

On the basis of the total rankings of all the sectors and data sets analysed, the ordering of the sectors are as follows: urban population, employment, highways, public capital expenditure and investment in the first set with relatively less disparities. Feeder roads and health facilities fall in the second set with relatively more disparities. The third set of sectors includes public sector-based projects and community-initiated projects with the highest level of disparities.

Convergence and divergence

The crucial question to answer now is why there has been such a persistent structure of disparity between the district localities as well as sectors within the Central Region. This underlies the argument on why there has continued to be divergence more than convergence (Schatzl, 1988). Indeed, there has been rather slim or negligible reduction in the intra-regional polarization, especially in relation to feeder roads. In almost all the data sets considered, the majority of districts falls in the worse-off categories. This means that they have become more disadvantaged in terms of the specific indicators used. Although the available data do not cover the whole period over which regional planning has been practised in Ghana, it is not likely that the emerging picture of socio-economic and spatial disparities would have been different.

An attempt is made to further explain this trend in the contexts of the views of the regional planners and the national planning consultants who were interviewed as well as the policy and theoretical constructs. According to the national planning consultant, this structure of intra-regional disparity is primarily due to the weakening of regional planning in design and practice. For example, it has been pointed out in chapters one and five how policy formulation and plan-making are not permitted, yet, at the regional level. This is also reflected in the weak political empowerment for regional planning. Therefore, the lack of a critical instrument of planning such as the regional plan has meant that initiatives have been undertaken largely on one-off and uncoordinated basis. Thus project implementation has also been disparate and inconsistent.

On its own as a substantive issue and as part of the practice, there had been no formal regional development policy nor strategic guidance. Indeed, the regional planners interviewed in the Central Region also pointed out the fact that regional planning has been non-executive and has lacked the context of formal governance to make formal policies and plans. According to the planners, this limitation also includes the lack of clarity of policy objectives and focus as well as the setting of targets. The regional planners also emphasized the point that the lack of formal making of regional development plans limits the opportunity for clearly expressing and implementing the regional policies.

Another explanation and the flipside or consequence of the one stated already is the practice of a formidable and sector-based policy-making; the emphasis has been on sector-based planning. Unfortunately, this has been characterized by ineffective co-ordination as well as weak communication between sector-based institutions. A further limitation relating to these is that of ineffective decentralization. The net effect of these inter-connected constraints is that resources tend to be concentrated within certain sectors as well as some localities, thus increasing and sustaining the various disparities.

Another valid explanation pointed out by the planning consultant relates to the nature of development projects and related aspects of the planning process. In relation to the limitations stated already, development initiatives amount to a listing of 'civic works', especially as, for example, indicated in the public investment programmes (e.g. Government of Ghana, 1987a). These are conceived, perceived and designed in the one-off format creating a culture of project planning that only seriously undermines effective co-ordination. This also undermines the potential and possibility of regional plan-making while it bolsters up the sector-based approach to socio-economic development. The consequence of this scenario is the entrenchment of the intra-regional disparities.

Moreover, the practice of the Regional Tender Board also contributes to structural-divergence situation. This is now the sole agency for approving regional projects, allocating funds and awarding the contracts for development to selected developers. According to the regional planners, the Board has no planning sub-committee and there has been the tendency for it to prefer particular sectors. Whatever project selection criteria used, therefore, the Tender Board has been making decisions in favour of sector-based and favoured-area development. A more detailed study of the functioning of the Board would be useful in shedding more light on the situation in relation to the impacts of its decisions on regional disparities. Nevertheless, the regional planners pointed out that these decisions have also contributed to the structural-divergence nature of the socio-economic and spatial disparities.

A further factor that explains the nature of the intra-regional disparities is the lack of effective regional project and programme evaluation. Sector-based practice poses an obstacle to the undertaking of such evaluation within the context of clear regional policy. While the objectives of the individual sectors are aimed at, the relations between sectors is not given due recognition. This denies regional planning of a regionally-based evaluation that would provide more valid information about project performance for further decision-making and action. Therefore, this contributes to limiting the determination of intra-regional disparities and effectiveness of the action aimed at reducing these.

Another explanation is based on the fact that there is no established methodology or an agreed *modus operandi* for identifying the regional problem. The regional planners did indicate how they identified depressed areas in terms of specific criteria in relation to the socio-economic outline, consumer levels and values of the target populations. However, this only applies to specific areas and not region-wide. Therefore, the lack of a region-based practice for clearly identifying regional problems in a balanced and co-ordinated way also contributes to the limited nature of the actions aimed at reducing the disparities.

Related to these forms of explanation and as highlighted in chapter one, is the historical inertia of intensified export commodity extraction and associated concentration of investment. It must be emphasized that the investment, in this, is itself polarized in space as well as between sectors. Indeed, the emphasis on the production of export commodity has been so pervasive that the territorial source is only important, in time and space, to the extent that the resource extraction can be undertaken. For example, the Twifo locality used to produce 10 per cent of national total cocoa output. Apart from the fact that the road infrastructure was poor, the area became depressed with the demise of the cocoa production as a result of the epidemic of pest attack. Thus producers had to destroy their plants by either cutting down or burning. It is only in recent times, with the introduction of 'modern' oil palm production that the area is being generated in terms of socio-economic and spatial development. This is only an isolated case in the national territorial space of Ghana (e.g. Songsore, 1979; Dickson, 1969). The regional planners in the Central Region confirmed that the area's depressed state had partly resulted from the demise of the cocoa economy, prior to the active introduction of oil palm cultivation. Therefore the social and basic needs aspects of poverty would be relatively more dominant and over longer time-scale.

The planners also pointed out the fact that the lack of formal and fully statutory regional planning also limits and constrains the participation of the local community in the planning and development process. As pointed out already, this includes the ineffective recognition for and promotion of individual as well as community-induced initiatives at the very local level (Ofori, 2000c). In the same way, private sector undertakers have not been given effective recognition. If this had happened, local initiative would have been an effective bottom-up development strategy. Certainly, this would have made an appreciable contribution to reducing intra-regional disparities.

A further explanation for the observed disparities is based on the way in which the vast resource potential of the Region is exploited. It was pointed out in chapter one that the Central Region has some mineral deposits, including gold, diamonds and other resources. One aspect of the problem here is the lack of a sustainable and appropriate technology to exploit all these resources. For example, the salt industry is not modernized to enable greater and efficient production. The same applies to the fishing industry which does not include a fish-processing plant in the Region, for example. The point is that if these resources are fully exploited and production effectively organized, the initiative would create substantial income, employment and socio-economic development that would also ripple out through the Region. This means that consistent and substantial investment has to be made in making things happen. Therefore, this is tied up with the availability of inward investment funds. While the scenario relating to this with respect to the public domain is a challenging one, it also reinforces the case for supporting local communities and the private sector to make effective contributions to the regional development effort.

The level and structure of the disparities can also be explained with respect to the lack of efficient and effective management of development projects and programmes. The factor of management is, for example, imbibed in the explanations relating to planning practice and the one-off nature of the development projects. It is also reflected in the absence of strategic resource development practices based on appropriate and sound technologies. Dunham (1977) has also pointed out the vital function of regional planners as managers. It was further noted in relation to the Harrod-Domar model and the other constructs how effective and quality management is a necessary condition for successful regional development. Indeed, the level of ineffectiveness of the regional planning practice and processes in reducing socio-economic and spatial disparities includes the absence or vitiated form of management practices. This will be further elaborated in chapter eight.

Furthermore, an ideological conflict in regional planning has also contributed to the trend of structural divergence. There is a conflict between social-distributive justice and populist values on one side and functionalist-capitalist practices on the other. The pervasive concern with 'efficiency' issues and selectively concentrated extraction of export commodity as well as development, therefore, creates the lopsided emphasis on economic aspects of the process. In this connection, the socio-cultural aspects tend to be left in the background and only grafted on, if at all, at some point in time. Therefore, there is the need for committed and consistent balance in the engaging dimensions of socio-economic and spatial development.

Equity versus growth

Bound up with the issue of convergence-divergence is that of equity versus growth. The urban-industrial approach to regional development is based on the notion of efficiency for growth; the alternative approaches stress more on equity. These two are often in conflict with each other. The macro-economic policies being pursued in Ghana now are fundamentally efficiency-oriented, and they have serious attendant equity problems as indicated in chapter four. Therefore, while socio-economic and spatial disparities may not be extirpated, the question of whether there can be equity with growth is important. This is also critical to answering the question as to whether poverty is being reduced and to what extent this is taking place or has been achieved.

It has been demonstrated that the same functional-urban-based structure leads and drives the disparities within the Region. This has been shown in terms of the few urban-based districts leading the remaining localities which are also more rural-based. The same situation has been noted with respect to sectors of the space-economy. In the case of urbanization, the majority of settlements is in the small and medium town categories which are also mostly in the 'lagging' districts. Therefore, it is concluded that the individuals, groups and communities in these more territorial localities are also less well off. It is also argued, by inference, that they have been growing poorer. It is strongly suggested that the lack of basic infrastructure in the poorer localities as well as policy to ensure that the resident populations are in rewarding and viable productive activity also limits the achievement of equity and poverty-reduction (Rao, 1978 p. 392; Logan, 1972). This puts emphasis on the private sector, including community initiative and less pervasive dependence on the public sector.

Indeed, the local community involvement illustrates the urgent importance of three qualitative aspects of making things happen in the territorial region. These include the spirit of initiative and attitudes of individuals and groups of which the former are part. In fact, this attitudinal aspect drives members of the community to be interested in their own development and the well-being of their neighbours. Attitude also underlies the perception of individuals and groups in the community by which they assess their environmental conditions and aim at changing them for the better. Third, the two aspects fuel up a spirit of co-operation and, in particular, partnership in the process of socio-economic development (Ofori, 2000a). The awareness and consciousness involved in all these also feed on individual and group experiential learning. Therefore, community spirit and initiatives, attitude, perception and partnership are crucial elements in the process of regional development.

The experience of Korea in poverty reduction is instructive. That country has successfully combined rapid growth with improved and enhanced equity. Crucial in this success story is the role of employment-generation with its multiplier effects. In fact, it has been seen as the principal generator of income for the poor and poorest in society. This growth was achieved through a distinctive and expanding labour-intensive manufacturing production with a highly active involvement of the private sector (Harris, 1986; Rao, 1978). However, the type of employment distinguishes between the highly and specially skilled and others that are not so demanding.

This labour-intensive manufacturing became the driver of equity. By this means, there was a drastic reduction in income inequalities between the rich and poor. The process also included substantial and effective achievement in distributive justice, with emphasis on meeting basic needs of the poor. This was done through direct public provision of leveraging infrastructure as well as organizing communities for self-initiated development activities. The latter included the construction of dams, building of roads and factories that were managed by the community.

Other elements of the Korean experience in reducing absolute poverty are through fiscal transfers and taxation and public subsidies. In the case of Ghana, under the structural adjustment and recovery programmes, subsidies are not encouraged. Fiscal transfer and taxation are indicated in the national development policy matrix and depend much on political decision-making. A critical element in the Korean case is the drastic reduction in its population growth rate.

By all the means and strategies, Korea succeeded in achieving substantial reduction in poverty and polarization-reversal between groups of people and places. While the capitalistic aspects of this experience may not exist in Ghana, it is the view, here, that production-based activities in the small and medium towns hold a promising alternative. The relevant details of the case of Korea and other

Third World countries are exemplary with respect to the poverty-reduction measures (Balogh, 1978; Rao, 1978; Griffin and Khan, 1978). In fact, Griffin and Khan (1978, p. 303) have argued that the remedy to alleviating poverty:

> lies in structural change, in changing the distribution of productive wealth (and consequently the distribution of economic power) and in increasing the participation of the poor in decision-making (and consequently enabling them to exercise political power).

This book is as concerned with the impact of regional policy on intra-regional socio-economic and spatial development as it is with economic growth therein. (Harris, 1986; Rao, 1978). While it may be said that some growth has been registered at the national level, this is not necessarily so within the regions. The claim by Aryeetey (1987) that intra-regional disparity has grown less rapidly, meaning more trends towards convergence, is not supported by the present analysis. The shifts between categories of districts and sectors do not show that any appreciable convergence is taking place. Indeed, it has been demonstrated that the more inter-regional growth and development there is, the less of it there is, if not in its worse form, at the intra-regional level (Stohr and Todtling 1977; Williamson, 1975). This implies more socio-economic disparity occurring at the latter. Nevertheless, the minimal achievement at the local community level indicates a potential for delivering through the initiatives therein.

The fact also remains that the very nature of the space-economy is characterized by this 'atrophied' distribution or occurrence of human settlements. It has already been implied that the lack of a comparable urban base in the peripheral regions is one of the factors behind their levels of disadvantage and deprivation. Therefore, in order to achieve relatively 'fair' equity with growth, an articulated settlement hierarchy is needed, especially for small, medium towns and village settlements. Quite apart from the substantial investment in infrastructure that central and local governments would have to make, there is need for clear identification of the productive activities to serve as the basis for economic growth (Ofori, 2000g; 2000c; Harris, 1986; Rao, 1978).

Testing hypothesis I

The analysis in this chapter has provided evidence in support of the observations and conclusions made. These are further reinforced by testing the first of two hypotheses stated in chapter three. This is done by the use of the technique of analysis-of-variance, Anova. Basically, this answers the question as to whether the variation between or among the districts in the Central Region as well as sectors of the space-economy is significantly greater than one would expect to see, given the amount of variation within the districts.

Variation is seen in terms of socio-economic impacts brought about by the implementation of public programmes and projects and the community-induced initiatives aimed at developing the localities. This has been measured in terms of specific indicators. The rankings of districts based on the plots of the z-scores as well as those derived from the other charts are used as a basis for ranking the districts. For example, if district 'A' appeared in category one with respect to time T_2 for health, that district is given the rank of 1 and so on. Time T_2 rankings are used because they are based on the more recent data. Rankings relating to data sets based on programme districts are not used as the individual and isolated localities are not indicated, yet contained in jurisdictional areas.

The calculated F value is 69.2 at 95 per cent significance level with $V_1 = 7$; and $V_2 = 88$. The critical F value is 2.10. Therefore, the null hypothesis is rejected in favour of the alternative one which states that intra-regional socio-economic and spatial disparities in the Central Region have continued to favour core-urban localities and isolated sectors. The other aspect of the alternative hypothesis is that there has been no reduction in divergence; the level and rate of convergence in socio-economic and spatial development have been consistently maintained. Therefore, this supports the observation that it is only by substantial and sustained investment in the social and productive infrastructure in the disadvantaged areas will real and greater regional development occur. The assumptions underlying the hypothesis are thus borne out. In addition, it means that the policy implications pointed out in chapter two also hold as will be discussed in chapter nine.

Summary

A number of data sets have been analysed to demonstrate the structural divergent nature of the policy-related aspects between the districts and sectors of the space-economy in the Central Region. The sets of data relate to health facilities, feeder roads and highways, employment and unemployment levels. Others are public expenditure and investment, public sector-based projects, and local community-initiated projects as well as inter-local urban population statistics. The charted z-scores as well as other charts are effective in showing the structure and trends in the disparities between districts. The coefficient of variation is equally effective in measuring the changes relating to the various sectors.

The results show consistent structural-divergent disparities between the districts as well as sectors. The three main urban-based districts have continued to dominate the other nine localities with respect to almost all the sets of data analysed. Most of the districts remain in the last category achieved in all cases. The same applies to the sectors with two of them leading the others. Only minimal shifts in categories of districts and slim reductions of disparities between the districts and a specific sector emerged. The data relating to disparities in urban population and number of towns as other settlements also showed that the medium-sized towns are the fastest growing settlements in the Central Region. It was pointed out how this had also been demonstrated for the Eastern Region.

The reasons that explain the observed disparities relate to the form of regional planning practice and the limited breadth of the democratic enterprise in social and economic functions as well as political-participatory terms. Another factor is the lack of formal regional governance to enable the statutory regional planning process. This is related to the fact that the current regional administrative and functional planning structures do not include the formulation of policy and plan-making. Others relate to the unutilized resource base of the Region; the lack of investment to enable this, at all. Besides, the greater concern with issues of 'urban-industrial', efficiency-driven and economic-based development which is after all sector-led conflicts with the socio-cultural aspects of regional development. Therefore, the ineffectiveness of planning programmes and projects also accounts for the trend of structural and consistent divergence. The losers are the territorial communities and the regional development process.

Apart from the reflective observations made on the results, the first hypothesis was also tested. This has provided further confirmation of the observations made. Therefore, this aspect of the study has produced two main sources of evidence in support of the conclusions made on the nature of the intra-regional disparities. Thus the assumptions underlying the hypothesis as stated in chapter three have been confirmed. These all imply that the objectives of the regional development policy as presented in chapter five have not been achieved in any significant measure, overall. However, the indication is that it is possible to achieve this if only the investment from both public and private sector sources are sustained. The process would also be promoted by placing it within the context of a fuller and formal planning practice and effective management.

7 Evaluating impacts of the Twifo Oil Palm Plantation and agro-industrial development programme

In the context of the regional planning policies and TOPP programme objectives stated in chapter five, an actual evaluation of the impacts of the latter initiative is now made. This engagement provides an opportunity to focus on the various aspects of the regional development process: economic, social, spatial, environmental and political within a single instrument (Ashcroft, 1983; 1982; 1978). The economic aspect is seen in terms of inward investment, employment, income and welfare, production as well as regional and external trade. The social aspect is in terms of infrastructure relating to education, health and housing. The impacts on road infrastructure development and urbanization processes are considered as the spatial component. In focusing on the impacts of the programme on land-use issues and in relation to food-stuff supply, the environmental aspects are also thus addressed. Subsequently, the political dimension of the process is seen in the focus on the social and community relations in the Twifo sub-region. In addition to all the evidence generated in support of the observed trends, the second of the two hypotheses stated in chapter three is tested.

Funding for the programme and inward investment

In both the level of formal funding and provision of inward investment, the TOPP programme has introduced substantial financial resources into the Twifo sub-region and the rest of the Central Region. The TOPP estate has been funded mainly by the European Union (EU) through the European Development Fund (EDF), under a technical assistance agreement with the Government of Ghana. As indicated in chapter five, the NIO, FMO and CDC are loan investors as indicated in Table 7.1. The FMO's loan which was used to finance the purchasing and installation of the mill has since been paid off by the TOPP

Table 7.1 TOPP programme: total initial project cost and investment

Source of finance		*Foreign currency*	*Cedi (¢) value*
TOPP Estate Project:			
	NIO	10 million Dfl	140,100,000
	FMO	10 million Dfl	140,100,000
	Commonwealth Development Corporation (CDC)	£3.36 million	208,800,000
	EEC	ECU 13 million	468,000,000
Sub-total			957,000,000
Smallholder Scheme:			
	EEC (a)	ECU 3.88 million	139,660,000
	EEC (b)*	ECU 2.48 million	89,280,000
Sub-total			228,940,000
Outgrower Scheme:			
	EEC (a)	ECU 1.0 million	36,000,000
	EEC (b)*	ECU1.667 million	60,010,000
Sub-total			96,010,000
Total			**1,281,950,000**

Source: Ministry of Finance and Economic Planning (MFEP) Accra; Office of TOPP Solicitor-Secretary; as at 1985, ECU 1 = ¢36.0 at time of initial project-costing; at time of earlier field-work: £1 = ¢400; at time of follow-up study, £1 = about ¢6,000; at time of writing, £1 = ¢9,000; * met by Government of Ghana

company. This is an indication that the TOPP company has performed successfully enough to have paid off the FMO loan. The total initial cost of this main core of the whole programme was over ¢1.2 billion as shown in Table 7.1.

The smallholder project was also funded mainly by the EU through the EDF under a Technical Assistance Agreement with the Government of Ghana. The total cost of this project component was ¢228.94 million of which ¢139.66 (ECU 3.88 million) was in foreign exchange for meeting the cost of externally imported inputs. Total operating costs were met by the Government from the EU Food Aid Counterpart Fund. This comprised salaries and wages of local staff, vehicles and equipment operating costs. The other elements covered here were building maintenance and general administrative costs. The initial off-shore cost was financed from the fifth EDF programme to Ghana and the 1981 Stabex Transfer Project. The EDF accounted for 61 per cent of the total project cost and an additional ECU 2.48 million was provided by the Government of Ghana. It also met all off-shore costs of the project up to the end of 1991, by which time the programme was financially self-supporting. The project unit is expected to produce 1,600 tonnes of palm oil and 300 tonnes of palm kernel per year. Its palm oil production is supposed to make gross savings of ECU 1.25 million, and the export of palm kernels to bring in ECU 720,000 per year. The target was also to complete all planting by the end of 1989.

The total cost of the outgrower scheme was ¢96.17 million, out of which ¢36.17 million (ECU 1.0 million) was in foreign exchange and the balance of ¢60.01 million met by the Government of Ghana. The outgrower unit also has a production target of 1,475 tonnes of palm oil to be absorbed by the local market. This is expected to make a saving of ECU 1.1 million in foreign exchange. It would also output 295 tonnes of palm kernels for export valued at ECU 85,100 per year in foreign exchange.

Altogether, the whole programme cost ¢1,281,950,000 to start up. The sources of this funding and investment are from the various Western organizations as well as the Government of Ghana. The NIO and FMO are Dutch, CDC is a private company with headquarters in the UK. Part of the funds have also come from the European Union with its main Commission based in Brussels. As indicated in chapter five, the main equity investors in the programme are Mobil UK Limited (Exxon-Mobil Corporation), Paterson Zochonis which is also based in the UK and Pasico Elders, an Australian company. The point is that the TOPP initiative has attracted substantial investment and from an array of sources. This is also a measure of TOPP's stature and profile. For an area that was depressed in socio-economic terms with barely any production capacity, the programme has acted as an appreciably powerful magnet for attracting this level of funding and inward investment. Altogether, this has been the driver of the initiative and regional change in the Twifo sub-region and the wider Central Region.

Employment

TOPP estates This core project was started in 1978 but the mill started production in 1987. It has already been observed that before the project-complex started, non-agricultural and paid employment was minimal in the area. Therefore, the TOPP programme has created a new form of paid employment and on a large scale.

The estate's employment by worker category is shown in Table 7.2. As the main employer in the area, the estate project employed 435 plantation officers, over the 1978-98 period. This includes estate managers, agronomists and extension officers. The other categories of employees over the same period are 1,678 administrators and accountants, 1,220 technical officers and 20,863 labourers including gardeners, weeders, pruners and harvesters. Technical staff comprise mechanical and electrical workers, mill operators, medical staff as well as drivers who also have auto-servicing skills.

Therefore, the TOPP estate component has introduced a new structure of employment in the Twifo sub-region. With this, there is also a newly structured distribution of income generated under the programme. All the various categories of employees and professionals did not exist in the sub-region's economy before

Table 7.2 Level and structure of TOPP estate employment, 1978-98

Year	*Number of plantation officers*	*Number of administrators and Accountants*	*Number of technical officers*	*Number of labourers*	*Row Total*
1978	18	10	35	509	572
1979	20	12	45	603	680
1980	22	13	49	691	776
1981	22	15	52	696	785
1982	24	18	63	791	896
1983	24	110	76	1,020	1,230
1984	24	132	98	1,116	1,370
1985	24	167	100	1,366	1,657
1986	24	160	114	1,286	1,584
1987	23	212	131	1,328	1,694
1988	23	218	170	1,103	1,514
1989	21	208	163	1,125	1,517
1990	18	45	13	1,313	1,389
1991	18	43	15	1,130	1,206
1992	19	44	13	1,038	1,114
1993	19	44	13	1,002	1,078
1994	19	44	13	990	1,066
1995	17	45	14	951	1,027
1996	17	46	13	1,015	1,091
1997	21	44	15	965	1,045
1998	18	47	15	825	905
Total	**435**	**1,678**	**1,220**	**20,863**	**24,196**

Source: Author's fieldwork

the project was introduced. In fact, it had been recognized that apart from logging operations, there has been an expansion in the local agricultural labour force market mainly because of TOPP (Government of Ghana, 1984, p. 10). As the Board's chairperson stated, the programme provides a breeding ground for training various professional groups. Some of these use their experience in working with TOPP as an 'incubator step' to transferring the skills they gain to other employment at a later stage in their working life. A further implication is that the project has contributed immensely to 'monetizing' the economy of the area. It is a very significant development because of the departure from the previous all-farm-labour hand market. Numerically, the significant point is that none of the jobs existed in the local labour market during the programme-off period.

The level of employment per category is only an indication of the level of demand over the entire period and on yearly basis. For example, the trends in the data as shown in Figure 7.1 indicate that there were more administrators and technical officers between 1983 and 1989. In a similar way, there were more labourers between 1983 and 1992. The row totals in Table 7.2 show a steady increase from the base year peaking up to the middle part of the period and a gradual decline towards 1998. It is clearer that there has been fewer plantation officers. The labourer category has provided the highest level of employment. However, many of these jobs are seasonal, casual and less stable. The trend of general decline in the core TOPP estate's employment is depicted in the chart. If this has continued, it means a less promising future performance of the

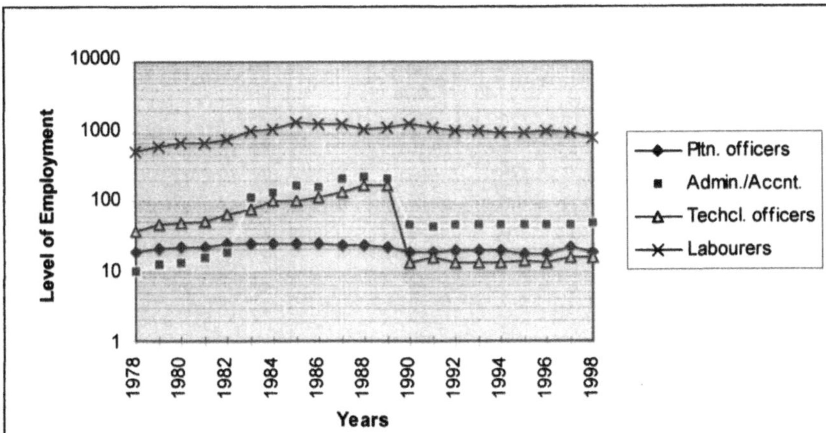

Figure 7.1 **Line chart of TOPP estate employment, 1978-98**

project component in terms of employment. It may indicate the fall in demand for the various employees and managers as a reflection of the nature of the operations or a slackening in the company's financial performance. It was hinted in chapter five that UniLever had acquired fifty per cent shares in TOPP and taken control of a similar company, Benso Oil Palm Plantations (BOPP). UniLever has further transferred part of the workforce from TOPP to BOPP in the Western Region. Therefore, the declining numbers of employees and managers may also be an indication of this rationalization and reorganization exercise by UniLever. These may be further related to a reduction in the volume of work at TOPP. Indeed, UniLever is emasculating in the palm oil industry.

Smallholder project Employment generated by the smallholder project is shown in Table 7.3. This project started in 1983 and is more limited in scale and structure than the core TOPP project. The data only refer to formal employment generated by the project; it does not include the actual smallholder producers. The data show a consistency in the employment of field supervisors, security staff and labourers. There is much less consistency in the number of mechanics and first-aid assistants. The relatively low scale of operations, compared with the estate component, is also reflected in the fact that only one accountant was

Table 7.3 Level and structure of smallholder project employment, 1983-98

Year	*Field Super-visor*	*Accounts*	*Over-seers*	*Head-men*	*Secur-ity*	*Drivers*	*Mecha-nics*	*First Aiders*	*Labo-urers*	*Row Total*
1983	1	-	2	4	4	-	-	-	80	91
1984	3	-	1	4	4	-	-	-	170	182
1985	3	-	-	4	4	-	-	-	112	123
1986	3	-	-	4	4	-	-	-	78	89
1987	8	1	4	28	8	2	2	1	553	607
1988	10	1	7	36	24	6	2	1	398	485
1989	10	1	7	34	23	6	2	1	371	455
1990	4	1	2	-	4	4	1	1	30	45
1991	4	1	2	-	4	4	1	1	3	20
1992	2	1	1	-	5	3	-	-	3	15
1993	2	1	1	-	5	3	-	-	3	15
1994	2	1	1	-	5	2	-	-	3	14
1995	2	1	1	-	20	2	-	-	3	29
1996	2	1	2	-	20	2	-	-	3	30
1997	2	1	2	-	20	2	-	-	3	30
1998	2	1	2	-	18	2	-	-	3	28
Total	**60**	**12**	**35**	**118**	**176**	**38**	**8**	**5**	**1,816**	**2,258**

Source: Author's fieldwork

employed over the 1987-98 period. Apart from the accountant, the transport workers, including mechanics and drivers as well as the other services consisting of security and first-aid assistants are all in the minority. Like the TOPP estate component, the smallholder unit created more labourer employment than all the categories of workers. The former group includes persons undertaking work in the form of weeding, pruning, harvesting and gardening. Once again, these are less stable and more casual as well as a seasonal form of employment. Therefore, the behaviour of these forms respond to the changing levels of the variously demanding activities.

The yearly employment over the 1983-98 period, as indicated by the row totals, shows a general increase from 1983 to 1989, a sharp decline in 1990 to less than 20 employees in 1994. Then there was a minimal increase from that level in 1995 to more than 20 employees per year. The greater number in the earlier part is related to the more involving development of the fields when initial planting was taking place. Therefore, the smallholder project also does not indicate a promising performance in relation to employment-creation, especially in the longer term. The project created a total of 2,258 jobs over the 1983-98 period.

In the case of the number of smallholders it was indicated in chapter five, the fact that the target population of 300 households were to be settled. As all the target of 1,200 hectares of oil palm would have been maturing by 1992, all smallholders were expected to have been settled by that year (Harrisons Fleming Advisory Services Limited, 1985). At the time of the earlier field-work for this study in 1989 only 43 of the target population had been settled, increasing to 89 by the end of that year. At the time of the follow-up survey in late 1998, 210 out of the total had been settled. The total target should have been achieved by then. In terms of smallholder employment, therefore, the project has generated significant levels but has not achieved the total target as planned, yet. The aspect relating to implementation would be dealt with later.

Outgrower project The outgrower project was started in 1987-88 and has generated the least formal employment as shown in Table 7.4. All the employee categories indicate the lowest levels of employment. Only the labourer group indicates yearly employment between 14 and 36 persons over 1988-93. Apart from the first two years for the driver category which show 7 and 10 employees, respectively, all the other numbers are 6 or less for all categories and years.

Table 7.4 Level and structure of outgrower project employment, 1988-98

Year	*Extension managers*	*Zonal managers*	*Supervisors*	*Overseers*	*Headmen*	*Clerks*	*Driver*	*Labourers & security*	*Row Total*
1988	1	2	3	3	4	2	7	36	58
1989	1	2	3	5	4	3	10	34	62
1990	1	1	1	4	3	2	1	18	29
1991	1	1	1	4	3	2	1	18	29
1992	1	-	-	4	3	3	-	14	25
1993	1	-	-	4	3	3	-	4	15
1994	1	-	-	4	3	3	-	4	15
1995	1	-	-	4	3	4	-	6	18
1996	1	-	-	4	3	4	-	6	18
1997	1	-	-	4	3	4	-	6	18
1998	1	-	-	4	3	4	-	6	18
Total	**11**	**6**	**8**	**44**	**35**	**34**	**19**	**74**	**305**

Source: Author's fieldwork

The trend in yearly employment, as indicated by the row totals, shows that the level of formal employment declined sharply after the second year of the scheme to less than 30 for the next two years. Subsequently, the level of employment declined further to 20 or less for the remaining years, 1993-98. Therefore, the formal employment generated by the outgrower unit is almost skeletal and steadily declining. If this trend has continued, the project has shed the shadow of a bleak future with respect to its employment.

In terms of structure, there is again a departure from the traditional all-farm-hand employment. The outgrower project has created employment for extension and zonal managers, supervisors, overseers, headmen, clerks and drivers. However, this is less finely-structured than the TOPP estate and smallholder projects. Thus in absolute and structural terms, the outgrower project is also making a positive impact with respect to employment; only the actual numbers of its employment are the lowest of all the programme unit.

However, there has been a phenomenal growth in the number of outgrower producers. They appear to be the producer group now driving the growth and successful performance of the entire TOPP company. In fact, the probable bright future of this project component can be gleaned from the sheer growth of outgrower participation. This is an indication of the future volume of work and demand for more full-time and formal employment. For example, the following statistics relating to 1987 only illustrate the popularity of the outgrower project. In May of that year, there were 216 outgrowers from 9 settlements with total area of newly planted oil palm of 1,199 hectares. In the month of June, the figure increased to 590 producers from 17 settlements and total area of newly planted oil palm of 2,699 hectares. Subsequently, in July, there were 1,491 producers from 21 settlements under a total area of newly planted oil palm of 3,957 hectares. Further in August, the statistics were 2,097 cultivators, from 19 settlements and with total area of newly planted oil palm of 5,963 hectares. All the actual total planted area far exceeded the expected and targeted amount of land to be planted for each of the months noted. This shows the explosive growth in the adoption of outgrower oil palm cultivation.

In fact, the phenomenal growth of the number of outgrowers and its steadily increasing popularity is further and more consistently illustrated by the data in Table 7.5, covering the period 1987 to 1998. There was a steady growth in the number of outgrowers from 1987 to 1991. Subsequently, there were three brackets of stabilized growth: at 1,500 for 1992-93; 1,710 for 1994-96; and 2,500 for 1997-98. This high rate and level of growth is due to the fact that the producers, in this case, are free to undertake the cultivation and production on their own farm sites within the zones indicated in Figure 5.3 in chapter five, unlike the smallholders.

The pattern and trend in outgrower growth is now graphically illustrated in Figure 7.2. It shows the drastic increase as well as periods of stabilization between 1992 and 1998. The periods of 'halt' may mark the stages of new and additional planting. Therefore, it is likely that this particular behaviour in the trend in outgrower growth has been consistent. Otherwise, it is likely that the

Table 7.5 Number of outgrowers, 1987-98

Year	*Number of outgrowers*
1987	67
1988	128
1989	389
1990	861
1991	1,200
1992	1,500
1993	1,500
1994	1,710
1995	1,710
1996	1,710
1997	2,500
1998	2,500

Source: Author's fieldwork

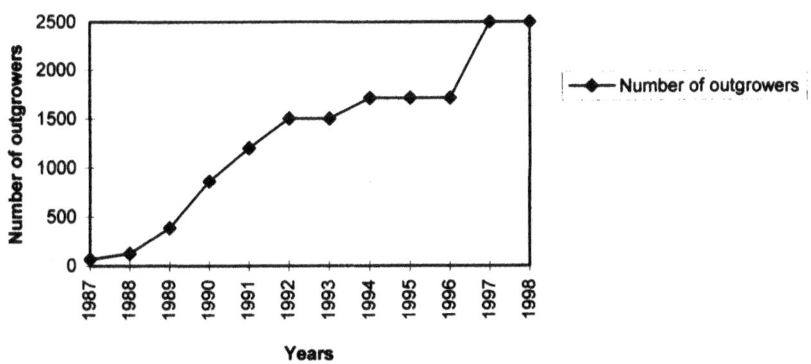

Figure 7.2 Line chart projection of outgrower population growth, 1987-98

trend of stable growth has continued. In either case, the outgrower project component has emerged as the fastest growing, compared with the smallholder unit. Indeed, the total hectares of planted land under the former continues to exceed the total target under the latter.

As indicated in chapter three, the simple regional multiplier model is now applied to the further analysis of the impact of the TOPP programme, on the basis of employment. For the reasons given already, the Keynesian and inter-regional trade model is not used. General impact analysis could also be done in terms of an input-output analysis which would also give an insight into the structure and level of industrial linkages (Armstrong and Taylor, 1978). However, the data inputs for this particular technique are not available. Simply, the regional multiplier, in this case, is stated as T/B, where T = total regional employment in the basic and non-basic sector; B = employment in the basic sector. The greater the multiplier, the greater the (potential) impact of the activity based on employment.

The results of the analyses are shown in Tables 7.6 and 7.7. The former covers 1989, based on data collected during the earlier study and the latter relates to data obtained during the recent follow-up fieldwork. Therefore, the objective is to compare the two sets of multipliers as a way of making a closer analysis of the employment impact of the whole programme. In each case, the basic component is obtained simply by adding up employment figures for the purely primary and basic sectors such as plantation work; and for the non-basic sectors - occupations such as accounting, administrative and clerical work (Glasson, 1978).

Table 7.6 TOPP programme: sub-regional employment multipliers, 1989

Project component	*Total employment*	*Basic employment*	*Non-basic employment*	*Regional multiplier*
Core TOPP	1,517	1,146	371	1.324
Smallholder	455	428	27	1.063
Outgrower	62	49	13	1.265
Total	2,034	1,623	411	n.a.
Group multiplier	*Total group employment*	*Total group basic employment*	*Non-basic group employment*	*Group regional employment multiplier*
Group total	2,034	1,623	411	n.a.
Multipier	-	-	-	1.253

Source: Author's calculation

The computed values of the regional multiplier are 1.324 for the core TOPP project, 1.063 for the smallholder project and 1.265 for the outgrower project in relation to Table 7.6. This shows that the TOPP estate unit confirms itself as the major employer and, therefore, is more likely than not to have greater multiplier effect on the regional economy. It is followed by the outgrower unit and then the smallholder. The position of the smallholder unit may be due to the level of categorization as pointed out already. I have introduced an innovation in this analysis by calculating the group sub-regional multiplier by the same approach. This produced 1.253 and indicates that the whole TOPP project complex has considerable potential to produce a greater multiplier effect.

The impact analysis relating to the data in Table 7.7 produced the following multiplier values: 1.055 for the core estate unit, 4.0 for the smallholder scheme and 1.286 for the outgrower section. The group regional multiplier, in this case, is also 1.082. The present and leading position of the smallholder unit, in this case, may be a compensation for its potential as at 1989. In the order of regional multiplier values, the smallholder is now followed by the outgrower before the TOPP estate. This means the first two units have grown more in their potential for greater impact than the estate component. The group regional multiplier values of 1.253 for 1989 and 1.082 for 1998 may also be an indication that the overall potential of the TOPP programme for making a greater impact on the regional economy has been slightly diminished over the period.

Table 7.7 TOPP programme: sub-regional employment multipliers, 1998

Project component	*Total employment*	*Base employment*	*Non-basic employment*	*Regional multiplier*
Core TOPP	905	858	47	1.055
Smallholder	28	7	21	4.0
Outgrower	18	14	4	1.286
Total	951	879	72	n.a.
Group multiplier	*Total group employment*	*Total group basic employment*	*Non-basic group employment*	*Group regional employment multiplier*
Group total	951	879	72	n.a.
Multiplier	-	-	-	1.082

Source: Author's calculation

All the categories have multipliers above 1.0. Although there is no level of statistical significance for the multiplier as in other tests, it is concluded that they are all above the accepted critical value of unity. Therefore, there is a significant potential multiplier effect to be made by the project complex in the Twifo sub-region as well as the wider Central Region. The basic component in all cases is considered as the 'prime mover' of the oil palm production activities. Therefore, any changes in this critical component would affect all the other aspects of the operations (Glasson, 1978). As pointed out, however, the quality of employment is not 'hard' enough: all the components show more non-skilled jobs.

The further implication of the multipliers is that an increase in the level of the basic component of the TOPP programme would produce various positive processes. One of these would be a rise in income flows into the Central Region. This would then create increasing demand for more goods and services. Consequently, there would be a corresponding increase in the amount of the non-basic part of the project-complex. On the reverse, a decrease in the level of basic activity would cause a lessening of income flows in the Twifo sub-region and Central Region as a whole. Subsequently, therefore, there would be a fall in demand for the output of the non-basic sector and so on.

Personal, group incomes and welfare

It has been stated that the generation of personal and group incomes for the target populations is one of the principal objectives of the entire programme. The basic question to ask is: has the programme succeeded in generating significant and sustainable levels of income for the participants? For the purpose of this particular aspect of the evaluation, an attempt is made to assess the socio-economic background of the respondents in order to determine relevant change against it.

TOPP estate employees: socio-economic background, migration trends, income and well-being effects As indicated in chapter two, 109 TOPP estate employees were interviewed (Table 7.8). Their background is seen in terms of their household responsibilities, whether or not they migrated into the sub-region and their expected duration of employment. This is a basis for assessing change in their income levels as well as welfare. The responses as indicated in Table 7.8 show that only 4 or 3.67 per cent are single with no dependants. The greater majority of 105 or 96.33 per cent are married with dependants. In fact, 41.28 per cent of the employees have 1 to 2 dependants; 27.52 per cent have between 3 and 4 dependants and 15.6 per cent, 39 and 40 dependants. In the case of the last two numbers, it must be explained that these are fairly old polygamist farmers. These dependants also include some members of extended relations. However, the data show that the estate employees interviewed are mostly responsible household heads. Therefore, there is a greater expenditure burden on them. In this case, the impact of the TOPP programme would be seen best in terms of their levels of welfare.

Origin and migration trends of estate employees The origins of the main estate employees is also assessed as a way of finding out the extent to which the project has attracted employment from the sub-region and wider Region. The data in Table 7.9 show that out of the total sample of 109, 86 or 78.90 per cent of the estate employees came from within the Central Region; 18 or 16.51 per cent migrated in from outside the Region to work there. However, of the 86 employees who had come from within the Region, 64 or 74.42 per cent of them

Table 7.8 Marital status and family responsibilities of TOPP estate employees

Marital status	*Count*	*%*
Single	4	3.67
Married	105	96.33
Total	**109**	**100**
No. of dependants:		
1 - 2	45	41.28
3 - 4	30	27.52
5 - 6	12	11.01
7 - 8	3	2.75
9 - 10	1	0.92
35 - 36	1	0.92
39 - 40	17	15.60
Total	**109**	**100**

Source: Author's fieldwork

Table 7.9 Migration and origin of TOPP estate employees

Original settlement	*Count*	*%*
All workers:		
Within Central Region	86	78.90
Outside Central Region	18	16.51
Did not say	5	4.59
Sub-total	**109**	**100**
Origin within Central Region:		
From another town outside project site	64	74.42
Did not move	22	25.58
Sub-total	**86**	**100**

Source: Author's fieldwork

had originated from settlements outside the project site and 22 or 25.58 per cent of them came from the more local settlements. This means that a minority of the estate employees came from outside the Central Region and a majority of them from within it. However, most of the latter came from outside the project site, within the Region. Thus the project has attracted substantial migration from within the Central Region and to a limited extent from outside it. This level of employee migration reflects the values of the regional multipliers presented already.

Former employment status An attempt was also made to find out the former occupations of the workers as a way of showing the value they attach to the TOPP employment (Table 7.10). This would, for example, emphasize their greater attractiveness to the estate project. The data show that 24 or 22.02 per cent had been farmers and 19 or 17.43 per cent, labourers. Twenty-one or 19.27 per cent had left various small-scale and skilled undertakings. Therefore, a majority of 64, in particular 43 out of it, had considered the TOPP estate attractive enough to have left their previous occupations to take up the new employment. In fact, it is significant that 37 or 33.95 had been unemployed. Therefore, for those who had been so worse off, TOPP has been a 'saver'. This also emphasizes the significant impact generated by the TOPP estate project.

Table 7.10 Former occupations of TOPP estate employees

Former occupations	*Count*	*%*
Farming	24	22.01
Trading	7	6.42
Unemployed	37	33.95
Labourer	19	17.43
Other skill	21	19.27
N.A.	1	0.92
Total	**109**	**100**

Source: Author's fieldwork

Estate employee incomes and well-being The actual levels of the income earned by the estate employees since their work with the TOPP company are now analysed. These provide a view of any changes that have taken place in their economic well-being. The responses relating to the sample of 109 estate employees are shown in Table 7.11. The data show that 49 of them or 44.95 per cent could not indicate any sources or levels of income. This also indicates their poverty situation before their new employment. For the estate employees who had some source of income before their entry into TOPP, 36 or 33.03 per cent of them were earning ¢1,250 or less per month. Another 12 or 11.01 per cent of them were earning between ¢1,666.7 and ¢4,166.7; 9 or 8.26 per cent were earning between ¢5,000 and ¢10,000 per month. Their top income bracket was between ¢10,000 and ¢13,333.3 monthly, with 2 or 1.84 per cent of them earning this level. Before their new employment, the 60 of them or 55.1 per cent who were engaged in undertaking various activities were earning a median income of ¢5,834.5 per month. This was significant at the prevailing market prices. Therefore, they must have perceived their entering TOPP's employment as a really attractive opportunity to have left their former occupations. Indeed, the majority of them were better off prior to their engagement with TOPP.

Table 7.11 Income levels of estate employees before the project

Income levels (Cedis)	*Count*	*%*
Less 83.3	5	4.59
83.3 - 416.7	12	11.01
416.7 - 833.3	14	12.84
833.3 - 1,250	5	4.59
1,250 - 1,666.7	2	1.83
1,666.7 - 2,083.3	7	6.42
2,083.3 - 2,500	1	0.92
2,500 - 2,916.7	1	0.92
2,916.7 - 3,333.3	2	1.83
3,333.3 - 4,166.7	1	0.92
5,000 - 5,833.3	1	0.92
5,833.3 - 6,666.7	3	2.75
6,666.7 - 7,500	1	0.92
7,500 - 9,166.7	2	1.83
9,166.7 - 10,000	1	0.92
10,000 - 10,833.3	1	0.92
12,500 - 13,333.3	1	0.92
n.a.	49	44.95
Total	**109**	**100**

Source: Author's fieldwork; (£1 = ¢400; prevailing national minimum daily wage = ¢218 (1990))

The data in Table 7.12 compare the estate employee income levels after they took up employment with the TOPP company. There was now no income below ¢2,000 with 15 of the employees or 13.76 earning between this and ¢4,000 monthly. This shows that the proportion of the interviewed estate employees were relatively better off than before their new employment. In fact, 30 or 27.52 of them now earned between ¢4,000 and ¢5,000 per month; only 2 of them earned within this range before their engagement with TOPP. Further, 27 of the estate employees or 24.78 per cent were earning between ¢5,000 and ¢10,000, against 9 of them or 8.26 per cent before their employment. In addition, 4 or 3.66 per cent earned between ¢10,000 and ¢13,000 and 1 person earned between ¢14,000 and ¢15,000, which no one did in the period before TOPP. Therefore, an assessment of the details and income brackets show that the employees were relatively better off after taking up employment with TOPP than before.

However, the median income was now ¢5,008.9, lower than the one before their work with the TOPP company. Thus the overall income situation of the estate employees was better before their employment. It must be noted, however, that the data in Table 7.12 are based on interviews with all the sampled 109 estate employees, against only 60 of them or 55.1 per cent in relation to the period before their participation in TOPP. It is also likely that valuation of labour and wages may have been different in the periods before and after their taking up work with TOPP. Nevertheless, the relatively low median income in the time after their employment shows that they were, generally, poorer than before.

Table 7.12 Income levels of estate employees after the project

Income levels (¢)	*Count*	%
Less 2,000	0	0
2,000 - 3,000	1	0.92
3,000 - 4,000	14	12.84
4,000 - 5,000	30	27.52
5,000 - 6,000	32	29.52
6,000 - 7,000	13	11.93
7,000 - 8,000	9	8.26
8,000 - 9,000	5	4.29
9,000 - 11,000	0	0
11,000 - 12,000	2	1.83
12,000 - 13,000	2	1.83
14,000 - 15,000	1	0.92
Total	**109**	**100**

Source: Author's fieldwork. (£1 = ¢400; prevailing national minimum daily wage = ¢218 (1990))

Estate employee expenditure levels An attempt was also made to find out the expenditure levels of the participants. This is the further test of the sufficiency and power of their earnings from their employment with TOPP. Data relating to this are indicated in Table 7.13. However, one finding is that most of the employees had supplementary sources of income. Therefore, their expenditure levels as indicated in Table 7.13 could not necessarily reflect their earnings from TOPP. Expenditure is seen as much as possible in terms of the material benefits that the earners were able to gain, using their earnings.

Nine or 8.26 per cent of the respondents spent part of their income on house building and maintenance; 7 or 6.42 per cent spent theirs on acquiring furniture; 5 or 4.59 per cent on acquiring personal items and 3 or 2.75 per cent on supplementing the cost of child education. One employee, in each case, spent their earnings on farm-making, livestock-keeping and other such activities. The overwhelming majority at 80 or 73.4 per cent achieved 'nothing' in such material

Table 7.13 Estate employee expenditure levels

Items of Expenditure	*Count*	*%*
House building; maintenance	9	8.26
Farm	1	0.92
Vehicle	1	0.92
Livestock	1	0.92
Other	1	0.92
Nothing	80	73.4
Furniture	7	6.42
Child education	3	2.75
Personal items	5	4.59
n.a.	1	0.92
Total	**109**	**100**

Source: Author's fieldwork

terms as noted. Thus they must have mostly spent their earnings as catering for their daily livelihood, including that of their dependants. Further data could not be obtained on the specific income levels of the particular employees who could not gain in such material terms as indicated. However, it is likely that these are mostly those who earned the lowest incomes as observed in relation to the data in Tables 7.11 and 7.12.

In further assessing the income effects on the employees, especially in terms of their consumption of services, the only available data relate to rent payments for those who did not live in their own houses (Table 7.14). Apart from 27 cases of 'missing' data, 42 of the respondents did not rent. In effect, only 40 of the respondents were actually renting. Many of the respondents were staying with relatives and friends or in their own houses as many homes in the locality are parent-family bases. For example, one could find three or more generations of the

Table 7.14 TOPP estate employee rent payments

Rent Levels (¢)	*Count*	*%*
100 - 200	4	3.67
200 - 300	10	9.17
400 - 500	20	18.34
500 - 600	3	2.75
700 - 800	2	1.83
800 - 900	1	0.91
No rent	42	38.53
Missing	27	24.8
Total	**109**	**100**

Source: Author's fieldwork; (£1 = ¢400 (1990)

same family living in the house and so on. Therefore, rented accommodation took up the income of only 36.7 per cent of the employees. Nevertheless, this indicates that the presence of estate employees in the area has generated a source of income for the rural property owners. The total level of this, however, could not be estimated.

Outgrower incomes and well-being The objective, here, with respect to the case of outgrowers is to find out what changes have been induced by the project. These are seen in terms of hectares of land, yield, net sales, and material benefits gained from the project. Data on hectares of land under oil palm are shown in Tables 7.15 and 7.16. Before the project, the majority of participants, being 15 or 34.88 per cent of the sample of 43 outgrowers, had between 3 and 4 hectares; 11 of them or 25.58 had between 1 and 2 hectares of oil palm crop. Five or 11.62 outgrowers had between 5 and 6 hectares; only two or 4.65 per cent farmers had between 27 and 28 hectares and 3 or 6.98 per cent, between 31 and 32 hectares of crop-land. Only one outgrower had between 31 and 32 hectares of crop-land, also

Table 7.15 Outgrower scheme: hectares of land before the project

Hectares	*Count*	*%*
1 - 2	11	25.58
3 - 4	15	34.88
5 - 6	5	11.62
7 - 8	2	4.65
9 - 10	3	6.98
11 - 12	1	2.33
19 - 20	2	4.65
25 - 26	2	4.65
27 - 28	1	2.33
31 - 32	1	2.33
Total	**43**	**100**

Source: Author's fieldwork

the highest bracket of hectares in the period before their participation in the project. The median hectare of oil palm cropped land for the outgrowers before the project was 10.50. This is fairly high, under usual farming practices in the Central Region as in other parts of Ghana.

Since they started participating in the project, 31 of the outgrowers or 72.39 per cent now had between 1 and 10 hectares of oil palm cropped land as against 36 of them or 83.71 per cent for the same amount of cropped land in the period before their participation in the project. However, at least one producer had between 35 and 36 hectares of crop land in the after-project period and no one fell into this bracket before the project. Another favourable element in the unit's performance

Table 7.16 Outgrower scheme: hectares of land after the project

Hectares	*Count*	*%*
1 - 2	8	18.30
3 - 4	6	13.95
5 - 6	9	20.93
7 - 8	7	16.28
9 - 10	1	2.33
13 - 14	1	2.33
15 - 16	1	2.33
19 - 20	1	2.33
25 - 26	3	6.98
27 - 28	1	2.33
35 - 36	1	2.33
n.a.	4	9.30
Total	**43**	**100**

Source: Author's fieldwork

after outgrower participation is the median hectare of cropped land of 13.30 which is higher than before. Therefore, there has been a relatively minimal improvement in outgrower cropped land in the period after the project than before. General and natural environmental factors account for this relative success. Another factor is the closer management control and attention provided by the TOPP company.

The same approach to assessment is applied to the data on outgrower yields as shown in Tables 7.17 and 7.18. Before the project, 5 or 11.63 per cent of the outgrowers harvested between 1 and 3 tonnes of oil palm. After the project, 12 or 27.91 per cent now harvested the same yield. Before the project, 12 or 27.9 per cent produced between 4 and 9 tonnes of oil palm fruit; after the project 20 or 46.5 per cent of them now did the same quantity of produce. However, for

Table 7.17 Outgrower yield levels before the project

Yield (tonnage)	*Count*	*%*
1 - 3	5	11.63
4 - 6	8	18.60
7 - 9	4	9.30
10 - 12	7	16.28
13 - 15	10	23.26
16 - 18	4	9.30
19 - 21	4	9.30
n.a	1	2.33
Total	**43**	**100**

Source: Author's fieldwork

Table 7.18 Outgrower yield levels after the project

Yield (tonnage)	*Count*	*%*
1 - 3	12	27.90
4 - 6	9	20.93
7 - 9	11	25.58
13 - 15	3	6.98
16 - 18	5	11.63
19 - 21	3	6.98
Total	**43**	**100**

Source: Author's fieldwork

outgrower production between 13 and 21 tonnes of oil palm fruits before the project, the number of producers decreased from 18 to 11 after the scheme was introduced. The median yield before the project was 11.0 tonnes and remained the same after the project. In relation to the first two tonnage brackets considered, therefore, the conclusion is that there was a minimal change in yields per outgrower. Otherwise, the overall picture does not indicate a significant change with respect to the median tonnage. It ought also be noted that some of the outgrowers do not sell all their produce to the mill. They have the independence and freedom to dispose of it as and when they wish.

The next items of impact assessment are the net sales and income levels of the outgrowers as shown in Tables 7.19 and 7.20. This community earned the highest incomes both before and after participation in the programme as the data in the two tables indicate. Before the programme, 14 or 32.56 per cent earned between ¢83.3 and ¢3,333.3; in the period after their participation, 3 or 6.98 per cent did. Again, none of the outgrowers fell in the income bracket between ¢17,500 and ¢33,333.3 in the period before, 37.1 per cent now did in that after. However, 19 or 44.18 per cent earned between ¢36,666.7 and ¢40,000 before TOPP and fewer did within the equivalent income range after their participation. Nevertheless, there was no income level above ¢43,333.3 in the period before; 11 or 25.57 per cent of the outgrowers earned between ¢45,833 and ¢125,000 per month in the period after their participation. Thus while the income levels in the period before were more contracted and concentrated, these were far more spread out and widely distributed in the period after.

The median outgrower net sales and income before their participation in the programme was ¢16,666.95. This is also appreciably high and may be because the producers have the independence to market their produce in various buyers which may further display a varied structure of pricing. It may as well be due to the fact that the outgrowers, as they own their fields, could additionally produce and sell food-crops. Moreover, the median income level of ¢33,334.1 after the project is greater than the one before their participation in the initiative.

Therefore, the outgrowers were far more better off in the period after the project than before.

Table 7.19 Outgrower net sales and income before the project

Income level (¢)	*Count*	*%*
83.3 - 3,333.3	14	32.56
3,333.3 - 6,666.7	4	9.30
6,666.7 - 10,000	2	4.65
10,000 - 13,333.3	1	2.33
16,666.7 - 20,000	2	4.65
36,666.7 - 40,000	19	44.18
40,000 - 43,000	1	2.33
Total	**43**	**100**

Source: Author's fieldwork; £1 = ¢400 (1990)

Table 7.20 Outgrower net sales and income after the project

Income level (¢)	*Count*	*%*
833.3 - 1,666.7	1	2.33
2,500 - 2,916.7	2	4.65
3,750 - 4,166.7	1	2.33
4,166 - 4,583.3	1	2.33
5,000 - 5,833.3	1	2.33
11,666.7 - 12,500	2	4.65
17,500 - 18,333.3	2	4.65
18,333.3 - 19,166.7	2	4.65
19,166.7 - 20,000	1	2.33
21,666.7 - 22,500	1	2.33
22,500 - 25,000	1	2.33
25,000 - 29,166.7	2	4.65
29,166.7 - 33,333.3	3	6.97
33,333.3 - 37,500	4	9.30
41,666.7 - 45,833.3	2	4.65
45,833.3 - 50,000	1	2.33
50,000 - 66,666.7	4	9.30
66,666.7 - 83,333.3	3	6.97
83,333.3 - 125,000	3	6.97
n.a.	2	4.65
Missing	4	9.30
Total	**43**	**100**

Source: Author's fieldwork; £1 = ¢400 (1990)

A further assessment of the project's impact on the well-being of the outgrowers is made on the basis of the material benefits that accrued to them from their participation in the programme. As indicated in Table 7.21, the responses show that the majority of 20 or 47.51 per cent outgrowers spent their earnings on general upkeep. Fourteen or 32.56 per cent of them spent theirs on child education, and 7 or 16.3 per cent invested in property, including farm expansion and new farm development. Therefore, for the majority of the outgrowers,

Table 7.21 Outgrowers: material benefits from earned income

Material benefits	*Counts*	*%*
General livelihood	20	46.51
Child education	14	32.56
Property	4	9.30
Farm expansion	2	4.65
New farm development	1	2.33
n. a.	2	4.65
Total	**43**	**100**

Source: Author's fieldwork

the project gives them the opportunity to benefit more in terms of daily expenditure. It has already been noted that they now earned more since taking part in the outgrower scheme. These further imply that apart from their daily livelihood, the outgrowers value their family responsibilities as well as the development of cropped land.

Smallholder incomes and well-being The family situation of the smallholders is analysed as a way of assessing change in their well-being (Table 7.22). A comparison is then made between their income levels and material benefits before and after their participation in the project. Thirty-three or 97.06 per cent of them were household heads and married. Thirteen or 37.14 per cent of the married smallholders had between 5 and 7 dependants including children and 8 or 22.86 per cent of them, between 8 and 10 dependants per family. Therefore, the majority of them have considerable family responsibilities with greater demand implications for their incomes. The significance of all these emphasize the fact that this target group are mostly very responsible people. Therefore, when their economies are disturbed they suffer harsher social and economic effects. Their situation is also more likely to create greater motivation and inducement for them to deal more seriously with their search for work: participation in the programme.

The income levels of the smallholders, as assembled in Tables 7.23 and 7.24 are now assessed. The data in Table 7.23 show that before the project, the lowest smallholder income bracket was between ¢83.3 and ¢166.7 per month. On the other hand, the data in Table 7.24 relating to the period after smallholder involvement does not show any income level below ¢1,666.7. In the period before, 18 or 51.4 per cent earned between ¢1,666.7 and ¢20,833.3. Besides, there were several more income brackets within this range in the period after than did exist before. These also confirm that the incomes were more dispersed and widely distributed in the period after than before for the smallholders. Furthermore, none of the smallholders earned above ¢25,000 in the period before; ten of them or 28.57 per cent did - between ¢25,000 and ¢58,333.3 - in

Table 7.22 Smallholders: marital status and family size of settled farmers

Marital status	*Count*	*%*
Married	33	94.28
Single	1	2.86
n.a.	1	2.86
Total	**35**	**100**
Children & other dependants:		
1 - 2	3	8.57
2 - 4	3	8.57
5 - 7	13	37.14
8 - 10	8	22.86
11 - 13	2	5.71
14 - 16	2	5.71
17 - 19	1	2.86
22 - 24	1	2.86
28 - 30	1	2.86
n. a.	1	2.86
Total	**35**	**100**

Source: Author's fieldwork

Table 7.23 Smallholder income levels before the project

Income levels (¢)	*Count*	*%*
83.3 - 166.7	4	11.4
1,666.7 - 3,333.3	2	5.7
3,333.3 - 5,000	5	14.3
5,000 - 6,666.7	1	2.9
8,333.3 - 12,500	5	14.3
12,500 - 16,666.7	4	11.4
16,666.7 - 20,833.3	1	2.9
20,833.3 - 25,000	1	2.9
n.a.	6	17.1
Missing	6	17.1
Total	**35**	**100**

Source: Author's fieldwork. £1 = ¢400 (1990)

the period after their entry into the programme. In addition, the median income of the smallholders before their entry into the programme was ¢12,500.13. This grew to ¢16,667.2 following their entry into the initiative. The two median income levels are also higher than the respective reference levels for the estate employees. Therefore, the smallholders have also fared better in the period after their participation in the programme than before.

Table 7.24 Smallholder income levels after the project

Income levels (¢)	*Count*	*%*
1,666.7 - 2,500	2	5.71
2,500 - 3,333.3	2	5.71
3,333.3 - 4,166.7	1	2.85
4,166.7 - 5,000	4	11.43
5,000 - 5,833.3	1	2.86
6,666.7 - 7,500	2	5.71
9,250 - 10,000	3	8.57
11,666.7 - 16,666.7	2	5.71
16,666.7 - 20,833.3	5	14.29
20,833.3 - 25,000	2	5.71
25,000 - 29,166.7	2	5.71
29,166.7 - 33,333.3	3	8.57
33,333.3 - 37,500	3	8.57
41,666.7 - 45,833.3	1	2.86
54,166.7 - 58,333.3	1	2.86
Missing	1	2.86
Total	**35**	**100**

Source: Author's fieldwork. £1 = ¢400 (1990)

The income levels of the settled smallholders are further analysed by comparing them with those of the targeted and potential farmers (Table 7.25). These have not yet been settled with allocations of cropped land. The data show far lower income levels. It is important to note that in this case, there were 15 respondents who could not indicate any income sources; and one 'missing case'. Therefore, 19 of them were, in effect, interviewed. The lowest income bracket here was ¢833.3 and ¢1,666.7 as against between ¢1666.7 and ¢2,500 for the settled smallholders in the period after. Fifteen or 48.57 per cent of them earned between ¢1,666.7 and ¢20,833.3 against 20 of the settled smallholders in the period after the latter members of the community started their participation in the project. As noted already, the highest income bracket for the settled smallholders in the period after the project took off, ranged between ¢20,833.3 and ¢58,333.3 and earned by ten of them. The highest income level for the non- settled was between ¢20,833.3 and ¢25,000. Moreover, the median income for the non-settled was ¢13,334.3 which is less than the one for the settled smallholders as well as that of the outgrowers, both in the period after the introduction of the projects.

However, the median incomes for the outgrowers, settled as well as the non-settled smallholders is also greater than the median income for the estate employees in the period after the initiation of the TOPP programme. However, the situation of the non-settled group, in relation to the other two main target groups, shows that they are worst off and their relative poverty deepened.

Table 7.25 Income levels of non-settled farmers

Income levels (¢)	*Count*	*%*
833.3 - 1,666.7	2	5.71
1,666.7 - 2,500	1	2.86
2,500 - 3,333.3	3	8.57
3,333.3 - 4,166.7	3	8.57
5,833 - 6,666.7	3	8.57
6,666.7 - 7,500	1	2.86
8,333.3 - 10,833.3	2	5.71
10,833.3 - 13,333.3	2	5.71
13,333.3 - 16,666.7	1	2.86
16,666.7 - 20,833.3	1	2.86
Missing	1	2.86
n. a.	15	42.86
Total	**35**	**100**

Source: Author's fieldwork

Therefore, it was of interest to find out how this 'control' group have been coping with a life of land-ejection and greater poverty, yet with a median income greater than that of the TOPP estate employees. The interviews with them indicate that they have been mostly engaged in very low-scale food-stuff production as well as cash-cropping, especially outside the locality. This will be further explained later in this chapter. Some of them are also engaged in petty retailing activities. Their efforts indicate that they could do better, if given oil palm plots like the 'experimental' group - the settled smallholders.

The material benefits that the settled smallholders gained from the programme were also assessed as indicated in Table 7.26. More than 50 per cent of the 35 smallholders interviewed indicated that they spent their earnings in various material ways: acquiring such personal items as radio sets and personal clothing. Others spent theirs on acquiring non-developed land, housing properties as well as investing in personal business plans. However, 16 or 45.7 per cent of the respondents did not find any questionnaire element, in this case, applicable to them. For those who did, they expended various sums of money ranging from ¢10,000 to over ¢100,000 within a year.

Table 7.26 Smallholders: form and value of material benefits

Type of material benefit	*Counts*	*%*
Radio set	2	5.7
Personal clothing	8	22.8
Land (undeveloped)	3	8.6
Investment (property)	1	2.9
Arrangement for other business	5	14.3
n.a.	16	45.7
Total	**35**	**100**
Cash value of benefit (¢):		
10,000 - 15,000	1	2.86
15,000 - 20,000	6	17.14
20,000 - 25,000	1	2.86
30,000 - 35,000	1	2.86
40,000 - 45,000	3	8.57
45,000 - 50,000	1	2.86
50,000 - 55,000	1	2.86
70,000 - 75,000	1	2.86
80,000 - 85,000	1	2.86
100,000 and over	1	2.86
n.a.	18	51.42
Total	**35**	**100**

Source: Author's fieldwork. £1 = ¢400 (1990)

The original business contract and establishment brief included the TOPP company occasionally providing the settled smallholders with building materials so the producers could improve their own housing structures as in (Table 7.27). Therefore, an attempt was made to investigate the specific contribution of the project income to settler housing improvement. Fourteen smallholders or 40.0 per cent had managed to improve their housing structures or build completely new ones. Similarly, 10 or 28.57 per cent of them had actually acquired their

Table 7.27 Smallholders: form and value of housing improvement

Type of improvement	*Count*	*%*
Extension of old structure	5	14.29
Refurbishment	4	11.43
Completely new building	5	14.29
Purchase of materials	10	28.57
N.A.	11	31.42
Total	**35**	**100**

Source: Author's fieldwork; £1 = ¢400 (June, 1990)

building materials to start new housing structures. These data show that the smallholders attach great value to their housing conditions.

Agro-industrial production: palm oil and kernel

Palm oil and kernel output In the final analysis, the success of the whole TOPP project-complex critically depends on the production levels achieved and thus, on consistent increase in its profits. Therefore, a significant question is whether the entire complex is in business. A feasibility study was undertaken by external consultants on behalf of TOPP in relation to its three components (Harrisons Fleming Advisory Services Limited, 1985). Appropriate projections were made, on this basis, for tonnage of palm oil and palm kernel production up to the year 2011. The projections also covered gross and net cash values. Therefore, the original intent was to study the current production levels and to compare them with the projections made by the consultants for the smallholder and outgrower projects. However, the TOPP company did not allow access to the original projections for the estate unit. Therefore, the comparisons could not be made.

The first level of analysis relates to the early years, 1987-89 (Table 7.28). Again, for the difficulty of data availability, it is not possible to disaggregate the figures in Table 7.28 for the three components. The data do not cover palm kernel sales. At any rate, the agreement between the loan investors and TOPP requires that all

Table 7.28 TOPP: palm oil tonnage and gross domestic sales,[1] 1987-89

Consumers	*Tonnage*		*% Gross Sales ¢ million*
	Tonnage	%	
UniLever (Ghana Limited)	6,129.62	59.33	53.85
Ameen Sangari Limited	1,046.64	10.13	17.64
Cash Sales	1,009.4064	9.77	10.46
Public Relations (TOPP)	1.986	0.02	0.02
Jogapa Enterprise	51.95	0.50	0.45
Anuanom Industrial project	28.97	0.28	0.22
Ghana Food Distribution Corp.	11.15	0.11	0.08
Paul & Adom Enterprise[2]	4.129	0.04	0.03
Volta Soap Industry	9.708	0.09	0.07
Appiah-Menka	444.19	4.30	0.04
Oils & Fats	1,321.38	12.79	12.88
Lovable Industries	204.57	1.98	1.95
Bea Soap Industries	16.81	0.16	0.15
Golfa Alou	50.71	0.49	0.16
Total	**10,331.2194**	**100.0**	**100.0**

Source: Author's fieldwork; (1) % of gross sales only (2) No longer in business

palm kernel output is exported to the European Union countries and paid for in kind: in the form of imported inputs, including vehicles, spare parts and so on.
lowest level for the period. However, the general picture shows a series of falls
These input resources are supplied to the level of the cost of palm kernel exports. Therefore, there are politics relating to the actual 'sales' of palm kernel that the TOPP company wishes to protect. Nor do the data in Table 7.28 relate to exports of palm oil output, only domestic sales. However, it was reported that in May 1990, TOPP repatriated $550,000 out of earnings from palm oil exports of 2,580 tonnes to a firm in Liverpool, England (*West Africa*, 1990, p. 2373). To the former also, the company did not allow access. According to the TOPP company, the total domestic sales of palm oil for the period, 1987-89, far exceeded the projected production for the period. The actual sales against which projects had been made are only available in percentages with some of the company's regular customers indicated. Those projections are not indicated in this book (Harrisons Fleming Advisory Services Limited, 1985). However, the company reported that the actual sales for the period also exceeded the projections, by far.

A more helpful picture of the company's production performance is provided by time-series data covering the 1989-98 period as shown for palm oil and kernel output in Table 7.29. The data relating to both palm oil and kernel show haphazard levels but fairly consistent and slightly steady increases. The statistics include minimal stable production at points over the period, especially for palm kernel over 1996-98. Production of palm oil dropped to 7,816 tonnes in 1998, the lowest level for the period. However, the general picture shows a series of falls and rises in production for both products over the twelve years. This implies that the overall behaviour of production is not really steady. The decreases may have

Table 7.29 TOPP mill: tonnage of palm oil and kernel produced, 1989-98

Year	*Tonnes of Palm Oil*	*Tonnes of Palm Kernels*
1987	2,445.86	497.55
1988	5,929.93	1,339.90
1989	11,155.00	2,188.00
1990	7,816.00	2,123.00
1991	13,186.00	4,075.00
1992	11,841.00	3,213.00
1993	13,602.00	2,679.00
1994	12,072.00	3,054.00
1995	11,601.00	2,551.00
1996	14,313.00	3,435.00
1997	11,623.00	3,021.00
1998	14,693.00	3,934.00
Total	**133,149.00**	**32,110.45**

Source: Author's fieldwork

been caused by the occasional increase in supply of palm oil and related products on the national market. For example, a glut of palm oil on the Ghanaian market had caused a stall in TOPP's implementation plans for a number of social projects. This will be further explained later.

The trend in palm oil and kernel production is further illustrated, graphically, in Figure 7.3. The line chart clearly illustrates the up-and-down behaviour of production over the period. If these trends have continued, they do not appear to indicate a future of increased growth and greater performance of the company. It may also be in the nature of the palm oil market as it is more of a seasonal product. The behaviour of UniLever (Ghana Limited), in its recent acquisition of 50 per cent shares in TOPP, following its being only a major customer of the company, must indicate its growing interest in the agro-industrial development programme.

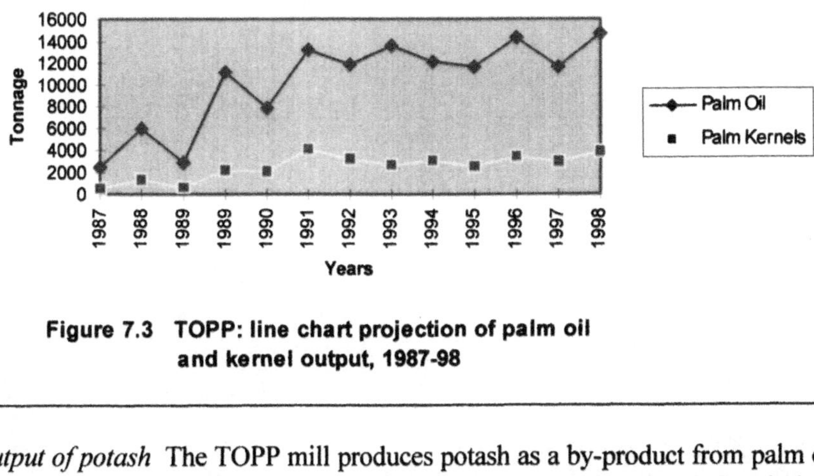

Figure 7.3 TOPP: line chart projection of palm oil and kernel output, 1987-98

Output of potash The TOPP mill produces potash as a by-product from palm oil processing. For example, 45.7 tonnes of potash were produced in 1987 and 126.3 tonnes in 1988. Immediate use is made of this by-product in the form of fertilizer on the oil palm plantations. However, it could not be indicated to what extent this had reduced cost of fertilizer purchases by the company. It could also not be indicated the quality effects of this on oil palm fruiting and yielding.

Regional and international trade

The TOPP programme has generated substantial regional as well as international trade. However, data relating to this aspect of the company's impacts are more limited. The various principal customers of the TOPP company have also been indicated in Table 7.28. 'Cash sales' in that table refers to factory gate sales to private individuals. According to the company, 'Public Relations' is also used to mean 'palm oil gifts' for protocol purposes and is included in the costing and considered as sales. The other customers range from the multinationals like UniLever (Ghana Limited) to smaller firms such as Paul & Adom, Volta Soap Industry or Bea Soap Industries. UniLever (Ghana Limited) consumed 59.3 per cent of all palm oil production and contributed 55.85 per cent of gross sales over the 1987-89 period. It is significant that one multinational company consumes over 50 per cent of TOPP's palm oil production and as well contributes 50 per cent of its gross sales. This time, it is not a wholesale international export. UniLever has factories in Ghana and processes the raw material directly into detergents and cosmetic products, among others. It would have been useful, though, to have identified the share of TOPP's product in UniLever's total raw material input but that kind of data were not available. Figure 7.4 shows some of the plantation workers preparing oil palm seedlings to be transferred to the planting fields. Figure 7.5 shows the central 'engine' of the TOPP programme,

Figure 7.4 TOPP: plantation workers loading oil palm seedlings from nursery grounds on to a tractor to be transferred to planting fields [photograph: author]

the mill, at the plantation site at Ntafrewaso. It was pointed out that on appreciably successful performance, TOPP has been able to pay off the FMO loan with which the mill was purchased.

Figure 7.5 TOPP: boiler section of palm oil mill [photograph: author]

At the regional level, it is of interest to note that Ameen Sangari Limited, based at Cape Coast, also consumed 10.13 per cent of total production and paid 17.64 per cent of gross sales. Anuanom Industrial Project, based at Winneba in the Central Region bought 0.28 per cent tonnes and contributed 0.22 per cent of total sales. Ghana Food Distribution Corporation (Central Region) also bought 0.11 per cent and contributed 0.08 per cent of sales. All the following are in the Greater Accra Region (Accra): Paul & Adom Enterprise which was closing down by the end of the earlier field-work; Volta Soap Industry, Oils and Fats Limited and Bea Soap Industries. Lovable Industries, which consumed 1.98 per cent of total output and paid 1.95 per cent of total sales is based at Takoradi in the Western Region. Figure 7.6 shows the reservoirs for storing the palm oil product prior to shipments with the company warehouse in the background.

The TOPP company's involvement in international trade is, so far, impressive. Apart from exports to Europe, the company has customers in the Republic of Mali. For example, Golfa Alou company which is based in that country bought

0.49 per cent and paid 0.16 per cent of total sales over the period. Thus TOPP is contributing to feeding national industries as well as exports and achieving one of the stated regional policy objectives. At the time of starting production in

Figure 7.6 TOPP: palm oil reservoirs; warehouse in the background [photograph: author]

1987, only UniLever (Ghana Limited) and Ameen Sangari Limited were industrial consumers. By mid-1989, there were ten others. Thus the demand for TOPP's product is growing and its consumer outlets expanding. The company serves many varied customers within the Central Region, other regions of Ghana as well as countries in Africa and Europe. This also underlies the strategic importance of such development-based companies as TOPP in the economy of the country as in that of the Central Region.

A consistent trend in this performance would promise greater and positive socio-economic change in the Region. This would also depend on whether the company continues to pay realistic prices for the production of all the smallholders, outgrowers as well as better wages for the formal employees in all three project components. The smallholders and outgrowers had no complaints about the prices they received. Indeed, they reported enjoying better levels of producer price than they would have done outside TOPP.

A further attempt is now made to project the future of oil palm sales, at least, at the domestic level, for which the available and more consistent data are indicated in Table 7.30 for the period 1991-98. The statistics show a steady increase, with a sharp rise from ¢7,376,297 to ¢12,987,322 over 1995-96 as well as from ¢13,453,901 to ¢20,564,452 during the 1997-98 period.

Table 7.30 TOPP: domestic sales of palm oil, 1991-98

Year	*Sales (¢million)*
1991	2,173,509.00
1992	2,302,034.00
1993	3,431,589.00
1994	4,463,864.00
1995	7,376,297.00
1996	12,987,322.00
1997	13,453,901.00
1998	20,564,452.00

Source: Author's fieldwork

The trends are clearly and graphically illustrated in the line chart in Figure 7.7. Despite the haphazard trends in production as indicated earlier, the domestic sales of palm oil has shown a consistent increase. This may also indicate the different behaviours of the prices on the domestic market as well as the trend of increase in price of the palm oil product over the period. Nevertheless, the recent behaviour of TOPP's main customers and the trends noted in Figure 7.3 do indicate a fairly good future, in terms of profits, for the company and programme.

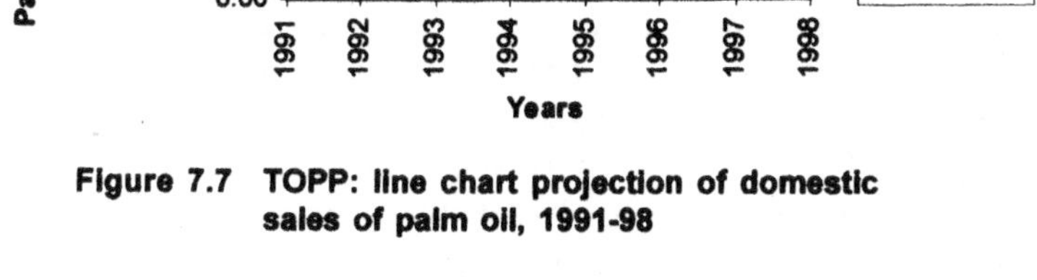

Figure 7.7 TOPP: line chart projection of domestic sales of palm oil, 1991-98

Social infrastructure: education, health and housing

Educational facilities and opportunities The TOPP company has built a kindergarten and nursery at the project site. Actually, these are meant to cater for wards of all categories of the formal staff and employees of the estate, smallholder and outgrower units. However, the facilities also cater for the children of some of the real oil palm producers in the smallholder and outgrower communities. Besides, some members of the wider Twifo communities also have their children enrolled at the school and nursery. The data in Table 7.31 are rather limited relating to 1985-89 only for the pre-stage one levels: kindergarten and nursery. These are not disaggregated by settlement. It is clear that enrolment for

Table 7.31 TOPP educational facility: pre-stage one

Stage	1985-86		1986-87		1987-88		1988-89	
	Boys	Girls	Boys	Girls	Boys	Girls	Boys	Girls
Kindergarten I	24	18	26	14	21	19	25	23
Kindergarten II	-	-	22	18	25	15	18	27
Nursery I	-	-	-	-	11	9	18	16

Source: TOPP Education Department

boys and girls has been growing; a total of 24 boys and girls in 1985-86 increased to 64 boys and 66 girls, respectively, over 1988-89. It is the expectation in this study that at this rate of enrolment, these numbers have since increased considerably; no further evidence is available. However, in this way, TOPP is making a significant impact to the extent that the educational facility provided is now being made accessible to all members of the wider community. These educational facilities did not exist before the project was introduced.

The company has also provided buildings and other facilities for a primary school and Junior Secondary School (JSS) as shown in Table 7.32. The data relate to the 1984-1989 period only and do not cover the provision of facilities for a Senior Secondary School (SSS). However, the facilities for the SSS have, since, been provided as the many batches of JSS have passed on from that stage. Indeed, the company expressed the intent to provide facilities for the former when the earlier field interviews were undertaken in 1989. There used to be only one SSS for the whole district, located at Twifo Praso.

The data in Table 7.32 cover the primary and JSS enrolment for the main settlements of Twifo Hemang, Twifo Mampong, Twifo Eduabeng, Ntafrewaso and Twifo Praso as well as the separate quarters for artisans and managers who all benefit from the primary school facilities. These did not exist before the

Table 7.32 TOPP educational facility: primary and junior secondary school enrolment by origin, 1984-89

Settlement	*Stage 1*	*Stage 2*	*Stage 3*	*Stage 4*	*Stage 5*	*Stage 6*	*JSS*
Twifo Hemang	8	7	8	9	11	4	5
Twifo Mampong	6	8	5	5	9	7	-
Twifo Eduabeng	5	9	2	-	1	5	-
Artisan Quarters	5	1	3	6	2	-	1
Management Quarters	9	3	8	8	6	5	3
Ntafrewaso	5	8	9	3	5	-	2
Twifo Praso	11	7	9	7	10	11	5
Total	**49**	**43**	**44**	**38**	**44**	**32**	**16**

Source: Author's fieldwork

TOPP programme was initiated. Figure 7.8 shows part of the school buildings with some of the students and staff in the veranda and compound. The TOPP company also provides free transport for the pupils to school and back on a daily basis. Many of the settlements are benefiting from these facilities and services.

Figure 7.8 TOPP educational facility: junior secondary school pupils and teachers standing in the veranda of school building and compound [photograph: author]

Twifo Praso used to be the destination of most pupils before the TOPP programme. This process has been reversed with pupils from Twifo Praso now making the TOPP school sites their destination.

Therefore, the TOPP project-complex has created vital and appreciable level of educational facilities and opportunities for the territorial communities in the Twifo sub-region. These are serving all the employees and their families across the developments and have thus significantly contributed to taking off pressure from the scanty resources provided by the public educational system in the area. Figure 7.9 shows part of the school building with some Junior Secondary School pupils being taught technical skills.

Figure 7.9 TOPP educational facility: junior secondary school pupils being taught technical skills [photograph: author]

Apart from providing these facilities, the TOPP company does also assist the wider community with their socio-economic development in other ways. For example, in 1988-89, the company provided iron roofing sheets for Junior Secondary School buildings at Ntafrewaso and Twifo Mampong costing over ¢350,000 at the prevailing market price. Perhaps this form of help could be formalized so that it happens on regular and rationalized basis. In this case, the company would be obligated to provide these as further forms of investment and development initiatives for the communities.

Health facilities and health-care The TOPP programme has also made an impact on health infrastructure in the Twifo sub-region. The company originally intended to build a 50-bed hospital as a principal project, expand and upgrade its own existing clinic unit. The planned hospital was meant to be a free service for all the company's employees and their dependants. All other members of the Twifo community were to be charged reasonable attendance fees. Another positive aspect of the hospital was its planned capacity to have employed some 40 additional workers.

However, this project did not materialize as planned. A newspaper reported in mid-1999 that the Cape Coast District of the Methodist Church of Ghana had acquired the uncompleted buildings and site of the hospital at Twifo Ntafrewaso in 1996. The Church paid ¢50 million for the assets which included a forty-bed ward, three operating theatre rooms and an out-patient department with the aim of developing the project into a modern hospital at a further investment of ¢1 billion. It was noted that the hospital initiative which was being undertaken by TOPP to serve the local community had been abandoned on technical grounds.

According to the TOPP company, it only suspended the project in 1990 because of funding problems. These had resulted principally from 'a country-wide palm oil glut' which meant the company was not achieving market price for its product. The company had also suspended 'a number of social projects in order to concentrate on the core business' (interviews with TOPP clinic staff, Ntafrewaso, 1998). However, TOPP decided in 1991 to continue the project on a partnership basis with any other local health-care provider. The Methodist Church appeared as an interested partner with the further intent of taking up the management of the hospital when it was completed.

The negotiation talks between the two organizations started in 1992. In 1993, there was a dramatic turn of events when the entire TOPP project-complex was listed by central government for divestiture. The government has been disposing of many public-sector and quasi-non-governmental projects as well as businesses by using the corporate-level strategy of reorganization or retrenchment. This was, certainly, the reason for UniLever's move to acquire 50 per cent shares in the company. Under this situation of uncertainty about the future of TOPP and the hospital project, the Methodist Church 'thought it wiser to acquire the project rather than enter into partnership'. In the follow-up interviews with the company management in 1998, it was stated that 'After a series of negotiations, the Project was offered for outright sale by the Company which was anxious to see the project completed to become operational as soon as possible' (interviews with TOPP clinic staff, Ntafrewaso, 1998).

It was as part of the deal that the Church decided to bring in some of its medical staff - from outside the area - to form the initial core personnel for the new hospital when the out-patient section became operational. However, the TOPP company has retained its own clinic to continue serving its employees and their dependants. Only serious cases such as those needing in-patient and surgery attention would be referred to the hospital. Thus it is also part of the deal for the new hospital to serve as the first referral point for TOPP employees and their families in the Twifo sub-region. This relationship between TOPP and the Methodist Church is also aimed at encouraging a collaboration and co-operation between the district hospital as a Level 'A' health provider and the TOPP clinic as a health centre, Level 'B' provider, within the national primary health-care system. Figure 7.10 shows part of the site of the acquired hospital buildings.

Figure 7.10 **TOPP: acquired new hospital buildings and site [photograph: author]**

The performance of the TOPP clinic was assessed against the other health-care providers. The data relating to 1988 and 1998, in this regard, are shown in Table 7.33. In 1988, the TOPP clinic served 87.6 per cent and more at 96.0 in 1998 of all patients who reported ill there. Of the total, 9.2 per cent of the reporting patients in 1988 were referred to Cape Coast hospital; this decreased drastically to 2.3 per cent in 1998. Hemang health post served 1.4 per cent of the referred patients in 1988 and 0.07 per cent in 1998. Similarly, Praso health centre served

0.6 per cent of the referred patients in 1988 and 0.26 per cent in 1998. All the other three providers served 1.2 per cent of the total number of patients referred from the TOPP clinic in 1988 and 1.37 per cent in 1998. This also confirms the critical role of the clinic in health-care in the sub-regional community.

Table 7.33 TOPP programme: health-care providers and number of patients treated, 1988 and 1998

Providers	*Number of patients*			
	1988	%	1998	%
TOPP estate clinic	24,015	87.6	27,728	96.0
Cape Coast hospital	2,516	9.2	658	2.3
Hemang health post	395	1.4	22	0.07
Praso health centre	168	0.6	75	0.26
Other providers	337	1.2	395	1.37
Total	**27,431**	**100**	**28,878**	**100**

Source: Absolute figures from TOPP clinic, Twifo Ntafrewaso; percentages by author

The trends are also graphically illustrated in Figure 7.11: the bars confirm the leading role of the TOPP clinic in serving the health-care needs of the territorial community. The further implication of these trends indicate that when the new hospital takes over most of the services of the clinic, it would involve a similar level of responsibility. The referrals to other providing places would be reduced or eliminated altogether, even with the continued services of the TOPP clinic.

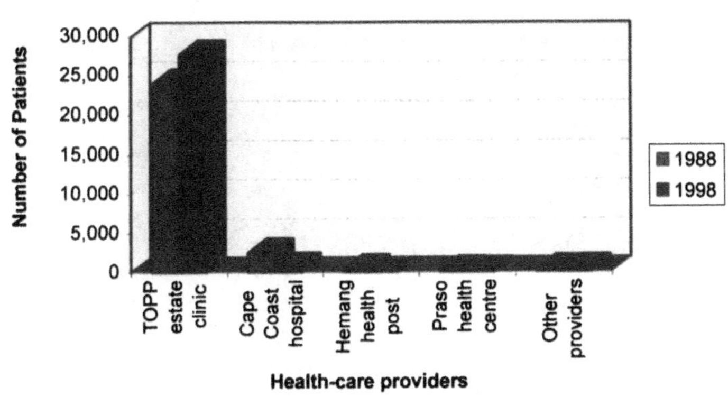

Figure 7.11 TOPP programme: group bar chart of health-care providers, 1988 and 1998

Furthermore, the impact of TOPP on health-care in the area is shown by the number of diseases treated at the clinic in 1988. It is also a way of showing the morbidity situation in the Twifo area as pointed out elsewhere (Ofori, 1991a). Of the 10 commonest diseases, malaria accounts for 29.85 per cent; respiratory infections, 13.30 per cent; chest pains, 12.88 per cent and rheumatic and joint pains for 10.40 per cent. The others are general bodily pains, 8.06 per cent; ulcers, 7.18 per cent; diarrhoea, 7.09 per cent; injuries, 5.84 per cent; worm infections, 2.93 per cent and skin diseases, 2.47 per cent. Again, the crucial point is that the company clinic is making a significant impact in terms of the treatment of the most common diseases plaguing the area. This pattern confirms malaria as the leading one among these. It is also typical of the other regions of Ghana. Therefore, the TOPP clinic has played a most vital role providing health-care in the Twifo territorial communities. Indeed, without this critical role, the health situation would have been worse than it is now. Thus the hospital has the potential to do even better in this regard.

Housing for programme workers and dependants The TOPP company has also contributed significantly to the provision of housing in the area by building modern units for its employees and their dependants. The available data cover the earlier life of the company, 1978-89 as shown in Table 7.34. Despite the fact that these are site developments and not meant for the communities at large, many of the housed employees would not have had such accommodation if the company had not provided these. From the author's experience of the social

Table 7.34 TOPP project site housing development, 1978-89

Project unit	*Number of units*		*Number of occupants*	
	Number	*%*	*Number*	*%*
Managers' quarters	51	22.7	104	22.37
A.T.P Timber company	3	1.34	6	1.29
Artisan quarters	14	6.25	50	10.75
Mill quarters (temporary)	60	26.79	117	25.16
Labourers' quarters	48	21.43	140	30.11
Mill village (permanent)	24*	10.71	24*	5.16
Mampong division	24*	10.71	24*	5.16
Total	**224**	**100.0**	**465**	**100.0**

Source: Public Relations Department, TOPP Headquarters, Twifo Ntafrewaso; * for families

organization and structure of families in the area, one comes across three or more generations of families living within the same compound of a set of rooms. Sometimes, this creates many difficulties including conflict. Therefore, the company is contributing to solving the housing problems of its employees and promoting its own work in this way (Ofori, 2000d). In fact, the company indicated that it had planned to provide more housing for its employees and their dependants. Therefore, one would expect that this has, since, happened to a greater extent.

The data show that the mill workers are more catered for, followed by the managerial group and labourers in that order; all the others fall in along. This is also an indication of the order of priority for the company's housing development. The temporary mill quarters was meant to provide initial housing till the construction of the permanent mill village was completed. Figures 7.12, 7.13, 7.14a and 7.14b show examples of the main housing types built by TOPP. The structured form of the houses also reflects the order of seniority as well as income levels in the company. These are further reflected in the variety of building materials used and implications for rent levels.

Figure 7.12 **TOPP: model of housing type for senior management [photograph: author]**

Apart from these on-site developments, the TOPP company also contributes to the development of other social infrastructure in the wider Twifo community as noted in relation to the case of educational facilities. For example, in 1988-89 the company built a football playing field for the communities at Twifo Praso

Figure 7.13 TOPP: model of housing type for middle-level management [photograph: author]

and Twifo Mampong. The pitch has been used for other sporting and recreational activities. In another such one-off act, the company donated roofing sheets costing ¢200,000 to members of the community whose houses had been destroyed by rainstorms at Eduabeng in 1987-88.

Once again, it would be more beneficial to the target community if these forms of one-off support given by the company were co-ordinated in a formal and consistent initiative. At the time of the follow-up survey in 1998, the company stated that they had suspended all such social projects, anyway, because of the reduced profits resulting from the glut of palm oil on the national market in Ghana. This implies that the community could not expect to receive even such limited and one-off forms of material support. However, if it were formalized, the company would be committed to delivering in whatever situation of change. Indeed, these kinds of situations indicate the opportunity for including social and community initiatives as part of regional programmes, the kind of TOPP. They also provide a vital link between the wider territorial community and the regional development instrument. These also point to the urgent need of a regional plan and clear, articulated objectives for specific programmes.

Figure 7.14a TOPP: model of junior staff housing type; external toilet systems in the mid-background; Ntafrewaso village in the farther background [photograph: author]

Figure 7.14b Mainly back-view of one of the junior staff housing sites

Road infrastructure and urbanization processes

Road infrastructure The TOPP programme has significantly influenced, if not catalyzed, the development of road infrastructure in the Twifo sub-region. If TOPP had not existed, it is probable that the Ministry of Roads and Transport, including the Ghana Highways Authority would have implemented their sector-based projects as sheer autonomous developments. The creation of TOPP promoted the up-grading of the main Cape Coast-Twifo Praso road link from a secondary route to a major secondary road. Figure 7.15 shows a section of the newly re-surfaced and improved road between Twifo Praso and Cape Coast. It was also planned to extend the development to Dunkwa-on-Offin, north of the area and possibly further north to Kumasi. The expected traffic flows, including those generated by TOPP and haulage of finished products influenced the priorities of the Ministry. Similarly, the Department of Feeder Roads included some feeder road connections in its programme with respect to the emerging network. These emphasize the effects of the TOPP programme on the development of highways as well as feeder roads in the Twifo sub-region.

Figure 7.15 **A section of the newly improved road between Cape Coast and Twifo Praso [photograph: author]**

Urbanization processes It has also been observed that the creation of the TOPP company and programme have generated certain processes towards urbanization in the Twifo sub-region. For example, the company stated that it was making a positive impact on the growth of community services. It ought to be pointed out, however, that it is has been difficult measuring these changes because some of them appear to be autonomous developments. With respect to growth in urban services like commerce and banking, it is probable that without TOPP such developments would not occur. In a similar way, the creation of many government administrative services based at Twifo Praso, the district capital, was also generating various growth processes. An interview held with 21 out of 25 District Assembly representatives in relation to the possible urbanization effects of the programme indicated that they did not see any connection between these two trends. This response from all 21 respondents is rather surprising.

Nevertheless, the author's view is that the urbanization effects resulting from the TOPP programme are, altogether, fairly significant. For example, the initiative has made an impact on the growth of commercial activities and various services by generating an in-migration of workers into the area as demonstrated earlier in this chapter. Their demand for commercial services has brought these into being at certain levels. Thus these services represent forms of multiplier effects of the TOPP instrument. For example, in an interview held with the manager of the local Ghana Commercial Bank he stated that TOPP was one of the critical factors that determined the siting of the local branch of the Bank. In a similar interview, it was observed that the creation of the local Branch of the Co-operative Bank was also encouraged by the location of TOPP. Indeed, all employees and programme participants are paid through the banking system as a requirement. Therefore, the TOPP company requires all these relevant stakeholders to open accounts with the local banks. In effect, TOPP has generated some growth in local financial services.

In other interviews with the tax officials of the Lower Denkyira-Twifo-Hemang District Assembly, it was noted that the creation of the TOPP system was causing a rapid growth in small businesses like 'drinking bars' or pubs, chemist shops, bakeries, 'chop bars' or local restaurants, corn-and-rice mill operators as well as leisure-based services. The same trend was also observed in the growth of local dress-makers or tailors, hair dressers, photographers, fuel-stations and chain-saw operators. The development potential of such small businesses as noted, here, was emphasized in chapter five of this book as elsewhere (Ofori, 2000g; 1994; 1981).

In fact, two local Tax Officers who were randomly interviewed stated that the populations of the bakers and chemists were growing at annual rates of 2 per cent and 10 per cent annually, respectively. Apart from the license fees paid by such businesses, there has also been an increase in the payment of market tolls as well as basic rates and property rates - the last two, together, constitute the equivalent of the council tax in the United Kingdom. The officials also pointed out that two of the most phenomenally growing of these elements, in these emerging economies of urban concentration, are market tolls and artisan-chain-saw operators. These urbanization economies emanate from the overall impact of urban developments (Richardson, 1969a; 1969b). For the market tolls, the monthly gross collected for the four months, January to April in 1989 were ¢174,170; ¢310,970; ¢446,300 and ¢597,300 respectively. The total licensing fees paid by the artisan and chain-saw operators over the same period were ¢10,800, ¢16,200, ¢24,300 and ¢41,300 respectively. It is clear that there were trends of increase in both cases. It is more likely that these positive trends have continued. Indeed, the author's personal interview with the District Secretary, at the time, confirmed all these processes as emanating from the existence and operations of TOPP and the public leveraging support.

Agricultural land supply, compensations and food-crop production

The arrangements for addressing the needs of the target population of 300 families under the smallholder project has been explained. The original objective was to allocate 5 hectares of land to each of the 300 targeted families, including 4 hectares for oil palm and 1 hectare set aside for food-cropping. However, it was later realised that even the allocation of 4 hectares per family was a problem and generated a lot of social and community conflict in the area. Sometimes, two or three such allocations went to a main and the same family because the kith and kin of the original household-head had established families of their own within the same compound. This meant that the same wider household of extended family relations contained more than one family unit within the same compound or 'house'. Meanwhile, some families had no allocations at all. Thus one of the difficulties facing the TOPP company is establishing the legitimate family unit in this system of social organization.

This situation has been a constraint on making the 4-hectare oil palm field allocations to all members of the original target population and has complicated its selection. Only a population of 300 families were to be selected from the - wider - universe of 5,826 registered landlords as well as tenants who had been ejected from their land. The selection is based on such criteria as age, farming experience and the availability of family labour. Many of the non-selected persons complained about the unfairness of the process of selection. This mix of factors had created separate local politics, stemming from the nature of the social organization of the extended family and the limited amount of land resources.

This meant that the objective of allocating one hectare per family for food-stuff cropping was defeated. So the settled participants unilaterally and altruistically decided to forgo their one-hectare plot per family in order that many more of their colleagues and neighbours could benefit from the project. In this way, those who had no oil palm farm allocations could now have extra four-hectare plots created for them in this way. Therefore, the project no longer caters for food-cropping for the personal benefit of the smallholder producers. This situation has created a number of other difficulties. Many of both the settled smallholders and non-settled land-ejectees, have to travel far and wide outside the sub-region in search of food-cropping land. This trend is also most likely to transform the traditional agricultural land-use and farming practice from a 'land fallowing' and rotation to one of permanent cultivation, *in situ*. In general, it might not be possible for farmers to move from one portion of land to another with each farming season, leaving the previous land to fallow and be rejuvenated (Ofori, 2000a).

Another problem created by this situation is the direct impact on the local supply and cost of food-stuffs. For the purpose of investigating this element of the problem, further interviews were held with the 21 District Assembly representatives whose responses are shown in Table 7.35. One participant or 4.76 per cent of the sample observed that food-stuff prices were rising; 2 or 9.52 per cent could not tell. However, 8 or 38.10 per cent agreed that food-stuff supply was falling simultaneously with rising prices. Ten or 47.62 per cent of the District Assembly representatives indicated that there was a shortage of land which

Table 7.35 Lower Denkyira-Twifo-Hemang territorial community: perception of land shortage and supply and food-stuff prices

Item	*Count*	%
Rising price of food-stuff	1	4.76
Cannot tell	2	9.52
Falling food supply and rising prices	8	38.10
Land shortage and decreasing food supply	10	47.62
Total	**21**	**100.0**

Source: Author's field-work

contributed to decreasing food-stuff supply. Although not a major survey in itself, these results clearly show that land supply for non-oil palm production has been affected by the implementation of the project-complex. This has created a prevailing upward spiral of local food-stuff prices as well as keen competition between food-cropping and oil-palm production.

Another difficulty was the fact that not all the persons who lost their land, through the government's compulsory purchase action, have been paid compensations. The project started in 1978 and by 1989 at the time of the earlier survey, 5,400 or 92.69 per cent of the total of 5,826 landowners had been paid compensations, leaving out 426 or 7.31 of them unpaid. In terms of actual payments, ¢129,660,707.83 had been paid out, remaining ¢3,816,789.53. Both those who had received compensation payment and those who had not complained about the unfairness of the levels and terms of payment. They pointed out that the payments were based on estimations which had not considered the realities of inflationary trends, for example. Many of them who had neither received compensations nor been allocated oil palm plots were totally deprived of their source of livelihood through the implementation of the programme.

In the midst of all these trends and turmoil, the problem of agricultural land supply and ineffective compensation payments have generated several social and community conflicts in the Twifo sub-region. Indeed, this situation only worsened an existing conflict relating to ownership of the lands in the sub-region and dating from the late nineteenth century (Harrisons Fleming Advisory Services Limited, 1985, pp. 15-18). As a result of this, some of the land-owners had refused to give up their lands, even though these had been acquired by compulsory purchase order. According to the assistant manager of the smallholder project, this has also affected the available amount of land to fully implement the smallholder scheme.

Testing hypothesis II

The analyses and assessments made, so far, in this chapter have provided multiple sources of evidence in support of the trends in regional change generated under the TOPP programme. The results of the analyses are now further subjected to testing by applying a non-parametric statistical technique because of the small sizes of the samples of respondents used for the purpose (Ofori, 1991a; Yeomans, 1968). These have also provided the opportunity for general phenomenological studies of the various target groups involved. Thus the second hypothesis as stated in chapter three is now tested. From the analysis in this chapter, it has emerged that the observed principal and direct impacts of the TOPP programme relate to employment, income and social infrastructure with respect to health, education and to an extent, local housing. The objective, here, is to show what the expected situation might have been in relation to the observed trends.

Therefore, the appropriate tool for performing this test is the chi-square (χ^2) technique. The χ^2 is a way of checking whether the difference between observed and expected numbers is greater than could reasonably be due to chance alone. Therefore, the objective is to compare the observed frequencies with which phenomena occur with what might have been expected if the two distributions had absolute independence. The χ^2 test is free from the assumption of normal distribution. Its capacity and capability in handling ordinal or classificatory data also makes it a useful non-parametric analytical tool. Therefore, it is more suited to analysing social and behavioural phenomena (Saunders, Lewis and Thornhill, 1997; Wyatt, 1989; Ofori-Cudjoe, 1981; Yeomans, 1968; Siegel, 1936).

The data used for testing this hypothesis relate to education in terms of total enrolment for stages 1-6, JSS I as well as the kindergarten and nursery grades; health, in terms of patients treated at the various providing centres. In the case of employment, the total number of employed persons for the two year-points, 1989 and 1998 are used in relation to the estate, smallholder and outgrower projects. The data relating to income are based on the 'before' (time T_1) and 'after' (time T_2) median values for all three project components.

Results of chi-square test On the basis of the employment data relating to all three project components, the calculated value of $\chi^2 = 51.9$. This is greater than the χ^2 critical value of 0.103 at 2^0 freedom and at 0.95 significance level. Therefore, the null hypothesis (H_0) is not accepted. The alternative (H_A) form of the second part of the hypothesis is accepted that the project-complex is making significant impact on employment in relation to the communities of outgrowers, smallholders and estate employees. However, a downward trend has been noted with respect to the estate employee employment. There are also many non-settled selected smallholders and the situation of those who lost their lands and were not selected to participate in the programme, at all, has grown worse. These results were not due to chance. However, only the alternative to the main hypothesis is accepted that the TOPP project-complex is not maximizing most rapidly and effectively the socio-economic development and well-being at the community, group and personal levels in the Central Region.

In the same way, the calculated χ^2 value for the median incomes is 546.41. At 2^0 freedom and at 0.95 significance level, the theoretical value of χ^2 is 0.103. Therefore, the H_0 is rejected in favour of the H_A. The χ^2 value is significant and shows that the results achieved under the programme emanated from the policy and programme actions taken. These also show there is a really high probability that the expected frequencies of the observed results might continue to occur. Therefore, the project-complex is making a significant impact with respect to income of the main groups of persons involved. It must be noted, however, that the median income for the estate employees has not shown any positive change. Otherwise, the alternative to the first part of the hypothesis is accepted that the TOPP programme is not maximizing most rapidly and effectively the socio-economic development and well-being at the community, group and personal levels in the Central Region.

With respect to the education-based data on the primary stage and JSS I, the calculated χ^2 value is 5.66. The critical χ^2 value is 1.635 at 6^0 freedom and 0.95 significance level. As the former is greater than the latter, the H_0 is rejected in favour of the H_A. Thus the difference between the observed pupil enrolment and the expected number is greater than could be attributed to chance alone. Similarly, the calculated χ^2 value for the pre-stage one enrolment data is 1.81. At 2^0 and 0.95 significance level, the critical value of χ^2 is 0.103. As the former is greater than the latter, the H_0 is not accepted in favour of the H_A. Therefore, the project-complex is making significant impact with respect to basic infant education in this regard. However, the alternative to the first part of the hypothesis is that the programme is not maximizing the socio-economic development and well-being in the Twifo territorial community in this way.

With regard to the data on the number of patients treated at the various health-care centres in 1988 and 1998, the calculated χ^2 value is 170.53. At 4^0 freedom and 0.95 significance level, the critical χ^2 is 0.711. Once again, the H_A is accepted against the H_0 that TOPP project-complex is making significant impact on well-being and socio-economic development, in terms of health-care, in the territorial community than could have been attributed to chance alone. The alternative to the first part of the hypothesis is accepted that the programme is not maximizing the socio-economic development and well-being in the Twifo territorial community.

Furthermore, testing of the data relating to housing produced a χ^2 value of 1.981 and a critical χ^2 of 1.145, at 0.95 significance level and 5^0 freedom. Therefore the H_0 is again rejected in favour of the H_A. It is, again, confirmed that the TOPP programme is making a significant impact on local housing than could have been attributed to chance alone. Furthermore, the null of the first part of the hypothesis is rejected in favour of its alternative: it is not maximizing the socio-economic development and well-being in the Twifo sub-region.

It must be emphasized, the rejection of the first part of the main hypothesis in relation to all the aspects of the χ^2 test does not remove the fact that the project-complex has the potential to make things happen. For example, this was established in the regional employment-based multiplier analysis.

The overall conclusion from these tests is that the TOPP project-complex has generated a significant socio-economic impact in terms of education, health, local housing, employment and participant income generation. These are the most direct impacts reaching the community at large and contributing significantly to the regional development objective of solving problems of a deeply territorial area. In this case, the TOPP company's one-off contributions to community services are not considered that significant. Urbanization effects were also difficult to measure in the face of severe paucity of data. Road infrastructure development is, in appreciable measure, an autonomous project. Although not included directly in the test, these are also significant effects.

The χ^2 test indicates that the project-complex has made some impacts because certain statistical relations hold. But it is naive to accept this on its own. The test is only a means to an end, not an absolute end on its own. It only demonstrates that differences between observed and expected numbers are greater than could reasonably be due to chance alone. Therefore, the noted impacts are those necessarily generated under the implementation of the project-complex. The assumptions underlying the hypothesis and its policy implications will be addressed in chapter nine.

Summary

It has been demonstrated that the TOPP programme has attracted and induced significant regional socio-economic change in the Twifo sub-region. The level of investment by foreign and domestic sources, under the initiative, has been phenomenal. This is further shown in the array of equity investors who remain actively involved in it. However, the increasing shares of UniLever coupled with the central government's shedding off part of its own shares would overwhelmingly tip the scale of power and control in favour of the former.

The programme has equally generated substantial levels of employment, especially in its first ten years. However the trends show a future of decline. Nevertheless, the regional multiplier analysis indicates that the programme has a greater potential impact on the basis of employment. Levels of production in palm oil and kernel also grew steadily in the initial stages and have since been indicating haphazard performance. However, the unstable nature of the performance is within a general trend of increase which is also supported by the phenomenal growth and driving lead of the outgrower population and production. The programme has also achieved appreciable market within the Central Region, in other regions of Ghana as well as in the EU countries and other parts of Africa. The objective of allowing an extra hectare of land for the targeted smallholders to produce their own food-stuff has not been achieved. The participating smallholders agreed to forgo this in order that some of their non-participating neighbours could be given oil palm plots. This has also created drastic shortage of food-cropping land, local food supplies and appreciable increases in the prices of food-stuffs.

With respect to incomes, not all the targeted groups have been well off. The outgrowers have achieved the highest incomes both before and after their participation in the initiative. They are followed by the participating smallholders. It is a surprise that the selected and yet-to-be smallholders are able to show some level of median income. This indicates their potential for earning their livelihood. Again, it is surprising that these non-participating people have not become as poor as the main estate employees. The entire sample of estate workers shows the lowest median income after their new employment. This may be due to their being in lowly-paid employment and not having their own private undertakings.

The programme has also created significant social infrastructure relating to education, health and housing. However, the company has had to sell off its hospital development project as a result of poor market performance. Other forms of assistance in support of social infrastructure-based development have been limited and rather one-off. Furthermore, the project-complex has promoted the up-grading of the main road infrastructure between Twifo Praso and Cape Coast. There is also evidence that the programme is generating a fairly significant rate of urbanization process in the sub-region. This is an important dynamic generated largely under the TOPP initiative in the sub-regional area that had always scored zero in relation to urbanization and urban development.

8 Effectiveness of implementing regional programmes and projects and managing regional change

The engagement in this chapter is with assessing the effectiveness of the implementation of the various programmes and projects that have been evaluated under the stated regional planning and development policies. The focus is on the effectiveness of functions, rates and quality of implementation processes; the roles of the actors involved in programme implementation as well as the effectiveness of managing regional change.

The planning process is only practically meaningful when its determined programmes and projects are implemented (Conyers and Hill, 1984; Hogwood and Gunn, 1984). Therefore, implementation represents a critical 'milestone' in the planning chain and involves a translation of policy, plan and programme into action. It is this that changes those aspects of the social, economic and physical environment constituting the goals of planning (Conyers and Hill, 1984; Rietveld, 1980). This further implies an interaction between goal-setting and the actions oriented to achieving the goals. Thus it represents the capacity of public policy to bring about change in the socio-economic behaviour of the target populations (Sabatier and Manzmanian, 1979). This also implies that there must be a clear relationship between the problem, goal, objective and action (Patton and Sawicki, 1986; Hogwood and Gunn; 1984; Sabatier and Manzmanian, 1979; Gunn, 1978; Friedmann, 1973). The expected change takes various periods of time to happen but the element of time is not necessarily indicated by theoretical constructs (Clark, Gertler and Whiteman, 1986; Friedmann, 1973).

Implementation involves mainly the co-ordination, not only of goals and actions, but also of agencies; control of all resources, including time and material forms, as well as effective communication (Gunn, 1978). This further highlights the importance of the management aspect of implementation (Patton and Sawicki, 1986; Meggison, Mosley and Pietri, 1986). Basically, it is 'getting things done' or 'making things happen', in this context, in the local and regional environment (Barrett and Fudge, 1981; Lewis and Flynn, 1979).

Effectiveness of main functions, rates and quality of implementation

The objective here is to discuss the rates of implementation performance with respect to the initiatives assessed as well as the quality of principal planning instruments in promoting the process. The main functions involved in making things happen are also addressed.

Rates of public sector-based and one-off project implementation The computed implementation rates of the one-off projects assessed in chapter five are shown in Tables 8.1 for 1981 and 8.2 for 1988. The original figures were obtained by calculating the means of all completion rates as estimated by the Regional Planning Co-ordination Unit for each district and by sector in the Central Region. The sector medians are obtained by calculating for the columns and rows in the tables. The median is used as a measure of central tendency because of the large range of implementation rates for some sectors and districts.

For 1981, the higher implementation rates as indicated by column medians are in the health, education and agriculture sectors and range between 40 and 63 per cent. This disparity was mainly due to the government's priority emphasis on these sectors. Another factor is the relatively less well performance of the agencies in the other sectors that lagged behind. In this situation, the rates of implementation achieved are significant. In terms of the districts, more urban areas had the highest rates in 1981 as indicated by the row medians: Cape Coast District, 69.4 per cent; Mfantsiman District, 57.9 per cent; and Agona Swedru

Table 8.1 Public project implementation rates by sector and district (%), 1981

District	*High-ways*	*Feeder roads*	*Water*	*Health*	*Agric.*	*Educ.*	*Row Median*
	%	%	%	%	%	%	%
Mfantsiman	51.0	93.5	0	64.8	80.0	0	57.9
Cape Coast	70.0	0	36.5	77.3	68.8	75.0	69.4
Komenda-Edina-Eguafo-Abrem	60.0	72.5	80.0	91.8	50.0	70.0	71.3
Awutu-Effutu-Senya	0	65.5	4.5	53.5	20.0	55.6	36.7
Gomoa	0	47.5	0	70.5	30.0	0	15.0
Upper Denkyira	0	57.5	0	50.0	0	30.0	15.0
Assin	0	52.7	0	63.0	0	62.5	26.4
Ajumako-Enyan-Esiam	0	0	0	70.0	0	0	0
Abura-Asebu-Kwamankese	0	0	15.0	62.7	65.0	95.0	38.9
Agona Swedru	0	0	90.0	55.0	57.0	77.5	56.0
Lower Denkyira-Twifo-Hemang	0	0	0	45.0	0	0	0
Asikuma-Odoben-Brakwa	0	0	0	95.0	57.0	50.0	25.0
Sector Median	0	23.8	0	63.9	40.0	52.8	-

Source: Author's computation, based on original project implementation rates provided by Regional Planning Co-ordinating Unit, Cape Coast; zero means no project

District, 56 per cent. The only rural district that emerged with a high median implementation rate was Komenda-Edina-Eguafo-Abrem, at 71.3 per cent. In view of the fact that this district appeared in category three for most of the eight sectors analysed in chapter six, this rate of implementation achievement was rather phenomenal. Ajumako-Enyan-Esiam and Lower Denkyira-Twifo-Hemang Districts registered zero per cent implementation rate. Four of the remaining and rural districts had below 30 per cent and two achieved between 36 and 40 per cent implementation rate.

While the reasons given already for the sectors also apply to the locality levels, the other constraint is the extent of data availability. Thus those districts that may appear as having achieved low rates of implementation may actually have done better. For example, Table 8.1 shows Komenda-Edina-Eguafo-Abrem District as having had the best data coverage on implementation rates. Nevertheless, the varying performance of the various developers, 'contractors' and other building agencies also accounts for these differences. The earliest 1980s were also the time of renewed reconstruction and economic reorganization in Ghana. Indeed, as noted already in chapter four, 1981 was the nadir of deterioration in the national economy.

By the late 1980s, all the six sectors of the regional economy indicated in the table showed consistently high rates of implementation, ranging between 50 per cent and 74 per cent (Table 8.2). The rates at the district levels ranged between 47 per cent and 76.2 per cent; 8 of the 12 districts achieved over 60 per cent implementation and 3 of these between 47 per cent and 56 per cent. However,

Table 8.2 Public project implementation rates by sector and district (%), 1988

District	*High-ways*	*Feeder roads*	*Water*	*Health*	*Agric.*	*Educ.*	*Row Median*
	%	%	%	%	%	%	%
Mfantsiman	65.0	75.0	49.0	70.0	75.0	89.0	72.5
Cape Coast	79.0	83.0	46.0	74.0	81.0	70.0	76.2
Komenda-Edina-Eguafo-Abrem	60.0	72.0	80.0	86.0	57.0	54.0	66.0
Awutu-Effutu-Senya	50.0	78.0	72.0	68.0	66.0	55.0	67.0
Gomoa	66.0	80.0	65.0	69.0	54.0	50.0	65.5
Upper Denkyira	54.0	69.0	73.0	68.0	21.0	54.0	61.0
Assin	66.0	67.0	28.0	65.0	0	30.0	47.5
Ajumako-Enyan-Esiam	0	64.0	67.0	47.0	0	0	23.5
Abura-Asebu-Kwamankese	74.0	100.0	60.0	72.0	49.0	50.0	66.0
Agona Swedru	61.0	83.0	39.0	62.0	45.0	73.0	61.5
Lower Denkyira-Twifo-Hemang	81.0	58.0	56.0	56.0	0	44.0	56.0
Asikuma-Odoben-Brakwa	47.0	42.0	34.0	56.0	51.0	56.0	49.0
Sector Median	63.0	73.5	58.0	68.0	50.0	54.0	-

Source: Author's computation, based on original project implementation rates provided by Regional Planning Co-ordinating Unit, Cape Coast,; zero means no project

Ajumako-Enyan-Esiam District which had registered only zero per cent in 1981 now made 23.5 per cent implementation rate. The same case applies to Lower Denkyira-Twifo-Hemang District. Indeed, there was appreciable improvement in project implementation rates by 1988.

Again, some of the reasons given for project implementation in 1981 apply here. By 1988, the national macro-economic recovery and adjustment programmes were in progress. The new local authorities were also preparing to begin or had begun their work. New planning legislation was being prepared which also created positions for co-ordinating planners within each government ministry and department. Therefore, apart from the regional planning officers, there came into being a formalized national-level function for programme implementation and co-ordination.

Rate of concrete regional programme implementation Further data on any aspects of the implementation of the CEDECOM programme are not available to the present study. Therefore, the assessment and discussion in this section are limited to the achievement of TOPP, so far. However, it is relevant to note that problems pointed out in relation to the former in chapter five could well constrain its implementation which would be well underway at the time of writing. These include the possible conflicts between the various governmental, quasi-non governmental and non-governmental organizations which were to be managed by CEDECOM. These conflicts would have the potential of limiting the new programme's effectiveness.

In the case of TOPP, the effectiveness of its implementation depends appreciably on the performance of the smallholder project. This is because it is the first real channel for delivering the public sector-driven development processes under the programme. In the original project plan and projection schedule, the settlement of smallholders and allocation of oil palm plots should have been achieved at 11 producers in 1983, 29 by 1984, and 30 by 1985; This should have produced a cumulative total of 70 by the end of 1985 (Harrisons Fleming Advisory Services, 1985). However, the TOPP company was only able to settle 11 smallholders, altogether, by the end of 1985; they could not settle any of the smallholders in 1983 and 1984.

By the same schedule, 80 more producers should have been settled in 1986 but the company only managed to settle a cumulative number of 34 by that year. By the projections, the company should have settled all the target population of 300 smallholders by 1988 (Harrisons Fleming Advisory Services, 1985). As at the time of the earlier fieldwork in 1989, TOPP had settled only 83 and by the end of the follow-up survey in 1998, 210 of them. This means 70 per cent of the entire target population that should have been settled by 1988 was only achieved in 1998 - a delay by ten years. While the company is still managing to settle the remaining 90 producers or 30 per cent of the original target population, it is far behind the projected and agreed schedule. It has been pointed out in chapter seven how the land-ejection and compulsory purchase action has worsened the poverty and socio-economic well-being of the non-settled smallholder producers.

The limitation on free availability of all the lands taken over by the TOPP company is one factor behind the delay in implementation. The entire area has been divided into blocks of land which are released by central government to the company as the programme proceeds. However, government has been reluctant to release land at some stages because of the disagreements and conflicts with the original landowners, some of whom were not agreeing to the compulsory purchase. These persons had either received minimal or no compensation payments at all. In view of the fact that they would have neither oil palm plots nor be able to undertake food-crop production, the landowners have had difficulties co-operating with the programme. Other constraints on effective implementation are the social organizational and cultural relationships of the sub-regional communities as explained in chapter seven. These have created difficulties in the process of identifying distinct and clear family units within each household. It has required long and complex negotiation and meetings between the company and representatives of the local communities to resolve, appreciably. Besides, TOPP has been recently faced with problems resulting from a glut of palm oil on the national market. The non-achievement of market price for its product has therefore meant a decline in profits and performance.

Quality of both regional planning policy and *development policy* The nature and state of planning policy also affects the rate and level of implementation (Alexander and Faludi, 1989; Sorensen and Ausler, 1989). Planning policy exists in terms of legitimacy and formal power only broadly at the national level. Regional policy has been purely advisory. This historical problem has only bolstered up sector-based policy and activities (i.e. development policy). Therefore, inter-sector co-ordination has been constrained at the regional level. When the various sectors within the regional space economy pursue their own agendas and not under the compulsion of formal regional planning policy, their attitudes and interests in this way tend to impede the rate and degree of implementation.

Apart from general co-ordination, there tends to be failure in agreeing values, objectives, as well as possible trade-offs. Indeed, a principal regional planning officer interviewed stated that 'national planning policies are passed on to departments, no targets; only specific projects within sectors'. An interview with the sector-based heads also confirmed this practice. For example, the regional feeder roads officer stated that: 'all sector heads operate in isolation - no co-ordination'. The regional health officer also indicated that 'no proper co-ordination ... Regional Council ineffective'. In a similar way, the regional highways engineer stated that 'no direct links with other sectors'. However, the regional engineer for the electricity corporation stated that: 'sectoral policies are incorporated in overall regional development policy but not integrated with other sectors'. This statement also implies that the sector-based policies are equally included in the advisory regional planning framework in the same stricture. A further implication of the making of development policy is that it amounts to a technical and 'routinized' exercise within each individual government ministry or department. The ineffectiveness of such practices could be seen for example, in the case of urbanization and urban development initiatives. The more fragmented and isolated the efforts are, the least opportunity there would be to achieve the development policy goals and objectives.

Quality and practices of plan-making and design of initiatives It has been emphasized that there is no formal regional-plan making, as yet. The best case of practice in the Central Region is at the level of informal and equally advisory plans. Indeed, it is further limited in providing strategic guidance for the various localities within the Region. This practice is also typical of the other regions of Ghana. The principal regional planner interviewed indicated that there were no formal regional plans 'because regional planning has no legal backing for plan-making'. The senior regional planner interviewed also indicated: 'no statutory plans'. In response to the question as to whether there were any real regional plans in the past, the principal regional planning officer stated that 'regional development plans are only academic; they are not statutory or gazetted'. The second principal planning officer interviewed also stated that the '1981-86 five-year development plan ... not implemented for political reasons'. These 'political reasons' include the problem of not having a formally instituted regional government. Another reason is the dominance of 'policy for regional development' - nationally-based regional policy. And the senior planning officer stated that '... regional planning unit not empowered to propose its own plans'. Moreover, this particular planning officer described the form of practice nearest to plan-making as 'sectoral adhocratism'. This illustrates the shifting and impermanent nature of anything near regional plan-making.

This practice simply influences the practice of project and programme design. For example, the regional education official interviewed described the mode of sector-based programme planning as 'top-down'. The regional agriculture officer also indicated that the sector-based planning is based on 'directives from headquarters ... technical officers from region'. However, the regional water engineer stated that 'some areas adopted by international agencies and NGOs - others under specific programmes'.

Therefore, while there is no formal making of regional plans, the quality of what might be a useful substitute is seriously impaired: strategic regional guidance instruments. While this situation further consolidates sector-based planning, it also limits more the form of practice in its co-ordination function.

The net impact is to limit the effectiveness of programme and project implementation.

Co-ordination of programme and project implementation The case here relates to the co-ordination of both inter-sector policies as well as of sector-based projects. One of the principal planning officers stated that a major problem facing regional planning practice is the 'lack of co-ordination and verticalization of development planning'. In any sector-based planning practice such as clearly identified and emphasized, co-ordination must be powerfully strengthened in order to achieve quality, integration and balance in implementation and results. Therefore, in the event that the co-ordination between sector-based policies as well as between projects is weak, programme implementation suffers a double fate of ineffectiveness. The responses from both the regional planners and sector departmental heads show that there is either limited or no co-ordination at all. In fact, the response from the electricity sector shows that although sector-based policies have some reflection in regional policies, this does not imply integration. Indeed, the point has been emphasized that planning, in this regard, is more of a top-down practice handed down from departmental or ministerial headquarters in the national capital city.

The total impact of all these problems is to limit the effectiveness of action, initiative and implementation. In the case of the TOPP programme, there has not been strong co-ordination between the settled smallholders and the company on one hand, between the latter and the non-settled people on the other. There is also limited co-ordination between the company and the other agencies, including the Central Regional Development Corporation and the Lower Denkyira-Twifo-Hemang District Assembly. This is also reflected in the relationship between the company and the local communities. Problems of socio-economic and spatial planning in the real world do not exist in isolation. Therefore, when effort aimed at solving them are fragmented and diverged, whatever development effort is seriously defeatist.

Communication in the implementation process This is a pervasive function in implementation and the whole planning process between various levels. This includes communication between the various sectors and the local community; between the various sector organizations as well as between other agencies; between levels of planning as well as between planners and the local community. With respect to the various sectors, the responses from the heads of sector departments as well as the regional planners show that communication is ineffective and that the sectors operate as vertical structures. As all the sector units control their budgets and have full independent implementation powers, they deal with their various contracting agencies on the ground. Thus even the Regional Co-ordinating Council which includes representation from the various sector departments and such organizations as CEDECOM is limited in its capital and real power to promote greater communication between the various sector ministries and departments.

In the case of communication between sector organizations and the local community, it is only in self-help projects that the latter participate fully. In relation to public projects, one role of the community is to prompt the regional and district authorities about their needs and problems. According to the regional planners interviewed, some of the local communities in the Region also do assist planners in project identification. Sometimes, the community also support planners and public officials with collection of relevant data and information in this regard. This is apart from being respondents in any surveys that the sector organizations undertake. Members of the District Assemblies and other community leaders make significant contributions to promoting communication between the local communities and planners as well as with the sector organizations. The efforts, in this regard in the Twifo sub-region, are demonstrated in the co-operation between community leaders. These include the men and women representatives of the District Assembly, in this case, and the TOPP company. However, this is not within the context of legitimate planning policy and regional plan.

Under the planning legislation, the local communities have a real opportunity of communicating with the planners and preparing a sub-district or action plan (Republic of Ghana, 1994b). They may be authorized by the District Planning Authority to do so. This would provide the opportunity for them to co-ordinate all their efforts, and resources as well as those of all the sectors. In this way, too, the local community would take advantage of the real opportunity for communicating with planners, sector organizations, local and regional governments. By these processes, they would effectively address the local environment in all its parts in the development process.

Control of resources and development processes Control is seen in relation to financial, physical and natural as well as temporal resources. The case of time resource control is considered in terms of monitoring and evaluation as measures for feeding back to on-going and subsequent implementation and checking on time schedules. Including time, 'control' is also applied to the development processes and planning standards these may involve.

The sector agency officials interviewed indicated that they do monitor their projects regularly. In fact, the highways personnel stated that they do so on daily basis. As to how such monitoring affected the overall implementation, the general response was that information collected was fed into the process by an internal feedback mechanism. With respect to the involvement of planners in this, the perception of sector-based organizations is that regional planning officials only issue approval certificates for project completion and for payment to be made to developers by central government. In other words, the Regional Planning Co-ordinating Unit is seen as performing a technical exercise as much as an administrative one. It is the principal responsibility of the Unit to ensure that all government-funded projects within the Region are completed according to schedule and standards. This is a condition for paying the developer or 'building contractor'.

Again, all the sectors undertake their own evaluations, except the highways department which indicated that they, occasionally, involve consultants. However, the involvement of external consultants in project evaluation is not necessarily typical across the sector-based organizations. Therefore, the sectors tend to have a good self-image. It has been argued that planning evaluation should involve both internal and external evaluations as part of ensuring the achievement of effective implementation (Bowden, 1988). The particular advantage is to provide the widest range of information about programme performance. Therefore, in the absence of this taking place, the net effect is a limitation on the rate of implementation success. The RPCU depends much on the information provided by the developers. In practice, however, this involves significant negotiation and agreement. The national planning consultant interviewed indicated that the quarterly reports prepared by the RPCU on the progress of implementing public projects 'are not effective because they only cover developments which are determined at the sectoral level'.

This role of the regional planners tends to be a rather passive one. Therefore, whatever the role the regional planning officials play in controlling project time, monitoring and evaluation are limited in effectiveness as these are primarily overshadowed by the power of the relevant sector organization. In all this role of the regional planner, the quality of the various individual projects has not been studied. However, it appears ensuring that planning and development standards are met is not well-adhered to and may be overlooked in many cases. For example, a number of projects that have been inspected to have been fully completed and paid for are later found to have been shoddily done. In situations such as these, the failures in the built structures may show only a while after these have been commissioned.

Programme and project funding, of course, has suffered an all-time constraint. Formerly, it was the practice for all contracting firms selected to execute government projects to be given the approved budgets for implementation. Under current practice, they have to bid on a competitive basis through the Regional Tender Board: compulsory competitive tendering. Then the 'contractors' spend their own funds and are later reimbursed by the Ministry of Finance. However, there is always an undue delay in the payment of these developers. Even so, changes in inflation rates - which can be very acrobatic in a Third World country - may affect the value of payment by the time the contractor actually receives it. Indeed, some projects are suspended by the contractors until they receive payment for their arrears. The net effect is to delay the realization of completion schedules. In relation to the 'scale element' introduced, the prosperous and viable contractors who are often urban-based are the ones in contact with local and regional government officials. Thus they exploit this locational advantage to their benefit (Ofori, 2000h). This is a more likely factor promoting the better implementation rates shown for most urban areas and districts. The problem is that the financial and budget allocation systems are not decentralized, and this represents another contradiction in public administration.

Another problem is the occasional shortage of material inputs, but this has to do directly with finance. As the contractors often have their contract payments delayed by the Ministry of Finance, this affects their rate of stock renewal. However, the regional planners pointed out the unhelpful attitudes of some contractors. For example, the building contracting companies occasionally do shoddy work (e.g. poor road or building quality). In this case, the particular contracts may be suspended or re-awarded. However, there can be government interference on its own, say through the unnecessary termination of a programme due to bad planning or sudden drying up of funds. The net effect of this mix of factors relating to the ready availability of input materials is to seriously delay implementation.

Another aspect of material or factor input relates more to land supply which is often a problem in the development process (e.g. Amissah, 1987). The case of the TOPP company in relation to this has been pointed out. Simply, if the amount of land needed to undertake the project is not supplied and on schedule, the result is a delay in implementation. Indeed, the land supply and availability problem, stemming from disagreements with the local communities, have caused considerable delay in achieving greater implementation success of the TOPP project-complex.

The regional planners also indicated 'bad weather' as one of the problems of implementation. Naturally, in a tropical country, the rainy season is not always a suitable and 'productive' time to undertake most projects for obvious reasons. Therefore, one expects that this would be taken care of in the time-scheduling. But it could so happen that budgetary allocations go through during such seasons and implementation must proceed immediately. Thus effective timing of starting project implementation is crucial to effective completion and achievement of the relevant development policy objectives. This is also an element in achieving and maintaining balance in the regional development process.

Decentralization and the implementation process The fact that the policy of decentralization has not seeped through all departments was pointed out in earlier chapters. It has also been indicated previously in this chapter that financial centralization is one of the constraints on effective implementation. Decentralization, so far, has only been administrative without any devolution of decision-making and political powers. Yet, even the so-intended administrative decentralization has not been complete. Examples include the Ministry of Agriculture; Ministry of Employment and Social Welfare which have not been fully decentralized in many district localities. This also means some services have not yet been decentralized.

Indeed, a most important and notable case is the ineffective decentralization of the system for allocating financial resources and for remunerating developers. It may be to ensure accountability for which there may yet be no decentralized structures in the regions and localities. All payments are concentrated in the Ministry of Finance. This tends to contribute to the delay in project completion and frustration for the developers. Ineffective decentralization also hampers project-planning since local level problem identification structures do not exist in many cases. This affects the rate of implementation, which is commonly based on quasi- or very minimal knowledge of the problem in the area (Hogwood and Gunn, 1984; Sabatier and Manzmanian, 1979; Gunn, 1978). It further limits the effectiveness of inter-sector co-ordination as well as related levels of communication.

Effectiveness of actor roles in the process implementation

It is equally important to assess the effectiveness of the actors who make things happen in the regional planning and development processes. For example, one needs to address the question whether the actions of the actors lead to an effective reduction or rather structural amplification at various levels of disparities. These include those between areas, sectors of the space economy, groups of persons as well as communities. While assessing the role effectiveness of individual actor-groups, it is also important to examine the interactive relationships between and among them. Their inter-relationships within the context of the planning process also reflect the essence and value of the democratic enterprise ethic as well as practices of partnership and team-working.

Central government It has been shown that regional policy is more of the 'policy for regional development' type, essentially formulated by central government and national-level policy makers. In the same way the sector-based organizations are directly controlled by their headquarters, despite the existence of the local government system which places many of them under the District Assemblies. These two factors have seriously limited and contributed to preventing the regional level from making its own policies. Again, despite the powers of the local government system, this culture only amounts to a top-down practice. This has also meant that central government has dominated and controlled the design as well as management of development programmes, the like of TOPP. While it is agreed that these are more strategic ventures and do involve substantial bilateral and multilateral agreements and protocol, it would serve the interests of the regional level best if it were allowed to play a direct and active and not a passive role.

Besides, this top-down management and control has limited the extent to which the regional level is able to identify its own socio-economic and environmental problems. Indeed, it has also contributed to the creation of the spatial separatist trend by making regional development sector-based and atomized. These also limit the achievement of balance and integration in the regional development process. The practices and attitudes of central government have contributed immensely to the situation of inflexibility and lack of strategic guidance at the regional level. Thus while it is appreciated that government is making an intervention to promote regional development, it is the nature of this that is limited in its effectiveness.

Regional governance and regional planning functions It is obvious, on the basis of the above reflective observation, that the advisory form of regional governance in Ghana has been far from adequate. Like the former Regional Consultative Council, the current Regional Co-ordinating Council does not have any formal options to formulate policies in regional development. While the former acted as a general 'watch-dog' and purely advisory body, the latter has some planning and management functions, still not of plan-making. Under the current planning legislation, the Regional Co-ordinating Council has the powers to co-ordinate plans and programmes as well as monitor and evaluate the implementation of development initiatives of the local authorities in the Region. The Regional Planning Co-ordinating Unit (RPCU) is also empowered to advise the RCC on these planning functions as well as development planning, in general. Yet still, this does not include the making of regional plans. In fact, the non-existence of formal regional governance has removed the opportunity for the regional level to play a really active role in the regional planning and development process.

However, a significant aspect of the legislation, in this regard, is that the RPCU is now empowered to advise the RCC on matters relating to sector-based and spatial policies. Furthermore, the RPCU represents central government at the regional level in relation to programmes and projects as may be designated. The RPCU's role in relation to all matters of development planning is only advisory. Therefore, the planning legislation is seriously limited in its power and effect. While all these functions may create an opportunity for the RCC and RPCU to provide strategic guidance, this would be characterized by vagueness and limited effectiveness. The reason is that the sector-based and other agencies would not necessarily be bound by such guidance. This limitation further bolsters up sector-based planning power, itself already strengthened by separate legislative provisions. While certain advisory forms of regional governance and regional planning agency roles could be advisory and still have effective powers (Wannop, 1995), the practices and legislation in Ghana do not, yet, fit into those categories.

Regional planners The regional planners interviewed pointed out a number of difficulties that constrained the effectiveness of their functions and duties. One of these is insufficient staffing of regional planners in the Central Region's RPCU. For example, of the required total number of five regional planners, there were only two at post. According to the two planners, regional planning professionals were not encouraged to stay in the Unit because the practice was only limited to project inspection as a form of development control - the basic function of issuing certificates of approval for completed projects. The quarterly report prepared by the regional planners is based on the various rates and levels of progress in monitoring and approval of the public-funded projects. This aspect of the role of regional planners in development administration also makes them function only as civil service administrators.

Despite the functions added to the work of regional planners in relation to advising on policy and programme matters, they are still not really empowered to act in the same way as are the more locally-based physical planners. Therefore, another aspect of the problem is that the professional skills and knowledge of the regional planners is not being fully utilized. Quite apart from this, regional administrators have often not consulted the regional planners as appropriate. For example the Regional Secretary (now Regional Minister) in the Central Region often depended on the regional administrators, to the neglect of the regional planners. The net effect is that full and realistic professionalism is not brought to bear on development planning work. The crucial point is that this affects policy-making and socio-economic as well as spatial planning. All the functions exercised by regional planners, so far, also point to the importance of management practice in the regional planning and development processes. Indeed, these reflect the argument made by Dunham (1977) in relation to the regional planner as a technician, negotiator and manager (Zetter, 1981).

It is also important to point out a limitation of regional planning education in Ghana. Regional planners were trained to gain skills and knowledge in a range of courses. These include regional analysis, regional economics, regional surveys and plan-making (development planning), natural resource development, transportation planning, agricultural economics, project and plan evaluation. Others are quantitative methods, planning law and administration, planning theory as well as principles of management. However, the lack of formal plan-making practice at the regional level has taken out an important context for regional planning education and practice in Ghana. Even the more recent legislation is limited in making this happen. If the District Assemblies have taken up the opportunity of producing local plans, this problem may have been tempered to a certain extent.

Besides these limitations, regional planning education which begun in the 1960s in Ghana later became limited in its content relating to urban and rural design as well as community-based planning. Perhaps this is related to the fact that Ghana, like many other African countries, is more rural-based in terms of population and, therefore, tends to promote a predominance of rural-oriented studies, emphasis on the economic aspects. However, the trends pointed out in chapters four, five and six show the need for an equally strong input relating to urban studies in regional planning education (Zetter, 1981). The kinds of issues and environments in which regional planners work in Ghana indicate the need to strengthen the urban and rural design studies aspects. When planning education lacks a context of real development planning in terms of plan-making as well as wider practices, it becomes limited in its full opportunity to deliver. A further aspect of planning, in this regard, is the bifurcation into urban-physical and regional planning. Perhaps, the case made here emphasizes the need to offer fully and firmly integrated planning studies in the form of 'urban and regional planning' and so on. This would also strengthen planning policy analysis.

In fact, when the post-graduate planning course was originally introduced, there were two separate masters programmes in 'urban planning' and 'regional planning'. The former was terminated due to the lack of appropriate instructors and tutors. The latter has since been reorganized into a combined international and in-country-based programme. The trends and material contexts do emphasize the need to provide a reformed instructional and explicitly integrated urban-regional planning programme of study at the post-graduate level in Ghana. There is also need for stronger emphasis on the planning process, especially in relation to policy formulation and implementation (Zetter, 1981). Planning law and planning practice are also of critical importance.

A realistic and non-truncated view of terrestrial space, in this way, would also promote the opportunities for the planners to engage in continuous learning about the planning process. Indeed, this enhances focus on the pervasive role of towns of all scales and rural centres in the process of regional planning. Ofori (2000b) Schon (1991) and Mattingly (1989) have argued strongly for applying concepts and practices of action and experiential learning in spatial planning. This is even more critical in a rapidly changing environmental context, more typical of Third World countries. In this way also, planners gain new experiences from which they can generate new learning and action. The regional planners who were interviewed indicated that they did not engage in any group learning outside formal staff meetings. Consultation between themselves and with other planners about urban and regional problems would offer opportunities for these kinds of interactive learning and work. This would also enhance the practice of self-assessment and evaluation in regional planning practice. While learning from their own experiences, they could also learn from the experiences of planners in the other regions of Ghana. For example, the regional planners would have the advantage of gaining new knowledge, skills, methods and techniques about policy formulation and planning activities. This would further create the opportunities for experimentation in the planning process (Mattingly, 1989).

Sub-regional community According to the regional planners and local community leaders interviewed, the local Twifo communities contribute to the regional development process by providing labour in the implementation of various initiatives. The local communities also do make contributions in cash and kind as a way of financing their own projects. They also contribute to data and information collection, as may be needed, by the RPCU. However, these roles are not in any way formalized except to the extent that there is now provision for community-led making of sub-district plans. They also have the right to examine in public any proposed district plans. Indeed, as the regional planners observed, 'no institutional arrangement to consider their participation yet; new planning law provides public comments on draft district plans though'.

Part of the analysis in chapter five shows the efforts being made by local communities in the Central Region to undertake various development projects. These are on self-help basis. The study in chapter seven shows the involvement of local communities in the actual process of development is of a different nature. They are not really involved with the TOPP company. In fact, there have been conflicts between some sections of the community and the company with respect to land supply, under the compulsory purchase order. It appears that this situation is exacerbated by the fact that the TOPP project-complex and company are not effectively accountable to the regional authorities. This also means they are not firmly within the statutory planning systems. In fact, this accounts for part of the justification for the introduction of CEDECOM which seeks to pull together all governmental and quasi-non-governmental organizations. The case of TOPP's relationship with the local community may reflect the situation pertaining to other parts of Ghana under similar development programmes. The fact must also be emphasized that the corporate members of the TOPP's actor-mix are muscling out, championed by UniLever.

Regional development institutions There are now two main organizations for development in the Central Region. One is the CEREDEC, which is a statutory and public corporate body. The other is the new non-statutory umbrella organization, CEDECOM. The general performance of the former has been questioned as indicated in chapter one (Ofori, 2000a). In a recent evaluative study of the Regional Development Corporations (RDCs) in all ten regions of Ghana, Ofori (2000a) has made a number of observations. While the RDCs are making some material impact through industrial and agricultural production, the greater emphasis is on economic considerations. There is significant control from international and multinational corporate organizations as well as central government forces. Therefore, the regional and local communities in the project areas are in a weaker position.

The real involvement of the RDCs has been limited, by legislation, in regional development. They also suffer the same limitation of severe under-funding. While they have power to borrow money, they are controlled and limited by central government in this regard. Bannerman (1984) had also pointed out that a critical problem facing the RDCs is frequent political interference from central government and the regional administrative establishment. Other difficulties appear to be inappropriate organizational arrangements. For example, the TOPP management actually report to the Ministry of Finance and Economic Planning, whereas the smallholder project component actually comes under the CEREDEC. This introduces some operational conflicts between the two bodies.

As part of this recent study, Ofori (2000a) proposed that the RDCs be placed under the control of a separate and specialized organization other than the State Enterprises Commission. This would promote the opportunities for them to focus on social and economic development in the territorial areas of the regions while they still maintain their corporate character (Ofori, 2000a). Nevertheless, CEREDEC has played a significant role in the development of the Central Region, apart from the TOPP project-complex (Ofori, 2000a).

The lack of regional development plans also limits the functioning of the RDCs. A statutory plan would indicate the place and roles of the agencies involved. The plan would, at least, have the potential to control and co-ordinate the functions of the RDC. It could, for instance, persuade the RDCs into undertaking more concrete socio-economic projects and programmes. In fact, apart from the TOPP complex, 90 per cent of CEREDEC's projects are located within or in the immediate surrounding area of Cape Coast District. This also reflects the situation in the other regions (Ofori-Cudjoe, 1990a). In one sense, it may represent 'efficiency' to do so under a structural-dualistic regional economy, with most of the available infrastructure supplied to the urban sector. Besides, in a situation where the RDC receives insignificant central government capitalization, its inward investment activities are much constrained. In fact, the CEREDEC's project officials seriously lacked transport facilities for making visits to sites in the peripheral districts and monitoring development initiatives (Rondinelli and Ruddell, 1978). All these problems limit implementation effectiveness and affect the achievement of equity and territorial justice.

As noted already, there has been no further data on the CEDECOM, apart from the original programme document available to the present study. Therefore only strategic statements with respect to what might have happened since its actual implementation are made here. It has already been noted that the size and design of the programme appears ambitious in seeking to bring rather too many organizations within its ambit. This is an attempt to put governmental, quasi-governmental organizations as well as NGOs under one giant institutional structure. There is the likelihood of this generating its own conflicts. These difficulties could also limit the effectiveness and robustness of the umbrella organization.

Funding and investment agencies It has been demonstrated that both the loan and equity investors have made substantial investments in the TOPP programme. It is expected that the United Nations Development Programme (UNDP) and other agencies, including the Government of Ghana, being the main funding sources for CEDECOM, would also have provided it with appreciable funding by now. It is critical upon the TOPP programme and CEDECOM to match the level and quality of funding through both efficient and effective performance, in particular, in terms of socio-economic development.

The behaviour of some of the equity investors and shareholders shows growing lopsided and corporate dominance under the TOPP programme. UniLever has taken up one-half of the shares in TOPP. In terms of the divestment strategy, it is likely that the government would dispose of its remaining shares. On the basis of the trends, it is also likely that UniLever would acquire more shares or take over the TOPP company altogether. UniLever (Ghana Limited) has been the principal and leading customer of TOPP and has every intent to controlling its own sources of raw material supply. It is likely that this situation has influenced the recent behaviour of Mobil UK (part of Mobil Corporation) which was seeking to withdraw from the company at the time of the follow-up survey in 1998. If these trends do take place, UniLever would become a 'monopolist' investor and enjoy absolute corporate power. This situation might limit the TOPP company's instrumental role in the socio-economic development of the Twifo sub-region if UniLever or the emerging dominant corporate investors have the intent to run TOPP on strictly commercial and business lines.

The democratic enterprise ethic and praxis In line with an underlying theme in this book, it is relevant to address the effectiveness of achieving the democratic enterprise in Ghanaian regional planning, based on the available evidence. In the absence of a political devolution form of decentralization at the regional level as well as of an elected form of regional governance, the opportunity for creating a really democratic enterprise is sacrificed. A number of factors contribute to the development of this situation - the lack of effective integration of projects; the position of TOPP; the form of regional administrative and institutional framework. One of the problems resulting from this situation is the fragmentation of the political and technical administration of TOPP among national, regional and programme management levels. This also limits the achievement of the democratic enterprise ethic. In any of these considerations, the real losers are the local sub-regional and territorial communities.

The situation of a seriously limited democratic enterprise has also created the opportunity for specific actors to initiate actions supposed to be in the interest of the regional community. For example, the Regional Minister's Office - then Regional Secretary - was in the process of introducing a new regional programme in the form of CEDECOM, with all the relevant forecasts and documentation prepared, without the knowledge of the RPCU which is also housed in the same building. The appointive nature of the representation on the CEDECOM as well as of the RCC itself contributes to intensifying the ineffectiveness of the democratic enterprise.

In the midst of all these, the opportunities for a genuinely shared decision-making as well as action-based and social learning are further seriously limited and vitiated at the regional level. The complex ineffective situation, in these regards, also limits the achievement of social distributive justice in the Region. Furthermore, these situations and tendencies are more likely to amplify and further intensify openings for class struggle and social conflicts. These could happen between any of the various communities identified in the study. The opportunities for genuine partnership and team-working as elements within the democratic enterprise in the regional planning and development processes also become limited.

The various communities identified in this study include the estate employees; outgrowers; and settled smallholder producers. Others are the non-settled, aggrieved and land-ejected persons; the wider Lower Denkyira-Twifo-Hemang sub-region, including the District Assembly. Further communities are those of the formal regional administrators, informal advisors and representatives on the RCC as well as regional planners. Another community is that of regional development agencies - including the TOPP executive company, CEREDEC and CEDECOM. The other community is that of sector-based organizations and central government. There is also the community of loan and equity investors (Ofori, 2000a).

While the domestic and regional private sector may be represented on the Regional Co-ordinating Council and perhaps CEDECOM, it appears to be one partner-group and team-member that is not clearly featured in this array of stakeholders. The attitudes of the regional development agencies, regional administrators and central government have not been fair in relation to compensations for some of the actual material producers: settled and non-settled land-ejected persons. For the latter group, their situation has been worsened. Therefore, these tendencies have limited the opportunities for partnership and team-working among these communities in the territorial region. The absence of an overarching structure for all these communities to be engaged together in decision-making and action also removes the opportunity for achieving partnership and team-working in a regional democratic enterprise.

The corporate investors are now growing stronger than central government, the latter becoming a weaker constituency in the regional development process. The wider sub-regional community is also growing weaker under the restructuring and emasculating dominance of corporate forces over the territorial ones as shown in the two regional programmes. This mix of forces also limits the chances of achieving the democratic enterprise, effective partnership and team-working. It is proposed that these would be best achieved through an elected regional government in which regional politicians, professional persons and the wider regional populace have a common stake and fair representation.

Effectiveness of managing territorial regional change

Managing regional change implies a response to a significant threat or opportunity emanating from both within the regional environment as well as the wider space-economy outside it (Gilgeous, 1997; Carnall, 1992). These include responding effectively to challenges, including uncertainties. Therefore, the attitude of planners, policy-makers and other stakeholders in it as well as their competence and capability to manage the process are also crucial to securing the relevant policy goals and programme objectives (Carnall, 1992; Webber, 1969). The element of uncertainty further underlies the urgent need to adopt a contingency approach to managing change in the local and regional environment (Ofori, 2000d; Christiansen, 1985). It is also relevant to assess the effectiveness of managing change in the Central Region in terms of its specific factors and instruments relating to the various initiatives, past and present. This aspect of the study is addressed in terms of the specific elements of managing change.

Strategies One of the declared and adopted strategies of regional planning within the stated policies is agro-industrial development as demonstrated under the TOPP programme. It has been shown that this strategy is effective in generating significant social and economic development in the programme region. This effectiveness is, however, limited by implementation problems in the form of constrained land supply, unfavourable macro-economic conditions of glut in palm oil and market performance. A further limitation of the potential is growing corporate dominance.

Another declared strategy is that of integrated rural development. This is only supposedly addressed through the earlier strategy mentioned and other individual strategies that will be mentioned. Thus there is no distinct and wholly concretely formulated rural development programme as such. One factor accounting for this is the lack of formal making of regional plans. At any rate, the sector-based nature of programme planning and implementation means that the effort at achieving an integrated development in the rural areas is defeated by the fragmentation of structures for delivering.

A further strategy is that of growth-and-service centres which includes elements of a sites-and-services approach as indicated in chapter five. Again this has not been implemented fully and comprehensively as formulated; aspects have been happening here and there. However, the successful implementation of a regional programme, in this regard, is constrained by the absence of a formally empowered, politically accountable and overarching agency. Therefore, it is self-contradictory attempting to solve problems that are integrated in nature and focused on settlements that exist as 'wholes' through institutional structures that are ineffectively co-ordinated and that undertake independently.

Furthermore, the provision and generation of social services, including appropriate infrastructure is another strategy of regional development in context. This has been shown to an extent in chapter five, six, and particularly seven. Once again, these are only one-off schemes, especially in relation to housing, education, leisure and recreation. Besides, there is no instituted and validated means of ensuring that these vital services are provided; nor does this happen within the framework of a regional plan.

An emerging and positive trend is the community-based and self-help initiative strategy. The two Departments of Community Development, Rural Development and Cottage Industries occasionally support the local communities with the procurement of input resources. However, the real opportunity to make more effective and better things happen through the development plan system has not been exploited by many of the local communities, yet.

There is also the more explicit and recent focus on tourism as a strategy. The Central Region is endowed with substantial resources for achieving the goals and objectives in this area. The high national premium on this sector is also encouraging and has appreciable promise to make significant contribution to the regional development process. No specific and material assessment of it has been made in this book. However, on the basis of the available information, the tourism sector in the Central Region looks a bright one which could make substantial contribution to effective regional change. This would need extensive surveys of all the resource bases as well as restoration and creation of other supporting infrastructure and facilities. Information relating to the actual implementation of CEDECOM is not available to this book.

Systems The relevant systems here for managing regional change are those of planning, legislation, administration, and governance. It is emphasized that the planning system has no provision, yet, for the making of regional plans. Although there has been an organizational change in the role and functions of regional planners in the form of the RPCU, the lack of a regional plan handicaps the process of regional development and 'sector reigns' more absolutely.

The regional administrative system tends to operate independent of the RPCU. Besides, the administrative function of the Regional Co-ordinating Council is not directly accountable to the regional community. The advisory role in this regard makes the administrative system a less active one. Moreover, the RCC lacks legislation-making powers. And the advisory system of regional governance has serious ineffectiveness relating to the lack of real political power, funding and effective strategic guidance. Nevertheless, the last item depends much on the extent to which the RPCU and RCC are able to advise the National Development Planning Commission (NDPC). In turn, it depends on the extent to which the activities of the latter are really influenced by such advice. In terms of the systems for managing change at the regional level, therefore, regional planning is much constrained.

Organizational and institutional structures Outside the District Assemblies, and within the arrangements for decentralization, there are supposed to be 'town councils', 'zones' and 'units', in the local communities (Ofori, 1991a). These had not been created at the time of the field-study for this book. However, the various producer communities under the TOPP programme had their own kind of 'union' structures or associations. Apparently, these are for industrial bargaining and commercial purposes. The community-led initiatives identified in chapter six also indicate the existence of social organizational structures for rallying and mobilizing the community to undertake their own initiatives.

However, this study did not make a detailed study of these structures. Nevertheless, the argument here is that the opportunity to manage territorial regional change would be promoted and enhanced if these various kinds of structures are formalized and made consistently active. The performance of the available social and organizational structures of the types that emerged in this study are limited in their effectiveness. This is reflected in the absence of a formal and legally-backed system for adequately assisting the community in a more significant way.

It was also noted during the field-study the gaping absence of any structure that brings all sector-based organizations together, outside the RCC. Perhaps the CEDECOM has addressed this already as reflected in its organization. However, in view of the fact that the real institutional framework for public-sector development initiatives is within the sector departments, an explicit structure of this type would also promote the effectiveness of change management in the territorial region. It has also been pointed out that the advisory role of the RCC has no real bite or bind.

Procedures The relevant processes here relate to the form of development control at the regional level and implementation activities. In relation to the first element, the practice of project completion inspection and certifying as a form of development control in itself is not an adequate instrument for monitoring the regional development process. The national-level planning consultant interviewed stated, in relation to the significance of the quarterly reports prepared by regional planning officers, that the 'reports are not effective because they only cover developments which are determined at the sectoral level'. Moreover the wide array of projects funded by the public sector do not fall within any clear regional plan or programme; just one-off and isolated initiatives. Therefore, the procedure and process for inspecting and certifying public projects may well be in need of radical reform. The capacity of this monitoring mechanism for managing regional change is limited.

Learning from experience of territorial regional change The sector-based practices of monitoring and evaluation do indicate that these have the potential to provide useful sources of learning. However, the effectiveness of such learning is limited as long as there are no instruments to actually integrate the sector-based initiatives.

A recent legislation has now made provision for regional planners to monitor programme and project performance (Republic of Ghana, 1994b). There has not been further surveys in relation to the monitoring function of the RPCU in the context of this book. However, it is likely that the new planner function, in this regard, is proving to be effective. The planners did indicate that such an opportunity would really facilitate and promote the effectiveness of their work. Therefore, it is expected that this provision would be providing sources of appreciable learning about the kind of regional planning processes taking place - no further indication was given as to how they intended to monitor the progress of development initiatives. The same trend is reflected in relation to evaluation practices as many of the sector-based organizations have their own specialized units or departments for this function.

However, the difficulty is that of actually monitoring and evaluating the real programme impacts on the social and economic well-being of the target populations. The analysis of the TOPP programme has proven that this does not take place. For example, the TOPP programme managers, RCC, RPCU and CEREDEC are not really informed about how the sub-regional communities fare under wider development programmes as demonstrated in chapter seven. Therefore, this limits learning in relation to the development processes and constrains the practice, if any, of managing territorial regional change.

Summary

The various initiatives undertaken and those that are being implemented in the Central Region are significant sources of socio-economic development. The various rates and levels of performance have, however, been appreciably limited. The reasons that account for this include the sector-based nature of programme planning and implementation, limited co-ordination between the sectors and various stakeholders in the regional development process. Others are equally ineffective control and communication. While the non-existence of formal regional plan-making only strengthens sector-based activities, this also limits the effectiveness and quality of programme design. There is no formal regional governance; the existing structure has no policy-making powers. The arrangements for decentralization have not seeped to the regional and sub-regional levels and this affects the payments of the wide range of developer companies for their work.

With respect to actor roles, the limitations relate to lack of full development planning powers for regional planners and what appears to be a limitation in regional planning education. Other limitations are the absence of formalized structures for promoting various relationships with the community, between the community on one side, planners and administrators on the other at the regional level. Others are the increasingly flexing power and role of corporate organizations which seems to be squeezing out the position of the sub-regional community. The role of the public sector may also weaken through its gradual withdrawal from active development processes. The political powers of the regional agencies and the RCC in managing regional change are limited.

9 Lessons and policies for future regional planning practice, development processes and implementation; conclusion

The lessons learned from the entire study are now presented. The assumptions underlying the hypotheses tested are addressed and the policy implications of these also pointed out. A number of policies that have variously emerged from the study are proposed for effective future regional planning in Ghana. It is relevant that the possible and probable implementation of the proposed policies are also prognosticated. The last two considerations mark both the 'final' stage and beginning of the cyclical and constantly engaging journey of regional planning.

As Coleman (1975, p. 31) states, 'policy research involves two acts of translation: translation of the problem from the world of reality and policy into the world of scientific method, and then a translation of the research results back into the world of reality and policy'. This book, however, has not been strictly based on 'scientific method' which only has theory refinement as its focus and object. Those of policy studies, as in this book, are on proposing and refining policy. Thus an attempt has been made to loosen the reins of the traditional positivism and to found inquiry in the additional contexts of relevant realist, rationalist and phenomenological epistemologies. The hypotheses tested are embedded in and derived from the material contexts of socio-economic and spatial development processes as well as shaped and informed by appropriate methodology and epistemology.

Main lessons learned

The lesson relating to the regional problem or question is about its nature and how it is perceived. The formal public reactions registered in chapter one as well as the reviews and stated policy frameworks in chapters four and five indicate that almost all aspects of the problem are recognized but the political one. The various discussions and reviews indicate that successful regional planning practice is severely limited without the political power for making valid decisions as well as policies that have legitimate force. Without such political power, the regional problem is denied full recognition and its perception is only a limited and distorted one. Therefore, this constrained view only emaciates regional planning action.

Another lesson learned in relation to the regional problem is the dominant and pervasive emphasis on the economic aspects, compared with the social and environmental components of planning and development. Certainly, this is one of the forces that underlie the strength of 'function' as against 'territory'. Indeed, it represents a contradiction in holistic regional planning that such an overloaded and lopsided emphasis exists. In a similar way, there is a dominance of the public sector on the supply side.

The regional problem as shown in the analyses of inter-district and between-sector disparities also points to another lesson. Whenever there is an increase in terms of supply, in a time T_2 indicator, there has been a decrease in the relevant coefficient of variation. This reflects the fact that the greater the sector-based investment, the greater the chance of reducing the level of disparity. However, as noted in chapters three and six, an essential requirement also lies in capable and competent project management to make things happen.

As part of the behaviour of the regional planning problem, it has also been learned that there is the potential to achieve significant or appreciable polarization-reversal. This is reflected in the evidence that Assin District which is more rural-based appeared in category one with respect to feeder roads as well as public capital expenditure and investment. Three other districts appeared in category two in relation to the feeder roads: Gomoa, Upper Denkyira, Lower Denkyira-Twifo-Hemang. It was also observed that another rural locality, Komenda-Edina-Eguafo-Abrem District also registered one of the highest rates of implementation in the early 1980s. Perhaps, the case of feeder roads is not discriminating enough as there is greater provision of this infrastructure in the rural areas. These changes may also be indications that such convergence may be initially sector-based before being amplified across all sectors and to the aggregate regional level. These are all bits of isolated cases that do not, in themselves, indicate any trend in convergence or polarization-reversal.

The regional problem has also shown itself between the various groups and communities in the Twifo sub-region. The fact that the programme has brought about an improvement in the well-being of a limited proportion of the target populations may also be an indication that intra-regional disparity decreases along a scale from a minority group towards the majority. In this case, however, those who lost their lands and would not be involved in the programme have no chance of ever reducing their level of poverty. Therefore, the 'continuum of disparity reduction' case suggested above does not apply to this group of people.

The nature and behaviour of poverty also provide avenues for learning lessons. While poverty is more prevalent in the most territorial communities, it also grows worse as the resource base is aggressively diminished through its intensified exploitation for export commodities. Some groups lose out in the process. The experience under TOPP shows that the process of regional development in that way enshrines a contradiction of increasing the levels of poverty, even when it is not necessarily the lot of elitist groups that is patently bettered. This is shown in the income disparity between the outgrowers, settled smallholders on one side, the non-settled part of the targeted smallholders and those who lost their lands and have no chance, at all, of being included in the programme on the other. The evidence also shows that the estate employers have not been better off, on the basis of their median income, as one would expect.

The kind of TOPP initiative also demonstrates the capability of Third World countries to undertake industrial activities in their deeply territorial regions. This is important in initiating the process of filling in a gap that was doubly created under the colonial policy of not initiating industrial development activities in those areas as noted in chapter one. If the metropolitan areas of these countries were starved of this component of economic development, their territorial parts have been the worst sufferers of this serious handicap. The greater potential of agro-based industrial activities in contributing to filling in this lacunae in Ghana's structure of territorial industrial activity is also thus demonstrated in the case of the TOPP programme.

The behaviour of the smallholder producers further illustrates important social values and attitudes that could be encouraged and nurtured through planning activities. They decided to give up the extra hectare each, meant for food-stuff cropping so that additional land could be made available for their neighbours and community folks to benefit from the programme. They incurred a cost of having to pay more for the available and now limited food-stuff supply. However, the smallholders interviewed indicated that they would rather they helped their colleagues in this way and paid a higher price than allowed the programme to favour only a more limited minority section of their community. These values and attitudes indicate good neighbourliness, positive action in promoting good community relationships and cohesion, selflessness, altruism as well as a positive perception of their own territorial region and community. These are worthy of emulation in other territorial areas as well as the wider national community in Ghana. Indeed, this achievement is part of the rationale and objectives of national development policy which were noted in chapter four.

In relation to the policy presence and context, the lesson learned is the illustration throughout the book how the lack of formal policy-making function hampers the effort at making things happen in the regions of Ghana. The role of the functional Regional Planning Co-ordinating Unit (RPCU) in advising the Regional Co-ordinating Council (RCC) on broad matters relating to development planning and including spatial policies, does not amount to the formal and legitimized policy formulation. The policy foundation and input in the planning processes is of such essence, pervasiveness and vital importance that an advisory, reactive and informal form, in this context, is limited in its effectiveness. Thus, for example, sector-based departments and agencies are not necessarily bound by the advisory policy provision of the RPCU.

The relation between policy-making and a certain amount of financial independence of the RCC is understood in the planning process, in theory and practice. However, Ghanaian regional planning policy-making is also limited by the absence of a formally elected regional government and significant financial independence at the regional level. Meanwhile, the existing situation has only historically and ironically encouraged the bolstering up of the culture and practice of sector-based policy-making.

In whatever form, the kind of regional policies noted are only of a general nature than focused: another lesson. For example, the latter would indicate clear levels of need and targets to be achieved in relation to the regional planning policies. Even at the former, there is hardly a practice of strategic regional guidance. Thus the policies also fail in indicating clear targets to be achieved. There is also a conflict or structural disagreement between regional planning policy and regional development policy. The former is not really empowered to enable the latter. Therefore, it is a weak or non-existent relationship between them. Thus regional development policy is sector-based and regional planning policy lacks the effective power to really co-ordinate the former.

The national development policies have substantial validity, concretion and comprehensiveness and reflect most of the concerns raised in the discussions, so far. However, the absence of a formal regional-level government constrains the translation of these policies into effective action. Thus, for example, it is shown in the limited coverage and content of the current broad regional policies.

The absence of formal regional plan-making has also removed a principal opportunity for effectively co-ordinating and controlling development activities as well as directing and guiding regional change. The lesson learned in this relation to the regional development initiatives is the fact that the erstwhile Regional Consultative Council introduced informal regional plans as noted in chapter five. In large part, these informal plans are forms of strategic guidance for the sector-based organizations and local authorities within the Central Region. Thus what was meant to be a regional plan was even far more informal. Nevertheless, the effort is significant in indicating the potentials of the regional planning agency and authority for making real regional plans. This must be encouraged to materialize into a formal practice than be suppressed and denigrated into passivity.

Another lesson has been learned in relation to a statutory authority and context for regional development programmes and projects. It has been illustrated that the development initiatives lack the context of a regional plan. In the absence of formal regional governance, this and the former factor, together, prevent the design of programmes under a clear authority. The introduction of CEDECOM, for example, is a reaction to this problem. Indeed, this body further illustrates the fact that regional planning and development must need a decision-making and executive body that has political and financial power. It is also a reaction to the failure of public sector business and development organizations to deliver effectively. The situation pertaining to 'regional planning' and 'regional development', in this regard, also illustrates the fact that these aspects are not integrated. This represents an apparent bifurcation and contradiction. However, CEDECOM also shows that the ambition in resolving all these problems runs into another one of fostering the potential to seriously limit robustness. It would require an emasculated, flexible, strategically responsive organization which also has sufficient managerial competence to make things happen in this case.

The type of TOPP programme does not come under the formal and direct control of a regional government or administrative organization. It is under the control of its own executive company, as well as the Ministry of Finance and Economic Planning. This split-up and fragmented management responsibility has created a source of interference and political-functional control and conflict. Indeed, this is a point of difference between TOPP and CEDECOM, the latter coming under a distinct and unitary organization. Besides, TOPP's structure and orientation make it far less accountable to the regional community. This situation has been growing worse as central government is gradually withdrawing from the programme and a customer of global corporate stature expands its involvement, gaining power and control in the process. The targeted beneficiaries of the programme are being limited in any power that they may have in relation to the programme. In fact, the total withdrawal of central government means that it would no longer have representation on the TOPP Board through CEREDEC. This would even deepen the socio-political crisis. Despite the historical emphasis on the economic and 'efficiency' aspects of the programme, there are indications of declining trends in production and in particular, employment.

The various policies, strategies and programmes indicated in chapter one as part of the evolution of regional planning also show the lack of a real context with respect to a politically empowered government. Like TOPP, the other initiatives were not under the direct control of the respective regional governments and planning agencies. Nor were these set within the frameworks of regional plans formulated by the respective regional governments. The involvement of some of the Regional Development Corporations and the Regional Administrative Offices in the case of some of these like NORRIP still did not put the development companies under the control of a regional government. Besides, the varying levels of achievement, even within the context of integrated rural-regional development, have not substantially reduced the intra-regional disparities. While CEDECOM is aimed at addressing this limitation, this initiative tends to lack sufficient robustness. Nevertheless, its particular establishment indicates the need to enshrine both political and executive powers within the same planning and implementation authority.

I have also learned how the kind of TOPP programme could be used to implement social and community initiatives in a formal way. The minimal and one-off projects undertaken by the TOPP company for the Twifo community could be a formal responsibility upon the former so that the initiatives would be on a consistent and regular basis. In the current situation, the TOPP company is not mandated and could not be accountable for providing such facilities as schools, leisure facilities and housing within the territorial community. If it were the practice, it would be best to place it in the context of a plan, project or development brief. However, the TOPP programme illustrates how its type could be used to address the various aspects of the regional development problem. These include the economic part and its elements: employment, income, regional and international trade, production and investment. Others are the social, political, environmental and spatial components. It also provides glimpses of the possible conflicts between these various facets.

A further lesson about the TOPP programme relates to its specific objectives as noted in chapter five. There has been no agreement among all the stakeholders with respect to the overall objectives of the programme. While it is accepted that it has created jobs and produced raw materials for export and domestic industries, anything goes for the concrete social aspects. It is the view that the various stated objectives are important and show the array of contributions that all stakeholders can make to the wider impact of the programme. In this way, it would mean, agreeing and formally negotiating goals and agenda for the programme within a formal institutional structure wider than the TOPP company, yet overarching the RCC or lesser than it. CEDECOM might be a guide in this particular respect. While there is no agreement on the objectives of the TOPP project-complex, the company interprets and legitimizes the role of its investors; any other objective is 'adjunctive' in its view. This attitude towards the social and wider territorial development being a graft-on and less of priority also makes the programme fraught with strategic ineffectiveness in this respect. This is further conflict within the public domain in using the kind of TOPP project-complex as a replication tool and strategy of regional development. On the basis of these constraints, the lopsided nature of the TOPP programme as well as its limitation in addressing the spatial separatist issue also emerge.

Furthermore, the TOPP programme illustrates the involvement of an array of global-corporate and Western investors in funding regional development programmes. The lesson learned is that these stakeholders, as confirmed by TOPP's executive, have a sole and commercial-financial interest in the project-complex: making profit. It is not their direct or indirect concern, the social and environmental development of the territorial community. Moreover, the increasing influence of this corporate-functional involvement only broadens out this bleak scenario in the strategic term.

The sector-based projects and changes analysed in chapter six also provide further lessons. One of these is the fact that the sector-based approach suffers ineffective co-ordination. The context of a region-wide plan is non-existent. If any district development plans, as provided for in the planning legislation have yet been prepared, these may begin to provide an 'inter-meshed' foundation for the sector-based activities.

The lesson is also illustrated that the regional planning and development process is predominantly the hold of the public domain. There is no significant drive provided for the private sector. Indeed, CEDECOM is a demonstration of the case that there has been failure in regional planning and development to formally recognize as well as actively involve the private sector. A related lesson, in this consideration, is the emerging bottom-up force of the local community effort. Still, this is not within the framework of any plan, programme, development brief or practice. The regional policies noted in chapter five show the lack of recognition for this local community effort. This is also reflective of the relative coarseness and limited effectiveness of the policies.

A further lesson relating to the sector-based analysis is the trend over the period studied that there continued to be structural disparities in favour of a few urban-based localities and against a greater and territorial part. Apart from feeder roads, this observation is reflected in all the data analysed. This has only meant a trend of divergence and rather minuscule-convergence, if any at all.

It is also instructive from the study the processes of territorial urbanization taking place. There is an increasing growth of small and medium towns, in particular the latter. This is characteristic of the Central Region, Eastern Region as well as other parts of Ghana. The territorial community is not homogeneously rural - it typifies rapid urbanization from the bottom-level. The increasing growth in local services in the Twifo sub-region, notably in the town of Twifo Praso, is also in support of this trend. The evidence has shown that this trend of growth in local social, commercial and financial services have stemmed, to a significant extent, from the presence of the TOPP programme. However, these trends of urban growth have not been really set within consciously formulated policy and strategy of territorial urbanization. The growth-and-service centre framework pointed out in chapter five has not so comprehensively been implemented. There is a strong case for territorial urbanization as a specific policy and strategy as an output of concrete and wider regional programmes.

Other lessons have also been learned in relation to the implementation aspect of the planning process. The development control system practised at the regional level is fairly effective, at least, in ensuring the completion of public sector projects. In the present practice, this provides a momentum for promoting the implementation of projects. However, this is not effective in addressing quality and standards of the developments - the experience shows that these limitations may not even be immediately apparent.

Another lesson illustrated is the fact that implementation is essentially sector-based. The existence of an advisory RCC and a functional RPCU have not the bite to provide an umbrella structure for ensuring project implementation across the Central Region; the same case applies in the other regions of Ghana. This is because of the RCC's, ironically, limited powers as noted already. The regulatory type of implementation, as it also relates to the financial and development control, is the one reflected in the practice for inspecting the completion of public-funded projects. The other type is distributive implementation as it relates to social and distributive justice. It has been pointed out in chapter six how this is limited in benefiting the wider regional community. It was also noted in chapter seven how this has not favoured all the affected persons and households and to the full extent, the specified target population. Therefore, both regulatory and distributive implementation have been limited.

A lesson is also learned in relation to the urgent need for creating overarching implementation teams. This was shown in chapter five with respect to the projects implemented over 1981-87 by the Central Regional Administration. It was also pointed out with respect to the efforts made to prepare an informal regional plan for the period. The structure of CEDECOM also reflects the greater need for a region-wide and co-ordinating management team. This kind of structure does not exist at the regional level, yet. For example, a separate representation that includes the RPCU, all heads of sector-based organizations and the development committee within the RCC would fill in the gap created by the non-existence of this kind of implementation-and-management team. Indeed, one of the regional planners interviewed did state that implementation was not only sector-based but really down to the actual contracting companies which undertake the development works. It is still emphasized that a practice of formal plan-making would promote the opportunity for creating the overarching and task-based teams. As part of this lesson and a substantive one on its own, the study shows that local communities and target populations have substantially limited opportunities, if any at all, for participating in implementation. It is also learning that this seriously limits the attainment of the democratic enterprise and strategic effectiveness of regional planning.

However, another lesson learned in relation to the team factor and direct involvement of the local community is the emergent opportunity for partnerships in the regional planning and development processes. These involve the forces of local and regional community, the public domain and the private sector. This was prised up in chapters five, six and seven. The policy and plan frameworks and contexts addressed in chapter four also point to the need for creation of such partnerships. These also have to be encouraged.

Another lesson derived from the study is that programme implementation is hampered by a strictly centralized financial system. This is absolutely centred within the Ministry of Finance. Apart from the possibility of low quality work being undertaken by contractors that may be immediately detected, this centralization does delay payments considerably. An effective decentralization in this system, too, could not be further delayed.

All these lessons also determine a further one in relation to the management of regional change and the instruments it involves. The minimal institutional structures are fragmented with respect to programme implementation. The systems, procedures and processes are not designed to promote effective management of change in the region. Nor are planning strategies set within concrete foundation of policies and plans. In fact, it is ironic that strategies intended to be 'integrated' are only implemented in a sector-based fashion.

There are also lessons to be learnt about the programme evaluation practices. It has been justified, the fact that this is a weaker link in the regional planning process as practised. In the absence of formal and region-wide policies and plans, the opportunity for programme evaluation, in context, has been substantially reduced. Indeed, apart from the TOPP programme, there was no such area-targeted initiatives. Yet, it has been demonstrated that neither the TOPP executive company nor regional and national-level organizations undertake any surveys aimed at evaluating the comprehensive material impacts of programmes such as TOPP.

Nor do they have any clear methodologies or practices for undertaking the evaluations with the wider community in focus. Apart from the practice of project completion inspection which is a form of monitoring and review, there is no evidence that evaluation in both the formative and summative form has been the practice. For example, a number of socio-economic indices could be specified in programme and project plans or briefs and as a basis for measuring material changes in the target communities. This would also clarify which organization undertakes such evaluation: whether the CEREDEC, the RPCU, the TOPP company, the development committee of the RCC, the Regional Administrative Office, an overarching body or a management task force or team. These lessons thus raise the issue of an appropriate methodology for exercising this function of evaluating regional development plans and programmes.

It is also important to have learned the working of the functional and territorial paradigms in real world regional planning. It was pointed out that the historical experience of the socio-economic and spatial development has taken the form of a small urban core dominating the extensive territorial area. It was noted in chapter one and four how 'function', in both its external and domestic forms, has dominated and exploited 'territory' in the regions. The rapid and almost explosive growth of small and medium-sized towns within the territorial areas has also been demonstrated.

Despite all these positive responses, 'function' has continued its persistent and notorious dominance in an almost consistent way. If the process of reversing the polarization involves a 'time lag' as a matter of historical trend, this has not been indicated in any theoretical construct. And it is not shown in any of the contextual experiences how long it takes to achieve this. It has been the central and cardinal goal of planning policy and process to achieve such polarization-reversal. A number of explanations were given for the state and trends of regional disparities; these also constitute new learning from the study.

However, further lessons should be pointed out in relation to the material relevance of the substantive theories reviewed in chapter three. The nature and process of regional development, so far, have shown the pervasive influence of urban-industrial strategies. Of course, these are underlain by urban-industrial theoretical and hypothetical constructs. For example, the structural-divergent nature of the socio-economic and spatial development as demonstrated illustrate and bear out these formulations.

The intensified commodity extraction as noted in chapter four and the further polarization in investment also conflict with the positive neo-populist tendencies. Indeed, the former contradict any effort at deploying endogenous and neo-populist strategies. These trends also reflect neo-classical and Keynesian tendencies of free market forces and investment in export activity and projects. This is based on cost-benefit assumptions. It also reflects the general efficiency orientation and macro-economic frameworks.

With respect to the territorial and neo-populist models, these are reflected, for example, in the emerging local community effort in undertaking self-initiated projects as shown in chapter six. The conflict between local land-ownership and the compulsory land acquisition action, in relation to the Twifo lands, also illustrates elements of neo-populist reactions. These further illustrate elements of the 'politics in the region' notions. However, all these trends are either limited and not being significantly promoted or suppressed. They are also not effectively negotiated out as shown in chapter seven.

The rapidly growing small and medium towns as well as the structural 'functional-divergence' situation reflect the pervasive need for endogenous and territorial urbanization efforts in the Central Region. Nevertheless, it must be noted that these areas are not attracting the same level of investment. This is also externally valid for the other regions of Ghana.

Further learning is also provided by the emerging evidence of radicalist-Marxist ideas and trends. Classes of producers and impoverished people are forming as a result of the TOPP programme. The outgrowers have the highest median income, followed by the settled smallholders. These two are categorized, here, into one class. These are also in a relatively better position to provide for their livelihood and have the greater potential towards creating wealth at the personal and household levels. Then there are the yet-to-be-settled and potential entrants into the smallholder producer class. Despite the fact that this group is not involved in the programme, yet, it has a median income above that of the estate employees; these constitute another class of people. However, there is a class of totally impoverished people who also lost their land and do not have the chance of ever being selected to participate in the programme. These have absolutely lost out and are much more poverty-stricken than any of the other classes before. The estate employees also constitute a separate class. Although their median income at time T_2 was less than that of the potential entrants into the smallholder class, the estate employees enjoy a more regular monthly income. Nevertheless, there is a trend of decline in their employment. On the other hand, the regional employment multipliers do indicate the potential of the TOPP programme to make significant impact. Thus, the TOPP project-complex has been in the process of sorting out classes of people in the Twifo sub-regional community. While an egalitarian factor has tempered the production and social relations among the smallholders, for example, there is no real political power play and intra-community dominance indicated in this local class formation processes.

Apart from this process of class formation, there is also a trend towards possible corporate acquisition and ownership of the means of production with respect to the resources of the project-complex, except land. The various reactions to shortages of land and food-stuff supply also indicate a social-political conflict between the central government and TOPP on one side, the local community on the other. In the midst of all these, there is an urgent need for a bolder, robust, stronger and dynamic public as well as regional planning policy.

Additional lessons have been learned in relation to the engaging themes introduced in chapter one. The absence of formal formulation of regional policies and plan seriously limits the robustness of regional planning practice. The isolated and weakly integrated nature of regional strategies in theory and practice also dent the value of robustness. Moreover, regional development programmes are also limited in breadth and depth, further weakening the opportunities for robustness. If CEDECOM has not kept an over-ambitious stature and limited managerial capability and low level of competence, it would have created opportunities for enhancing such noted robustness in regional planning. This implies that it must have a broadened and fair spread of concerns and intents. The evidence from the whole study shows opportunities for achieving the process. This is, for example, indicated in the structure and organization of the TOPP project-complex, properly set within the statutory planning system and process.

The limited extent of strategic effectiveness is also displayed in the absence of formal making of regional policies and plans. It is further reflected in the limited content and coverage of development programmes. This includes the limited effectiveness in choice of indicators: socio-economic and spatial development.

Thus the futuristic aspect of planning policy and programme is also limited in scope and perspective. Implementation, in this consideration, also suffers strategic ineffectiveness on the basis of its limited distributive form. This is also reflected in the apparent gap between 'planning' and 'development' aspects of spatial-socio-economic policy action and process. Certainly, the level of implementation further reflects limited strategic effectiveness in being sector-based and poorly co-ordinated. Moreover, the regional private sector is not formally involved or encouraged to participate in the regional planning process. Besides, local community efforts and initiatives are not registered and recognized as part of the regional development effort. Therefore, regional planning is missing out on auspicious opportunities for making things happen. In addition to these, the limited and weak communicative aspect of programme implementation only increases the amount of strategic ineffectiveness in Ghanaian regional planning.

The provisions and opportunities for creating an effective democratic enterprise in Ghanaian regional planning are also limited, if any exist at all. There is not a properly instituted system of public participation in the regional planning process, as there is of a local planning one, in general. For example, this practice of participation in policy formulation and plan-making are virtually non-existent. The current decentralization in government and public administration has swept the regional level by, to an appreciable extent. In fact, not all government departments and agencies have been decentralized even at the local level. Thus the 'new decentralism' and neo-populism in Ghana are not promoting opportunities for a viable and effective democratic enterprise in regional planning. Of course, this limitation is reflected in the need for public participation in a decentralized social and economic system as is the case with the political-administrative aspect at the regional level.

The crucial issue of environmental sustainability, as already addressed in the study, also provides avenues for learning lessons. In the first place, the national development policy framework does contain useful elements of sustainable development. However, these are not reflected in the regional policy framework. Nevertheless, some of the aspects studied do contain elements of environmental sustainability. For example, the CEDECOM programme, as far as the available information shows, does include a project for the development of wildlife and ecological resources. This is used as a strategy for protecting the regional environment. Apart from this, there is no other indication of needed effort at doing this in the informal plans examined. However, most of the projects and other potential resources do involve substantial tempering with the integrity and quality of the regional environment. This cuts across all components of the CEDECOM programme, for example.

The TOPP programme involves even a greater measure of natural land resource developments. Some of the immediate environmental effects, for example, are seen in the form of soil erosion in the oil palm fields. The company manages this through appropriate planting culture and land management. However, this is by no means comprehensive. For example, all the hydrological by-product from the processing of palm oil at the TOPP mill is drained into a large and exposed pit dug for the purpose and a distance away, between the main office building and part of the Ntafrewaso junior quarters. This only provides the best habitat for mosquitoes to breed. Already, malaria is the leading health hazard in the Twifo sub-region and is only symptomatic of the high mosquito population in the area.

Besides, the competition between food-cropping land and oil palm production raises serious issues of environmental sustainability. Moreover, it illustrates the fact of 'function' and 'efficiency' invading and supplanting the 'social' and 'environmental' factors. For example, it has been pointed out that many of the land-ejected people have gone out of the programme area in search of food-cropping land.

The sector-based projects analysed in chapter six do not offer any significant glimpses into issues and practices of environmental sustainability. However, it is inferred from the active local growth of small and medium towns as well as emerging local community development initiatives that there is urgent need to address the issues of environmental sustainability. This pressing need would even be clearer if all these one-off and strictly sector-based projects are set within formal regional or sub-regional plans. The regional development plan, then, becomes the appropriate instrument for ensuring environmental sustainability.

Assumptions behind hypotheses

A number of assumptions were made with respect to the first hypothesis underlying the nature of inter-local and between-sector disparities and which was tested in chapter six. The results of the test favoured the acceptance of the alternative hypothesis: that socio-economic and spatial disparities have continued to favour the lopsided urban core of a few localities and sectors of the regional space economy. Therefore, the first assumption, in this regard, is not borne out. Rather, the favoured localities are still the urbanized districts and more segmented economic sectors which have also continued to receive relatively greater investments and more development projects.

However, there is an indication that one rural-based district appeared in the first category in relation to feeder roads. The data set relating to feeder roads may not be discriminating enough as these tend to be provided more in the territorial parts. However, the rate of occurrence of feeder roads in the more rural localities is also limited. Therefore, the second assumption holds to a very large extent: the levels and rates of socio-economic and spatial disparity have increased consistently in favour of the urban core within the Region. In fact, apart from one rural-based district ranking in the first category, two other such districts fell in the second category in relation to the analysis of feeder roads. Therefore, on the whole, the alternative assumption has been accepted here. The alternative to the third assumption, is also accepted, that the noted levels of public sector funding for the sector-based development projects have clearly favoured the few urban district localities and limited sectors. This is also reflected, very closely, in terms of the number of public projects per district and reinforces the accepted alternative hypothesis related to this.

Fourth, the assumption relating to the level of effectiveness of project implementation between district localities as well as sectors is retained. The urban localities, notably Mfantsipim and Cape Coast Districts still showed higher rates of project implementation over the period considered. However, Komenda-Edina-Eguafo-Abrem which is more rural-based appeared in the top category in the early 1980s. The more urban-based districts still dominated in terms of the implementation rates in the late 1980s. However, the evidence shows that a few more rural-based localities registered better rates in the later than earlier part of the period. This may be an indication that the greater data availability for this time T_2 shows improved implementation rates over time. It is also reflective of the fact that when there is an increase with respect to the particular indicator, the coefficient of variation shows a decrease.

An alternative to the fifth assumption relating to the community and self-induced initiatives is accepted. Indeed, the pervasive structural-divergence and dominance of the few urban-based districts remains. This shows that in terms of the levels of funding, community involvement and effort, there is greater concentration in the urban districts. However, there is an exception here as Agona District scored zero just as the rural localities of Abura-Asebu-Kwamankese and Gomoa did. Indeed, the more urbanized district of Awutu-Effutu-Senya fell in the third category. This illustrates the fact that despite the structural urban lead, the rural localities show a significant potential for self-initiated community development. Nevertheless, most of the rural-based districts were also in this category. The further analyses and discussions in chapter eight also indicate that this must require effective project management and territorial change to achieve the objectives.

The main alternative to the second hypothesis tested in chapter seven was accepted against its null. This means that socio-economic development and well-being at the community, group and personal levels in the Central Region are not being maximized most rapidly and effectively by implementing local resource-utilizing programmes and projects such as TOPP. Indeed, a principal goal of wider planning and regional planning is maximizing the social, environmental and economic benefits of the development initiatives. However, the level of significant impact achieved was also pointed out.

Four main assumptions were made in support of the whole of the second hypothesis. The first one relates to the limitation in design of the kind of TOPP programme in addressing the socio-economic development and well-being of the target population and territorial area. It has been noted that the capacity for providing the necessary social infrastructure aspects of territorial development in the wider sub-regional community is not formally provided for in the company's functions. Some of these are only one-off 'donations' depending on the 'goodwill' of the TOPP company.

The assumption that the TOPP project components are not clearly set within the context of formal regional planning policy and practice has also been borne out. While TOPP comes under the control of national macro-economic policy managers, its statutory regional planning and policy context is lacking. The fact that the company's executive management reports to separate and divided institutions further complicates the problem. This is also because there is no formal policy-formulation and plan-making at the regional level. Another reason is the pervasive emphasis on the economic aspects of the programme. In fact, there is no general agreement on the principal objectives of the project-complex. Furthermore, the growing involvement of global corporate stakeholders also bolsters up the dominant and faceted interests.

The other assumption that all the targeted participants in the TOPP programme have not experienced a real change has also been confirmed: the situation of those selected persons who were yet to be given developed plots of oil palm crop. Neither has it provided any source of hope for those who lost their land but have no chance, at all, of being included in the fixed targeted population of 300 participants.

The fourth assumption relates to the fact that the well-being of the target population and development of the area are not monitored as an integral part of the whole programme, in particular for feeding back to implementation. Certainly, this has not been provided for because of the other limitations that have been pointed out in relation to statutory regional planning and related programme management. This would, for example, have been assessed against defined criteria of social, economic, spatial, and environmental developments.

Policy implications of hypotheses

Four main implications are pointed out here in relation to the first hypothesis tested in chapter five. The first policy implication is the fact that there is need to significantly increase and maintain sustained investment levels in the peripheral regions by keeping to priority sectors and targeted areas at each round of investment. This is legitimate as it has been shown in all terms that those areas have continued to be famished of inward investment funds. The needed investment would have to be based on soundly identified problems and scientifically formulated development programmes and projects for the real benefits to be achieved.

An examination of aspects of central government's macro-economic policies and the budgetary allocation by sectors showed those of education, agriculture, health and industry, to be priority areas. But it is doubtful whether at the regional-local level this is based on the critical awareness of the real problems on the ground. Even so, as there are no regional development plans, there has been no specific study of intra-regional socio-economic disparities to determine and formally establish such needs. Therefore, a clear, formal and scientific study of sectors and territorial units with respect to these is necessary for functional programming and territorial regional management.

Further, the first hypothesis implies the need to achieve an effective horizontal development of the sector-based functions through a formal regional development plan. It has been pointed out that it is a contradiction to solve the problem of ineffective co-ordination of sectors by an equally dysfunctional form of co-ordination. A proper strategy towards functional co-ordination is by the creation of appropriate regional governance and regional plan-making practice.

Another policy implication of the first hypothesis bears out the need to design and implement a functional urban development strategy, particularly in the disadvantaged areas i.e. territorial urbanization. This implies that in line with an emerging school of thought in the field of urban and regional planning, the current alternative development strategy should include the development of secondary towns especially in peripheral regions. However, this strategy of secondary town development must happen in conjunction with other strategies. The trends also show the potential of local community and private sector efforts.

The policy implications of hypothesis II are now pointed out. The first one is that principal and wider regional programmes should be of an integrated type. These should also be formulated on the basis of productive activity in the local-regional economy. It has been emphasized that no greater significant, maximum and effective impact can be made if the various dimensions of an area's development are not linked to the particular instrumental initiative. A function of formal policy-making at the regional level would promote the practice of this integrated form of programme planning.

A second policy implication is the pervasive need to give other facets of the development process equal premium as the economic aspect. These include the social and environmental factors. Besides, the psychological aspect, including attitudes and perception of the planners, administrators and policy makers as well as those of the target population and community.

Another implication of this second hypothesis is the need to enter into some form of agreement with investors and developers so that they are obligated to contribute additionally to the development of the area in which the initiative is undertaken. This should be done in a clearly formalized way. For example, such contribution could be a determined proportion of their investment or profits. This kind of contribution could, for example, be used to meet certain targets or needs in the regional or local development plan in exchange for some concession to the investor-developer; this is on top of the regular or main budget. It would provide a further basis for negotiation in the regional planning process.

Furthermore, the hypothesis implies the need to actively involve local communities in the entire process of planning, in particular, the implementation stage. It has emerged from this study that most of the people who lost their lands to the programme were not selected, at all, to participate in it. The median income of the potential entrants into the smallholder class also shows that they are managing to earn a certain level of livelihood, though fragile. The local community efforts analysed in chapter five also show the dominance of the urban-based districts in this regard. The majority of the local and regional communities are not really involved in all these cases noted.

Proposed policies for futuristic regional planning

The proposed policies are guided by the identified points of intervention as well as the underlying assumptions and policy implications of the hypotheses tested. Other informing and underpinning considerations are the theoretical formulations, planning instruments and nature of the activity environment. Possible constraints to the implementation of the policy proposals are also noted. Emphasis is put on the external validity of these policies to all the political-administrative and planning regions of Ghana.

Policy of formalized planning policy formulation practice and explicit strategic regional guidance: emphasis on territoriality A policy of active and direct regional policy formulation practice is proposed with greater emphasis on the territorial component. It would require new legislation to implement this. It is also recommended that the National Development Planning Commission (NDPC) gives broad strategic guidance to the RCC-RPCU to enable them engage in the formal practice of formulating policies for regional development.

One objective of the policy proposed here is to formulate clear policies on matters of relevance and validity in the region's development. In guiding its own work, the RCC-RPCU would also, in turn, provide much needed strategic planning guidance for the District Planning Authorities (DPAs). Another objective is to make more specific and targeted policies for sub-regional purposes, as may be needed. A third objective is to make region-wide policies in relation to both single sector and multi-sector initiatives. Furthermore, the policy-making practice in the region should have the objective to promote social cohesion, a sense of community, attitude of co-operation and participation.

This proposed policy would also strengthen the planning research and problem identification capabilities of the RPCU because it would provide legal force and legitimacy to undertake these necessary activities. It would also create a close relationship between policy determination and formulation as well as implementation and evaluation functions. The RCC-RPCU would be more involved in all three aspects; it shares implementation with the DPAs and the sector-based organizations. This focused and formalized policy-making would also contribute to eliminating the problem of 'spatial separatism' which is so pervasive in the 'policy for regional development' approach. Certainly, it would further promote the practice and enhance the quality of co-ordinated policy-making and action in the region.

A problem with direct and formal making of regional policy is one of financial independence and region-based spending systems. This would also have direct implications for a second level of taxation, after that made by the District Planning Authorities - it would create additional tax burdens for the regional populace. Therefore, it is recommended that the RCC-RPCU's planning and development policy frameworks should be based on an independent control of public sector-based financial resources. The policy-making function of the statutory regional bodies should also include the purpose of enabling the work of the DPAs and providing a legitimate arrangement for targeted regional action. It should also seek to encourage partnership ventures. In this case too, the RCC-RPCU would be a principal enabling force in the region.

Policy of formal region-wide plan-making There is need for an equally innovative approach to regional plan-making. The rationale here is that the gap between national and local level planning is rather too wide to make for effectiveness. Indeed, the function of co-ordination is best achieved through a formal regional plan and effective strategic guidance. While local-tactical policy action is more short term, there is need for longer term indications of broad areas of development planning guidance.

The policy proposed here is one of a formal introduction and establishment of a practice of plan-making at the regional level. Like the earlier proposed policy, this one would also require new legislation to implement it. One objective is to make the RPCU responsible for plan-making and development guidance at the regional level. Another objective is to provide the RPCU with the facilities and resources to enable it undertake effective planning research in the region as in support of the first objective. It is also essential to create an effective, more legitimate and representative regional government to have the powers for making regional policies and plans. A possible constraint could be resistance on the part of the sector ministries and agencies to the region-wide plan-making. However, appropriate planning legislation would have the force to check this.

Policy for regional governance and functional integration of sector-based organizations and agencies It is proposed that the RCC should be re-organized and widely-based as much as possible, with its members still appointed, only initially. Indeed, as financial independence for this new body will be an appreciably intractable issue, the option of non-elected regional government could be considered. One objective here is to make formal electoral areas, various associations, gender-based and pressure groups and so on the sources of appointment to membership of the new regional government. Another objective is to back the enhanced appointive role with legislation for planning and political powers. A further objective is to ensure the formalized participatory role of the regional populace. It should also be the objective to ensure the accountability of the new regional government to the law and the people in the region. A strategic intent is to prepare a tested basis for a more formally elected system of regional governance with appreciable financial independence, without subjecting the regional community to further taxation.

Apart from a formal system of regional governance, it is also proposed that there should be a formal introduction of a structure for co-ordinating the functioning of the various sector-based ministries and agencies. This structure would be analogous to the cross-functional planning groups that the National Development Planning Commission is required to create under its Act. One objective is to establish a formal and regular meeting of all organizations and institutions outside the decision-making processes of the regional governing body. Another is to create additional sources of professional advice and community consultation for the new regional government, outside the RPCU.

It is further proposed that financial independence of the new regional government and effective co-ordination of the sector-based ministries should be based on the creation of a Consolidated Regional Budget (CRB). This should integrate the individual budgets of all the various sector organizations and departments at the regional level and be controlled by the new regional government. Of course, this would be part of placing the sector departments and ministries, within the region, under the effective control of the regional government. Apart from this CRB, the regional government should have the power to enter into agreement with the private sector within the region as well as bilateral and multilateral agencies to fund targeted development programmes. In this case, all the investors would share in the returns unless it is a purely non-profit-making and social service to the community. The regional government would then have the effective responsibility of determining and designing the regional programmes and projects in collaboration and co-operation with the sector departments and ministries in the region. This would also mean making modifications to the current practice of preparing sector-based plans.

An objective here is to promote the achievement of effective distributive justice because of the integrated spending framework. Another is to further promote all-inclusiveness and effective co-ordinative function in the region's development processes. A further objective is to promote and enforce a proactive planning role for the RCC-RPCU. It is also to pre-empt any possible conflicts between the regional and district levels as well as between any of these and the national level.

The RPCU would also be strengthened in being a professional and technical arm of the NDPC and its National Development Planning Secretariat (NDPS). This organizational arrangement would also promote a closer working between the RCC-RPCU and the national-level planning units which are based within each sector ministry's headquarters. It is emphasized that this proposed form of regional governance should only be the initial stage to providing an elective version of it in the strategic future.

Policy of formulating and designing integrated programmes, projects and strategies The policy proposed here is essentially one of integrated practice relating to project and programme formulation as well as strategy design. If formal policy formulation and regional plan-making are accepted, these would create the conditions for achieving integrated programme and strategy design. Therefore, it is important that in any formulation of development initiatives, emphasis should be on the multifaceted and multidimensional aspects. All possible and feasible beneficial effects of the initiatives should be explored to reap maximum benefits from these. It is also emphasized that regional development programmes should be targeted as much as possible. It is further proposed, as part of the integrated programme approach, that there should be a policy of prioritized investment planning. This would also facilitate the clear identification of needs and specification of targets.

One objective of this policy proposal is to integrate one-off projects within the framework of area-based or regional and sub-regional plans. Another objective is to ensure balanced integration of the various aspects of the projects and to enhance its potential for generating maximum impact. A further one is to effectively co-ordinate the activities and strategies of implementing agencies.

The approach of explicit and effective integration, in this way, would also promote the advisory roles of the RCC-RPCU in relation to the identification of Joint Development Planning Areas (JDPAs) as well as Special Development Areas (SDAs). It ought to be noted that the planning authority that would have jurisdiction over a JDPA or SDA would have the power to formulate a development plan, unlike the Regional Co-ordinating Council in its present form and structure.

The implementation of the policy proposed here would require a re-organization of the RPCU along similar lines as the District Planning Co-ordinating Unit (DPCU), the planning agent of the District Planning Authority (Figure 1.1). It is suggested that a 'new' RPCU, in this consideration, should be structured into a number of components, apart from its technical section of draughts-persons as well as in-house administrative office which are already in existence. In this case, the RPCU's first proposed component should be a planning research and data management section. The second section should be one for initial policy formulation, plan-making, programme design and budgeting. The third one which could also be constituted as part of the second section should be for programme implementation and management. The function of the third or fourth section, depending on the alternative consideration, should be one for monitoring, evaluation and development control.

Policy for territorial urban development: small and medium-size towns It is proposed that a deliberate policy for territorial urbanization be introduced for the integrated development of the identified settlements; the specific focus should be on small and medium-size towns and viable production bases of these.

One of the objectives here should be to identify the functional bases of small and medium settlements in the regions as a way of clearly establishing their economic support systems and diversifying their production bases. Another objective is to revise the criteria for identifying growth and service centres with a view to emphasizing the inclusion of those relating to production-based potentials. The criteria being used currently relate more to services and limited primary activity as shown in chapter five. A further objective is to clearly identify the various linkages between and among the sets of settlements within the territorial context. The point is to strengthen these linkages, or create them where these are not existent, in a functional and robust way.

Possible constraints with respect to this policy proposal could be lack of needed investment in the development of the relevant social and economic infrastructure. However, if the other policies proposed already are accepted and implemented, this one of territorial urbanization could be contained, leveraged. For example, a policy of integrated programme formulation and design would create significant spin-offs for the development of small and medium settlements.

Policy of formalized social responsibility of investors and development agencies It is proposed that all investors and development agencies contribute a certain percentage of their profits or investments to the development of particular sectors of the project area on a mandatory and consistent basis. This can be justified on the basis of the social responsibility of investors and developers. In this case, this 'special and obligatory' undertaking by the particular investor or developer would be clearly indicated in the programme document or development brief or development permit (planning permission). The developer could be given some concession in return for the inclusion of some additional development as a contribution to local amenity. Therefore, the project area gains in the form of this additional development, apart from the main initiative.

An objective is to co-ordinate such mandatory contributions within the statutory budgetary allocation or Consolidated Regional Budget for the area. Another is to ensure that the investor contributes in this way to social and economic development in the area. The receiving communities should be given the opportunity to decide in which areas to invest the funds. Another option is to allow the investor or company the freedom of contributing, additionally, to the development of a particular sector of their choice e.g. water facilities, schools, markets or health infrastructure as may be agreed or negotiated in the programme brief or schedule. This would also be a built-in flexibility for the developer-investor to contribute to various developments over the duration of its profit-generating operations or investment activities. These additional contributions should also be an advantage for the developer when development permit and contract applications go before the Regional Tender Board.

A possible constraint to this policy is opposition from the companies or investing agencies and suspicions on their part of greater increases in their social overheads and total investment costs. However, the problem could be managed through fair and mediated negotiation between politicians, planners and administrators on one side and investor-developers on the other. Any legislation aimed at enforcing such agreements would also require wide consultations with the developer and investor communities.

Policy for effective compensation under compulsory land acquisition A policy of realistic, flexible and effective system of compensation is proposed in relation to compulsory land purchase actions. It is also proposed that a mandatory comprehensive programme budgeting is introduced to ensure that the arrangements for compensating the affected persons and the levels of such compensations are included in all programme schedules and briefs.

One objective here is to base compensation payments on realistic valuations of cropped and non-cropped land and other properties. Another objective is to make all project costing and payment estimations exhaustively rigorous and realistic. A further objective is to make the compensation payments strictly on time to the affected persons to have 'full' benefit for their acquired lands and properties. All these mean that project costing is done at the prevailing market rates and consideration given to inflationary realities in all the estimations and payments.

A possible constraint to the realization of this kind of policy is the ineffective valuations and co-ordination of the implementation agencies. Another constraint is the possible delay in aspects of comprehensive budgeting such as forwarding the necessary valuations by the appropriate statutory body or funding agency. The latter implies the urgent need for effective time-scheduling in programme planning and implementation. All these constraints also mean that there must be appropriate and legitimate regional governance as proposed.

Policy of more effective participation of regional and local community in the planning and development processes All the available opportunities do not, yet, provide for effective participation and involvement of the local communities in the processes of planning and development. Therefore, the policy proposal is the formalization and articulation of public and local community involvement in regional planning and development processes. There would be need for specific analysis of the issues and opportunities for public participation at the regional level in this connection. This would also provide a basis for further promulgating appropriate legislation for the formal introduction of structures to involve the local communities in an active, responsive and proactive way. For example, the specific meaning and notions of 'local community participation' or 'public participation' need be clarified and put into an operational form.

The main objective of this policy is to create empowered structures for actively involving the local community in planning and development outside and as part of the District Planning Authority. A possible constraint of duplication of functions and roles could be avoided if this policy is carefully implemented in a way that is more sensible, sensitive and sympathetic to the needs of the wider regional communities.

Policy for actively involving the private sector in the process of regional development The proposed policy is that there should be stronger representation of the private sector within the region, in terms of all the categories of industry and recognized undertakers, on the RCC. It is also proposed that legitimate representation of the region's private sector attend regularly meetings of the sector-based ministries and agencies as proposed already.

The objective is to encourage the proactive as well as active participation of the private sector in regional development. A more specific objective is to encourage them to undertake profit-generating activities and ventures which also have significant potential for creating employment in the region. Another objective is to assist the private sector with finding solutions to generic problems that face them. For example, these relate to business establishment services and investment opportunities. The RCC could create a business advisory service unit to help the private sector with business advice and services in this way. The purpose here is to provide some leverage and further encouragement for the private sector to locate and establish in the region.

Policy of ensuring environmental sustainability in regional development and planning practice The proposal here is one of enforcement because elements of it have been expressed in the national development policy matrix presented in chapter four. The proposed policy is that regional policies, development plans, programmes and projects should reflect as well as flavour the criteria and elements of environmental sustainability. It is further proposed that measures of environmental sustainability be included in planning standards, rationale and principles.

One of the objectives, in this case, is to build in strategic effectiveness and facilitate implementation processes. Another objective is to promote the effectiveness and efficiency of development control, monitoring and evaluation functions. A further objective is to ensure quality and standards in all development programmes and projects. Therefore, it is pervasively essential for the function of policy and plan formulation as well as regional strategic guidance to be formally and explicitly established as proposed earlier.

Policy for proactive resource surveys and strategic feasibility studies It is proposed that the RCC and RPCU in the region create a proactive practice of undertaking resource surveys and preparing strategic feasibility reports and proposals as a way of attracting potential investors into the region. The implementation of this policy should include efforts such as public relations initiatives and place-marketing to promote the region's investment potential and future development activities. These kinds of proactive studies and reports should be those that attract and promote inward investments.

An objective of this policy is to give potential investors the initial confidence about the intentions and initiative of the regional government as well as encourage them to enter into the various development ventures. Another objective is to encourage and promote the formation of partnerships for regional development activities. Therefore, there is great need for the suggested studies to be very well founded and justified. The cost of undertaking these strategic resource surveys and making the project proposals should also be considered as part of leveraging regional development. This strategic approach to resource development would also promote opportunities for the creation of partnerships and other joint ventures in the region.

Policy of integrated urban-regional planning education and learning The policy proposed is that an explicit and formally integrated urban-regional planning focus be included in planning education and training, especially at the post-graduate levels. This should entail appreciable emphasis on the urban-rural interface as on the small-medium town growth and wider territorial urbanization. Of course, it is essential to emphasize the interactive relationships among these settlements as well as the internal processes, including the design of the built environments: urban and rural environmental design. Another emphasis should be on the processes and practices of robust policy analysis and formulation as well as implementation. There should also be explicit inclusion of the aspects relating to planning and environmental law.

The objective is to set regional planning education clearly and distinctively in a real world and material-based context. Another objective is to encourage reflective professionalism, action and experiential learning in regional planning and wider planning education.

Conclusion

The nature of the 'region' in Ghana in constraining regional planning has been demonstrated. The Ghanaian territorial region lacks the political power to make things happen. It has neither policy formulation nor plan-making powers. In this way, the national planning system enshrines a serious weakness for regional planning. This has also the potential and reality of constraining the opportunities for divergence-reversal and poverty reduction.

It has been demonstrated that the territorial region is a scene of buoyant urbanization trends in relation to small and medium-size town growth. These settlements also have substantial potential for reducing the structural-divergent, socio-economic and spatial disparities within the region. Indeed, the small and intermediate towns must contain appreciable opportunities for local economic growth and development. Therefore, the lack of within-region policy formulation and plan-making further diminish the chances of effectively co-ordinating these small and medium-size town developments and any initiatives.

The Ghanaian state's perception of the regional problem is also as limited as the instruments it deploys to solve them. The cases relating to the absence of intra-regional policy formulation and plan-making have been noted. The one-off nature of some of the initiatives and lack of effective co-ordination is also a limitation. Further, the sector-based nature of planning and implementation and practices in these regards also contribute to the fragmented, truncated and inconsistent view of the regional problem. Apart from being a problem on its own, this sector-based culture also promotes the over-loading, now and again, of a dimension or facet of regional development; the typicality here is the economic aspect. Thus the social and environmental components tend to be left in the background or do not feature. All these weaknesses have the effect of severely constraining the perception and action in relation to the regional problem. These thus contribute to limiting any efforts at reducing socio-economic disparities and poverty. This state of fragmentation also weakens the opportunities for achieving environmental sustainability and robustness in regional planning.

The more concrete and wider regional programmes have the greater promise for making things happen in the territorial communities. However, the lack of formal plan-making and policy formulation powers as well as non-existence of a more legitimate regional government constrain this potential. Therefore, there is also the need to re-organize regional governance. Despite the advantage of the wider development programme, there is still the dominant emphasis on single facets as in the one-off type of projects. Indeed, these principal limitations also contribute to reproducing the problem of socio-economic and intra-community disparities by satisfying the interests of only a minority within the targeted population under the wider programme. The problem is further exacerbated by the ineffective arrangements for compensations when compulsory purchase orders apply.

Regional planning in Ghana is also lacking in legitimate and formalized arrangements for actively involving the territorial communities in planning and development processes. While the wider regional programme evaluated more demonstrates this, the problem is worst with the one-off projects. The emerging significant and self-inducing efforts of the territorial communities indicate the potential for reducing disparities and poverty in this regard. However, the frameworks for co-ordinating these local community efforts are also lacking. Therefore, appropriate legislation, practices of regional policy formulation and plan-making as well as integrated programme design have the potential to make things happen in this regard. Apart from these, all the evidence indicate opportunities for the effective creation of partnerships as an approach to regional development: among local-regional communities, regional-central government, the private sector and well-intending international investors.

A popularity and greater value of the wider regional programme lie in the vast opportunities it provides for inward investment in the territorial region. The various domestic, bilateral and multilateral sources of funding and stakeholder interests are registered enough. The increasing importance of corporate organizations of global stature, their attitudes and values of profit maximizing must stir up concern. These problems have the effect of generating conflicts with territorial forces and the various levels of government. The emasculating corporate power of the global capitalists is being felt in the territorial regions. While they become entrenched in growth-generating ventures, they are over-powering government and running over the targeted population, especially at a time when regional governance is not strong enough. The spate of processes also harbours the potential of limiting the reduction of socio-economic disparities and poverty.

Another conclusion relates to the need to re-organize the RPCU, its processes, procedures and operations. It is essential to create specialized sections within the Unit and provide adequate professional and intellectual guidance, leadership and services. Without an effectively functional and robust role for the RPCU, the public domain's efforts at reducing intra-regional disparities and poverty would be choked of the needed amount and level of planning knowledge and practice. A re-organization of the RPCU, its functions and roles, in this way, would also promote the opportunities for professional reflection and experiential learning for the planners.

A further conclusion relates to the role of professional planning education, particular focus on training and studies in regional planning. Without an integrated and responsive practice in this regard, the making of regional planners would have been denied of an opportunity to promote the comprehensiveness required of their professional activities. The pervasive emphasis and orientation to rural-based issues has only promoted homogeneity and played down the essential urban focus. This contradiction has also fed up the fallacy of spatial separatism. Therefore, an abolition of both this contradiction and spatial separatist factor must mean a necessary reform and re-organization of regional planning education and training.

Without further reforms and changes to the planning system and practices, any arrangements and opportunities for managing inward investment and funding for regional development would continue to be limited and weakened. An innovative, responsive, flexible and proactive approach to regional planning in the context of more legitimate regional governance hold far greater promise to deliver effectively than a mimetic and play-it-over-again engagement. It is hoped that the observations, suggestions and policy proposals made in this book will make useful contributions to the process of making things happen in the regions of Ghana, in particular the territorial communities.

Bibliography

Abe, H. and Alden, J.D. (1988), 'Regional development planning in Japan', *Regional Studies*, vol. 22, no. 5, pp. 429-438.

Adams, G.R. and Schevaneveldt, J.D. (1985), *Understanding research methods*, Longman, New York.

Adarkwa, K. (1983), 'Spatial analysis of rural development policies in the Upper Region of Ghana', *Rural Africana*, 17, Fall, pp. 5-18.

Adelman, I. and Morris, C.T. (1971), 'Analysis-of-variance techniques for the study of economic development', *Journal of Development Studies*, vol. 8, no. 1, pp. 91-105.

Ahluwalia, M.S. (1974), 'Inequality, poverty and development', *Journal of Development Economics*, no. 3, pp. 307-342.

Alden, J. and Morgan, R. (1974), *Regional planning: a comprehensive view*, Leonard Hill Books, Bedfordshire.

Alexander, E.R. and Faludi, A. (1989), 'Planning and plan implementation: note on criteria', *Environment and Planning B: Planning and Design*, vol. 16, pp. 127-140.

Allen, K. (1979), *Some national approaches to regional inequality*, Studies in Public Policy no. 41, Centre for the Study of Public Policy, University of Strathclyde, Glasgow.

Allen, K., Bachtler, J. and Yuill, D. (1988), *Alternatives in regional incentive policy design*, Research Paper no.1, Regional and Industrial Policy Research Series, Centre for European Policies Research, University of Strathclyde, Glasgow.

Amissah, S.B. (1987), 'Some issues in housing and urban development' in *World: problems and solutions*, UST/LARC, Kumasi, pp. 183-193.

Andrae, G. (1981), *Industry in Ghana: production, form and spatial structure*, Scandinavian Institute of African Studies, Uppsala with Department of Human Geography, University of Stockholm, Stockholm.

Armstrong, H. and Taylor, J. (1978), *Regional economic policy and its analysis*, Philip Allan, Oxford.

Armstrong, H. and Taylor, J. (1985), *Regional economics and policy*, Philip Allan, Oxford.

Aryeetey, E. (1987), *Inter-regional development disparities in Ghana: a reconsideration*, Discussion Paper no. 24, Institute of Statistical, Social and Economic Research (ISSER), University of Ghana, Legon.

Aryeetey, E. (1989), 'Functional and structural changes in small- and medium-sized towns of Ghana since 1970', Paper presented at an Inter-Faculty Lecture, 27 April, University of Ghana, Legon, Accra.

Aryeetey-Attoh, S. and Chatterjee, L. (1988), 'Regional inequalities in Ghana: assessment and policy issues', *Tijdschrift voor econ. en soc. geografie*, 79, no. 1, pp. 31-38.

Ashcroft, B. (1978), *The evaluation of regional economic policy: the case of the United Kingdom*, Studies in Public Policy no. 12, Centre for the Study of Public Policy, University of Strathclyde, Glasgow.

Ashcroft, B. (1982), 'The measurement of the impact of regional policies in Europe: a survey and critique', *Regional Studies*, vol. 16.4, pp. 287-305.

Ashcroft, B. (1983), *Regional policy evaluation and the disaggregation of policy effects*, Studies in Public Policy no. 113, Centre for the Study of Public Policy, University of Strathclyde, Glasgow.

Ayee, J.R.A. (1994), *An anatomy of public policy implementation: The case of decentralization policies in Ghana*, Avebury, Aldershot.

Balogh, T. (1978), 'Failures in the strategy against poverty', *World Development*, vol. 6, no. 1, pp. 11-22.

Bannerman, J.E. (1971), 'Problems and policies of regional planning in Ghana', in Dunham, D.M. and Hilhorst, J.G.M. (eds) (1971), *Issues in regional planning: a selection of seminar papers*, Mouton, The Hague, pp. 125-140.

Bannerman, J.E. (1984), 'Regionalization of planning in Ghana: regional development and Regional Development Corporations', *Ghanaplan*, vol. 1, no. 1, pp. 48-68.

Barnekov, T., Boyle, R. and Rich, D. (1989), *Privatism and urban policy in Britain and the United States*, Oxford University Press, Oxford.

Barrett, S. and Fudge, C. (1981), *Policy and action: essays in the implementation of public policy*, Methuen, London.

Bartlett, C.A. and Ghoshal, S. (1989), *Managing across borders*, Harvard Business School Press, Boston.

Baster, N. (1972), 'Development indicators: an introduction', in Baster, N. (ed.), *Measuring development: the role and adequacy of indicators*, Frank Cass, London, pp. 1-20.

Baxter, R.S. (1976), *Computer and statistical techniques for planners*, Methuen, London.

Belbin, R.M. (1996), *Management teams: why they succeed or fail*, Butterworth-Heinemann, Oxford.

Bentley, I., Alcock, A., Murrain, S. and Smith, G. (1985), *Responsive environments, a manual for designers*, The Architectural Press, London.

Berry, R. and Jackson, R. (1981), 'Inter-provincial inequalities and decentralization in Papua New Guinea', *Third World Planning Review*, vol. 3, no. 1, pp. 57-76.

Biehl, D. (1980), 'Determinants of regional disparities and the role of public finance', *Public Finance*, vol. 35, no. 1, pp. 44-71.

Bigstern, A. (1980), *Regional inequality and development*, Gower, Aldershot.

Birmingham, D. (1990), *Makers of the twentieth century: Kwame Nkrumah*, Sphere, London.

Birmingham, W., Neustadt, I. and Omaboe, E.N. (1966), *A study of contemporary Ghana*, vol. I, George Allen and Unwin, London.

Boateng, C.N.K. (1987), 'Planning for development: some lessons from Ghana's experience', in Amissah, S.B. (ed.) (1987), *Planning for development in the Third World: problems and solutions*, LARC/UST, Kumasi, pp. 23-30.

Borts, G.H. (1960), 'The equalization of returns and regional economic growth', *American Economic Review*, 50, pp. 319-347.

Boserup, E. (1965), *The conditions of agricultural growth: the economics of economic change under population pressure*, Aldine, New York.

Boudeville, J-R (1966), *Problems of regional economic planning*, Edinburgh University Press, Edinburgh.

Bowden, P. (1988), *National monitoring and evaluation: development programmes in the Third World*, Avebury/Gower, Aldershot.

Brown, C.K. (ed.) (1986), *Rural development in Ghana*, Ghana Universities Press, Accra.

Bruton, M. and Nicholson, D. (1987), *Local planning in practice*, Hutchinson, London.

Bunker, R. (1971), *Town and country or city and region?*, Melbourne University Press, Carton, pp. 2-23.

Burke, G. (1980), *Town planning and the surveyor*, The Estates Gazette, London.

Camhis, M. (1979), *Planning theory and philosophy*, Tavistock, London.

Cappellin, R. and Molle, W. (1988), 'The co-ordination problem in theory and Policy', in Molle, W. and Cappellin, R. (eds), *Regional impact of community policies in Europe*, Avebury/Gower, Aldershot, pp. 1-22.

Cardoso, F.H. (1972), 'Dependency and development in Latin America', *new left review*, no. 74, pp. 83-95.

Carnall, C. (1992), *Managing change*, Routledge, London.

Casley, D.J. and Kumar, K. (1988), *The collection, analysis and use of monitoring and evaluation data*, John Hopkins University Press, Baltimore.

Casley, D.J. and Lury, D.A. (1981), *Data collection in developing countries*, Clarendon Press, Oxford.

Casley, D.J. and Lury, D.A. (1982), *Monitoring and evaluation of agriculture and rural development projects*, John Hopkins University Press, Baltimore.

Castells, M. (1977), *The urban question*, Edward Arnold, London.

Central Regional Administration (1987), *Central Region: guidelines for three-year development plan 1987/89*, Central Regional Administration, Cape Coast.

Central Regional Development Commission (1989), *Central Regional Integrated Development Scheme*, UNDP Sponsored Programme, Central Regional Administration, Cape Coast.

Chadwick, G. (1978), *A systems view of planning*, second edition, Pergamon Press, Oxford.

Chadwick, G. (1987), *Urban and regional systems in developing countries*, second edition, Pergamon, Oxford.

Chatterjee, L. and Nijkamp, P. (1983), *Urban and regional policy analysis in developing countries*, Gower, Aldershot.

Christiansen, K.S. (1985), 'Coping with uncertainty in planning', *Journal of the American Planning Association*, vol. 51, no. 1, pp. 63-73.

Clark, G.L., Gertler, M.S. and Whiteman, J.E.M. (1986), *Regional dynamics: studies in adjustment theory*, Allen and Unwin, Boston.

Coates, B.E., Johnson, R.J. and Knox, P.L. (1977), *Geography and inequality*, Oxford University Press, Oxford.

Coffey, W.J. and Polese, M. (1984), 'The concept of local development: a stages model of endogenous regional growth', *Papers of the Regional Science Association*, vol. 55, pp. 1-12.

Coffey, W.J. and Polese, M. (1985), 'Local development: conceptual bases and policy implications', *Regional Studies*, vol. 19.2, pp. 85-93.

Coleman, J.S. (1975), 'Problems of conceptualisation and measurement in studying policy impacts', in Dolbeare, K.M. (ed.), *Public policy evaluation*, Sage, Beverly Hills, pp. 19-40.

Conyers, D. (1981), 'Papua New Guinea: decentralization and development from the middle', in Stohr, W.B. and Taylor, D.R.F. (eds), *Development from above or below: dialectics of regional planning*, Wiley, Chichester, pp. 209-229.

Conyers, D. (1984b), 'Bridging the gap between North and South: towards a common approach to intra-regional planning', *Third World Planning Review*, vol. 6, no. 4, pp. 339-353.

Conyers, D. (1985), *Rural-regional planning: towards an operational theory*, Progress in Planning, vol. 23, part 1, pp. 001-036.

Conyers, D. (1986), 'In search of the practical academic: lessons from the study of regional administration', *Regional Studies*, vol. 20.6, pp. 579-584.

Conyers, D. and Hill, P. (1984a), *Introduction to development planning in developing countries*, Wiley, Chichester, pp. 209-229.

Cooke, P. (1983), *Theories of planning and spatial development*, Hutchinson, London.

Cooke, P. and Hulme, D. (1988), 'The compatibility of market liberalization and local economic development strategies', *Regional Studies*, vol. 22, no. 3, pp. 221-231.

Cooke, P. and Kirkpatrick, C. (eds) (1988), *Privatization in less developed countries*, Wheatsheaf, Brighton.

Dewar, D., Todes, A. and Watson, V. (1986), *Regional development and settlement policy*, Allen and Unwin, London.

Diamond, D. and Spence, N. (1983), *Regional policy evaluation*, Gower, Aldershot.

Dickson, K.B. (1969), *A historical geography of Ghana*, Cambridge University Press, Cambridge.

Dickson, K.B. (1970), *Urbanization in pre-colonial Ghana*, Annual Museum Lectures, Ghana Museums and Monuments Board, Accra.

Dickson, K.B. (1971), *The Ghanaian town: its nature and function*, Ghana Universities Press, Accra.

Dickson, K.B. (1975), 'Development planning and national integration in Ghana', in Smock, D.R. and Bentsi-Enchill, K. (eds), *The search for national integration in Africa*, The Free Press, New York, pp. 100-116.

Dickson, K.B. (1978), *Report on the possible regional impact of the Twifo Oil Palm Plantation (TOPP) project*, Department of Geography, University of Ghana, Legon.

Dickson, K.B. (1984), *Urban-rural contrasts in Ghana: its implications for development*, Ghana Academy of Arts and Sciences, Accra.

Donkor, K. (1977), *Structural adjustment and mass poverty in Ghana*, Ashgate, Aldershot.

Doyle, K. (1997), *Marketing management and strategy*, Prentice Hall, Hemel Hempstead.

Dugbaza, T. (1978/79), 'Some demographic measures and pointers to socio-economic inequalities in Ghana', *Ghana Journal of Sociology*, vol. 12, no. 1, pp. 107-132.

Dunham, D.M. (1977), *Group interests and spatial structures: a study of regional development in southern Ghana*, Geboren Lincoln, England.

El-Shankhs, S. and Obudho, R. (eds) (1974), *Urbanization, national development and regional planning in Africa*, Praeger, New York.

Emmanuel, A. (1972), *Unequal exchange*, New Left Books, London.

Ewers, H-J. and Wettman, R.W. (1980), 'Innovation-oriented regional policy', *Regional Studies*, vol. 14, pp. 161-179.

Ewusi, K. (1973), *Economic development planning in Ghana*, Exposition Press, New York.

Ewusi, K. (1976), 'Disparities in levels of regional development in Ghana', *Social Indicators Research*, 3, pp. 75-100.

Ewusi, K. (1977), *The spatial distribution of manufacturing industries in Ghana: implications for balanced development*, seminar paper, Institute of Statistical, Social and Economic Research (ISSER), University of Ghana, Legon.

Ewusi, K. (1986), *Industrialization, employment generation and income distribution in Ghana*, Adwensa, Accra.

Ewusi, K. (1987), *Structural adjustment and stabilization policies in developing countries: a case study of Ghana's experience in 1983-86*, Ghana Publishing Corporation, Tema.

Faludi, A. (1970), 'The planning environment and the meaning of "Planning"', *Regional Studies*, vol. 4, pp. 1-9.

Faludi, A. (1973a), *Planning theory*, Pergamon, Oxford.

Faludi, A. (1973b), *Planning theory: a reader*, Pergamon, Oxford.

Faludi, A. (1986), *Critical rationalism and planning methodology*, Pion, London.

Faludi, A. (1987), *A decision-centred view of environmental planning*, Pergamon, Oxford.

Folmer, H. (1986), *Regional economic policy: measurement of its effects*, Dordrecht, Hingham and Martinus Nijhoff, Boston.

Franklin, G.H. (1976), *An introduction to programme evaluation*, Wiley, London.

Franklin J.L. and Thrasher, J.H. (1976), *An introduction to programme evaluation*, John Wiley and Sons, London.

Freeman, H.E., Rossi, P.H. and Sonia, R.W. (1979), *Evaluating social projects in developing countries*, OECD, Paris.

Friedmann, J. (1966), *Regional development policy: Venezuela, a case study*, M.I.T., Cambridge, Massachusetts.

Friedmann, J. (1972), 'A polarized theory of development', Hansen, N.M. (ed.), *Growth centres in regional economic development*, Methuen, London.

Friedmann, J. (1973), *Urbanization, planning and national development*, M.I.T., Cambridge, Massachusetts.

Friedmann, J. (1974), *Retracking America: a theory of transactive planning*, Doubleday, New York.

Friedmann, J. (1975), 'Regional development planning: the progress of a decade', in Friedmann, J. and Alonso W. (eds), *Regional policy: readings in theory and applications*, M.I.T., Massachusetts, pp. 791-808.

Friedmann, J. and Forest, Y. (1988), 'The politics of place: toward a political economy of territorial planning', in Higgins, B. and Savoie, D.J. (eds), *Regional economic development: essays in honour of François Perroux*, Unwin Hyman, Boston, pp. 115-130.

Friedmann, J. and Weaver, C. (1979), *Territory and function: the evolution of regional planning*, Edward Arnold, London.

Frimpong-Ansah, J.H. (1991), *The vampire state of Africa: the political economy of decline in Ghana*, Africa World and James Currey, London.

Gattoni, D. (1989), 'Decentralisation shows diverse face in Africa', *The Urban Fringe*, vol. 13, no. 4, pp. 5-6.

George, S. (1976), *How the other half dies: the real reason for world hunger*, Penguin, Harmondsworth.

Giese, F. and Hecht, A. (1983), 'Regional variations in the standard of living in the Soviet Union', in Giese, F. and Hecht, A. (eds), *Regional development in the peripheries of Canada and Europe*, Department of Geography, University of Manitoba, Winnipeg, pp. 205-243.

Gilbert, A. and Gugler, T. (1981), *Cities, poverty and development: urbanization in the Third World*, Oxford University Press, New York.

Gilgeous, V. (1997), *Operations and the management of change*, Pitman, London.

Gillingwater, D. (1975), *Regional planning and social change: a responsive approach*, Saxon/Lexington Books, Farnborough.

Gillingwater, D. and Hart, D.A. (1978), *The regional planning process*, Saxon House, Westmead.

Glasson, J. (1978), *An introduction to regional planning: concepts, theory and practice,* second edition, Hutchinson, London.

Gooneratne, W. (1997), 'Regionalization of local and regional economies: potentials and preconditions', in Gooneratne, W. and Obhudo, R.A. (eds), *Contemporary issues in regional development policy: perspectives from Eastern and Southern Africa*, Ashgate, Aldershot, pp. 15-36.

Gooneratne, W. and Obhudo, R.A. (eds) (1997), *Contemporary issues in regional development policy: perspectives from Eastern and Southern Africa*, Ashgate, Aldershot.

Gore, C. (1984), *Regions in question: space, development theory and regional policy*, Methuen, London.

Government of Ghana (1959), *Second development plan, 1959-64*, The Government printer, Accra.

Government of Ghana (1982), *Decentralisation in Ghana*, Information Services, Department, Accra.

Government of Ghana (1983a), *Economic Recovery Programme, 1984-86*, vol. I, Report prepared by the Government of Ghana for the Meeting of the Consultants Group for Ghana, Paris, November.

Government of Ghana (1983b), *Economic Recovery Programme, 1984-86: Review of Progress and Goals for 1985-86*, Ministry of Finance and Economic Planning, Accra.

Government of Ghana (1983c), *Central and Greater Accra Regions Rural Integrated Programme (CARRIP)*, Ministry of Finance and Economic Planning, Management and Investment Consultants Limited, Halcrow-ULG Limited and Commission of the European Union, Accra.

Government of Ghana (1984), *Central and Greater Accra Regions Rural Integrated Programme (CARRIP) Report*, vol. 2: (a) Technical development proposals; (b) Twifo Zone, Ministry of Finance and Economic Planning, Management and Investment Consultants Limited, Halcrow-ULG Limited and Commission of the European Union, Accra.

Government of Ghana (1987a), *Programme of actions to mitigate the social costs of adjustment (PAMSCAD)*, Dames, Accra.

Government of Ghana (1987b), *Public investment programme 1986-88*, vol. 1: Project profiles and summary tables, Ministry of Finance and Economic Planning, Accra.

Government of Ghana (1987c), *National programme for economic development (revised)*, Ghana Publishing Corporation, Accra.

Government of Ghana (1988a), *Ghana Living Standards Survey*, Ghana Statistical Service, Accra.

Government of Ghana (1988b), *Local Government Law, 1988*; *PNDC Law 207*, Ghana Publishing Corporation, Accra.

Greed, C. (1993), *Introducing town planning*, Longman, London.

Greed, C. (1994), *Women and planning: creating gendered realities*, Routledge, London.

Griffin, K. and Khan, D.R. (1978), 'Poverty in the Third World: ugly facts and fancy models', *World Developments*, vol. 6, no. 3, pp. 293-304.

Grove, D. and Huszar, L. (1964), *The towns of Ghana: the role of social services*, Ghana Universities Press, Accra.

Gruchman, B. (1972), 'Growth poles in the spatial structure of the Libyan Economy', in Kuklinski, A. (ed.), *Growth poles and growth centres in regional planning*, Mouton, The Hague, pp. 195-304.

Gunn, L.A. (1978), 'Why is implementation so difficult?', *Management Series in Gulf*, vol. 33(4), pp. 169-176.

Hakim, C. (1987), *Research design: strategies and choices in the design of social research*, Allen and Unwin, London.

Hallet, G., Randall, P. and West, E.G. (1973), *Regional policy for ever? essays on the history, theory and political economy of forty years of 'regionalism'*, The Institute of Economic Affairs, London.

Hampden-Turner, C. and Trompenaars, F. (1994), *The seven cultures of capitalism*, Piatkus, London.

Hansen, N.M. (1988), 'Small and medium-size cities in development', in Higgins, B. and Savoie, D.J. (eds), *Regional economic development*, Unwin Hyman, Boston, pp. 318-329.

Hardoy, J.E and Satterthwaite, D. (1986), *Small and intermediate urban centres: their role in national and regional developments in the Third World*, Hodder and Stoughton, London.

Harris, N. (1986), *The end of the Third World: newly industrializing countries and the decline of an ideology*, Penguin Books, London.

Harris, N. (1989), 'Aid and urbanization: an overview', *Cities*, vol. 6, no. 3, pp. 174-185.

Harris, N. (1990), *Urbanization, economic development and policy in developing countries*, Working Paper no. 19, Developing Planning Unit, University College London (UCL), University of London.

Harris, N. (ed.) (1992), *Cities in the 1990s: the challenge for developing countries*, UCL Press, London.

Harrison, P. (1987), *Inside the Third World*, fourth edition, Longman, New York.

Harrisons Fleming Advisory Services Limited (1985), *Study of the smallholder scheme for Twifo oil palm and evaluation of profitability of Jukwa plantation*, Harrisons Fleming Advisory Services Limited, London, in Association with E.N. Omaboe and Associates, Accra.

Harsch, E. (1989), 'On the road to recovery', *Africa Report*, July-August, pp. 21-26.

Hastings, C. (1992), 'Teamworking', in Lock, D. (ed.), *Handbook of management*, Gower, Aldershot, pp. 933-941.

Hatry, H.P., Winnie, R.F. and Fish, D.M. (1973), *Practical programme evaluations for state and local government officials*, The Urban Institute, Washington.

Hautumaki, L. (1986), 'An Analysis of the mechanisms of regional development - a theoretical analysis', in Department of Regional Studies (ed.), *Approaches to regional development: two decades of research*, University of Tampere, Research Reports, Series B 37, second edition, pp. 26-70.

Haveman, R.H. (1976), 'Evaluating the impact of public policies on regional Welfare', *Regional Studies*, vol. 10, pp. 449-463.

Healey, P. (1991), 'Debates in planning thought', in Thomas, H. and Healey, P. (eds), *Dilemmas of planning practice: ethics, legitimacy and the validation of knowledge*, Avebury, Aldershot, pp. 11-33.
Healey, P. (1993), 'Planning through debate: the communicative turn in planning theory', in Fischer, F. and Forester, J. (eds), *The argumentative turn in policy analysis and planning*, UCL Press, London, pp. 233-253.
Hebbert, M. (1982), 'The new decentralisation - a critique of the territorial approach', in Healey, P., McDougall, G. and Thomas M.J. (eds), *Planning theory*, Pergamon, Oxford, pp. 102-119.
Helmsing, A.H.J. (1986), *Firms, farms and the state in Columbia: a study of rural, urban and regional dimensions of change*, Allen and Hyman, Boston.
Higgins, B. and Savoie, D. (eds) (1988), *Regional economic development: essays in honour of François Perroux*, Unwin Hyman, Boston.
Hilhorst, J. (1969), 'Regional development theory: an attempt to synthesize', in OECD (ed.), *Multidisciplinary aspects of regional development*, OECD, Paris, pp. 21-34.
Hilhorst, J. (1971), *Regional planning: a systems approach*, Rotterdam University Press, Rotterdam.
Hilhorst, J.G.M. (1981), *Territory and function: a new paradigm?*, ISS Occasional Papers, August, Institute of Social Studies, The Hague.
Hill, C.W.L. and Jones, G.R. (1995), *Strategic management: an integrated approach*, Houghton Miffin, Boston.
Hinderink, T. and Sterkenburg, J. (1975), *Anatomy of an African town: a socio-economic study of Cape Coast, Ghana*, Department of Geography of Developing Countries, Geographical Institute, State University of Utrecht, Utrecht.
Hirschman, A.O. (1958), *The strategy of economic growth*, Yale University Press, New Haven, Connecticut.
Hogwood, B.W. and Gunn, L.A. (1984), *Policy analysis for the real world*, Oxford University Press, New York.
Holland, S. (1976a), *Capital versus the region*, Macmillan, London.
Holland, S. (1976b), *The regional problem*, Macmillan, London.
Howard, R. (1978), *Colonialism and underdevelopment in Ghana*, Croom Helm, London.
Hoyle, B.S. (1974), *Spatial aspects of development*, Wiley, London.
Huq, M.M. (1989), *The economy of Ghana: the first 25 years since Independence*, Macmillan, Basingstoke.
Hyde, D. (2000), 'Idealism should be at the heart of planning', *Planning*, issue 1366, p. 19.
Jeannet, J.R. and Hennessey, H.D. (1994), *Global marketing strategies*, Houghton Miffin, Boston.

Johnfia, K. (1983), *Strategy for regional/district planning for accelerated development*, Regional Planning Co-ordinating Unit (RPCU), Ministry of Economic Planning and Finance, Central Regional Administration, Cape Coast.

Johnson, E.A. (1970), *Organised space in developing countries*, Praeger, New York.

Johnson, G. and Scholes, K. (1999), *Exploring corporate strategy*, fifth edition, Prentice-Hall, London.

Joseph, K. and Sumption, J. (1979), *Equality*, John Murray, London.

Kafe, M. and Nuer, F. (2000), 'Ghana economic review', *West Africa*, Issue no. 4241, pp. 26-29.

Kay, C.B. (ed.) (1972), *The political economy of colonialism in Ghana: a collection of documents of statistics 1900-1960*, Cambridge University Press, Cambridge.

Kiamba, K.M., Mitullah, W., Musah, A.E., Nwaka, G.R. and Ofori-Cudjoe, S. (1990), 'The rural areas in some African countries', *Prospect*, 3/4, pp. 20-24.

Kudiabor C.D.K. (1972), 'Regional development planning in Ghana - problems, objectives and strategies', in German Foundation for Developing Countries (ed.), *Regional Development Alternatives*, Institute Seminar Report, Berlin, pp. 137-162.

Kudiabor, C.D.K. (1977), 'Urbanization and growth pole strategy for regional development in Ghana', in Mabogunje, A.L. and Faniran, A. (eds), *Regional planning and national development in tropical Africa*, Ibadan University Press, Ibadan, pp. 86-92.

Kudiabor, C.D.K. (1986), 'Policy objectives and strategies for integrated rural development in Ghana', in Brown, C.K. (ed.), *Rural development in Ghana*, Ghana Universities Press, Accra, pp. 26-32.

Kuklinski, A.R. (1970), 'Regional development, regional policies and regional planning: problems and issues', *Regional Studies*, vol. 4, pp. 269-278.

Leone, R.A. and Struyk, R. (1976), 'The incubator hypothesis: evidence from five SMSAs', *Urban Studies*, vol. 13, pp. 325-331.

Levitt, R. (1980), *Implementing public policy*, Croom Helm, London.

Lewis, T. and Flynn, R. (1979), 'The implementation of urban and regional planning policies', *Policy and Politics*, vol. 7, no. 2, pp. 123-142.

Lewis, W. (1966), *Development planning: the essentials of economic policy*, George Allen and Unwin, London, pp. 38-42.

Lichfield, M., Kettle, P. and Whitbread, M. (1975), *Evaluation in the planning process*, Pergamon, Oxford.

Linn, J.F. (1979), *Policies for efficient and equitable growth of cities in developing countries*, World Bank Staff Working Paper no. 342, New York.

Lipton, M. (1977), *Why poor people stay poor: urban bias in world development*, Maurice Temple Smith, London.
Logan, I.M. (1982), 'The spatial system and planning strategies in developing countries', *The Geographical Review*, vol. 62, pp. 229-244.
Mabogunje, A.L. (1980), *The development process*, Hutchinson, London.
Mabogunje, A.L. and Faniran, A. (1977), *Regional planning and national development in Tropical Africa*, Ibadan University Press.
Magnifico, G. *et al.* (1985), *Regional imbalances and national economic performance*, Commission of the European Communities, Luxembourg.
Martins, M.R. (1986), *An organisational approach to regional planning*, Gower, Aldershot.
Martinson, O.B. and Schulman, M. (1977), 'Support for growth centres: the case of rural N.W. Wisconsin', *Growth and Change*, April, pp. 31-32.
Massey, D. (1979), 'In what sense a regional problem?', *Regional Studies*, vol. 13, pp. 233-240.
Massimo, Q. (1982), *Geography and Marxism*, Basil Blackwell, Oxford.
Mattingly, M. (1989), 'Implementing planning with teaching: using training to make it happen', *Third World Planning Review*, 11(4), pp. 417-528.
McCrone, G. (1969), *Regional policy in Britain*, Allen and Unwin, London.
McGranahan, D. (1972), 'Development indicators and development models', in Baster, N. (1972), *Measuring development*, Frank Cass, London.
McLoughlin, B.T. (1969), *Urban and regional planning: a systems approach*, Faber and Faber, London.
McNeil, D. (1985), 'Planning with implementation in view', *Third World Review*, vol. 7, pp. 575-579.
Meggison, L.C., Mosley, D.C. and Pietry, P.H. Jr. (1986), *Management concepts and applications*, second edition, Harper and Row, New York.
Miliband, R. (1969), *The state in capitalist society*, Weidenfeld and Nicolson, London.
Miliband, R. (1977), *Marxism and politics*, Oxford University Press, Oxford.
Mobil Corporation (1998), *Annual report*, Mobil Corporation, Fairfax, Virginia.
Molle, W. and Cappellin, R. (eds) (1988), *Regional impact of community policies in Europe*, Avebury/Gower, Aldershot.
Molle, W., van Holst, B. and Smit, H. (eds) (1980), *Regional disparity and economic development in the European community*, Saxon House, Aldershot.
Moser, C.A. and Kalton, C. (1971), *Survey methods for social investigations*, Heinemann, London.
Moyo, B. (2000), 'The economy in distress', *West Africa*, Issue no. 4238, pp. 12-14.

Myrdal, G. (1957), *Economic development and underdeveloped regions*, Duckworth, London.

Nacer, M. (1979), *Regional disparities and development in Algeria*, unpublished MA (town and regional planning) thesis, Department of Town and Regional Planning, University of Sheffield, Sheffield.

Nge'the, N., Mitullah, W.V. and Nguyi, M. (1990), 'Government-NGO relationship in the context of alternative development strategies in Kenya', Paper prepared for the conference on NGOs in Africa, Centre for African Studies, University of Edinburgh, Edinburgh.

Nijkamp, P. and van Pelt, M. (1983), 'Urban and regional impact analysis in development planning', in Chatterjee, L. and Nijkamp, P. (eds), *Urban and regional policy analysis in developing countries*, Gower, Aldershot, pp. 171-179.

North, D. (1964), 'Location theory and regional economic growth', in Friedmann, J. and Alonso, A. (eds), *Regional development and planning: a reader*, M.I.T. Press, Cambridge, Massachusetts.

OECD (1988), *Regional problems and politics in Turkey*, OECD, Paris.

Ofori-Cudjoe, S. (1981), *Small-scale industries and regional development in the Eastern Region*, MSc (regional planning) thesis, Department of Planning, Faculty of Environmental and Development Studies [formerly Faculty of Architecture], University of Science and Technology, Kumasi.

Ofori-Cudjoe, S. (1987), 'The regional planning process in Ghana: the case of the Central Region', Paper presented at the Open Lecture Series, Faculty of Social Sciences, University of Cape Coast, Cape Coast.

Ofori-Cudjoe, S. (1990), 'Development policy and planning for rural urbanization in Ghana: small and medium towns for the Central Region', Paper presented at the 40th World Congress of the International Federation for Housing and Planning Dublin, Ireland, September.

Ofori, S.C. (1991a), *Regional planning policy and intra-regional socio-economic disparities in the Central Region, Ghana: evaluating the impact of development programmes*, PhD (urban and regional planning) thesis, Department of Environmental Planning [formerly Centre for Planning], Strathclyde Business School, University of Strathclyde, Glasgow.

Ofori, S.C. (1991b), 'Drought mitigation and water resource schemes in pastoral Northern Ghana: some aspects of international agency programmes', in Stone J.C. (ed.), *Pastoral economies in Africa and long-term responses to drought*, Aberdeen University African Studies Group, Aberdeen, pp. 206-220.

Ofori, S.C. (1994), 'Small-scale industries and the local economic development process in a developing country: the Eastern Region, Ghana - towards an effective local development policy', in Erkelens, P.A. and van der Meulen, G.G. (eds), *Urban environment in developing countries;*

futures, ideas, directions; Faculty of Architecture, Eindhoven University of Technology, pp. 274-288.

Ofori, S.C. (1995a), *Regional policy and planning in the Third World: achieving results in developing regions*, Research Paper Series no. 14, Faculty of Built Environment, University of Central England, Birmingham.

Ofori, S.C. (1995b), *Strategic regional planning guidance in the West Midlands: regenerating the Black Country; putting it altogether*, Draft planning policy and programme document prepared for the Department of Environment and Development Services, Sandwell Metropolitan Borough Council, West Midlands.

Ofori, S.C. (1998), *Managing change in small and medium enterprises, A.P. Smith and Son Limited: responsive management and success*, Individual Management Project, submission for Diploma in Management Studies (DMS), Division of Management, University of Central England Business School, Birmingham.

Ofori, S.C. (2000a), *Assessing Regional Development Corporations and regional development in Ghana and the Third World*, Working Paper Series no. 76, School of Planning, Faculty of the Built Environment, University of Central England, Birmingham.

Ofori, S.C. (2000b), *Epistemology, evaluation of regional planning research and experiential learning*, Working Paper Series no. 78, School of Planning, Faculty of the Built Environment, University of Central England, Birmingham.

Ofori, S.C. (2000c), *Inter-district disparities in socio-economic development: the effectiveness of regional planning policy in the Central Region, Ghana*, Working Paper Series no. 79, School of Planning, Faculty of the Built Environment, University of Central England, Birmingham.

Ofori, S.C. (2000d), *Regenerating the urban regions: regional policy and strategic regional planning in Emscher Park and the Black Country*, Working Paper Series no. 77, School of Planning, Faculty of the Built Environment, University of Central England, Birmingham.

Ofori, S.C. (2000e), *Culturally-diverse and product-market environments in a process of globalization, a European focus: influences on and responses of a manufacturing organization*, final project submission for Boundary Management 3, module within the Master of Business Administration (MBA) programme, Division of Management, University of Central England Business School, Birmingham.

Ofori, S.C. (2000f), *Corporate strategy and human resource management: strategic effectiveness and praxis in a manufacturing organisation*, Master of Business Administration (MBA) dissertation, Division of Management, University of Central England Business School, Birmingham.

Ofori, S.C. (2000g), *The spatial context and potential roles of small firms in Ghana: informing foundations of regional planning policy and development processes*, Working Paper Series no. 80, School of Planning, Faculty of Built Environment, University of Central England, Birmingham.

Ofori, S.C. (2000h), *Processes of socio-economic generation and locality development in sub-Saharan Africa*, Working Paper Series no. 83, School of Planning, Faculty of Built Environment, University of Central England, Birmingham.

Ohmae, K. (1990), *The borderless world: power and strategy in the global marketplace*, Harper Collins, London.

Okonjo, C. (1986), 'The concept of development', in Brown, C.K. (ed.), *Rural development in Ghana*, Ghana Universities Press, Accra, pp. 3-26.

Omuta, G.E.D. and Onokerhoraye, A.G. (1986), *Regional development and planning for Africa*, The Editorial Committee, Geography and Planning Studies, University of Benin.

Paterson Zochonis Plc (1998), *Annual report and accounts*, Cussons House, Stockport.

Paterson Zochonis Plc (2000), *Annual report and accounts*, Cussons House, Stockport.

Patton, C.V. and Sawicki, D.S. (1986), *Basic methods of policy analysis and planning*, Prentice Hall, Englewood Cliff.

Perloff, H. and Wingo, L. (1964), 'Natural resource endowment and regional economic growth', in Friedmann, J. and Alonso, W. (eds), *Regional development and planning: a reader*, M.I.T. Press, Cambridge, Massachusetts, pp. 215-239.

Perroux, F. (1955), 'Notes sur la notion de pôle de croissance', *Economy Appliquée*, 7, pp. 307-320.

Potter, M. (1998), *Competitive advantage: creating and sustaining superior performance*, The Free Press, New York.

Poulantzas, N. (1969), 'The problem of the capitalist state', *new left review*, no. 58, November-December, pp. 67-78.

Poulantzas, N. (1973), *Political power and social classes*, New Left Books, London.

Rambanapasi, C.O. (1989), 'Regional development policy and its impact on regional planning practice in Zimbabwe', *Planning Perspective*, 4, pp. 271-294.

Rao, D.C. (1978), 'Economic growth and equity in the Republic of Korea', *World Development*, vol. 6, no. 3, pp. 383-396.

Rao, H. (1984), *Regional disparities and development in India*, Ashish, New Delhi.

Ravetz, A. (1986), *The government of space: town planning in modern society*, Faber and Faber, London.

Republic of Ghana (1963), *Seven-year development for reconstruction and development, 1963-64 to 1969-70*, Planning Commission, Accra.
Republic of Ghana (1968), *Two-year development plan from stabilization to development (mid-1968 to mid-1970)*, Ghana Publishing Company, Accra.
Republic of Ghana (1970), *One-year development plan*, Ghana Publishing Company, Accra.
Republic of Ghana (1973), *Regional Development Corporations Decree, 1973 (NRCD 140)*, Ghana Publishing Corporation, Accra.
Republic of Ghana (1977a), *Guidelines to the five-year development plan of 1973-80*, Ministry of Town Planning, Accra.
Republic of Ghana (1977b), *Five-year development plan, 1975/76 to 1979-80* (part 1), Ministry of Town Planning, Accra.
Republic of Ghana (1979), *Budget statement for 1979-80,* Ghana Publishing Company, Accra.
Republic of Ghana (1994a), *National Development Planning Commission Act*, Ghana Publishing Corporation, Accra.
Republic of Ghana (1994b), *National Development Planning Commission (System) Act*, Ghana Publishing Corporation, Accra.
Richardson, H.W. (1969a), *Elements of regional economics*, Penguin, Middlesex.
Richardson, H.W. (1969b), *Regional economics: location theory, urban structures and regional change*, Weidenfeld and Nicolson, London.
Richardson, H.W. (1969c), *Regional economics: a reader*, Macmillan/St Martins, London.
Richardson, H.W. (1973), *Regional growth theory*, Methuen, London.
Richardson, H.W. (1975), *Regional development policy and planning in Spain*, Saxon House/Lexington, London.
Richardson H.W. (1978a), 'Growth centers rural development and national urban policy: a defense', *International Regional Science Review*, vol. 3, no. 2, pp. 133-152.
Richardson, H.W. (1978b), *Regional economics*, Penguin, Middlesex.
Richardson, H.W. (1980), 'Polarisation reversal in developing countries', in *Papers of the Regional Science Association*, vol. 45, pp. 63-85.
Richardson, H.W. and Townroe, P.M. (1986), 'Regional policies in developing countries', in Nijkamp, P. (ed.), *Handbook of regional and urban economics*, North-Holland, Amsterdam, pp. 647-678.
Rietveld, P. (1980), *Multiple objective decision methods and regional planning*, North-Holland, Amsterdam.
Roberts, M. (1974), *An introduction to town planning techniques*, Hutchinson, London.
Robson, C. (1993), *Real world research: a resource for social scientists and practitioner-researchers*, Blackwell, Oxford.

Rodwin, L. (1978), 'Regional planning in less developed countries: a retrospective view of the literature and experience', *International Regional Science Review*, vol. 3, no. 2, pp. 113-131.
Rondinelli, D.A. (1983a), *Development projects as policy experiments: an adaptive approach to development administration*, Methuen, London.
Rondinelli, D.A. (1983b), *Secondary cities in developing countries: policies for diffusing urbanisation*, Sage, Beverly Hills.
Rondinelli, D.A. (1987), 'Linking decentralisation and regional development planning: the IRD project in Peru', *Journal of the American Planning Association*, Summer, pp. 348-357.
Rondinelli, D.A. and Ruddel, K. (1978), *Urbanization and rural development: a spatial policy for equitable growth*, Praeger, New York.
Rose, E.A. (1974), 'Philosophy and purpose in planning', in Bruton, M.J. (ed.), *The spirit and purpose of planning*, Hutchinson, London.
Rostow, W.W. (1960), *The stages of economic growth: a non-communist manifesto*, Cambridge University Press, New York.
Rye, T.R. (1987), *Understanding public policy*, Prentice Hall, Englewood Cliff.
Sabatier, P. and Manzmanian, D. (1979), 'The conditions of effective implementation: a guide to accomplishing policy objectives', *Policy Analysis*, no. 3, Summer, pp. 481-483.
Santos, D. (1970), 'The structure of dependence', *American Economic Review*, vol. 60, no. 2, pp. 231-236.
Santos, M. (1979), *The shared space: the two circuits of the urban economy in underdeveloped countries*, Methuen, London and New York.
Saunders, M.N.K., Lewis, P. and Thornhill, A. (1987), *Research methods for business students*, Pitman, London.
Sayer, A. (1988), *Method in social science: a realist approach*, Hutchinson, London.
Schatzl, L.H. (1988), *Growth and spatial equity in West Malaysia,* Institute of South East Asia Studies, Singapore.
Schofield, J. (1987), *Cost-benefit analysis in urban and regional planning*, Unwin Hyman, London.
Schon, D.A. (1991), *The reflective practitioner: how professionals think in action*, Avebury, London.
Scott, G.C. (1978), 'The basis for regional policy for economic development', *Ekistics*, vol. 45, no. 267, pp. 77-82.
Seers, D. (1973), 'What are we trying to measure?', *Journal of Development Studies*, vol. 8, no.3, pp 5-17.
Seitz, J.L. (1988), *The politics of development: an introduction to global issues*, Basil Blackwell, Oxford.

Sharp, J.A. and Howard, K. (1996), *The management of student research project*, second edition, Gower, Aldershot.

Shillington, D. (1992), *Ghana and the Rawlings factor*, Macmillan, London.

Siegel, S. (1936), *Non-parametric statistics for the behavioural sciences*, McGraw-Hill, Tokyo, pp. 30-34.

Simon, D. (1990a), 'The question of regions', in Simon, D. (ed.), *Third World regional development: a reappraisal*, Paul Chapman, London, pp. 1-23.

Simon, D. (ed.) (1990b), *Third World regional development: a reappraisal*, Paul Chapman, London.

Singer, H.W. and Ansari, J.A. (1977), *Rich and poor countries*, George Allen and Unwin, London.

Skelcher, C. (1982), 'Planning context and planning methodology in regional planning', in Leach, S. and Stewart, J. (eds), *Approaches in public policy*, George Allen and Unwin, London, pp. 120-148.

Slater, D. (1975), 'Underdevelopment of spatial inequality: approaches to the problems of regional planning in the Third World', *Progress in Planning*, vol. 4, no. 2, pp. 97-167.

Songsore, J. (1979), *Structural crisis, dependent capitalism, development and regional inequality in Ghana*, I.S.S. Occasional Papers, July, Institute of Social Studies, The Hague.

Sorensen, A.D. and Ausler, M.L. (1989), 'Fatal remedies: the sources of ineffectiveness in planning', *Town Planning Review*, vol. 60, no. 1, pp. 29-43.

Spiegel, M.R. (1974), *Theory and problems of statistics*, McGraw-Hill, New York.

Stewart, J. (1982), 'Guidelines to policy derivation', in Leach. S.W. and Stewart, J. (eds), *Approaches to public policy*, George Allen and Unwin, London, pp. 120-148.

Stohr, W.B. and Taylor, D.R.F. (eds.) (1981), *Development from above or below?: the dialectics of regional planning*, John Wiley and Son, Chichester.

Stohr, W.B. and Todtling, F. (1977), 'Spatial equity - some anti-theses to current regional development doctrine', *Papers of the Regional Science Association*, vol. 38, pp. 33-53.

Sutton, K. (1988), 'The growth of Algiers and regional development in Algeria', *Third World Planning Review*, vol. 10, no. 2, pp. 130-157.

Szereszewski, R. (1966), 'Regional aspects of the structure of the economy', in Birmingham, W., Newstadt, I. and Omaboe, E.N. (eds), *A study of contemporary Ghana*, vol. 2, George Allen and Unwin, London, chapter 4.

Tang, F. (1981), 'Regional planning in developing countries: the case of Taiwan, Republic of China', *Papers of the Regional Science Association*, vol. 46, pp. 97-107.

Teriba, O. and Kayode, M.O. (1977), 'The concept of a planning region', in Mabogunje, A.L. and Faniran, A. (eds.), *Regional planning and national development in tropical Africa*, Ibadan University Press, Ibadan, pp. 17-25.

The Ghanaian Times Corporation (1982), 'Editorial', *The Ghanaian Times*, Monday 13, Accra, p.2.

The Gold Coast (1951a), *The development plan*, The Government Printers, Accra.

The Gold Coast (1951b), *Second development plan (1959-1968)*, The Gold Coast, Government Printers, Accra.

Thirlwall, A.P. (1972), *Growth and development with special reference to developing economies*, Macmillan, London.

Thomi, W.H. and Yankson, P.W.K. (1985), *Small-scale industries and decentralization in Ghana*, Department of Geography, University of Ghana and Institute für Wirtschafts-und Sozialgeographie, J.W. Goethe Universität, Frankfurt.

Thornley, A. (1991), *Urban planning under Thatcherism: the challenge of the market*, Routledge, London.

Thwaites, A.T. (1982), 'Some evidence of regional variations in the introduction and diffusion of industrial products and process within British manufacturing industry', *Regional Studies*, vol. 16, 5, pp. 371-381.

Tiebout, C.M. (1964), 'Exports and regional economic growth', in Friedmann, J. and Alonso, W. (eds), *Regional development and planning: a reader*, M.I.T. Press, Cambridge, Massachusetts, pp. 256-265.

Todaro, M.P. (1989), *Economic development in the Third World*, fourth edition, Longman, New York, pp. 67-77.

Trevallion, B.A.W. (1989), 'The role and output of the transition implementation team for streamlining the central planning system and the decentralisation of development decision-making and budgeting', Paper presented at the National Workshop on 'Establishing local level system in support of decentralisation', UNDP Project, GHA/85/003, Accra.

Twifo Oil Palm Plantation (TOPP) (1988a), *TOPP Newsletter*, vol. 24, December, TOPP Head Office, Twifo Ntafrewaso.

Twifo Oil Palm Plantation (TOPP) (1988b), *TOPP Newsletter*, vol. 24, September, TOPP Head Office, Twifo Ntafrewaso.

Twifo Oil Palm Plantation (TOPP) (1989a), *TOPP Newsletter*, vol. 26, March, TOPP Head Office, Twifo Ntafrewaso.

Twifo Oil Palm Plantation (TOPP) (1989b), *TOPP Newsletter*, vol. 27, May, TOPP Head Office, Twifo Ntafrewaso.

UniLever (1994), *Annual review and summary financial statement*, UniLever House, London.

UniLever (1997), *Annual review and summary financial statement*, UniLever House, London.

United Nations Centre for Human Settlements (UNCHS) and United Nations Environment Programme (UNEP) (1987), *Environmental considerations in regional planning and management*, UNCHS and UNEP, Nairobi.

van Buren, L. (2001), 'Economy', section under 'Ghana', in Europa Publications, *Africa South of the Sahara 2001*, 30th edition, Europa Publications, London, pp. 550-571.

van Staveren, J.M. and van Dusseldorp, D.B.W.M. (1980), *Framework for regional planning in developing countries: methodology for an inter-disciplinary approach to the planned development of predominantly rural areas*, International Institute for Land Reclamation and Improvement, Wageningen, The Netherlands.

Wadley, P. (1986), *Restructuring the regions*, OECD, Paris.

Walden Publishing Limited (1999), 'Ghana', in *African Review*, 22nd edition, Walden Publishing Limited, London, pp. 109-114.

Wannop, U.A. (1988), 'Do we need regional local government and is the Scottish model relevant?', *Regional Studies*, vol. 22, no. 5, pp. 439-452.

Wannop, U.A. (1995), *The regional imperative: regional planning and governance in Britain, Europe and the United States*, Jessica Kingsley and Regional Studies Association, London.

Wannop, U. and Smith, R. (1985), 'Robustness in regional planning: an evaluation of the Clyde Valley Regional Plan', in Smith, R. and Wannop, U. (eds) (1985), *Strategic planning in action*, Gower, Aldershot, pp. 210-241.

Waterston, A. (1966), *Development planning: lessons of experience*, The John Hopkins University Press, Baltimore.

Weaver, C. (1978), 'Regional theory and regionalism: towards rethinking the regional question', *Geoforum*, vol. 9, pp. 397-413.

Weaver, C. (1981), 'Development theory and the regional question: a critique of spatial planning and its detractors', in Stohr, W.B. and Taylor, D.R.F. (eds), *Development plans above or below*, Wiley, Chichester, pp. 73-103.

Weaver, C. (1984), *Regional development and the local community: planning, policies and social context*, Wiley, Chichester.

Weaver, C. (1989), 'Urban systems theory and Third World development: a review', Paper presented to the 19th Annual Meeting of the Urban Affairs Association in Baltimore, Maryland, March 15-18; also presented to academic staff and research students, the Department of Environmental Planning [formerly Centre for Planning], University of Strathclyde, Glasgow, June, 1990.

Webber, M.J. (1984), *Explanation, prediction and planning*, Pion, London.

Webber, M.M. (1969), 'Planning in an environment of change', *Town Planning Review*, January, pp. 291-292.

Wenban-Smith, A. and Beeston, J. (1990), *Negotiation with planning authorities*, Estates Gazette, London.
West Africa Magazine (1990), 'Dateline', in *West Africa*, no. 3809, p. 2373.
Williamson, J.G. (1975), 'Regional inequality and the process of national development: a description of the patterns', in Friedmann, J. and Alonso, W. (eds), *Regional Policy*, M.I.T., Cambridge, Massachusetts, pp. 158-200.
Wonnacott, P. and Wonnacott, R. (1990), *Economics*, fourth edition, John Wiley, New York.
World Bank (1989a), *Ghana: structural adjustment for growth*, Washington D.C.
World Bank (1989b), *Confronting poverty in developing countries: definitions, information and politics*, ISMS Measurement Study Working Paper no. 48, Washington D.C.
World Bank and International Finance Corporation (1988), *Ghana: Preliminary Results of Living Standards Survey*, World Bank and International Finance Corporation, Washington D.C.
World Council for Environment and Development (WCED) (1987), *Our common inheritance*, Oxford University Press, Oxford.
Wyatt, R.G. (1989), *Intelligent planning: meaningful methods for sensitive situations*, Unwin Hyman, London.
Yankson, P.W.K. (1986), 'Intra-regional inequalities in development and implications for regional planning: the example of the region in Ghana', in *Zeitschrift für Wirtschaftsgeographie*, 30, Heft 3/4, pp. 85-95.
Yeomans, K.A. (1968), *Statistics for the social scientist: 2*, Penguin, Harmondsworth.
Yin, R.K. (1989), *Case study research: design and methods*, Sage, Newbury Park.
Zetter, R. (1981), 'Imported or indigenous planning education?: some observations on the needs of developing countries', *Third World Planning Review*, vol. 3, no. 1, pp. 21-42.

For Product Safety Concerns and Information please contact our EU representative GPSR@taylorandfrancis.com Taylor & Francis Verlag GmbH, Kaufingerstraße 24, 80331 München, Germany

Batch number: 10726013

Printed by Printforce, the Netherlands